THE PANOPTIC SORT

Critical Studies in Communication and in the Cultural Industries

Herbert I. Schiller, Series Editor

The Panoptic Sort: A Political Economy of Personal Information,
Oscar H. Gandy, Jr.

Triumph of the Image: The Media's War in the Persian Gulf—A Global Perspective,
edited by Hamid Mowlana, George Gerbner, and Herbert I. Schiller

The Persian Gulf TV War, Douglas Kellner

Mass Communications and American Empire, Second Edition, Updated,
Herbert I. Schiller

FORTHCOMING

The Social Uses of Photography: Images in the Age of Reproduction, Hanno Hardt

Introduction to Media Studies, edited by Stuart Ewen, Elizabeth Ewen, Serafina
Bathrick, and Andrew Mattson

Music Television, Jack Banks

Media Transformations in the Age of Persuasion, Robin K. Anderson

A Different Road Taken: Profiles of Five Critical Communication Scholars,
John A. Lent

Hot Shots: An Alternative Video Production Handbook, Tami Gold and
Kelly Anderson

The Dallas Smythe Reader, edited by Thomas Guback

Public Television Versus the Market, William Hoynes

The Communications Industry in the American Economy, Thomas Guback

THE PANOPTIC SORT

A Political Economy
of Personal Information

Oscar H. Gandy, Jr.

Westview Press

BOULDER · SAN FRANCISCO · OXFORD

Critical Studies in Communication and in the Cultural Industries

Copyright © 1993 by Westview Press, Inc.

Published in 1993 in the United States of America by Westview Press, Inc., 5500 Central Avenue, Boulder, Colorado 80301-2877, and in the United Kingdom by Westview Press, 36 Lonsdale Road, Summertown, Oxford OX2 7EW

Library of Congress Cataloging-in-Publication Data
Gandy, Oscar H.
   The panoptic sort : a political economy of personal information /
Oscar H. Gandy, Jr.
      p.   cm.—(Critical studies in communication and in the
cultural industries)
   Includes bibliographical references and index.
   ISBN 0-8133-1656-1 (hc.)—ISBN 0-8133-1657-X (pbk.)
   1. Privacy, Right of—United States.   2. Records—United States—
Access control.   I. Title.   II. Series.
JC596.2.U5G36   1993
323.44′8′0973—dc20
                                                                                   92-37434
                                                                                   CIP

Printed and bound in the United States of America

   The paper used in this publication meets the requirements
of the American National Standard for Permanence of Paper
for Printed Library Materials Z39.48-1984.

10   9   8   7   6   5   4   3   2   1

CONTENTS

TABLES AND FIGURES

ACKNOWLEDGMENTS

This project has been a long time in development. It began to pick up steam once I decided to move from Howard University to the University of Pennsylvania. George Gerbner is largely responsible for that move and for many of the good things that have happened as a result. Among those things was an introduction to Ken Laker, the head of Penn's computer science department and guiding force for the Penn/AT&T Telecommunications Technology Program that provided three years of support for my research. Ben Peterson's confidence in my potential led an understandably cautious organization to eventually pair me with Emmanuel Gardner, whose generous assistance led to my national telephone survey. With the AT&T grant, and with support from the Annenberg School, I was privileged to work with a continually changing but always wonderful team of graduate research assistants including Jerry Baber, Todd Kristel, Eleanor Novek, Catherine Preston, Michael Schunck, Nikhil Sinha, Beth Van Horn, and Csilla Voros.

As I began to share my thoughts about privacy and the panoptic sort, I was pleased to be included in the stream of comment and conversations about technology, rights, and responsibilities. Although we did not always agree, I value the advice and counsel of Ed Baker, Mary Culnan, Janlori Goldman, Jim Katz, Gary Marx, Robert Posch, Priscilla Regan, James Rule, Rohan Samarajiva, and Alan Westin. As the final hours approached and it seemed as though I would never take the next critical step, Kathleen Jamieson made an offer that I could not refuse. Time off and an implied deadline made it both possible and necessary to transform boxes into pages. Her support and encouragement are much appreciated.

I would also like to thank Herb Schiller and Gordon Massman whose perseverance put me in the capable hands of Shena Redmond, Sabina Vanish, and the other good folks at Westview who have helped to finish this project in good form and in record time.

Finally, I would like to acknowledge the continued support and understanding of my wife, Judy, whose gentle counsel and editorial insights were always on call. For our daughter, Imani, who always wanted to know "how many pages is it?" I can now say "ask your mom!"

Oscar H. Gandy, Jr.

1

PROLOGUE

INTRODUCTION

In 1934, the Spiegel corporation was an industry leader in the development of a pointing system, which it used to evaluate applications for credit. Spiegel developed what it called the "vital question system," which gathered data in four critical areas that were then used as the primary factors in the decision to grant credit. The four questions were (1) amount of the order, (2) occupation of the applicant, (3) marital status, and (4) race of the applicant. Other data gathered in the rating process included an assessment of the importance of the geographic territory to the overall marketing plan.[1] Although race and marital status are no longer *legally* permissible components of the credit authorization process, the evidence is clear that a similar discriminatory process that sorts individuals on the basis of their estimated value or worth has become even more important today and reaches into every aspect of individuals lives in their roles as citizens, employees, and consumers.

I refer to this process as the "panoptic sort," the all-seeing eye of the difference machine that guides the global capitalist system. Kevin Robins and Frank Webster have coined the phrase "cybernetic capitalism" to underscore the nature of the totalizing system of social control that depends on the ability of state and corporate bureaucracies to collect, process, and share massive amounts of personal information to track, command, coordinate, and control each and every one of us to an extent we would not have considered possible.[2] Other descriptive terms appeared over the years as I have gathered examples and insights about the nature of this process. One that still holds an attraction is the notion of triage. The popular understanding of the term is that associated with medical decision making: "the sorting and allocation of treatment to patients, especially battle and disaster victims, according to a system of priorities designed to maximize the number of survivors."[3] The original meaning of the term,[4] however, is derived from the French *trier,* meaning to pick or to cull, but the word emerged into the English language as having to do with the "grading of marketable produce," and more specifically, referring to "the lowest grade of coffee berries, consisting of broken material."[5] Although some metaphors speak for themselves, let me be clear. I see the panoptic sort as a kind of high-tech, cybernetic triage through which individuals and groups of people are being sorted according to their presumed economic or polit-

1

ical value. The poor, especially poor people of color, are increasingly being treated as broken material or damaged goods to be discarded or sold at bargain prices to scavengers in the marketplace.

This book is a project in critical theory. The purpose of critical theory is generally to understand the world in order to change it, to make possible the realization of some social ideal. Critical theory should then, ultimately, contain both an analysis and a prescription. This book can claim to meet only the first requirement. It provides a critical assessment of the character and consequences of the development and implementation of the panoptic sort. In my view, this sorting mechanism cannot help but exacerbate the massive and destructive inequalities that characterize the U.S. political economy as it moves forward into the information age. It is a process that feeds on itself. Although there are already some signs of resistance that have emerged in some quarters, the response of the panoptic system is very much like that of a child's straw finger puzzle: Once you have placed your fingers in either end of the tube, the more you stuggle to escape, the more it tightens its grip. I would like to suggest that these inequalities are emerging in an area that is critical to the maintenance of a democratic polity and to the operation of an efficient market. These inequalities have to do with differential access to information that is necessary for informed decision making.

The operation of the panoptic sort increases the ability of organized interests, whether they are selling shoes, toothpaste, or political platforms, to identify, isolate, and communicate differentially with individuals in order to increase their influence over how consumers make selections among these options. At the same time that the panoptic sort operates to increase the precision with which individuals are classified according to their perceived value in the marketplace and their susceptibility to particular appeals, the commoditization of information increases the dependence of these interests on subsidized information.[6] To the extent that the panoptic sort, as an extension of technical rationalization into the social realm of consumer and political behavior, depends on a reduction of the skills of individuals in the same way that automation reduces the skills of laborers in the factory or the modern office, the market and the political or public sphere as we understand them are transformed and are placed at risk.[7]

As the panoptic sort matures and increases in scale and scope, a number of contradictory developments seem likely. First, because the sorting mechanism utilizes data about past behaviors, it tends to limit the options that are presented for individuals to choose. When the options concern choices about information, this tendency has the potential to increase the knowledge and information gap between the haves and the have nots. Also, to the extent that these conservative models aim at the lowest common denominator, the panoptic sort will contribute to a generalized lowering of the average level of public understanding. Second, because the sorting mechanism is based on theoretical models that reflect quite transitory fads or trends in social, economic, and political thought, increasing instability in markets and political action will become the rule rather than the exception. Third, as people's awareness of the panoptic machine grows, some will find ways to resist, and others will attempt to withdraw. Both responses will invite further attempts at inclusion and containment within the panoptic sphere. The same technology that threatens the autonomy of the individual seems destined to frustrate attempts to reestablish community and shared responsibility because it destroys the essential components of trust and accountability.

Whereas Jürgen Habermas holds out hope for the liberatory potential of the rationalist program, I argue that it is this very rationalism that is at the core of the panoptic sort.[8] The freedom that Habermas seeks and necessarily assumes for communication to produce understanding, is consistently threatened by the strategic rationalism of this technology, which is designed to identify, classify, evaluate, and assign individuals on the basis of a remote, invisible, automatic, and comprehensive sensing of personhood. What is left of the public sphere will be described as little more than a phantasm, a ghostly afterimage that will appear in different forms to different individuals according to their profiles. The communications competence—that Habermas suggests is required before the ideal speech situation can emerge—will be systematically denied to individuals and groups.[9] Although communication may take place within more narrowly defined sociocultural communities, the ability of people to engage in communication across these lines will be lost as segmentation moves apace.

THE DIVERSE THEORETICAL ORIGINS
OF PANOPTIC THINKING

This book represents an effort to integrate the perspectives from several social science disciplines. A political economy of personal information is at once set apart from the mainstream focus and approach of economics. The narrow vision and unrealistic assumptions of the neoclassical canon would make it impossible to take note of the real influence of people's everyday lives, the influence of powerful institutions, and, indeed, the presence of power itself. Randall Bartlett suggests that "there is, as yet, no well-structured theory of power in economic relationships that can be used to look for power," and although institutionalists and Marxists have made power a central part of their analysis, he finds it either merely declared or assumed, rather than defined or explored.[10] Multiple sources in sociology, economics, and political science have contributed to the sense of disciplinary power that is inherently a part of the operation of the panoptic sort.

These sources have helped to construct an understanding of power as a complex relationship rather than as something to be weighed and measured. This power is seen as a dynamic relationship, one that changes as it changes those who are part of the relationships that define it. Although there are any number of relationships that might be described in terms of the relative inequalities that obtain, my primary focus is on the inequality that obtains between the individual and the bureaucratic organizations of business and government interests. And within this nexus, the focus will be sharper still on the asymmetry between individuals and business establishments.

From Marx, a Dialectical View

The influence of Karl Marx on my thinking about social change is difficult to measure, but there is little doubt that it is pervasive. In part, this difficulty is a reflection of the extent to which other writers who have influenced my thinking have not recognized or have failed to acknowledge Marx's influence on their own sociology, philosophy, history, economics, and yes, even psychology.[11] Thus, much of what these writers have contributed to my understanding of technology and social change has been enhanced by Marx's social theory, but the credit lines have become blurred. Ideology is thought to have been a victim of its own success. The choosing of sides within Marxist social theory has transformed this core construct into a contested battle site where each contending group seeks to strip off the distasteful or vulgar aspects of its derived meaning and keep only those that justify the study of a particular social practice.[12] Because arguments about relative autonomy and determination have challenged the traditional force with which the terms *economic base* and *superstructure* might be offered as an anchor for a materialist theory of social change, the formal concepts have also fallen into relative disuse.[13] It is clear, however, that the same conceptual elements in less obvious Marxian garb are at the heart of much contemporary theorizing about an Information Age.

We are regularly challenged to examine the relationships between changes in technology, which occasion, or are necessitated by, changes in the structure of the market, the regulatory infrastructure, or the perceptions of consumers. New devices that facilitate production, distribution, display, or reproduction of mass media products nearly always threaten the equilibrium of the marketplace, and those actors most at risk from competitive alternatives are first in line to demand regulatory protection—in the public interest, of course.[14] Anne Branscomb underscored the impact of technological change on the ability of individuals and corporations to exercise what they have come to see as their rights to information.[15] Changes in technology make it easier for relatively unsophisticated users to make high-quality copies of information, thereby transforming private resources into public goods. The call by media firms for copyright enforcement falls on deaf ears when it is recognized that the general public believes that making copies of television programs for later viewing or personal tapes of favorite songs for use in portable or automobile tape players is a perfectly legitimate use. Changes in technology heighten our awareness of the strictures that old laws, old contracts, and old customs represent for the exploration of the newly possible. The real possibility of genetic engineering of humans, in addition to rodents and plants, raises an ethical storm.[16]

In the modern discourse of the science policy debate, the language of Marx appears stodgy and old-fashioned. Why speak of "fetters" when the linguistic currency demands talk about hyperghettoization and the incontestability of markets? However, the dynamic tension between the technological means of production and the traditional or contractual relationships through which goods are finally exchanged against capital, revenue, and wages continues to be played out in the superstructural realm of the "legal, political, religious, aesthetic or philosophi-cal—in short ideological, forms in which men become conscious of this conflict and fight it out."[17]

The debates within Marxism over the nature of nonproductive labor bring me closest to the root of my search for a political economy of personal information.[18] It is Marx's labor theory of value and through that his explication of the core con-cept of surplus value and capitalist exploitation that serve as the critical distinc-tion between a Marxian political economy and the mainstream neoclassical or-thodoxy.[19] Although Joseph Schumpeter was generous in his praise of Marx's social theory, including much of his economics, he suggested that Marx need not have placed all his bets on a concept as weak as that of surplus value.[20] We even find a curious revisionism in the writing of Arun Bose, whose assessment of mod-ern Marxian political economy includes the claim that

> Marx himself had doubts and misgivings about this labour value approach, from the beginning to the end of his career as a political economist. A few years before his death in 1883 (in 1875 to be precise), he finally called for its rejection for mystically and "falsely ascribing *supernatural creative power* to labour." In other words, Marx renounced the labour value approach because it was based on a *mystique* about la-bour which was as unacceptable to him as the *mystique* about capital inherent in the trinity formula.[21]

Dan Schiller suggests that this association between productive labor, which is defined as labor that produces surplus value for the capitalist, and nonproductive labor, much of which may be expended in marketing and other activities neces-sary for the realization of surplus value, stands in the way of the development of a Marxian analysis of the information economy.[22] To the extent that those who are involved in the design and administration of the panoptic sort are nonproductive by traditional definition, their growing importance for capitalist economic devel-opment must be realized and their status as "peripheral phenomena" must be changed.

From Ellul, a Perspective
on the Technological Imperative

The panoptic sort is a technological system. Its rationale is technicist. To some de-gree, concern about the panoptic sort reflects a reticence to embrace technology. It is a posture that is well founded. Jacques Ellul stands as the most visible exem-plar of those who see technology as guaranteeing a dystopic future. Ellul's is an untempered pessimistic view. His view of technology is a totalizing model that evokes a sense of resignation and hopelessness, although that is not his purpose. Those who do not share his view of technology are seen as simply misinformed:

> It has not yet been appreciated that this entry of technology means control over all the persons involved, all the powers, all the decisions and changes, and that technology imposes its own law on the different social organizations, disturbing fundamentally what is thought to be permanent ... , and making politics totally futile. ... No decisions can be made that run contrary to technological growth. All decisions are dictated by the necessity of technological development. Nothing else matters.[23]

In Ellul's view, it is not only the physical world and the social institutions that must adapt to the demands of the technological imperative, even human nature itself must ultimately be transformed. He suggests, for example, that

> genetic manipulation is designed to produce exactly the type of people that we need. ... From birth, individuals are to be adapted specially to perform various services in society. They are to be so perfectly adapted physiologically that there will be no maladjustment, no revolt, no looking elsewhere. The combination of genetic makeup and educational specialization will make people adequate to fulfill their technological functions.[24]

This chilling vision of the future does not promise an egalitarian transformation by which perfection is the lot of all,[25] but reveals a landscape of shameful inequality of the sort that William Julius Wilson[26] has described with many contemporary examples:

> On the one hand there will be a kind of aristocracy marked by its total and infallible adaption to technical gadgets and the technological system, and on the other hand there will be a vast number of people who are outdated, who cannot use the technology, who are powerless, who are still at the social stage but who live in a technological environment for which they are totally unprepared.[27]

Ellul is frequently criticized for a tendency to represent technology as an autonomous force, one that is guided by the goal of efficiency.[28] Robert K. Merton, in his Foreword to the Knopf edition of Ellul's *The Technological Society,* makes this autonomous trajectory clear: "The essential point, according to Ellul, is that technique produces all this without plan; no one wills it or arranges that it be so. Our technical civilization does not result from a Machiavellian scheme. It is a response to the 'laws of development' of technique."[29] Technologies seem to demand, because they require for their own efficient operation, the development of ancillary or support technologies. The technological imperative then generates something akin to an inflationary spiral or a positive feedback, deviation amplifying loop, with each response cycle increasing the level of technological sophistication. Although the process may be dialectical, Ellul's system seems to be devoid of any conceptual role for human agency, beyond those who serve rather than direct the technological wave.[30] Joseph Schumpeter shares Ellul's sense of the importance of technological development and offers a similarly dialectical vision of dynamic change. However, Schumpeter's "gales of creative destruction" are not autonomous but are the result of entreprenurial investment in product and process innovations valued for their potential contribution to the capitalist's "bottom line."[31]

From Weber, an Understanding of Rationalization

Although Max Weber's contribution to modern social science is extensive and is enjoying a sort of rebirth, not unlike that which had been enjoyed by Marx, two aspects of his theoretical project have emerged as central to my analysis of the panoptic sort. The first aspect is Weber's development of the theme of rationality as a characteristic of Western industrialization, and the second is his exemplification of that theme in the rationalization of human activity through the mechanism of bureaucratization. The dominant theme of the contemporary discourse on modern society is one of efficiency, but efficiency is only one aspect of Weber's construct. And more important, perhaps, the current elevation of efficiency to the level of a moral imperative ignores Weber's warnings about the negative consequences of rationalization. "In no sphere of life according to Weber, has rationalization unambiguously advanced human well-being. The rationalization of economic production, for example, has created the 'iron cage' of capitalism, a 'tremendous cosmos' that constrains individuals from without, determining their lives 'with irresistible force.'"[32] This rationalization, especially the formal instrumental rationality, assumes that everything is subject to measurement and calculation. Substantively rational goals and purposes are pursued in markets, where the transactions are guided by reliable calculations of demand. Bureaucratization ensures calculability by organizing the factors of production in ways that guarantee their centralized control.

Perhaps we might see Weber's emphasis on the influence of bureaucracy as reflecting a similar degree of comfort with the notion of an autonomous, self-directed technology. For Weber as for Ellul, those associated with bureaucratization act to ensure its continued growth. Weber expressed the sense that "bureaucracy had an inherent tendency to exceed its instrumental function, and to become a separate force within society, capable of influencing the goals and character of that society. It constituted a separate power group within the state, a separate status stratum within society at large."[33] Bureaucracy is an organizational technology, and the spread of this technology is seen as inevitable. According to Reinhard Bendix, we must find in Weber's work a view that "a system of bureaucratic rule is inescapable. ... Universal bureaucratization was for Weber the symbol of a cultural transformation that would affect all phases of modern society. If this development ran its full course it would result in a new despotism more rigid even than the ancient Egyptian dynasties because it would have a technically efficient administration at its disposal."[34]

The somewhat tempered pessimism of Weber may be based in part on his appreciation of the potential for meaningful action on the part of individuals. Like Marx, Weber believed that history is the product of individual action, even if the designs and circumstances are not of any actor's choosing. David Beetham's exploration of Weber's political activism reflected the similarity in the analyses of Marx and Weber but also noted the differences. "Both Marx and Weber, therefore, recognized the same power relationships, the same structure of power, in modern society; where they differed was the point at which they sought to apply the level of political action to this structure."[35] Weber recognized, however, that the political opposition would not really be able to resist the siren call of bureaucratization but would be required, if it hoped to succeed, to develop its own "counterbureaucracy." Thus for Weber, unlike Marx, socialism offered no promise of escape, but rather an even more extensive bureaucracy. We find signs of this Weberian criticism in Frank Webster and Kevin Robins's exploration of various responses by the Left to information technology and its promise for socialism. With few differences among writers on the Left they noted "a remarkable consensus as to how it should be approached: neutral, inevitably to be accepted, and, more or less, determining."[36] For them, this view sees the scientific and technological revolution as something to which people must learn to adapt and perhaps to enjoy under the guidance of a beneficent state. I find clear parallels in the disclaimers offered by representatives of progressive political action groups who invest in and use the same manipulative and exclusionary technologies of segmentation and targeting as those used by reactionary conservative groups because they believe that without these technologies they must surely lose.[37]

A critical aspect of Weber's view of bureaucracy was his association of power with knowledge—the knowledge of official statistics, which, when linked to the science of mathematics, provided an additional margin of legitimacy. Christopher Dandeker emphasized the surveillance aspect of bureaucratic administrative power and underscored the importance of controlled access to the files developed by the bureaucratic organization in ways that ensure "that administrative reasoning can in principle be understood and replicated by anyone with access to the same information."[38]

Weber's economics is valued for its recognition of the existence and power of institutions and for his criticism of marginal utility analyses, which depend on unrealistic assumptions about the distribution of that power. For Weber, consumer sovereignty is denied by the existence of power inequities, including the power of producers to influence consumers' preference functions. It is suggested that Weber "rejected any view that market relations within a capitalist society were or could be 'free,' in the sense that they dispensed with unequal power relations."[39] Weber's assessment of the rationality of the legal system also took note of the persistence of inequality. From Rogers Brubaker's reading, we see that Weber understood that

> formal freedom of contract does not guarantee that everyone will be equally able to stipulate the terms of contractual agreements, for legally protected inequalities in the distribution of property generate inequalities in bargaining power. Freedom of contract enables an economically powerful employer, for example, to "impose his terms" on the worker who is constrained to accept them by his "more pressing economic need."[40]

This is what is meant by the claim that individuals are largely "contract term takers" in the bulk of their economic relations with organizations, especially with regard to those in which personal information is required before the transaction can move forward.[41] Weber's distinction between formal and substantive rationality finds expression in this area as well. The formally rational pursuit of capitalist goals is seen to generate greater substantively irrational inequality and scorn. Indeed as Brubaker suggests, to the extent that it is "characterized by a high degree of formal rationality, the modern capitalist economic order maximizes the value of calculability, efficiency and impersonality but it is deeply inhospitable to egalitarian, fraternal and caritative values," because formal rationality favors economically powerful groups.[42] Bartlett's generously detailed exemplifications of the broad range of inequalities in the relations between consumers and employers, producers, and government officials largely finishes the critique that Weber's analyses had begun.[43]

From Foucault, the Underlying Concept of Panopticism

The influence of Michel Foucault on my work is so substantial that it threatens to dominate the construction of my arguments about power and social control. It is from Foucault that I derive the underlying concept of panopticism as a technology of power realized through the practice of disciplinary classification and surveillance referred to as the panoptic sort.[44] The Panopticon is the name given by Jeremy Bentham to the design for a prison that would facilitate the efficient observation or surveillance of prisoners by guards or supervisors who might periodically occupy a central tower. The major effect of the design was to create a "state of conscious and permanent visibility that assures the automatic functioning of power."[45] In Foucault's view, the panoptic design need not be limited to prisons but would apply equally well to other institutions that share a disciplinary, educational, or rehabilitative purpose. The panoptic technology was not limited to surveillance alone but included the classification and isolation of subjects by category or type. Once divided, a panoptic structure could be used as a "laboratory; it could be used as a machine to carry out experiments, to alter behavior, to train or correct individuals. To experiment with medicines and monitor their effects. To try out different punishments on prisoners, according to their crimes and character, and to seek the most efficient ones."[46] Thus, panopticism serves as a powerful metaphorical resource for representing the contemporary technology of segmentation and targeting, which involves surveillance of consumers, their isolation into classes and categories, and their use in market tests that have the character of experiments.[47] Kevin Robins and Frank Webster are explicit in their suggestion that the new communications and information technologies provide "the same dissemination of power and control, but freed from the architectural constraints of Bentham's stone and brick prototype. On the basis of the 'information revolution,' not just the prison or factory, but the social totality, comes to function as the hierarchical and disciplinary Panoptic machine."[48]

More generally, Foucault is to be credited with emphasizing the linkage, indeed, the inseparability of power and knowledge. An important focus of his historical work was to describe those forms of power/knowledge that are bound up in the classificatory activities Foucault refers to as "dividing practices," which identify and then separate the deviant, the diseased, or the dissenters.[49] "Essentially, 'dividing practices' are modes of manipulation that combine the mediation of a science (or pseudo-science) and the practice of exclusion—usually in a spatial sense, but always in a social one."[50] The process of the "objectification of the subject," which is implied by the dividing practices, finds an important match in the more subjective forms through which the individual actively participates in transforming himself or herself into a disciplinary subject. From my perspective on marketing, I see this subjectification in consumers' identification of themselves with products and brands, as well as in standards of consumption that marketers have defined for "yuppies" or the "thirty-something" generation. The distinguishable character of popular dress is the prominent display of the name of a particular brand of garment, car, or beverage preferred by the "in" group. Mary Douglas suggests in this regard that "as fast as new medical categories (hitherto unimagined) were invented, or new criminal or sexual or moral categories, new kinds of people spontaneously came forward in hordes to accept the labels and to live accordingly. The responsiveness to new labels suggests extraordinary readiness to fall into new slots and to let selfhood be redefined."[51] This process of "active self-formation" is one that Foucault described as being mediated by some external authority figure. In the contemporary stage of this process, such authority figures may be selected and defined instrumentally but reinforced by an autonomous cadre of cultural experts whom we rely on to tell us "what's in, and what's not!"

This process of objectification involves yet another aspect of the power/knowledge relationship that informs my critical project. Foucault is credited with adding the concept of normalization to that of efficiency as the goal of rationalization. "By 'normalization,' Foucault means a system of finely graded and measurable intervals in which individuals can be distributed around a norm—a norm which both organizes and is the result of this controlled distribution."[52] The importance of statistical measures in the definition of what is normal serves to pull the logic of the law away from strict definitions of right and wrong. We find in the process of normalization the emergence of the empirically derived standard of the "public's interests" replacing a more ethically derived definition of the public interest.[53] This process of normalization may also be seen in the increasing centrality of economic efficiency considerations in the ruling of judges and courts, as well as the emergence of risk analysis as a statistical basis for the offer of contractual services.[54]

This process of normalization contains an inherent contradiction that is evident in the increasing fractionalization of markets. Just as specialists emerge to discipline and correct new classes of deviants, another branch of the same technostructure identifies new forms of perversion and new classes of deviants. As the ability to measure and classify expands, so, almost automatically, do the emergent classes come to be filled with cases demanding attention. According to one observer, "this is what Foucault meant when reminding us that power is not just a force which excludes and says 'No,' but a form of creation."[55] Having heard and understood Foucault, Stanley Cohen then turns away to issue his own plea: "Some ways must be found to halt the seemingly inexorable process by which society keeps classifying, controlling, excluding more and more groups according to age, sex, race, behavior, moral status, ability or psychic state."[56] As will be suggested in the pages that follow, success appears nowhere on the horizon.

From Giddens, a Perspective on Complexity

Contemporary theoretical debates within the social sciences reflect the ebb and flow of fashion as well as insight. In opposition to the heavy-handed theories of social domination that characterize much of the critical theory associated with the Frankfurt School before attempts at its rehabilitation by Jürgen Habermas, we find a growing number of neo-Althusserians who suggest that existence and change in social systems are the product of a complex of influences that almost defies description.[57] This claim of complexity is referred to as "overdetermination," in the sense that entities are mutually constitutive. In the most extreme or radical view, this mutuality means that it is impossible to identify any cause or influence as being more important than any other. This "antiessentialist" posture leaves theorists free to choose an "entry point" from which to begin the ongoing process of describing the complex relations between entities.[58]

Anthony Giddens's theory of structuration provides a useful analytical framework through which one might begin to examine the relations between entities in a way that does not deny the possibility of assessing the nature of influence or power within those relations.[59] Giddens's contribution to this project is quite substantial, as I will attempt to make clear in this brief introduction.

The concept of structuration implies a dynamic rather than a static vision of influence. Although there is well-deserved criticism of the haziness of Giddens's explication of the concept of structuration, it is more than suggestive of a way to understand the production and reproduction of a given social order as a recursive process through which knowledgeable actors, in pursuit of goals, interact with other actors and institutions in ways that reproduce or reconstitute both the actors and the relations.[60] Giddens's emphasis on the knowledgeable actor's understanding of her circumstances and her interests represents an important distinction between structuration and the dominant versions of Antonio Gramsci's notion of hegemony.[61] Hegemony describes a circumstance or status in which a dominant, or hegemonic, view of reality comes to be diffused throughout a society. This hegemonic ideology is that which George Gerbner et al. finds in the "mainstream," toward which people are moved through a process of "cultivation," primarily attributed to television as the dominant cultural form.[62] This equilibrium status is arrived at through a process of leadership and negotiated consensus, rather than through more coercive forms of social control. However, the privileged position that Giddens assigns to the agency of individuals stops well in advance of the extreme positions taken by some cultural theorists who deny influence all together. Indeed, Giddens's definitions of knowledgeability invites efforts to describe the sorts of limiting constraints that other actors' resources may represent.

Part of Giddens's contribution to our understanding of the influence of structure is his identification of the "rules and resources" that are implemented through the routine interactions that make up the daily lives of his agents. Individuals come to understand the rules they have to follow when they interact with other actors and institutions, and they also come to understand and appreciate the differences in the resources that they can bring to bear in these interactions. Thus, we see the exercise of power and influence in the context of what people accept as legitimate or appropriate demands and sanctions. Actors are limited by the contemporary rules and resources that govern a variety of interactions between them. Some of these rules and resources develop such a stability and reach that they rise to the level of institutions or social systems.

Giddens's elaboration of the theory of structuration involves his expansion of relations into the dimensions of time and space. There are important differences between interactions that take place between individuals face-to-face in real time and those that take place across vast distances through the means of advanced communications technology. The absence of authority in space and time is no longer a limit on the ability of agents in power to coordinate the system. Modern communication technology provides a means of remote control.

With Giddens's notion of distanciation, it becomes possible to theorize the interaction between individuals and figures of authority who are not only not present but who are conceivably "interacting" with hundreds, even millions, of others at the same time. The testimonial advertisement in a prime time television program places youngsters in an interaction with an established cultural hero who develops or is assigned authority in a related area as he or she declares how much he or she likes or depends on a particular brand of shoes. A somewhat different form of "distanced" authority can be seen in the "authorization code," which is received from a transaction processing organization handling a vendor's point of purchase request for a charge against a customer's credit line. This distanced interaction differs from, but has much in common with, the remote monitoring of a telemarketer's processing of an inquiry to an 800 number. Giddens is rather explicit in his analysis of the power inherent in this remote surveillance capacity of communications systems.[63]

> Administrative power now increasingly enters into the minutiae of daily life and the most intimate of personal actions and relationships. In an age more and more invaded by electronic modes of storage, collation and dissemination of information, the possibility of accumulating information relevant to the practice of government is almost endless. Control of information can be directly integrated with the supervision of conduct in such a way as to produce a high concentration of state power.[64]

Of course, it is not necessary to limit one's examination of structured relationships and interactions to those between citizens and the state. Indeed, the primary emphasis in this book will be on relations between individuals and the corporate private sector.

With the knowledgeable actor as a focal point for an analysis of the emerging institutionalization of the panoptic sort, Giddens's critical project suggests a number of key empirical targets: (1) practical consciousness and the relations between personality and social perceptions, attitudes, and opinions; (2) routinization and the relation between repetitive interactions with bureaucratic organizations that collect and claim rights in personal information; (3) social positioning, through which different social roles are adopted, assigned, or denied on the basis of computer-aided assessments; and (4) the ever-expanding settings and locales in which interactions and relationships become defined and structured. Each of these will be examined in some detail in the pages that follow.

2

INFORMATION AND POWER

INTRODUCTION

The panoptic sort is the name I have assigned to the complex technology that involves the collection, processing, and sharing of information about individuals and groups that is generated through their daily lives as citizens, employees, and consumers and is used to coordinate and control their access to the goods and services that define life in the modern capitalist economy.

The panoptic sort is a system of disciplinary surveillance that is widespread but continues to expand its reach. The operation of the panoptic system is guided by a generalized concern with rationalization of social, economic, and political systems. The panoptic sort is a difference machine that sorts individuals into categories and classes on the basis of routine measurements. It is a discriminatory technology that allocates options and opportunities on the basis of those measures and the administrative models that they inform. The panoptic sort has been institutionalized. It is standard operating procedure. It is expected. It has its place. Its operation is even required by law.[1] And where it is not, people call out for its installation. Its work is never done. Each use generates new uses. Each application justifies another. It is efficient, having largely been automated. Like a voice-activated recorder, it moves into action solely in response to an action by the object of its control. The panoptic sort is a system of actions that governs other actions.[2] The panoptic sort is a system of power.

Identification

The panoptic sort can be understood to involve three integrated functions or processes: identification, classification, and assessment. Although its operation is by no means limited to identifiable individuals, it depends to a large part on the ability of its users to reliably identify the objects to be controlled. The identification will never move to the level of personhood as we may understand the person as the subject of religion, philosophy, and idealized systems of justice. The attention of the panoptic sort moves only to levels of identification that have administrative and instrumental relevance. Here we refer to the identification of persons with histories, records, and resources when those persons or agents of those persons present a card, form, signature, claim, or response, or when they present themselves at a particular place or time. Identification is associated with authorization and authentication of claims. Identification is associated with the assumption of responsibility for actions, transactions, interactions, and reactions, which may be recorded by the panoptic system.

The level of identification required by the panoptic system is indicated by the importance of the transaction that is about to take place. As the level of risk increases, more sophisticated technologies are called into play. The signature gives way to the physical description, which gives way to the photograph, which gives way to the fingerprint, or the voice print, or the retinal scan. But that is not enough.

The panoptic sort frequently requires third-party validation. You may be *who* you say you are, but we need verification that you are *what* you say you are. Are you old enough? Are you, perhaps, too old? Are you trained and certified; is your license currently in force? Are you creditworthy, reliable, stable, honest, entitled? Are you one of us? This form of identification, more often than not, involves some form of classification.

Classification

Classification involves the assignment of individuals to conceptual groups on the basis of identifying information. Class membership is based on measurement of one or more attributes of an individual's identifying array of attributes. As we have suggested with regard to identification, the data matrix may be infinitely complex, depending on the requirements and resources of the panoptic system brought into play at any given point of interaction. The identification of class membership will always be made on the basis of less information than is at hand or is readily available. As we have suggested with regard to preprocessing, information is thrown away so that more efficient means of control may be put in place.

In discussing the process of classification in the emergence of natural history as a scientific discipline, Foucault suggested that "it reduces the whole area of the visible to a system of variables all of whose values can be designated, if not by a quantity, at least by a perfectly clear and always finite description. It is therefore possible to establish the system of identities and the order of differences between natural entities."[3] Of course, as Foucault later reminded us, not all classification and differentiation were limited to the visible. Important transformations in the classificatory enterprise involved making connections between the seen and the unseen, drawing inferences about deep structure from surface appearance. Estimates of honesty, based on the movement of pens on moving paper or pencils checking boxes on lengthy questionnaires, have become commonplace, and uneasiness about the accuracy, reliability, and validity of these measures does little to restrict their use.

The panoptic sort institutionalizes bias because the blind spots in its visual field are compensated for by a common tendency to fill in the missing with the familiar or with that which is expected. When the paradigmatic vision of the panoptic machine is linked with the futures of bureaucratic organizations and the individuals who stand at their helms, the incentive to find precisely what has been predicted is often too powerful to resist. A disciplinary profession that depends on treating a particular kind of problem has every incentive to calibrate its instruments to find ever more cases of the dysfunction that are in need of expert attention. The discovery of epidemics is very difficult to separate from the interests of the agencies whose responsibility it is to keep them under control. Bureaucratic records reflect the local custom. The definition of what is a crime depends as much on the social status of the perpetrator and the victim as it does on the actions that have allegedly taken place. Troy Duster notes that "if one looks at the record in 250 years of U.S. history, no white man ever committed the crime of rape on a black woman in twelve southern states."[4] Is this a statement about the violent sexual behavior of southern white males, or is it a statement about a racially biased system of classification? There are no objective standards; classification always includes an assessment, whether expressed or not.

Assessment

Assessment represents a particular form of comparative classification. Individuals are compared with others. Individuals are compared with hundreds and thousands of others whose measured attributes help to establish norms and the bounds of reasonableness and acceptability. Assessment involves the use of standards and assumptions about the normality and the independence of distributions. Social distributions are often highly skewed rather than normal. Social distributions are often highly correlated, because they share a common cause, rather than being independent.

Once classification has occurred, assessment frequently involves the examination of probabilities—that is, the likelihood that a person will act, react, or interact in a particular way to a situation or circumstance. Individuals may be classed and evaluated on the basis of the responses they give, as well as on estimates of how likely similar responses are to occur. As with the requirement for precision in identification, the demand for precision in assessment is based on an assessment of the consequentiality of error. Given the tendency of humans to be risk averse, the privileging of avoidance over gain is not without a basis in fact.[5]

The panoptic sort is more concerned with the avoidance of loss than with the realization of gain. Although on the face of it this statement may seem to be in conflict with assumptions about profit maximization, if we recognize that cost reduction and the avoidance of loss are what make the realization of profit possible, the emphasis is not so far afield. Yet the claim made here is meant to be as provocative as it sounds. The panoptic sort is primarily a defensive technology. It operates through victimization, through avoidance. Although marketing targets are eventually identified and selected, these targets are the individuals who remain on the list after the high risks and the sure losers have been eliminated from the pool.

The panoptic sort is a screen that excludes, a filter that blocks, a magnet that ignores fine wood in preference for base metals. The sorting process works primarily by eliminating those who are too much, too little, too late ... too bad! By establishing a criterion, such as those in the 95th percentile and above, the panoptic sort requires that you discard 95 pecent of the population. That is unequivocally what it means to sort and then choose.

The panoptic sort victimizes because it decontextualizes. Status is divorced from circumstance. The circumstance cannot be recaptured; an assessment will always be incomplete. However, the ways in which context is misrepresented are not randomly distributed but reflect an institutionalized bias; a bias established by race, gender, age, class, culture, and consciousness.

Just as capitalism as a form of social organization has neither fully matured nor been extended to the same degree in all areas of social existence in even the most advanced industrial societies, the spread of panoptic technology is uneven and incomplete. This chapter is organized so as to provide a vantage point from which to observe the development and spread of the panoptic sort as an institutionalized system of power.

A QUESTION OF POWER

Randall Bartlett offers a definition of power that may serve us well as we venture into battle with those who would ignore the role that information plays in its use. He defines power as "the ability of one actor to alter the decisions made and/or welfare experienced by another actor relative to the choices that would have been made and/or welfare that would have been experienced had the first actor not existed or acted."[6] Defined in this way, power is a relative measure. All actors may be seen to have some power. The importance of the question is based in the desire to determine, or to demonstrate, which is perhaps more clearly the intention of this work, that the power of individuals is frequently overwhelmed by the power of bureaucratic organizations.

Bartlett identifies several forms of power that are useful in characterizing our response to the various manifestations and influences of the panoptic sort. Ungranted event power describes a circumstance in which the other creates a situation, or a situation may be created by accident or by an unrelated superior force, in which an invididual's options are limited. What economists refer to as externalities are seen to be exemplary forms of ungranted event power. The telemarketing call that disturbs your train of thought is an externality. It is an objective reduction in your welfare for which you are unable to claim compensation. The person who is able to make such a call has ungranted event power. An organization with a computerized telemarketing operation is able to exercise this power simultaneously on hundreds of individuals. This power has a particular irony if the call is from the local Bell operating company offering you caller identification service, which would protect you against just this sort of unwanted telephone harassment.

Bartlett also includes in this category of ungranted event power the influence on welfare that might flow from a lobbyist's modification of the regime of rights that affects the welfare of thousands of individuals. Few if any of the persons affected by this modification of their rights willingly consented to this change. Agenda power is related to this, in that some actors may influence how other actors understand the options that are available to them. As this understanding influences the choices of the latter, it may represent substantial power. Finally, in the same vein, Bartlett identifies what he calls value power—the ability to influence the subjective evaluation of events. For example, in combination with ungranted event power, "If I can actually 'make you like' an item that you previously did not, I have exercised power of an extraordinary kind."[7]

Amitai Etzioni's discussion of value power adds the dimension of social or moral value as an additional force beyond the economic evaluations of worth common to the neoclassical economic paradigm.[8] And, as the moral dimension is influenced by the dominant values of the society, oppositional stances are less powerful in that it would take a greater investment to change the average value position. This is an issue to which we will return because of this critical claim that individual preferences are not given. Instead, preferences are learned, indeed taught, and more often than not, reflect structures of domination.[9]

As we explore the political economy of personal information, the relative power of individuals in comparison with that of institutions and organizations becomes highly relevant. As Bartlett suggests, "Whenever knowledge is a scarce good, it confers power on its possessors."[10] But the power that the individual is able to exercise over the organization when she withholds personal information is almost always insignificant in comparison with the power brought to bear when the organization chooses to withhold goods or services unless the information is provided. This inequality is inherent in the concept of a market in which there is a large number of sellers facing a large number of buyers. Theoretically, none has power over the other because there is always another place to buy or there is always another person to sell to. In reality, however, economic transactions always take place in the context of substantial inequality. When sellers are organizations, they are few, rather than many, and they have acted through marketing to create the impression that the options are fewer still.

Samuel Bowles and Herbert Gintis join Bartlett in identifying similar inequalities in power that characterize the relation of labor to capital.[11] Bowles and Gintis suggest that the "effectiveness of capitalist command over workers depends ultimately on the capitalist's power to terminate the labor contract."[12] They suggest that capital is different from labor in that it is able to move more freely. Unlike labor, which is embodied in people, capital can move across the globe instantaneously at the push of a button.[13] To the extent that information is capital, its ability to move is unprecedented. This heightened mobility increases the power of capital relative to that of labor. The laborer, on his own, generally does not perceive the option of voluntary unemployment or the breaking of an unsatisfactory contract as a viable option. The theoretical labor market, in which there are no costs associated with the negotiation of new labor contracts, does not exist. There are substantial costs that flow from laborers who quit, as well as from those who are fired. More important, in terms of the panoptic sort,

> to the extent that being fired is a signal that G must carry with her into the market, they may reduce the quality of jobs made available. If she is able to hide the particular job experience, she is also hiding the positive experience aspects of that position, and perhaps raising questions about the hole in her employment record. C's ability to fire is an ability to return G to the labor market with a published statement of her incompetence. That is a potential ability to alter the agenda of job opportunities available to G in the future.[14]

Thus, employers have substantial power over labor, which limits the worker's options regarding the labor contract. On the one hand, the actions of an employer, without the consent of the employee, can change the present and future welfare of any worker by influencing the record that follows an employee throughout working life. A chain reaction may also set in. A period of unemployment may cause an arrears in the payment of bills, which will adversely affect a worker's credit rating. As access to a credit report is considered to be a legitimate business need for an employment decision, a poor credit report may thus mean that future employment possibilities are also limited. This is substantial ungranted event power. Awareness of these consequences makes the average employee highly cautious about testing the limits of her power. On the other hand, unless they are barred by the presence of a strong union or by the threat of government action, capital strikes or reductions in force are commonplace and are initiated without apparent risk to the owners of the firm.

Although it will not be developed here to the extent it deserves, there is an approach to power that focuses not on individuals, firms, or the state, but on the networks that the elites in each of these spheres develop and maintain in the pursuit of their common interests and objectives.[15] Here I refer to the tradition of power structure research associated with G. William Domhoff, resurrected in part in a treatise on the policy process.[16] Domhoff finds himself in an argument between the instrumentalists, with whom he is most closely aligned, and the structuralists, who discuss the limitations on the ability of the state to act independently. The articulated structuralist view, represented by the work of Nicos Poulantzas, suggests that "ultimately, even a president cannot press beyond the constraints of government structure and must succumb to the internal dynamics which push government to maintain stability, provide a favorable investment climate for privately held businesses, and suppress any discontent with the outcomes of these policies."[17] Against this view, the instrumentalists explore the power and influence of organizations and institutions outside of the formal structure of the government apparatus, such as the foundations, policy centers, or think tanks, and the business organizations and political action committees (PACs). A more comprehensive analysis of the organizational influence on policy is to be found in the work of Edward Laumann and David Knoke.[18] Particularly useful about their analysis is their focus on the ability of organizations to mobilize and process information as a resource in the production of influence.

Michel Foucault's primary project was concerned with the exploration of the techniques—the microphysics of power—that were involved in the formation of the individual as the object of a disciplinary technology.[19] His project was radical and intentionally destabilizing. In a conversation in which he answered criticisms from those involved in the penal system, such as social workers, Foucault responded forthrightly to the challenge that he provided little guidance:

> It's true that certain people, such as those who work in the institutional setting of the prison—which is not the same as being in prison—are not likely to find advice or instructions in my books that tell them "what is to be done." But my project is precisely to bring it about that they "no longer know what to do," so that the acts, gestures, discourses which up until then had seemed to go without saying become problematic, difficult, dangerous. This effect is intentional.[20]

Foucault's conception of the relation between power and knowledge is complex. Rather than to claim, as was (and is) popular, that power equals knowledge, Foucault discussed the two as being inextricably linked and mutually constitutive. Power cannot operate without a constitutive field of knowledge, and the operation of power reveals both its possibilities and its limits; knowledge is necessary for power to continue to operate. The social science disciplines that were the focus of much of Foucault's writing about power are defined in terms of their specialized and evolving knowledge of persons as objects of power. This knowledge is gained through a form of disciplinary surveillance that he defined as panopticism.

PANOPTICISM

Panopticism is based on the belief that control over individuals is made possible through a system that facilitates the continuous, automatic, disciplinary surveillance of persons who have been determined to be in need of correction or normalization. As a technology of power it involves the organization of individuals into space through their partition into categories that are at their base dichotomous, either inside or outside.[21] Subsequent examination of people through observation and surveillance serves the goals of correction and control.

Foucault began his discussion of panopticism with a description of late seventeenth-century efforts to control the plague. The panoptic procedures of segmentation and surveillance are readily identifiable in the routines described for locating, observing, and taking note of the status of the residents of the town. Locked into their individual homes, the residents were required to appear at a

window and report the status of their health, under pain of death. The surveillance depended on the creation of a record of every resident that formed the basis
of a permanent registration and that could be added to after each inspection. In
this description Foucault found the underlying principles of panopticism
through which we will see clear reflections of the much more sophisticated systems in place today:

> This enclosed, segmented space, observed at every point, in which the individuals
> are inserted in a fixed place, in which the slightest movements are supervised, in
> which all events are recorded, in which an uninterrupted work of writing links the
> centre and periphery, in which power is exercised without division, according to a
> continuous hierarchical figure, in which each individual is constantly located, exam-
> ined and distributed among the living beings, the sick and the dead—all this consti-
> tutes a compact model of the disciplinary mechanism.[22]

And the power of the mechanism lay in its analysis.

Foucault identified the Panopticon of Jeremy Bentham as an architectural realization of the disciplinary principle.[23] The prison that Bentham wanted to have
built was a model of efficiency. Bentham believed that this design, orginally developed by his brother, a naval architect, would serve a utilitarian purpose of the
highest order. His presentation of the design to the National Assembly of
postrevolutionary France won him the distinction of honorary citizenship.[24]
Bentham's vision was not limited to the use of the panoptic form as a prison, per
se; he also thought that it might serve a dual function as a self-sufficient, even
profitable workhouse for the indigent and unemployed who were unwilling or
unable to join the emerging proletariat.

The Panopticon, as designed, would be a many-sided construction with a central observation tower. Each cell would be supplied with two windows, one to provide backlighting for the occupant, the other to allow the observer in the tower
unimpeded visual access. Unlike the dungeon, which locked prisoners away in
darkness, the panoptic design provided control through complete visibility. Because each occupant of a cell would be isolated from others, it would reduce the
possibility of the collective, cooperative, or infectious spread of problematic conditions or behavior. In Foucault's assessment, the design could be readily adapted
for any number of uses, to house patients, students, soldiers, or workers. All could
be managed more efficiently if isolation and surveillance could be facilitated. In
Bentham's design, power would operate because it was both visible and unverifi-
able. The central tower, visible at all times, would be a constant reminder that an
unseen observer might be watching at any time. The Panopticon would be efficient because it would require fewer guards or supervisory personnel. In one
sense, the system was self-monitoring in that residents would soon come to expect
continuous surveillance or, at the very least, would always be uncertain about
when the next glance would fall on their cell. The likelihood of periodic observa-

tion would operate like random reinforcement in conditioning each person to his status.

The efficiency of the panoptic design was also ensured by the fact that it did not matter who exercised the power of observation. Almost anyone could perform the function. Indeed, as Foucault suggested, there need not even be uniformity of purpose or motivation behind the operation of the Panopticon by observers with access to the tower—any would serve as well. "The more numerous these anonymous and temporary observers, the greater the risk for the inmate of being surprised and the greater his anxious awareness of being observed."[25] Anyone could be watching, and nearly all would tell someone should a prisoner step out of line.

The fact that the Panopticon was never built says more about Bentham's failings as a politician than it says about the utility of the Panopticon as a metaphor for a system of control. Foucault was clear on this point. He suggested that the Panopticon must "be understood as a generalizable model of functioning; a way of defining power relations in terms of the everyday life of men."[26] The metaphor is powerful. Although some may find its totalizing character harsh and unrealistic, it is not one from which I shrink. Instead, I wish to echo Foucault's claim, and to offer extensions of my own:

> It is polyvalent in its applications; it serves to reform prisoners, but also to treat patients, to instruct schoolchildren, to confine the insane, to supervise workers, to put beggars and idlers to work. It is a type of location of bodies in space, of distribution of individuals in relation to one another, of hierarchical organization, of disposition of centres and channels of power, of definition of the instruments and modes of intervention of power, which can be implemented in hospitals, workshops, schools, prisons. Whenever one is dealing with a multiplicity of individuals on whom a task or a particular form of behavior must be imposed, the panoptic schema may be used.[27]

It is only the locational constraints, the notion of separation by space, occasioned by the initial conceptualization of the panoptic system as a building and by the surveillance as visual that limits Foucault's construct. But in an age of electronic networks, virtual memory, and remote access to distributed intelligence and data, disciplinary surveillance is no longer limited to single buildings, and observation is no longer limited to line of sight. This fact has been stated forcefully by Frank Webster and Kevin Robins, whose work has been influential in guiding my pursuit of the mechanics of the panoptic sort.[28]

Disciplinary Surveillance

Foucault's emphasis on the social sciences, the disciplines of sociology, psychology, criminology, and psychiatry, reflected his interest in particularly salient forms of social control that have historically been legitimated behind the cloak of science. The professionals involved in market research and risk analysis are not substantially less scientific in their methods and certainly no less consequential in their conditioning of behavior than any who fall within Foucault's category of the objectifying social sciences. They are all characterized by the same "vast compilation of data, the proliferation of dossiers, and the continuous expansion of new areas of research developed concurrently with a refinement and flourishing of disciplinary techniques for observing and analyzing the body, so as to make it more available for manipulation and control."[29]

It is critical to note that the purpose of the modern prison and of other panoptic systems that imitate its technology is not punishment, but transformation, rehabilitation, and correct training. The same may be said of the panoptic sort: It is not limited to identification, classification, and assessment, but includes the goal of normalizing behavior within categories. This process of correct training involves three simple components, one of which we already met—surveillance, or hierarchical observation. The second component, normalizing judgment, which seeks to punish nonconformity, or deviation from the norm, may teach conformity more efficiently through judicious supply of rewards. The distribution of rewards, or of freedoms on the basis of ranks, grades, or scores, describes and defines at the same time that it instructs. Like the colors of the epaulettes on the boys at the École Militarie,[30] the colors of American Express (Amex) cards, green, gold, and platinum, are only glimpses of the much finer gradations that operate to lead cardmembers through their paces.[31] The possibilities for discipline with the Amex membership are quite similar to the possibilities within the military academy, and the process of normalization is the same because it depends on a system that "compares, differentiates, hierarchizes, homogenizes, [and] excludes."[32]

The third component of correct training is the examination, which facilitates the process of normalization. It is through examination that the evaluation on which normalization is based may be produced. Amex is reported to examine each of its cardmembers on as many as 450 categories on a daily basis, because such an examination facilitates both the authorization of charges and the marketing of cardmember, auxiliary, and affiliate services. For Foucault, the examination is important because it not only places individuals within the field of surveillance, but it also "situates them in a network of writing; it engages them in a whole mass of documents that capture and fix them. The procedures of examination were accompanied at the same time by a system of intense registration and documentary accumulation."[33] In addition to the creation of an individual record, which defines the individual as a case, this documentation eases the disciplinary accumulation of records, which eases further classification, and the establishment of empirical norms. The computerization and linkage of these written documents via telecommunications move the panoptic sort to a different level of significance.

Part of the challenge we face in the integration of Foucault's vision of a system of dispersed but continually evolving sytems of power is understanding how these systems come to be institutionalized and legitimated at different levels of social systems. We are especially interested in the ways in which these sytems of power come to be integrated with other systems of domination that may be mutually reinforcing. The evolution and elaboration of systems of power may be seen as a process of structuration.

STRUCTURATION

Structuration is one of the more acceptable neologisms generated by Anthony Giddens as he has labored to produce a theoretical alternative to functionalism. Giddens is unremitting in his criticism of all forms and varieties of functionalism, even to the finding of damaging traces of its presence in Marx and Marxists of a variety of stripes.[34] His major criticism of functionalism has been that it provides no true explanation in a claim that a system has *needs* for some thing or some relationships that may come to characterize it. Saying that a capitalist system needs a reserve army of the unemployed does nothing to explain *how* it is that a reserve army comes to be. Giddens suggests that functionalist theories ought to pursue an explanation through consideration of the counterfactual—what would happen to the system in the event that there were no such army? What would *it* do to ensure that such an army developed and was maintained? It is clear that Giddens's critique in part attacks the tendency of functionalism to assign an intelligence to a system as though it were an entity, a life form, or, at best, an organization with a leadership. To say that capitalism as a system needs something is quite different from saying that a group of capitalists, an elite core that recognizes a common class interest, may act in ways its leaders believe will serve those needs. This is also different from arguing that a capitalist logic *demands* certain choices, because that logic, so defined, is one that is either implemented or not by capitalists themselves. Similarly, leaders of the state as an organization may perceive what the needs of groups and organizations may be and may act to meet some of those needs as a part of their mission and presumed responsibility. But in each of these examples, knowledgeable human beings are acting on the basis of an analysis of circumstances and options. This is a continuing problem in the pursuit of analysis at the level of institutions.

Organizations and institutions do not think. American Telephone and Telegraph (AT&T) has no mind, no consciousness, and no social conscience other than that which may be written down, reproduced, and transmitted to its leadership through a process of socialization. Social systems have no needs, because systems are not entities but are theoretical constructs. Social systems cannot act, but they may be seen to *operate* in a particular fashion. It may even be argued that social systems have requirements, but this claim cannot be demonstrated conclusively unless the definition of the system is tautological in that its requirement is part of its definition—a capitalist system is one that requires the exploitation of labor.

Giddens's emphasis on knowledgeable human beings, acting in pursuit of their interests as they understand them, provides an entry point through which to begin thinking about structuration as a process, rather than as a static framework. For Giddens, "social systems are composed of patterns of relationships between actors or collectivities reproduced across time and space."[35] Giddens's knowledgeable agents are privileged in terms of their individual and collective agency. Knowledgeable actors not only have an understanding, but also act on the basis of that understanding. This action, taken primarily through interaction with other knowledgeable agents, produces and reproduces the social system. Giddens's concept of structuration is not unlike the process of socialization, except that his emphasis on agency avoids defining a process through which persons are acted *on.* Rather, structuration describes a process that unfolds by working *through.* Furthermore, structuration differs from socialization in that relationships, as well as beliefs and values, are reproduced through the process.

This notion of reproduction is to be distinguished from the familiar biological sense of reproduction in which similar, perhaps functionally identical, beings are produced through genetic rules and biological resources contributed by parents, but it is more recursive in the sense of being constitutive of itself. That is, in the process of engaging in interactive and contextually situated practices, in which the actors are constrained by the rules as well as by the resources that they bring to the relationship, each actor is produced again, or reproduced, in an identifiable relationship that we may understand to be structured.

Interactions between parents and children take place in a variety of sites and circumstances, each characterized by a particular set of expectations and governed by a set of rules and understandings about the powers and freedoms of each knowledgeable agent. To the extent that each individual acts consistently with historically and idiosyncratically generated sets of expectations, the parent-child relationship is reproduced. Of course, parent-child relationships usually change. Sometimes the changes are conflictual and unpleasant. The nature of the change is not mysterious. Most parents are able to understand and accommodate these changes, which they accept as part of a normal, if ritualized, process by which their children pass into adulthood and independence. These are the sorts of changes that Giddens's emphasis on time and space might suggest we explore through a focus on the middle range of historical time, which is captured by the concept of the life cycle. Beyond the minute-by-minute, day-by-day, even year-by-year spans of time, which characterize the dimension of temporality, we find a much longer period that Giddens associates with institutions. The primary emphasis in this book will be within the shorter historical moments of people's time, although I do not wish to lose sight of the structures of time in which institutions are seen to change.

Roles, Resources, and Routines

Giddens has been subjected to considerable criticism for the often frustrating lack of clarity with which he defines some of the core concepts in his theory of structuration. Among the most problematic areas are those having to do with the use of power in various interactions. Knowledgeable agents understandably differ in terms of the resources that they can bring to bear to increase the probability that the outcomes of those interactions are ones that they favor. The use of an agent's resources, however, is constrained by the existence of rules that govern the use of rewards as well as sanctions. Rules are moral, professional, social, and inherited and may even be negotiated on the spot and apply only in limited special circumstances. These rules apply to communications as well as more overt forms of behavior that define any interaction. For Giddens, "all human interaction involves the communication of meaning, the operation of power, and modes of normative sanctioning."[36]

Depending on the site and the nature of the interaction, referred to as a structural set, Giddens suggests that we may focus on different structural properties, which he labels signification, domination, and legitimation. Structures of domination are further distinguished in terms of capabilities relating to influence over persons (authorization) and command over material resources (allocation). Giddens suggests that through rules the structuring may acquire a certain degree of stability as the rules permeate social systems, and in this way they may be seen as having become institutionalized. That is, some rules become institutionalized in bureaucratic forms and have the force of law, and the instrumentations of precedent and expertise help to guide their interpretation.

Different institutions may therefore be characterized in terms of the modalities of domination that are most characteristic of their process. Although all three structural properties are always present and interacting, legitimation may be seen to be in the forefront of the legal realm, and allocative considerations might characterize the economic realm. The authoritative modality is in the forefront of interactions within political institutions.[37]

John Thompson suggests that there are numerous problems with the concept of rules in Giddens's theoretical system.[38] Part of the difficulty has to do with the fact that "the rules which comprise structure are embroiled in struggles, are subject to rival interpretations and are continually transformed in their very application. Rules, in other words, cannot be conceptualized in isolation from the resources which facilitate the exercise of power."[39] Rules, therefore, cannot be specified objectively because, like systems and relationships, they are conceptual and vary in the degree to which they are believed to be operative in any interaction. An agent's awareness of the rules that apply in any interaction may be influenced strategically by another actor, as well as by a habitually structured process of "checking" as an individual takes stock reflexively of the circumstances in which he or she finds himself or herself at any point in time.

Consciousness

This checking may take place at different levels of consciousness or with different degrees of self-awareness. Giddens makes an important contribution in his discussion of the differences between two levels of consciousness. As I have suggested, individuals acting in the pursuit of their interests are guided by their understandings of the environment, the rules of the game, and their own capacities and resources. Much of this knowledge is seen to operate below the level of one's conscious awareness, a kind of autopilot that draws on the accumulated knowledge and experience that individuals have stored, perhaps even at the neurological level. People may *know* how to drive a car, ride a bicycle, throw a ball, return a serve, dodge a wild pitch, and perhaps even how to get their computer to print out a design onto a page. They also know how to engage in a conversation, an argument, or a negotiation. Yet they may be far from articulate about the mechanics involved in any of these activities. This is a distinction that Giddens makes between practical consciousness and discursive consciousness, in which language is required to give knowledge and reason expression. Discursive consciousness is not limited to communication with others, but includes communication with oneself—the ability to reflexively examine the reasons, the arguments, and the meanings behind the myriad of choices that might be involved in the completion of any routine process, such as preparing an evening meal or voting for a referendum issue. Giddens helps us to understand the methodological difficulties involved in trying to understand how what people know influences what they do. "Where what agents know about what they do is restricted to what they can say about it, in whatever discursive style, a very wide area of knowledgeability is simply occluded from view."[40]

Giddens introduces the influence of history and culture into his theoretical mix through his suggestion that consciousness, both practical and discursive, has multiple sources, personal, direct, and mediated. The "stocks of knowledge," on which actors draw as they engage in the interactions that produce and reproduce the systems in which they are situated, are neither fixed nor fully given. It is important to understand the extent to which the power within the various relationships that define a system may be bound up in the structuring of access to knowledge.

Although a distinction is made between practical and discursive consciousness, I take from Giddens an emphasis on an individual's reflexive monitoring of her own actions, in the context of reassessments of progress and purpose: "All (competent) actors in a society are expected to 'keep in touch' with why they act as they do, as a routine element of action, such that they can 'account' for what they do when asked to do so by others."[41] It is important at this stage to note that Giddens recognizes that the reflexive monitoring of individuals is almost by definition incomplete and inadequate. When Giddens characterizes his agents as knowledgeable, he admits to the limitations on that knowledge. It is clear, for example, that an actor will not fully apprehend all of the conditions that constrain (help or hinder) the actions she may pursue. Similarly, this actor will not know, indeed cannot possibly know, of all of the unintended consequences of whatever actions she may take. Indeed, as Bartlett suggests, many of the actions that an individual will take will be constrained by actions taken by other actors, and not all of those constraints will have been planned by those actors; they may be uncontrolled externalities.[42]

An individual's motivation for action works through her reasons for the action, which include both her sense of her present status, assessed reflexively, and her sense of the conditions in which actions are taken in pursuit of purposeful goals. We may add, although Giddens is unclear on this point, that the unknown may also include the unconscious motivations, reasons, and awarenesses that may interact with and influence understanding and action. The monitoring of actions will take note of those that were intended and those that were unintended. Because vision is physiologically as well as psychologically limited, however, even many of the unintended consequences will not be noticed. I might also suggest, consistent with the notions I share with Bartlett and others, that much that is unacknowledged in the conditions, including the unintended consequences, is not available for monitoring because other interested actors have purposively hidden it from view. It is through this vision of agency that Giddens is able to make an association with Marx's dictum about agency. People make (and are made by) the world, but it is not a world constructed according to their designs.

As has been suggested in the discussion of rules and resources, a critical aspect of knowledgeability has to do with self-identification and estimates of the presumed appropriateness or legitimacy of one's claims or of the claims that others make on the basis of that identification. Relations among individuals that are defined or are definable in terms of class involve considerations of differential resources appropriate to one's position or status. Awareness of the rules governing interactions, which is also likely to involve an evaluation of the appropriateness or fairness of the rules, may be seen as an index of class consciousness.

Class Consciousness

Critical consciousness frequently involves an analysis of the power of others as having unjustly limited the life chances of entire groups or classes of individuals. Group consciousness, defined as a recognition of commonality of status, options, and purpose, has been seen as a necesssary precondition of resistance and social transformation. Class consciousness has been identified as the primary condition necessary for a revolutionary transformation of capitalism. The failure of class consciousness to develop into a revolutionary form has been a core problem in social theory.[43]

The definition of class and the origins of its consciousness have been fundamental concerns of Marxists and reflect the centrality of the concept of class consciousness in Marx's writings. Contemporary Marxist scholars struggle to explain the considerable variety in class orientations that can be found within the working class. Erik Olin Wright has pursued his concept of contradictory class positions as a way to understand the complexity of class relations and to reclaim class analysis as a theoretical force.[44] Wright recognizes that one's existence in a class location means that one is subject to a set of mechanisms and forces that influence one's class consciousness. For Wright, the "task is to understand the ways in which macro-structural contexts constrain micro-level processes, and the ways in which the micro-level choices and strategies of individuals can affect macro-stuctural arrangements."[45] Class consciousness, as a common understanding, is derived from shared material interests, which may or may not be derived from their common experience as labor. Wright's empirical work has been troubled, as has been the work of many who sought the link between experience and consciousness, by the fact that people within the same objective class will have quite different life experiences and, as a result, will understand the world and their place in it quite differently. Wright finds in Giddens a failure to specify an alternative to the determinations of class consciousness that are based on property relations. Indeed, he suggests that many of the examples that Giddens provides are in fact very close to Marxist understandings of class.[46] He finds in Giddens no reason to doubt that the influence of class is primary: "This does not imply that individuals are necessarily 'class conscious' in the sense of being aware of their class position and class interests, but simply that their forms of social consciousness are more systematically shaped by class relations than by any other relations and should therefore be accorded primacy."[47] Wright has also expressed a reluctance to join the Weberian bandwagon and to set aside theory in preference for an empiricist glance toward whatever relationships may appear.

Max Weber distinguished between class and status groups in ways that set him apart from Marx. The distinctions between Marx and Weber on the question of class were not limited to their differential emphases on class conflict as a primary force in the transformation of society. The distinction for Weber between classes and status groups reflected a difference in his conception of the nature of power within a society. With slightly different terms, Weber's conception of the relations between the economic base and the superstructure can be read from his discussion of power, wherein he finds a determination of class situation in a person's market situation.[48] An individual's class situation is determined by economic conditions, based on that person's position in the commodity or labor markets. Such a position is defined in terms of an individual's possession of goods and opportunities for income. Weber suggests that we can speak of a class when a given number of people share, in common, these determinations of life chances. These classes are not communities of common interest, but definitional sets.

Weber steps back from the Marxian position that class position determines class consciousness. Although he recognizes that a common class situation *may* generate "similar" reactions, such a result is far from certain. Instead, Weber argues that social consciousness, which may be reflected in associations and social action, is developed in the cultural realm, in intellectual discourse. Class situation has to be understood before it can support class action, and this understanding is not inextricably linked to one's position in the market. The kind of social consciousness that can lead to social action is, in Weber's view, more likely to take place in status groups, which are real, rather than conceptual, social forms.

Status groups, differentiated in terms of the status honor its members may claim, are expressed by a "style of life" that their members and those who aspire to membership must adopt.[49] The difference between classes and status groups is seen ultimately to turn on their relation to the production or the consumption spheres. Class situation is defined and determined by the relations of production and the acquisition of wealth, whereas "status groups are stratified according to the principles of their *consumption* of goods as represented by special styles of life."[50] This is not to suggest that status position is independent of class position, because the ability to maintain a life-style is largely dependent on economics, but only to indicate that the correlation is far from perfect.

Wright's desire to find a more clearly theoretical basis for understanding the variance in class consciousness may also be seen in the empirically grounded theorizing of Arthur Stinchcombe. Stinchcombe defines class consciousness as the "tendency of people to think of their position in the larger society in terms of their position in an employing organization. Workers are class conscious when they think of their grievances at work and their interests in politics as both derived from their employment relation to particular organizations."[51] Similarities among workers in industrial societies reflect the similarities in the contracts that determine which "slots" workers are assigned to within a particular production system. The political content of class consciousness is based on the interaction between the processes that assign workers to slots and on the rights and freedoms that are common to workers in particular slots. Stinchcombe utilizes the contributions of E. P. Thompson and David Lockwood to aid our understanding of the diffuse and nonrevolutionary class consciousness that has come to characterize workers in the service or information sectors of modern economies.

In contrast to the neoclassical notions of free labor negotiating contracts with employers, industrialization involved a "bureaucratization of the wage contract," by means of which workers found themselves in a "take it or leave it" situation with regard to a standard contract. The uniformity in the labor contract is seen to have been matched by a kind of uniformity in the political contract defined in terms of democratic suffrage. The uniformity in the labor contract makes it possible for labor to identify its common interest in seeking a general improvement in the wage payment in general, rather than in terms of a personal contract. Collective bargaining through unions is an understandably bureaucratic response to such an analysis of common interests deriving from common circumstance.

After noting substantial differences in the nature of the labor movements in the United Kingdom, the United States, and Japan, Stinchcombe focuses on the cultural aspects of the process through which class consciousness develops. The development of the left-wing Enlightenment project of Thomas Paine is seen to have departed from the rightist commitment to tradition and the wisdom of one's betters, which restricted the development of class consciousness among some. Stinchcombe finds in Thompson a thread that is central to Giddens's theory of structuration. The development of class consciousness was the result of the ongoing "intellectual struggles of a bunch of workers to figure out what was going on, in terms of the cultural heritage that they had."[52] Class consciousness was the product of a process involving a goal oriented search for understanding, conditioned but not fully determined by class position. A common conclusion that emerged from this process was that the system was not trustworthy. It was *not* "a system in which the rulers cared about their fates, respected their action to defend those fates, and regarded them as persons with inherent value to be respected and protected."[53] As we shall see quite clearly as we examine public understanding of the panoptic sort, the question of *trust* is a critical component in the formation of consciousness and the demand for state action.

Problems with trust emerge when organizations create the expectation that the standard contract will guarantee standard treatment, but when the concrete, objective experience of workers is anything but equal. Ensuring equal treatment has been traditionally a prime concern of unions, but the decline in unionization in the U.S. work force may be seen as both cause and consequence of ill-formed class consciousness.

Stinchcome identifies two factors to explain the absence of class consciousness among workers. The first is the creation of a dual labor market in which the subordinate market contains low-skilled, low-commitment workers, generally female, young, and minority group members. These workers tend to be excluded from positions that have strong union control, and they fail to perceive a common purpose in standard contracts because such contracts do not exist where turnover, or the flow of labor between jobs, is so rapid.[54] The second and more interesting factor in terms of our efforts to understand the cultural component of consciousness is the claim that one's consciousness *as* a worker comes from interaction and contact *with* workers.

It is the nature of work in the service sector that "many service jobs isolate the person from social contact with other workers and require intense contact with clients."[55] This influence does not work in a unified direction but rather works similarly to the mainstreaming process identified by George Gerbner and his colleagues.[56] Contacts with clients in upper-class professions are seen to lead service workers leftward, whereas contacts with clients in lower-class professions lead those workers rightward. Neither movement leads to the development of a progressive class consciousness.

The strength of this influence is determined by the extent of a worker's contact with clients. "The more the demography of the workplace includes clients, and the more intense the interaction of service workers with clients is, the more those who might otherwise be disposed to join unions or to vote left will instead be nonunion and vote to the right."[57] This confusion in class consciousness is heightened by the fact that many service workers are themselves engaged in selling the symbols of class status. To sell effectively, service workers must place themselves "inside the heads" of their clients. This process cannot help but influence their own consciousness and values. You become what you sell.

Stinchcombe suggests that when the interaction with clients involves a necessary deference to the client, a similar form of identification takes place. He suggests further that the nature of the organization of the service sector means that many workers will be in smaller organizations where they will be in close direct contact with the profit-oriented owner of the enterprise. The influence on consciousness from this contact is far greater than anyone would imagine might result from such contact between workers and owners in a massive organization such as AT&T. The scale of the organization and the individualization of the labor contract also support the development of a conservatizing ambition, which is less likely to develop on the factory floor or at a telemarketing console.

It is through this focus on the nature of the work process that Stinchcombe helps us to understand some of the conflicting and contradictory aspects of class consciousness that are derived from Wright's notion of contradictory class locations. It is his emphasis on the day-to-day, routine interactions that help to condition, structure, and reproduce class orientations that are among the most useful, especially as they are closely linked to Giddens's construct of structuration. However, in the modern (or postmodern) era, a great many routine interactions no longer take place face-to-face.

Distanciation

Giddens's concept of distanciation helps one understand the significance of telecommunications and telecommunications networks. Interactions, which involve situated practices generally conceived of as taking place in a restricted time-space nexus, increase in variety through the technology of communication. The technology of communication, no doubt including communication across distances by means of the drum, but perhaps more significantly, the communication that spans temporal limits as well through writing, changes the structures of domination. Allocative and authoritative resources may be used to coordinate social systems across time and space by means of communication. This process of distanciation, which transforms the presence/absence character of the power that is reproduced through interaction, is qualitatively different in the context of modern communications networks. Communications networks change the nature of the resources that are required to maintain a level of domination within a social system. Geoff Mulgan suggests that the "social organization of control is substantially dependent on available communications technologies. Without direct and rapid communication, control must depend on the use of agents."[58] Coordination is a fundamental aspect of structuration and involves the application of authoritative resources. The ability of some actors to exercise this authority remotely and to effectively multiply the presence of any given authority by allowing its appearance in multiple sites at a fraction of the cost that would have been required for a physical presence is a resource of great importance and historical moment. Giddens suggests that "in general (although certainly not universally) it is true that the greater the time-space distanciation of social systems—the more their institutions bite into time and space—the more resistant they are to manipulation or change by any individual agent."[59]

Giddens also suggests that we give due consideration to the storage and access qualities of media that help to determine the nature of time-space distanciation:

> The storage of authoritative and allocative resources may be understood as involving the retention and control of information or knowledge whereby social relations are perpetuated across time-space. Storage presumes *media* of informational representation, modes of information *retrieval* or recall and, as with all power resources, modes of its dissemination. Notches on wood, written lists, books, files, films, tapes—all these are media of information storage of widely varying capacity and detail. All depend for their retrieval on the recall capacities of the human memory but also on skills of interpretation that may be possessed by only a minority within any given population.[60]

As I have suggested elsewhere, the inequality in the distribution of individual capacities to access and retrieve information is compounded when similar limitations also constrain the ability of individuals to express their knowledge discursively in ways that have force.[61]

Derek Gregory's criticism of Giddens's theoretical project focuses on the challenges of empirical research that might be involved in the coordination that is facilitated through interactions with others who are absent rather than present in time-space.[62] Gregory notes that Giddens places capitalist societies in a structure of domination that is characterized by a high degree of time-space distanciation, which supports the realization of power through the control of allocative (economic) resources through surveillance and commoditizatio He suggests, however, that Giddens draws back too soon from hisn. responsibility to specify what some of the locales and settings might be in which this modern form of structuration takes place. Clearly, he suggests that "actors routinely encounter locales in the conduct of everyday life, no doubt, but any genuinely critical theory must surely go beyond these mundanities to show how particular places and spaces are *produced.* "[63] Gregory's demand for geographical specificity misapprehends the aspects of a virtual reality in a networked environment that defies locational precision. It is not a geographical space but a transactional space that begins to identify and define the structurational reality of the panoptic sort.

As we have suggested with regard to Foucault's reconstruction of the Panopticon, the operation of the panoptic machine has escaped the constraints of location or space just as effectively as it has overcome limitations on time. Gregory is correct, however, in his charge that Giddens's contribution remains, for the most part, at a very high level of abstraction, and perhaps it falls to us to push those insights into the empirical realm to discover how technology, markets, and culture enable as well as constrain the freedom of knowledgeable agents.

TECHNOLOGY, MARKETS, AND CULTURE

It is my goal in this book to explore the changes in technology, especially the integrated technical system that I refer to as the panoptic sort, in the context of the changes that are taking place in the markets of late capitalism. In the face of the collapse of the communist, or state capitalist, forms of governance that have occurred so dramatically as the decade of the 1990s began to reveal its character, I would only invite ridicule by speaking as though capitalism was nearing its end. Yet the transformations in capitalism that have been predicted by Marx, Weber, and Schumpeter have surely produced a kind of capitalism that Adam Smith would quickly disown. When some social theorist succeeds in popularizing a name for this new form of socioeconomic organization, then capitalism will have come to an end. Thus, to the extent that the old nomenclature no longer fits the data very well, lateness is a fitting characterization.

The cultural changes of interest are those that reflect and are reflected in the laws, practices, and customs regarding the treatment of personal information, as the coordination of capitalism requires ready access to increasingly detailed information about the history and status of individuals. The panoptic sort is an integrated system that is involved in the identification, classification, assessment, and distribution of individuals to their places in the array of life chances, which are determined in the play of tensions within late capitalism. The operation of the sort reflects the extent to which individuals and institutions share understandings about the necessity as well as the fairness, appropriateness, or legitimacy of the system that is evolving at the same time as it is being put into place. It may operate smoothly, or it may operate in fits and starts, like an automobile that is out of adjustment or under the control of a new driver unsure and unskilled in the operation of the clutch.

The Role of Technology

The automobile is a useful metaphor for thinking about the panoptic sort in the context of late capitalism. The automobile is certainly a technology. It has become quite sophisticated in terms of the number of its systems that are under the control of microprocessors. Although it is not difficult to imagine a time when the amount of active control by drivers will have been reduced to a bare minimum and the level of any operator's knowledge of its systems will be negligible at best, we are not well served by thinking of automotive technology as autonomous. The automobile serves a variety of instrumental goals, not limited to getting us from here to there. The use of automotive technology for transportation, as well as for status enhancement and the expression of personality, has had an immeasurable influence on the environment and on the social, economic, and legal systems that have developed to structure its use. Yet refusing to accept a perspective that views technology as an autonomous force does not at the same time mean that one must deny the fact of technological influence.

Technology and technological systems represent resources that knowledgeable actors may use in their interactions with other actors that may systematically constrain their options. An orientation toward technology may also come to characterize the ways in which these knowledgeable actors understand their goals and options. I believe that there is a technological imperative. It resides not in the machines but in the people who use them. By locating the imperative in individuals, rather than in machines, I do not mean to associate myself with those who suggest that technologies are neutral.[64] This is simply not so. Technologies are designed by humans for specific uses. Although creative (or destructive) individuals may discover or invent novel uses or applications for particular technologies, the range of those applications is limited by the character of the technology. Some technologies are more flexible in this regard than others. By design they have a broad range of applications. The disclaimer "guns don't kill, people do" is true as far as it goes. But it is also true that guns can be used far more efficiently for killing than they can for hammering nails into plasterboard. Automobiles also kill, but they have been designed for other ends, which they serve more efficiently. Information technologies may be seen to have quite a broad range of applications and may even be argued to have a great potential for increasing the democratic potential of societies. Part of this apparent flexibility is inherent in the fact that the technology of the computer-based information system is not limited to the hardware but includes the applications software, which more completely defines its use.

The operational effectiveness of any inherent technological constraint depends on the awareness, understanding, and acceptance of this apparent limitation by different individuals. Jacques Ellul helps us to see that this understanding is also subject to the influence of technical systems in use. Ellul is generally identified as belonging to the class of technophobics. Yet it is his mission to teach understanding and to engender resistance rather than fear. His master work on the nature of technology has stood the test of time as an articulate expression of insights into a way of thinking that permeates all spheres of social existence.[65] It is important to understand Ellul's thinking with regard to propaganda as being integrally related to his views on technique in general.[66] In his Preface, Ellul suggests that "not only is propaganda itself a technique, it is also an indispensable condition for the development of technical progress and the establishment of a technological civilization. And, as with all techniques, propaganda is subject to the law of efficiency."[67] Later he continues, "propaganda is called on to solve problems created by technology, to play on maladjustments, and to integrate the individual into a technological world."[68]

Clifford Christians[69] finds Ellul's vision of the technological society and its totalizing systems of control to be superior to the theory of ideological hegemony associated with Antonio Gramsci,[70] in that Ellul understands that the sophisti-

cated use of mass media to eviscerate public opinion is one that is itself guided by
the rule of efficiency. This same technicism that distorts the public sphere is also
seen to have transformed political participation into an abstract illusion.[71] This
conclusion is directly opposed to those who believe that communications technology can never be a democratizing force.

John Wilkinson, translator of the Knopf version of Ellul's *The Technological Society,* warns the readers that Ellul's writing betrays an "insistence on rendering a
purely phenomenological account of fact, without causal explanation of the inter-
relation of the subordinate facts. ... The important questions concerning the
technological society rarely turn for Ellul on how or why things came to be so, but
rather on whether his description of them is a true one."[72] Yet it is difficult to avoid
the bald functionalism that Ellul uses to personify technique. Although there are
alternative ways to read Ellul to bring his vision more in line with the theoretical
construction we have in mind, the most damaging criticism launched against
Ellul is that he sees technology as autonomous. This, in common with his tendency to give technique an anthropomorphic stance, leads one to wince when
reading a passage such as this:

> Thus technique theoretically and systematically assumes to itself that liberty which it
> has been able to win practically. Since it has put itself beyond good and evil, it need
> fear no limitation whatever. It was long claimed that technique was neutral. Today
> this is no longer a useful distinction. The power and autonomy of technique are so
> well secured that it, in its turn, has become the judge of what is moral, the creator of
> a new reality.[73]

Yet Ellul's descriptions of what has taken place and his predictions of what lies
ahead are so clear, sharp, and ripe with illustrative potential that they cannot be
abandoned on the basis of this partially stylistic flaw. There is, as C. George
Benello suggests, a need to find a way to introduce the concept of instrumental rationality as a behavioral orientation into the history that Ellul writes for us.[74] In
this way we can produce another reading of the hundreds of examples of a decision pertaining to technology, made in the context of technicist vision, which
leads to yet another set of decisions made along the path of technical efficiency.
This is part of our search to find insights into the patterns that emerge as we include social systems of larger and larger scale within our vision. For us the problem of theory is to find an explanation for the empirical fact that local actions lead
to global patterns. The problem of elusive theoretical closure is reflected in the
isolated struggles of analysts who focus on the macroscopic level of systems and
institutions and refuse to engage those who toil at the microscopic level of individuals, cognitive processes, or even the molecular level of communication between cells.

In Ellul's description of the attempt to mechanize the production of bread, we
find that an attribute of the wheat made it difficult for the machines as designed

to reproduce the characteristic flour of a premechanical age; the result was a different kind of bread. "In the last resort, the ultimate success of mechanization turned on the transformation of human taste. Whenever technique collides with a natural obstacle, it tends to get around it either by replacing the living organism by a machine, or by modifying the organism so that it no longer presents any specifically organic reaction."[75] The "it" in the example is not truly any kind of autonomous technology, but an entrepreneur seeking to find a way to make use of a technology that facilitated an efficient (read: profitable) processing of grain. All that was necessary for this entrepreneur to realize his goals was the creation of a demand for a new kind of bread. David Lovekin offers a contemporary example to demonstrate the lengths to which this process has come:

> Thus, a simple food like potatoes becomes Tater-Tots, something that is not clearly food at all, and that contains elements of no clearly known nutritional value. What is clear is that each piece is made to look like the other piece, identities which are also different, new. McDonald's markets and produces sameness. ... To understand fast food, a purely technological phenomenon, one must look to the walls and notice the pictures of the food. One buys the picture, which will never nourish, but which will always keep the customer coming back for more, the ever-perfect, indeed, the same hamburger, designed in the laboratory and cooked by computers.[76]

This does not suggest that humans are not somehow convinced that it makes good sense to accommodate themselves to the limitations of technological design, nor does it suggest that they are not also somehow transformed in the process. All that we resist is the assignment of the power, design, and reason to a machine or a tool. Technique is an orientation, not an entity.

Rationalization and Technique

Reading Ellul with the sideways glance that he adopts in his book on propaganda assists us in finding an instrumentalist position from which to understand technique as it emerged at the time of the industrial revolution. In *Propaganda: The Formation of Men's Attitudes*, Ellul identifies propagandists as goal-oriented, technologically sophisticated individuals, organized through institutions, who act with purpose.[77] Although he also suggests that the technique that is propaganda constrains those who would use it, the sense of instrumentalism can be easily identified and then found throughout his work on technique: "From this point of view, it might be said that technique is the translation into action of man's concern to master things by means of reason, to account for what is subconscious, make quantitative what is qualitative, make clear and precise the outlines of nature, take hold of chaos and put order into it."[78] He finds a transformation in the rationale behind science that in the eighteenth century began to admit more and more of a concern with utility, rather than knowledge, for the sake of curiosity and discovery. The latter parts of the century were characterized by a kind of optimism, and for Ellul this "state of mind created ... a kind of good conscience on the part of scientists who devoted their research to practical objectives. They believed that happiness and justice would result from their investigations; and it is here that the myth of progress had its beginning."[79] A form of technical consciousness was seen to be derived from the influence of special interests, not only those of capital, but also those of a revolutionary state, as in France. Ellul even saddles Marx with the responsibility for having "rehabilitated technique in the eyes of the workers. He preached that technique can be liberating. Those who exploited it enslaved the workers, but that was the fault of the masters and not of technique itself."[80] Technique expands in response to the expression of interest, and interest, with the aid of propaganda, has been expanded over the years to accommodate the reach of technique.

Ellul's examination of the role of technology in the economy and the role of economists as social technologists is an insightful extension of Marx's contributions to our understanding of the role of a technological change in the economic base by reminding us that, despite their protestations to the contrary, economists have taken Marx's challenge to heart: The goal is not to understand the world, but to change it! Ellul argues that "at the same time that the economist has created a technique for knowing, he has created a technique for acting," and this involves the introduction of plans and norms that, over time, assume a coercive force.[81] Positive in method, normative in purpose, economics and economists have helped to spread a technicist orientation into all corners of the society, not merely those clearly defined as economic.[82] Ellul's discussion of the human technologies bears much in common with Foucault's emphasis on the disciplines.

For Ellul, the technologically oriented human sciences are being aimed toward the task of "rounding up those elements of the human personality that are still free and forcing ('reintegrating') them into the expanding technical order of things. What yet remains of private life must be forced into line by invisible techniques, which are also implacable because they are derived from personal convictions."[83] This all-encompassing grasp of technique seeks to eliminate all forms of "social maladjustment or neurosis. Man is to be smoothed out, like a pair of pants under a steam iron."[84]

Ellul asks rhetorically, why did history produce such a dramatic growth in technique at the time at which it occurred. James Beniger asks the same question but limits it to information technology.[85] Beniger ignores Ellul's response in favor of his own version of Weberian rationalization—an instrumental need to reestablish control through the efficient management of information.

Progressive rationalization has been identified as the unifying theme of Weber's assessment of Western civilization. Rationalization is clearly akin to Ellul's notions of technique. By rationalization "Weber meant the process by which explicit, abstract, intellectually calculable rules and procedures are increasingly substituted for sentiment, tradition, and rule of thumb in all spheres of activity."[86] Rogers Brubaker suggests that there are a great variety of meanings of rational in Weber's work, yet we can see most of them as being inherently compatible with an underlying theme. Brubaker includes "deliberate, systematic, calculable, impersonal, instrumental, exact, quantitative, rule-governed, predictable, methodical, purposeful, sober, scrupulous, efficacious, intelligible and consistent."[87]

Although Weber identified rationalization as a characteristic of Western society, he was less than sanguine about the results that flowed from its adoption and spread. The rationalism that undergirds capitalism creates a constraining "iron cage." With regard to bureaucratic organization, rationalism has dehumanization as its consequence. Scientific rationalism in Weber's view also heightens the possibility for political, social, and economic manipulation.[88]

Rationalization involves the application of method to the pursuit of identifiable goals in administration in the same ways that method supports the discovery of knowledge in the science of sociology. Yet there are problems and contradictions. Robert Holton and Bryan Turner join Christopher Dandeker in noting Weber's ambivalence about the demand for equality as a matter of social rationality.[89] "To guarantee equality of condition or equality of outcome requires extensive political intervention, which may involve the increasing surveillance and subordination of population to government regulation."[90] Thus, equality and freedom are placed in opposition by the structural and procedural requirements of rationalization.

Although rationalization was a goal, Weber recognized the existence of problematic, perhaps insurmountable, methodological difficulties involved in the rationalization of social policy. Indeed, David Beetham's comments suggest that although Weber's emphasis on rationalization and the technical superiority of the bureaucratic form runs throughout his economic writing, Weber's "political writings were concentrated explicitly on its negative, on what it could not achieve."[91] Holton and Turner suggest that "Weber was particularly adamant on the impossibility of aggregated measures of welfare, due to the incommensurable subjective values given by individuals to their utilities."[92] This problem continues to vex efforts to develop measures of well-being that might serve in the contemporary administration of social justice.[93]

Weber held that there was a critical distinction between substantive and formal rationality. The formal calculative aspects of rationality were generally not at issue. Individuals will depart in their specifications and assessments at the level of goals and values and, as a result, their subjective estimates of rationality will differ. As Holton and Turner note, "what counts as substantively rational within a group or a culture cannot be reduced to a consideration of the formal rationality of the process of want-satisfaction. Hence the conflict between optimal economic rationality and the substantive rationality of protesting classes or disprivileged status groups striving for justice is endemic."[94]

Weber's analysis of the development of a rationalized system of law took note of the preference that patriarchal and theocratic powers had for a system of laws that reflected a substantive rationality. The law that worked best was one that served their interests best, and this often meant that formality or even logical consistency represented a hindrance.[95] However, when the interests of an emerging bourgeoisie coincided with the willingness of the monarch to exchange legal flexibility for economic support, the movement of the law toward formal rationality accelerated. Of some interest is the emergence of the disciplinary specialization of trained jurists who would come to replace the "lay notables of the old folk justice." This transition was brought about in part by "the growing need for their special skills in the administration of justice. These skills consisted above all in the 'capacity to state clearly and unambiguously the legal issues involved in a complicated situation,' and that capacity resulted from special professional training in a university."[96] Here, as elsewhere, rationalization involved professionalization and the emergence of yet another discipline.

Efficiency

Weber's economic sociology was not concerned directly with microeconomic questions of efficiency. Marxist scholars have made the most influential contributions to our understanding of the social consequences that flow from the rationalization of the process of exploitation under capitalism. Harry Braverman has been identified as having made one of the most significant contributions to our understanding of rationalization in the manufacturing process.[97] Braverman's discussion of the progressive division of labor emphasizes the instrumental pursuit of savings in labor time. The less paid labor time that might be required for each unit of manufacture produced would mean an increase in the amount of surplus value that became available for capitalist investment or consumption. Frank Webster and Kevin Robins explore the pursuit of efficiency and control over labor as a joint product and goal of the technological system.[98] This process of rationalism is seen to have moved from the time-and-motion studies of Frederick Winslow Taylor, through the intensification of managerial control, to the assembly line referred to as Fordism.

Characteristic of this pursuit of efficient control is the "separation of head from hand," which is involved in capturing and installing the knowledge and intelligence of skilled labor into the hardware and software of automated process and control.[99] The "deskilling" of the work force may be seen as an externality rather than as an explicit goal of management. Webster and Robins describe the extension of Fordist principles to the realm of governance and political rationalism under the rubric of Social Taylorism, which reaches its extreme in the complete mobilization of society within the panoptic system.[100]

Webster and Robins's analysis shares much in common with Beniger's analysis of the "control revolution."[101] Crisis and a technological response to crisis are at the heart of Beniger's dialectical chain of events. Beniger explains the growth in the use of information technologies as a response to crises that emerged in production as information controlled technology and managerial authority increased output beyond the ability of the transportation system to move goods to market. The need to coordinate the schedules of railroads was satisfied, at least temporarily, by the invention of timetables and was facilitated by the spread of control through the telegraph. Crises of consumption, which emerged as the distributional bottlenecks were overcome, were themselves regulated by the development of controls over mass consumption through marketing, retailing, and marketing research. This application of scientific management to the consumption function is described by Robins and Webster as "Sloanism," after Alfred P. Sloan of General Motors who presaged "just in time manufacturing" by not producing an automobile until a buyer for it had been identified.[102] Similar control of governance is described in the spread of the bureaucratic system.

A key aspect of Beniger's definition of rationalization is the efficiency gains associated with what he calls preprocessing. Control is enhanced through the elimination of "unnecessary" information. That is, rationalization, as preprocessing, "might be defined as the destruction or ignoring of information in order to facilitate its processing."[103] In asking us to think about the amount of paperwork that might be involved in the processing of the hundreds of forms that are generated as increasing complexity in systems of production, distribution, or governance requires more information for the management of the entire process, Beniger suggests we ought to imagine "how much more processing would be required, however, if each new case were recorded in an unstructured way, including every nuance and in full detail, rather than by checking boxes, filling blanks, or in some other way reducing the burdens of the bureaucratic system to only the limited range of formal, objective, and impersonal information required by the standardized forms."[104] This preprocessing accelerates the dehumanizing standardization and the disciplinary normalization that depersonalizes and restricts the freedom of individuals who are, as Ellul suggests, made to fit the technology, which has become part and parcel of the panoptic sort.

Preprocessing is a standardizing technology. As Beniger suggests, standardization increases the efficiency of most technical systems. It makes the processing of information efficient in the same ways that efficiencies are realized in material production. Standardization facilitates routinization, reduces the skill needed, and allows for the replacement of labor with machines. The efficiencies realized through standardization are not costless. Success in marketing involves, at least to some degree, the creation of the impression of difference. The control of workers and consumers alike, at some level, requires the appearance of individuation.

Standardization is relative, is conceptual, and may take place at the level of appearance. Thus, as Spiros Simitis suggests, the appearance of great variety and choice in the marketplace is fundamentally illusionary, as consumers must choose not from an infinite range but from within the predetermined and highly standardized categories presented by the market. With reference to "high-tech," interactive media offerings, Simitis suggests that "the media supplier dictates the conditions under which communication takes place, fixes the possible subjects of the dialogue, and, due to the personal data collected, is in an increasingly better position to influence the subscriber's behavior. Interactive systems, therefore, suggest individual activity where in fact no more than stereotyped reactions occur."[105] What is important for us to emphasize at this stage is that the creation of standards, categories, classes, and options, although they may be contested from time to time, is the product of a process dominated by agents in organizations, not individuals who are the objects of a system of power.

Measurement and Calculation

Preprocessing and standardization, wherever they occur, involve measurement, calculation, and comparison with a priori or empirical standards or distributions. The measurement, almost by definition, is imprecise.[106] Think for a moment about the simple measurements that might be required to facilitate the identification of persons: gender, race, age, height, and weight are all standard measures with varying degrees of imprecision. Although sexuality and sexual identity have become issues of some importance in recent times, we need not be informed about the core of these debates to agree that we could differentiate between individuals along some continuum that we might identify as maleness/femaleness. Preprocessing allows only a dichotomous response: You are one or the other. Questions of individual choice in self-definition arise in this area almost as readily as they do in terms of classification by race. Where is the line one crosses in order to become black rather than white? Is there a blood test? When racial identification becomes a question of ethnicity, the question of "who is Jewish" or "who is a Native American" becomes a question of considerable political and economic concern. The rules tend to be determined administratively, for administrative purposes, and reflect powers inherent in traditions that have become institutionalized in law.

Not even measures of height and weight are immune from a challenge to their accuracy. Many of the measures are based on self-report and tend toward what people believe to be socially preferred. The tendency to ignore that which cannot be easily measured is a criticism that is frequently directed at empiricist social science. It is an especially important aspect of the radical critique of political economy.[107] Benefits and costs that are not easily measured in terms of dollars and cents are excluded from models seeking to evaluate the welfare effects of a given social policy. Emphasizing the easily measured cannot help but distort the decisions of actors whose reflexive monitoring is influenced by the limited availability of environmental cues. The same distortions play through and reproduce systemic constraints when institutional decision making comes to depend on the accessible.

It might be argued that each of the measurements that become part of a person's history ought to include relatively detailed information about the circumstances in which an action, such as being fired, laid off, or even changing jobs voluntarily, has taken place. The same actions are bound to have had quite different structuring circumstances, and this information is lost to a system that forces that complexity into a form that demands that you "list the jobs you have held in the past ten years." The same is also the case with regard to the record of late or missed payments that might come to seriously mar a person's credit history. Yet, from the perspective of the record keeper, who wants to either include or exclude an event from a specific class, the details are unnecessary, and the costs of organizing and storing them are excessive. Mario Bunge adds: "The elements of the collection will be the same *in certain respects,* never in all particulars."[108]

It is in the context of measurement as interpretation that Giddens's notion of the double hermaneutic demands consideration.[109] In the social sciences, probably more than in the case of the physical sciences,[110] the concern with reactivity is well founded.[111] Yet Giddens describes a more circuitous route through which measurement and analysis transform an object. The theories and concepts that are developed by social scientists are routinely incorporated into the language and understandings that help to structure the societies that they have studied. Giddens suggests:

> Because in some respects it is only possible for the social scientist to keep "one jump ahead" of those whose behavior he or she is investigating, much social science appears relatively banal to lay members of society. Yet this seeming banality disguises the tremendous practical impact which social science has had and which is in substantial part constitutive of modernity. ... My point is not just that social science concepts and findings "influence" "the ways in which we think," but that they become in large part *constitutive of the practices which form institutions of modernity.*[112]

Social interest in measurement is not limited entirely or even primarily to a concern with the explanation of causation. Bunge identifies a complex of determinations, none of which are necessarily causal.[113] As he suggests, "determination is a vector in a space of a large, as yet unknown number of dimensions, causal determination being just one of its components or projections."[114] Beyond causal determination, Bunge identifies quantitative self-determination, such as we see when physical systems in motion continue in motion (to the extent that motion is not hindered by gravity and/or friction) through the force of inertia. Social systems may be argued to continue in a similar manner until changed by some force. In biological systems, there is also a form of interactional-reciprocal causation, a functional interdependence of the sort that describes some glandular function. In addition to mechanical and statistical determination, Bunge identifies structural determination, which describes the influence of an organism on its constituent parts. Social organisms, such as groups and organizations, may be seen to be determinative, although not causal, with regard to the behavior of their members. The members of an organization may be influenced by a form of teleological determinism, wherein the ends determine the means. A biological example can be seen in the production of saliva in the presence of, or even in response to the mention of, a lemon. Clearly the lemon did not cause the salivation, but the body's preparation for processing and consumption (goal) helped to determine the means (saliva). In the social realm, we might consider the influence of goals on the behavior of group members who are committed to those goals as determinative.

Bunge also identifies a form of qualified self-determination, which he refers to as dialectical determination. Here we find the contrasting interests of contending groups acting to change the very social structure of these groups in a qualitative rather than a quantitative manner. In recognition of the complexity of determination, it is frequently sufficient to demonstrate a relationship. In the context of the exercise of power, the value of a demonstrated relationship is in the interpretation of a consistent pattern as an instrumentalism we know as prediction.

Prediction and Coordination

Prediction is of central importance to the panoptic sort. It is not only the insurance industry that is interested in predictions of the outcomes likely for classes of individuals. Predictability, the reduction of uncertainty about individual behavior, is a valued aspect of social systems and the social relations within them. Power may be seen as the ability to act in such as a way as to induce a desired and predictable reaction. It is in the pursuit of improved predictability that the panoptic sort is engaged, and it is calibrated on the basis of a limited amount of information about a great number of individuals.

In the context of predictability, we see the interplay between generality and specificity. Whereas disciplinary power operates on individuals through their membership in groups, the systemic orientation to groups is based on information gathered about the experience of individuals. "Very few facts in the concrete world are predictable with near certainty, and none in all detail, because scientific forecast is based on the knowledge of laws and of specific information regarding singular facts, neither of which is ever complete and exact."[115] In addition, with regard to Giddens's insights about the influence of social theory, the identification of the criterion as well as the independent variables in any predictive model are reflective of the thinking of the time, rather than determined by any ontologically determined necessity. Interdependence was certainly a fact long before social theorists recognized it and demanded that it be incorporated into analytical models.[116] According to Thomas Haskell,

> Social scientists in the 1890's and in the Progressive era located the effective causation of human affairs sometimes in heredity, sometimes in environment; sometimes in the play of economic interests, sometimes in particular historical conditions, such as the frontier experience; sometimes in stimulus-response associations, sometimes in instinct, sometimes in culture, sometimes in that alien area within the person but remote from his conscious mind, the subconscious. They seldom located causation close to the surface of events or in the conscious, willing minds of individuals.[117]

Giddens's emphasis on human agency may take us closer to this surface, but because he places agency in the context of a theory of structuration, the heritage of positivism still weighs heavily on his thinking.

Yet it is not clear that the operation of the panoptic sort depends on a comprehensive theory of causation. Indeed, incompatible theories of agency may characterize its application at different sites, and at the intersections between them.

Bureaucratization and Surveillance

Christopher Dandeker's investigation of surveillance since the 1700s links both the collection and the maintenance of information in files as essential characteristics of the bureaucratic form of organization. As a technology, the bureaucratic organization depends on information and knowledge being controlled and modified if necessary by the organization. For Weber, the ability of the bureaucratic form to manage this information efficiently explained the growth of bureaucracy:

> The decisive reason for the advance of bureaucratic organisation has always been its purely technical superiority over every other form. A fully developed bureaucratic apparatus stands to these other forms in much the same relation as a machine does to non-mechanical means of production. Precision, dispatch, clarity, familiarity with the documents, continuity, discretion, uniformity, rigid subordination, savings in friction and in material and personal costs—all these things are raised much more effectively to the optimal level by a strong bureaucratic, especially a monocratic, administration with trained individual officials than by any form of collegiate, honorific or avocational administration.[118]

Centralized control of a common informational core introduces a reliable standardization, avoiding the rigidity of traditional authority and, at the same time, avoiding the apparent irrationality of individual personality and style. In Dandeker's view, the bureaucracy is very much like a machine "to the extent to which subjective or irrational elements of will and mood are eliminated."[119]

Dandeker suggests that there is considerable variety in the capacity of bureaucracies to engage in surveillance. Organizations vary in terms of the amount of information they gather and maintain in centralized files, in terms of the speed with which information flows into and out of files and between members of the organization, and also in terms of the number of points of contact between the organization and the population under surveillance. Advances in computerization and telecommunications have the potential to increase each of these indices of bureaucratic scope, which, by definition, increases the power and reach of the bureaucracy.

Dandeker intimates that, historically, surveillance of the work force was both facilitated and necessitated by the application of the principles of scientific management in ways that resulted in an increased division of labor. Standardization, monitoring, record keeping, and statistical analysis were the cornerstones of bureaucratic surveillance and control of the labor process. This detailed bureaucratic specification not only increased managerial control, but it also reduced the level of skill and the training time required to reach it. This deskilling further reduced the bargaining power of individual laborers because they could easily be replaced by others who could learn to perform the job just as well in a relatively short time. Bureaucratic rationalization through surveillance made it possible for management to compare individual workers to empirical or managerial norms of output or method, and performance could be linked with compensation.

With computerization, remote surveillance of labor has come to mean that a supervisor in another town might be responsible for assigning calls to telephone operators on the basis of continuous assessment of their performance and the performance of others.[120] Employees in the growing telemarketing sector are under continuous surveillance, and some even receive computer-generated printouts at the end of the day that locate their average performance plotted against organizational norms.[121]

Bureaucratization of the capitalist firm involved an expansion of scope from the surveillance and control of its employees to include surveillance of its customers and competitors. Just as surveillance of the work force has moved beyond the confines of the factory and the office into the personal lives and the psychology of the workers, surveillance of consumers has moved into life-styles and psychographics deemed relevant to the rationalization of the marketing function. As the modern corporation grows in size and global reach,[122] telecommunications becomes even more important:

> Taking advantage of electronic means of surveillance and techniques of transferring information, financial and other resources, such enterprises have sub-divided their operations and located them in different countries depending on product markets, labour costs and so on. Modern large corporations can control these dispersed operational units because electronic techniques of surveillance break through the space-time limitations of communications systems based on word of mouth, handwriting and the printed word.[123]

Dandeker shares with Weber the belief (although perhaps not the same level of concern) that bureaucracy will continue to expand, and he rejects the claims of the futurists such as Alvin Toffler who project the emergence of an "ad hocracy," or some other post-Fordist organization of economic activity. This is not to suggest that Dandeker does not envision changes in the nature of organizations, as there are clearly changes under way, especially with regard to the specification of the boundaries between organizations. He suggests that we should not see these changes in terms of a "decline in the significance of the vertical principle of bureaucratic organization" because a decentralized structure does not mean a weak center; it suggests only that there is an alternative and perhaps less visible system of power.[124] Whether the structure of power and authority is centralized or dispersed and operated interdependently, there is no question that postmodern systems will still depend on knowledge of their parts and a shared sense of the legitimacy of the actions taken by seemingly autonomous units.

Legitimation

Weber believed that "every type of domination depends on an administrative apparatus under a chief or ruling body and on a shared belief in the legitimacy of rules or decisions."[125] The apparent predominance of rules and regulations in the bureaucracy, with its formal policies and procedures manuals outlining standard practices, provides one form of legitimation seen as the absence of arbitrariness. Legal authority differs from traditional or charismatic authority in that it is based on the presumed rationality of the laws, policies, or procedures that have been developed.[126] The formal bureaucracy represents the institutionalization of the rules and resources that are at the heart of Giddens's process of structuration. Not only are rules in bureaucratic organizations operational, they are written down and available to all and provide an external source of legitimation of action in that rules can be referred to as a source of guidance in the case of dispute. The bureaucratic organization also specifies which individuals have which resources or powers. The rules define spheres of competence and responsibility. The resources within a bureaucratic organization rest not with the individual but with the position. This "separation of the office from the incumbent" allows a bureaucratically structured organization to function more efficiently because it can function continuously through the routine replacement of individuals.[127] Thus, even though the popularity of professional specializations may ebb and flow, the importance of legitimacy applies to expertise. For the power of disciplines to have their force, legitimacy has meant that the professions have to be invested with the cloak of authority. Thomas Haskell suggests that the professionalization of social science was a movement to establish authority, and, further, "with ironic regularity, the movement to establish authority rose above even its most selfish intentions to defend not class interest, but *authority* as a general principle."[128]

With regard to the function of a state bureaucracy, however, a lack of stability in the norms and goals of the political center can serve to threaten the efficient operation of the governmental systems and raise questions about the legitimacy of its decisions. Reaganism and Thatcherism, which represented attempts to redirect the focus and priorities of the state and involved an attack on the government bureaucracy through privitization, are modern examples of the kinds of disturbances that bureaucratic systems have to overcome in the face of contradictions between structure and goals.[129] The "Reagan revolution" represented a challenge to the Keynesian model of an economically active state and elevated "the market" to a position of centrality in the ideology of change. In the view of one analyst, we find that the "market is reconstituted as a major ideological force and crucial distinctions between the productive and unproductive, private and public, wealth creating and wealth consuming, come to be the yardsticks for judging policy."[130]

In one sense, the market stands in opposition to the bureaucratic ideal. The market as a conceptual entity is autonomous and unpredictable in all but the character of its theoretical equilibria. Yet its hypothetical flexibility was thought to make its efficiency superior to that of a government bureaucracy rigidified by the interests of bureaucrats and professionals, as well as the pervasive influence of organized interests that had come to depend on the government budget. The pursuit of "rule by markets" changed the purpose of government surveillance to a more explicitly disciplinary focus, and it legitimated its expanded scope on the basis of a critical need to "eliminate waste, fraud, and abuse" in government.[131]

According to Andrew Gamble, the "achievement of the New Right was to place the supporters of public provision and public services on the defensive. The New Right attacks on the grounds of cost and efficiency were predictable, but what was less expected was the New Right claim that they had a superior moral vision of what a free society should be like. Their concept of citizenship saw freedom and equality being achieved through the daily plebiscite in the market, not through the infrequent plebiscite in the political system."[132] The government bureaucracy faced a legitimation crisis that was heightened by the fact that the executive branch saw its professionals as enemies and its rank and file as dishonest slackards.[133]

Thus we see that as social systems evolve differences in ideology can modify the approaches taken by knowledgeable agents to realize their goals. Changes in policy reflect changes in beliefs about which technologies, including those of a state bureaucracy, are the most efficient means available for the realization of identifiable goals. In the next section, I examine information technology as a particular response to the demand for rationalization.

Information Technology
and the Rationalization of Control

A considerable amount of work has been put forward that attempts to distinguish between the structures and orientations that characterize the United States and other advanced industrial economies from those of earlier stages after their entry into the industrial revolution. A good part of the debate has surrounded the issue of whether or not this period, which is characterized as an Information Age, represents a significant, epochal change or is merely a continuation of capitalism as we have known it. Without suggesting that the issue is really a nonquestion, let us consider the possibility that it really will not matter unless the response of people and the institutions they control behave in a fundamentally different way because they do or do not accept that view. We are, for example, somewhat at odds as to whether the Information Age is upon us or whether it is just ahead in the not too distant future.

Wilson Dizard entitles his book *The Coming Information Age.*[134] On the one hand, he discusses changes that are taking place but he suggests that we are only in the first stages of this new age. On the other hand, James Beniger speaks of his control revolution as having begun more than a century ago. Peter Hall and Paschal Preston, reflecting the views of long wave theorists, suggest that we are not approaching an epoch at all but are merely on the verge of the fifth Kondratieff upswing.[135] Jorge Schement and Leah Lievrouw's chapter in their edited volume offers a compromise position that suggests that "the information phenomena reflect the continuing evolution of industrial capitalism, which has resulted in an information-oriented society in the United States."[136] Some of the distinctions drawn by these analysts revolve around precisely what it is that observers take as markers of significance in defining the period of interest.

Dizard notes a flood of publications that discuss the current period as being post-something-or-other (as in postindustrial from Daniel Bell) and takes due note of the variety in indexes that these authors use as markers of this change. A chain of researchers from Fritz Machlup through Daniel Bell and, more recently, Marc Porat, have emphasized the changes in the composition of the labor force, the members of which can be identified as working primarily in the production or transformation of information or knowledge, rather than in agriculture, manufacturing, or noninformation services. Porat's work[137] stimulated hundreds of imitative studies that sought to determine the extent to which other nations were or were about to become information societies.[138] If, on the one hand, one's primary concern is the projection of the character of the labor force and the demand for a particular kind of labor, such predictions are perhaps meaningful.

If, on the other hand, one's interests are more general and one is concerned with economic planning at a national level, then perhaps with the aid of an input-output model, questions of investment, trade, and sectoral linkage become more important than labor force character per se.[139] For example, Merheroo Jussawalla discusses several input-output analyses of Pacific rim countries and notes that Singapore's investments in information networks appear to be appropriate given the tight information related linkages of five of the ten most important sectors in the economy.[140]

However, if one's interests lean toward a critique of capital and an understanding of the ways in which the new technologies have been incorporated into (all the while transforming) capitalist social relations, then other measures become more important. Traditional Marxists struggle with the conceptualization of productive and nonproductive labor and wonder aloud if the growth in the number of nonproductive information workers represents a critical crisis.[141] Although the theoretical basis for the construct is markedly different from that of neoclassical economics, there is an underlying commonality in the concern about the contribution of information technology and the information work force in the realization of the goals of capitalism. Information, information technology, and the informational work force all represent the products of a broadly shared instrumental rationalism linked to the realization of profit, or surplus value. Part of the challenge in making sense of the apparently cyclical "swarms" of innovations[142] that are differentially linked to a decline in economic expansion is to identify the underlying logic that selects data processing, pattern recognition, or mobile communications as the leading edge technologies at one period rather than another.[143] The nature of the interaction of organizations with their environments helps to determine the kinds of information and information technology that their leaders adopt and adapt to meet their objectives.[144]

Although Beniger identifies information technologies as basic as the manual typewriter, most contemporary writing about the Information Age is focused on the twin technologies of the computer and the telecommunications networks that facilitate their interoperability.[145] Advances in both technologies are discussed in terms of the increased speed, capacity, reliability, and ease of operation that characterize these systems. This increase in capacity, or power, has been accompanied by a phenomenal reduction in the costs of processing or transmission. Miniaturization increases the number and variety of devices that can be made more "intelligent" with the addition of microprocessors. Miniaturization also increases the ease with which individuals can be tied into the telecommunications network, no longer bound by wires, cables, or unwieldy interface devices.[146]

A good part of the contribution of computer and telecommunications systems to the character of the Information Age is based on the ability of these systems to process information in a way that provides intelligence about the environment. The computer—high speed, high capacity, perhaps designed to operate in parallel with hundreds of other microprocessors—can scan unimaginable amounts of information in search of patterns and relationships that help decision makers make sense of the world. Although a great many observers are quick to challenge the accuracy, and warn of the consequences, that flow from acting on this intelligence, the computer makes it possible to take far more information into consideration than has ever been possible.[147] The telecommunications network makes it possible to access this capacity from virtually any place on the earth (and of course, places not on the earth, as well). This low-cost capacity to collect, store, process, and share intelligence increases the pressures on institutionalized actors to gather and make use of even more information.[148] A question remains as to the effect that this intelligence has on the productivity of individuals, organizations, or economies as a whole.[149]

The claims of the Futurists, from Daniel Bell through the popularizers such as Alvin Toffler, are challenged by Marxist and non-Marxist analyses of the productivity of the information work force. Charles Jonscher's analysis suggests that in the United States, at least, the rapid growth in the size of the information work force had already peaked and was beginning to decline as continued rationalization required the introduction of labor-saving technology in the office just as surely as it had been introduced into the factory and on the farm.[150] Webster and Robins take special note of the likely consequences of this rationalization on women in the work force, who happen to be concentrated in the routine information jobs most susceptible to elimination through automation.[151] Yet it is also clear that the pressure to develop intelligent systems through a process of knowledge engineering not unlike the time-and-motion studies of Frederick Taylor will only increase in the future, and reductions in force will be visited on the ranks of middle-level managers.[152]

As recognized by Katz[153] and Arriaga[154] and others, much of the information work force in Third World nations, especially those on the verge of economic development, is actually employed in nonproductive government bureaucracies. Internally and externally applied pressure to accelerate privatization will require substantial reduction in this part of the information economy.

Futurists, economists, and Marxists alike have identified another aspect of this period that demands more attention than it has been given to date. Not only is information a critical input into the process of rationalization and control, but it has also emerged as a commodity in its own right. Information producers have been organized into independent organizations that serve a variety of clients. The commoditization of information has not proceeded smoothly, in part because of the peculiarities of information as a resource. Critical questions emerged and remain about the ownership of information, not the least of which has to do with the ownership of information about individuals that is produced as a byproduct of their interaction with organizations in their roles as employees, citizens, and consumers. The panoptic sort, as the integrated control technology of the Information Age, depends for its operation on ready access to information about individuals. The debates about informational privacy are a reflexive index of the stresses and strains that are created as knowledgeable actors, at various sites in independent and intersecting systems, struggle to identify, define, and institutionalize an orientation toward personal information that will allow the process of rationalization to continue in ways that are consistent with their goals.

Yet the issue is not simply a question of privacy. In the report to the Club of Rome regarding the role of information, Klaus Lenk suggests that there is an error in focusing our attention on the issue of privacy as it is generally formulated. "The real issue at stake is not personal privacy, which is an ill-defined concept, greatly varying according to the cultural context. It is power gains of bureaucracies, both private and public, at the expense of individuals and the non-organized sectors of society, by means of gathering of information through direct observation and by means of intensive record keeping."[155] The issue is the panoptic sort.

3

OPERATING THE PANOPTIC SORT

DATA AND THE PANOPTIC SORT

The panoptic sort depends on data that are made from the raw material of human experience. This chapter will explore the ways in which this information is gathered, data are generated, and intelligence is shared among the bureaucracies of business and government.

The panoptic sort, as a discriminatory technology, has much in common with content analysis as a technique for drawing inferences about the source of symbolic materials. Klaus Krippendorff's discussion of the kinds of methods used and inferences drawn by content analysts over the years helps to make the connection clear.[1] Core figures involved in the development of the method share an interest in the pragmatic, instrumental uses of a technology that will support the development of inferences about the causes, circumstances, or unseen states of the source of communications. The source has been defined variously to include individuals, especially political actors, as well as entire nations. Krippendorff defines content analysis as "a research technique for making replicable and valid inferences from data to their context."[2] This context may be understood to refer to the environmental circumstances, which may include the psychological state of the communicative source, which gives rise to symbolic content with a particular character.

> The target is what the analysis will want to know about. Since content analysis provides vicarious knowledge, information about something not directly observed, this target is located in the variable portion of the context of available data. ... The task is to *make inferences* from data to certain aspects of their context and to justify these inferences in terms of the knowledge about the stable factors in the system of interest.[3]

The use of content analysis in the study of propaganda to assess military strategy, to predict troop movements and the readiness of an enemy for surrender, has ready parallels in the assessment of consumer culture and the prediction of trends, fads, and tendencies on the basis of content analysis of newspapers and popular media. Both military and marketing strategists rely heavily on such assessments to plan their moves against targets.

In the production of intelligence about the relationship between context and content, analysts frequently rely on independent sources of information about the environment. Studies that link the content of presidential speeches to the status of the economy must depend upon government and corporate statistics to define the environment. The panoptic sort is similarly dependent on multiple sources for information about the contexts in which its targets exist. Concerns about the reliability and validity of such data are common, but the panoptic system acts to address the problems of data standards and compatability in ways that clearly exceed the resources and vision of any single content analyst.[4]

The panoptic sort differs from content analysis in other dimensions as well. Content analysis avoids sources of reactive error in that it is generally an unobtrusive technique and does not depend on compliance of the source as long as the symbolic materials are readily available (as is the case with mass media content). The panoptic sort, however, depends in part on subjects' awareness of the fact (or at least the possibility) that their behavior is under surveillance at the numerous points of contact they have with bureaucratic systems. A similarity with content analysis emerges again, however, in the fact that individuals are never aware of the variety of interests that will have access to personal information, nor can they imagine all the analytical and strategic uses to which this personal information may be put. Thus, at many levels of the system, analysts engaged in surveillance and in the production of strategic information about citizens, employees, and consumers function behind a cloak of invisibility—a one-way mirror.

The panoptic sort, as a technical system, has an orientation to data similar to that of content analysis. Both analytical systems must be able to handle large volumes of data. Both must develop methodological strategies to ensure the usefulness of the intelligence or the inferences that are produced by the analysis. Krippendorff refers to an analytical process that includes four primary steps: data making, data reduction, inference, and analysis. The process of data making involves establishing a link between attributes and measures and always contains the risk of error, both systematic bias and errors associated with the instability in the behavior of interest. Errors are introduced into the panoptic sort in the same ways that they are introduced into a content analysis. The errors may be inherent in the specification of the construct, or they may reflect unreliability in the process that captures the behavior through observation and transforms it into data suitable for processing.

Content analysis may involve unmanageable amounts of data, such as a count of the number of times in which a female character is physically abused by a male character in a year's productions of theatrical film. Because the behavior is so common, a method of sampling these films is necessary for the task to be made manageable. By the same token, for some purposes, the panoptic sort must rely on data generated from probability or purposive samples. For many purposive samples, the panoptic technology searches for key words, events, or relationships. Files that display any of those key markers may be selected for further analysis. This analysis of raw hits is common to the disciplinary surveillance of bureaucracies concerned with taxes, credit, and insurance.

Data reduction in content analysis finds ready parallels within the panoptic sort. It is part of the analytical process but is similar to the strategy of preprocessing that seeks to reduce the amount of information to that which is the minimal efficient scale for the production and sharing of useful intelligence. Data reduction involves the search for similarity and difference expressed in convenient, communicable terms. It may be visual—charts, maps, graphs, or models—and it may be linguistic, as in the labels assigned to the forty geodemographic clusters like "back-country folks" used by Claritas/PRIZM to help marketers understand their clientele or their circumstances.[5]

Finally, the panoptic sort, like content analysis, is a dynamic process. Measures and methods are constantly being adjusted as the inferences about the targets of surveillance are evaluated in terms of their contribution to the realization of the organization's goals.

GOVERNMENT INFORMATION GATHERING

The U.S. government is a major source of information in the economy and about the economy: that which it produces on its own and that which it brings forward through a system of contracts and grants. My emphasis here is on the role of the government at the federal and state levels in the collection or generation of information about individuals and groups in society. A distinction is to be made between government statistics and personal data gathered by agencies of the government for the purposes of administering a particular bureaucratic function. The distinction is a tenuous one because there is considerable evidence that data move back and forth between administrative files and those of statistical agencies, and more important, representations of normality and deviance derived from general statistics are used in bureaucratic decisions about the benefits or services that individuals are to receive. The distinction between government data and the data collected and maintained by private bureaucracies is also difficult to maintain. Data gathered by government agencies find ready use by private firms, and private surveillance is increasingly relied on by government agencies to enhance their own investigations.

The numbers of computerized files maintained by the agencies of government continue to grow at a nearly exponential rate, despite efforts by the Office of Management and Budget (OMB) to restrict reporting requirements for business and industry.[6] A study of the U.S. Office of Technology Assessment (USOTA) revealed that 12 government agencies maintained some 539 records systems classified under the Privacy Act, and that these systems contained more than 3.5 billion records, 60 percent of which had been computerized. Estimates of the number of such records are likely to be grossly underestimated, because the act of recording their existence has been complicated by the growth in the use of personal computers by workers in these government agencies.[7]

Much of the public's concern about government data gathering has been focused on the system of files maintained by those government agencies responsible
for law enforcement, tax collection, and the protection of national security interests against domestic and foreign enemies, real and imagined. Herbert Mitgang,
former president of the Authors' Guild, compiled a detailed analysis of the use of
clandestine surveillance to develop files on thousands of writers and artists believed to represent some threat to the U.S. government.[8] A quote from John
Kenneth Galbraith illustrates the tension between actual and potential harm that
might result from the development of such files: "While the impression of other
people's paranoia is great, my own was diminished by the fact that while the documents are full of deeply damaging intentions, virtually nothing unpleasant ever
happened as a consequence. But one can see how the only slightly more vulnera-
ble must have suffered."[9]

Frank Donner's analysis of government surveillance is much less sanguine.[10]
As director of the American Civil Liberties Union (ACLU) Project on Political
Surveillance, Donner is of the opinion that government surveillance represents a
substantial threat to political freedom in the United States. He suggests that the
Congress, the Federal Bureau of Investigation (FBI), the Central Intelligence
Agency (CIA), the various armed services, and grand juries have all abused their
power in the search for enemies. This continuing search for subversives by the FBI
included a program that would recruit librarians to identify "suspicious" users of
unclassified material of a "sensitive" nature who might conceivably represent a
threat to the competitive or security status of the United States.[11] In a recent book,
Gary Marx focuses on the techniques of undercover police surveillance that include a variety of "stings," which brutally distort the definition of entrapment.[12]
Marx, like Donner, emphasizes the development of data through surveillance as a
means of prevention that facilitates an anticipatory controlling response. For
Donner, "open-ended political surveillance is really the collection of evidence of
potential criminal conduct."[13]

It is important to note that the files gathered for purposes of surveillance are
different from the files that are part of records of the criminal justice system—
such as the Criminal History System, which provides a national electronic index
to the files of persons with any federal or state criminal history.[14] However, the integration of such files with surveillance records can be triggered in a great variety
of ways, making for a distinction without a difference. A recent proposal to implement a point-of-sale system of automated record checks for persons attempting to
purchase firearms would access a proposed "national felons file," which would
conceivably include "suspect" flags triggering a notification to the FBI or other
agency.[15] Citing 1974 data, Donner reports that the FBI had some 6.5 million files
containing a great variety of raw data in different forms: photographs, memo-
randa, and transcripts. Those largely paper files expanded and were tranformed as
the computer and its digital storage replaced some 58 million index cards. Donner
also calls our attention to the history of the Internal Revenue Service (IRS) and

notes its frequent subversion to political ends unrelated to its primary function of tax collection. Donner claims that "the undercover capacity of the IRS outweighs that of all the other federal civilian agencies combined."[16]

Political surveillance is not the only purpose for which the government maintains files on individuals. The criminal justice system and the records of the courts have already been noted. The administration of the public welfare system represents a massive system of files and has been identified as a primary mobilizing force behind the expansion of file matching programs.[17] For the purposes of verifying the eligibility of individuals for social services or economic support, the federal government, under the Deficit Reduction Act of 1984, required states to match records in their files against dozens of other computerized files maintained by public and private organizations.[18] The involvement of the government in the maintenance of public health has also stimulated the creation of personal files. Persons who are patients or who have received care in government facilities, who have participated in government research programs, or even who have been diagnosed as possessing a genetic "defect" will become part of a government file, list, or record.[19] David Flaherty suggests that the Social Security Administration has data that "constitute one of the richest single aggregations of current demographic and economic information on individuals in the United States."[20]

Government data at the state levels include the countless public records noting births, deaths, weddings, divorces, transfers of real property, voter registration, and the issuance of licenses to drive or to provide professional services. In addition to the administrative purposes they may serve, these extensive records are a valuable resource to countless providers of private goods and services, including those who provide insurance, credit, and related financial services.

The Census

Paul Starr reminds us that the original purpose of the census was somewhat different from its present administrative purpose and dominant use.[21] Rather than serving as a source of quantitative data, the census was primarily an aid to a state's efforts in the surveillance of its population, especially with regard to the assessment and collection of taxes. The differences between the current census and those of the premodern age are striking. The modern census is a count of the entire population, whereas earlier counts may have been limited to households, and within households, to adult males. For a considerable period, the census of old was taken continuously, whereas the modern census process demands the expenditure of substantial effort and expense to complete the count within a limited time. Although Starr sees the most important difference between pre- and postmodern census forms in the contemporary separation of the activities of the collection of government statistics from the collection of taxes, from the perspective of the panoptic sort an equally important distinction is the fact "that statistical data from modern censuses are typically expected to be published; premodern censuses were generally state secrets."[22]

Starr's emphasis on the transformation of the census from an instrument of surveillance to a source of government social statistics can be understood as an attempt by government to ensure the public trust and ready compliance with its data gathering requirements. Concerns about privacy have generally lowered individual responsiveness to a variety of surveys, including the U.S. census. Such concerns have resulted in the cancellation of the census in the Federal Republic of Germany because of fears about the use of the data by the state for the purposes of disciplinary surveillance. David Flaherty's discussion of German surveillance notes that in 1983, some 53 percent of the population had indicated a mistrust of the census, and at least 25 percent of the households would not cooperate by filling out the forms. Flaherty echoes the sentiment of Starr in suggesting that the "fundamental problem with the planned census was the failure to maintain an absolute functional separation between statistical and administrative uses of personal data."[23] The 1983 German census was postponed, and the government began a process of legislative and bureaucratic adjustment in response to the protest, but the initial response was not enough. In 1987, political opposition to the census became part of the platforms of the Green party and the Social Democrats, leading the statistical office to spend some 45 million deutsche marks on public relations to calm the fears that the political rhetoric had stirred.[24]

In the United States, the Bureau of the Census has been more successful in maintaining public trust in the confidentiality of the data that it gathers. The primary means of guaranteeing confidentiality is the separation of individually identifiable information from their records if there is to be any transmission of the information in the records to other parties, including other agencies of the government.[25] It is suggested that in an effort to reduce the possibility of reestablishing the linkage between a name and a particular record, the bureau will not even return records to other government agencies that initially provided them for verification or for estimation use if the borrowed records were individually identifiable.[26]

The United States has been a leader in the collection of government statistics by means of the census. The role of the census in apportionment was defined by its inclusion in the Constitution. A regular population census, established in 1790, did more than count the population, however; it made distinctions on the basis of race, gender, and status as slave. The numbers of questions and the range of their coverage of personal information increased steadily after 1840.[27] In planning for the 1990 census, interested parties, such as those represented by the American Planning Association, petitioned the bureau not to eliminate questions about housing, especially estimates of house sale and rental value. Despite the fact that census data are not to be used to the detriment of anyone complying with the request for information, planners suggested that they feared the loss of valuable data that they used for rental housing administration and enforcement.[28] Although the use of the data may not be the proximal cause, it is not difficult to establish the linkage between census data and the redlining of neighborhoods and communities in ways that bring unquestionable harm. As will be discussed later, the commercial and political importance and consequentiality of census data far exceed the formal purpose of providing guidance to the federal government.

In addition to the periodic censuses, the Census Bureau conducts hundreds of surveys each year tracking population trends, trends in employment, and trends in consumer expenditures. Because of its expertise, it conducts many of these surveys for other agencies of the government.

Leadership in the development of the census in the United States was not matched in other areas of statistical information gathering at the federal level. One interpretation of the lag was a distrust of centralized government, which found the state governments collecting and publishing most of the public statistics before the Civil War.[29] It was because of the expansion of federal government responsibilities during and after the Civil War that the collection of statistics began to expand and involve other departments and bureaucratic units. The creation of federal agencies and departments, such as the Department of Agriculture, the Bureau of Education, and the Fish Commission, which became the Bureau of Fisheries, and later the Department of Commerce, ensured a steady expansion of the statistical reach of the government.

Several government agencies with responsibility for regulatory oversight emerged during times of heightened concern about harmful business practices at the turn of the century. The creation of a federal income tax and an IRS after passage of the Sixteenth Amendment marked the birth of still another magnet for personal data and statistics. The demands of war and military preparedness saw the creation of a statistics branch within the War Department in 1918. The inflationary impact of war mobilization increased the importance of data about prices, and the Bureau of Labor Statistics increased its responsibility during the war, including its work on the development of the cost-of-living index.

After 1942 government statistics took a dramatic turn as a result of the wholesale adoption of the methods of probability sampling. These methods increased the efficiency with which the government could keep tabs on more and more aspects of the economy under its charge. The Census Bureau developed a sampling method to facilitate more efficient estimation of the rather extensive list of personal attributes that was being sought at the time. Although there remained a set of questions that the heads of every household would complete, other questions would be asked of one out of five, one out of fifteen, and one out of twenty households.[30] In the 1970s the Statistical Reporting Service played a significant role in the development of remote sensing methods to estimate crop production. In one sense, we might consider all statistics based on probability samples as a form of *remote sensing*, in that data presumed to represent classes or categories of individuals are generated without any direct contact with the overwhelming majority to whom the statistics apply.

Social scientists[31] and others have expressed concern over the fact that more and more of the data generated by government is available only through electronic means, which may serve to limit professional as well as public access to those data.[32] This concern is heightened by a concurrent tendency on the part of the federal govenment to implement a policy of privatization, which makes access to these data dependent on an ability to pay the third-party vendors who have been brought into competition with traditional government information sources.[33] At the same time that the electronic storage and access to government data and statistics are made more efficient, a technical resource and skill barrier has been introduced that serves to concentrate power at the centers, or nodes, of the panoptic network.

THE CORPORATE DATA MACHINE

As with government, modern business enterprise depends on data. Corporate decision makers require accurate and timely information about their own competitive environments, the efficiency of their production process, and the extent of success that is currently enjoyed by each of their product lines. In addition, the modern business enterprise needs information about the future to use as a critical input into strategic planning.[34] Information about the environment includes assessments of the competitive potential of products in development compared with those of their competitors. Industrial espionage represents the underside of a search for intelligence that includes more legitimate data gathering methods such as the continuous scanning of scientific, technical, and trade publications, participation in conferences and seminars, and the anxious perusal of costly, limited distribution consultants' reports.

The short-term competitive advantages derived from product and process innovations require access to information that is generated by internal research and development, infused into the organization through mutually beneficial linkages with former competitors or through purchase on the open market. Arthur Stinchcombe suggests that the form of the organization will reflect the uncertainties it faces and the means that it develops to deliver necessary information to decision points within the system.[35] Information about employees as components in the organization's production function is of particular importance with regard to the panoptic sort.

Organizations face an almost impossible task of selecting employees with whom they will enter into a long-term contractual relationship if that selection is to include an assessment of that employee's potential contribution to a variety of tasks that have yet to be defined. There is only a slight improvement when the employer must make decisions about which tasks to assign to workers already inside the organization. Stinchcombe suggests that there is tremendous uncertainty in the labor contract from the perspective of the employer, which is due to the great difficulty in predicting performance. Still, he suggests, "an organization needs information about the immediate past work performance of a worker so as to allocate rewards fairly, and it needs information about future work performance in decisions about hiring, promotion and retention."[36] The bureaucratic imperative demands that this information be "auditable" or quantifiable so that it can be used more easily in analytical models of performance and potential. This demand for auditability leads organizations to increase the collection of those bits of information that are more easily gathered, including that which may be gathered more efficiently through automation. Yet, because the quality of the information is so suspect, susceptible as it is to errors of measurement, misinterpretation, and strategic modification by workers who are aware of the monitoring, firms compound the errors by increasing the reach of the informational net. More flawed information does not improve the analysis, it only compounds the errors.

Drug testing of current and prospective employees represents just one of the more controversial aspects of the modern corporation's attempt to reduce uncertainty about its work force. The demand for information by business and government organizations has stimulated the development of a drug testing industry estimated to exceed $1 billion in revenues by 1990.[37] The rationales for such testing are varied and controversial. One concern is the risk of harm to consumers or other "innocent bystanders" when a person under the influence of drugs causes an accident. A second concern is associated with the loss to society when popular athletes and cultural heroes die as the result of drug use. The primary concern for business is that associated with the assumed relationship between drug use and productivity. This relationship is not well established, and some critics argue that the selective emphasis on "illegal" drugs is primarily ideological because most testing ignores the more serious productivity losses associated with use of alcohol, tobacco, and prescription drugs, all of which are legal at the present time.[38]

The political aspect of the almost faddish demand for information about drug use was revealed when the Reagan administration made drug abuse a focal point of its domestic campaign to reduce crime and eliminate waste in the U.S. economy. The report from the President's Commission on Organized Crime, which was released coincidentally with a scheduled conference on drug testing by the National Institute on Drug Abuse (NIDA) in 1986, marked a dramatic shift in corporate policy, made possible by an apparent shift in public opinion. No longer was it radical to suggest the testing of persons who were employed in critical, sensitive, or high-risk positions. The dominant line, echoed by the press, established the necessity of testing everyone who wanted to work.[39]

Information about the actual and potential consumers of goods and services represents an area of the most explosive growth and ultimate significance for the reach of the panoptic sort. Information about the quantities and prices of goods sold represents a critical form of feedback to the decisions by firms inside and outside a given market. Firms naturally keep track of their own sales, but information about the sales made by other firms also provides important strategic insight. Information about sales and purchases within and between industries provides the basis for economic planners to assess the status of the economy. Data gathered by the Department of Commerce and the Bureau of the Census provide critical assessments of the nature and status of U.S. business. Input-output analysis of the flows of goods and services within and between sectors provides the basis for sophisticated assessments of the status of a nation's economy and its potential for competition in the global marketplace.[40]

Most of this information is at a fairly high level of aggregation. It is when firms seek to improve their performance in the market by increasing the precision with which they are able to assess the responsiveness of consumers to variations in price, quality, and representation that the demand for personal information grows more quickly. Corporate planners come to believe that it is no longer sufficient to gather information about the fact that a product was sold at a given price, in response to a particular advertisement, at a particular time of the year. Businesses increasingly demand to know more about the *kinds* of people who bought and the kinds of people who did not. Information about their own customers takes on a new value as the technology of database marketing makes it possible for firms to target their promotions to those most likely to respond to similar appeals in the future. Information about potential customers who are not already known to the firm represents the critical aspect of a growing demand for personal information about consumers. Firms can gather this information through their own research and they can purchase it in the growing market of primary and secondary sources. Frequently, organizations that advertise will be provided with information about potential consumers by media representatives who seek to increase the perceived value of the audience produced by their publication or information service.

The Corporate File:
It Begins with the Application

Although corporate bureaucracies are not the source for all the personal information that enters the panoptic sort through applications and bureaucratic interaction (Table 3.1), all of the data generated have become readily available through electronic means.

Applications are not generally involved in the purchase of most consumer goods. They are more likely in the realm of services. The justification for the creation of a file in the area of services is based in part on the length of the relationship and the likelihood that more than one person may be involved in delivering that service over the life of the relationship. Occasionally applications are required to classify the applicant in terms of eligibility or in relation to the assignment of the applicant to one or more classes of service. Insurance represents a unique category of service that begins with the limited amount of information that can be gathered on a simple form but that may expand to include microscopic levels of detail.

H. Laurence Ross's assessment of the extent of personal information in insurance files in the late 1960s was that it was extremely limited.[41] The application forms for individual insurance policies gathered information that located the in-

TABLE 3.1   Personal Contributions to Machine-readable, Network-linked Data Files

1. *Personal Information for Identification and Qualification.*
   Includes birth certificate, driver's license, passport, voter's registration, automobile registration, school records, marriage certification, etc.
2. *Financial Information.*
   Includes bank records, savings passbooks, ATM cards, credit cards, credit reports/files, tax returns, stock/brokerage accounts, traveler's checks.
3. *Insurance Information.*
   Includes insurance for health, automobile, home, business, general and specific liability, group and individual policies.
4. *Social Services Information.*
   Includes social security, health care, employment benefits, unemployment benefits, disability, pensions, food stamps and other government assistance, veterans' benefits, senior citizens' benefits/subsidies.
5. *Utility Services Information.*
   Includes telephone, electricity, gas, cable television, sanitation, heating, garbage, security, delivery.
6. *Real Estate Information.*
   Involved with purchase, sale, rental, lease.
7. *Entertainment/Leisure Information.*
   Includes travel itineraries, recreational profiles, automobile and other rentals/leases, lodging reservations, airplane and ship reservations, entertainment tickets/reservations, newspaper and periodical subscriptions, television/cable ratings.
8. *Consumer Information.*
   Includes store credit cards, accounts, lay-aways; leases and rentals; purchases; purchase inquiries; subscriber lists; dress, hat, and shoe sizes.
9. *Employment Information.*
   Includes applications, medical examinations, references, performance assessments, employment histories, employment agency applications.
10. *Educational Information.*
    Includes school applications, academic records, references, extracurricular activities/memberships, awards and sanctions, rankings.
11. *Legal Information.*
    Includes records of the court, attorney's records, newspaper reports, index and abstract services.

dividual by name, residence, and place of employment. A second class of descriptors approached the construction of a profile of the applicant from the perspective of risks associated with a particular life-style, but the primary indicator was age, because of its statistical association with life expectancy. Life-style information about occupations and hobbies could have been used to adjust life expectancy, as some activities are revealed to be statistically more dangerous than others. A detailed medical history, including questions about the health of close relatives, was frequently expanded or validated by physical examination. Related documents from the applicant's medical history might have been obtained on the basis of a broad release form signed as part of the application.

This initial application frequently triggered what Ross euphemistically referred to as an "inspection," which seems more akin to an investigation, through which specialized firms gathered behavioral information from friends, neighbors, and associates. These inspections were particularly concerned with gathering information about an individual's personal "habits," including the use of alcohol and other drugs. The information generated by applications and inspections joined the medical record and moved to a centralized data exchange called the Medical Information Bureau (MIB). The MIB functions very much like a parallel system of credit bureaus in that organizations in the insurance industry and the medical field submit information for their mutual benefit and use in making decisions about individuals. Unlike the case of credit bureaus, however, consumer access to the information in their medical files is many times more difficult. At the time of Ross's writing, computerization was just becoming a factor in the insurance business. Ross's predictions about their use were very much on target: "It would seem reasonable that among the uses to which these computers will be put is sharing available and relevant personal information concerning insureds within and between departments of individual companies, as well as among companies."[42]

Ross suggested that a trend in the area of life insurance toward more group insurance would reduce the need for personal information. The same would not be true for automobile insurance, for which information about personal habits, driving records, and environmental risks would maintain its instrumental value. Homeowners' insurance would also reflect a continuing need for personal information.

Surveys and Samples

The simple and direct way to gather information about consumers is to ask for it through a marketing survey or questionnaire. Surveys are mailed to people in their homes, completed over the telephone, and filled out in response to appeals on the street or in shopping malls. Consumers respond freely to marketing surveys inserted in their newspapers and magazines. Information about consumers is gathered when customers complete the questions asked on the warrantee forms usually included with electronics and home appliances. Generally, there is no compensation provided in exchange for the information or for the time involved in providing it. Opinion researchers have noted that a substantial proportion of the population believes that such information helps manufacturers better meet their individual needs, and thus an improvement in the quality of goods is reward enough. Occasionally there are small premiums or the possibility of winning prizes of one sort or another, which are offered as compensation for the inconvenience and value of the personal information provided. Increasingly, data about consumers is gathered under false pretenses, such as when sales representatives pose as members of a public opinion research firm.[43] This practice, as well as the dramatic increase in the number of marketing surveys attempted by phone, has apparently brought about a decline in the willingness of people to participate.[44]

Refusal to participate in surveys or the exclusion of some categories of respondents from the surveys threatens the reliability and validity of the information that such surveys produce. Increased demand for access to personal information from consumers directly has begun to produce a variety of responses that may distort this information in critical ways. As more consumers refuse to participate, there is an increase in the use of those who do respond as being representative of those who do not. This occurs in two ways. The first way is through weighting. The responses of those in the sample are multiplied by a weighting factor to make their proportion in the sample match that of a presumably reliable assessment of their presence in the population. As a result, the attitudes, opinions, and behaviors of willing participants then are overrepresented in the subsequent analyses of data. This problem had been pointed out in the criticism by minority broadcasters of the dominant ratings services. Because African-Americans who agreed to participate in surveys or who were "qualified" to receive a meter or were able to complete a diary were different from those who listened to "black-formatted" radio, the audiences for these stations were seriously underestimated.[45]

The same overrepresentation occurs when the same people are called on to participate in more and more surveys because they are known to be willing. These consumers develop a kind of expertise as professional subjects, and their responses are less valuable as cues about the distribution or the characteristic responses of the population. This problem has particular implications for marketing research:

> While public opinion surveys typically sample a cross-section of the general public, marketers' growing use of market segmentation requires that they look for specific population groups which are thought to be the best consumers for their goods or services. This study suggests that some of these groups—the young, better educated, higher income, females—are of particular interest to many, and that they are being oversurveyed. If the trend continues, it may become more difficult to interview these popular segments, and both refusal rates and repeat participation may rise.[46]

In the face of continuing concerns about the representativeness of the samples that are drawn to serve as panels for the estimation of the media consumption behavior of Americans, there is increased pressure to speed the development and implementation of more precise and reliable means of audience measurement.[47] The eventual domination of the market for People Meter technology by the A. C. Nielsen Company has not led to any noticeable slowdown in corporate willingness to pay for more precise estimates of individual media use. The Nielsen company was reported to be working in cooperation with the David Sarnoff Research Center on the development of a scanning technology that would utilize infrared sensors to take note of the entry and exit of individuals from the television viewing space. This technology would use optical pattern recognition to identify individuals and whether or not their faces were oriented toward the screen.[48] This automation of the process of identification is designed to lessen concerns about the tendency of some members of the family, especially youngsters, to forget to indicate when they are or are not watching the program.

Transaction Records

The initiation of an individually identifiable file in a corporate database may begin with the first transaction. It is easy to understand why a file may be initiated when consumer purchases are made on credit, such as with a store card, with personal checks, or even with a bank or nonbank credit card. For security and for record keeping purposes, stores have traditionally requested that consumers provide additional personal identification, which is either printed on checks or added by clerks. It is only recently that some firms, such as American Express, have warned their clients not to allow their card numbers to be written on checks nor to allow their telephone numbers to be added to charge slips to reduce fraudulent use of that information. However, even cash transactions in some establishments generate a computerized record. The electronics firm, Radio Shack, uses an inventory management system that generates a computerized sales slip as well as a customer file. The customer who buys even a single battery either initiates a file or adds to an existing file with each purchase. The key to the files is the last four digits of the consumer's telephone number. Customer refusal to provide these numbers, the absence of a previously keyed file, or the provision of a fictional number generates a receipt with the name J. Doe.

The importance of the development of scanning technology cannot be overstated. Scanning from point-of-purchase terminals, such as the checkout counters in the supermarket, provides data at high speed and in real time about the status of the market as well as the responsiveness of consumers to variations in price and representation. This information helps in the coordination of the distribution system that supplies the market with products in the right size, style, color, and so on to match the apparent tastes of the shoppers who frequent a particular store. Such coordination reduces the losses associated with excess or insufficient inventory in a region or in a particular store. But the scanning technology also provides the organization with the option of gathering this information at the level of purchases by identified individuals. Special mailings or other distributions of promotional materials to persons whose identities are scanned at the time they pay for their purchases facilitate the linkage between inventory control and marketing central to the emerging just-in-time approach to manufacturing, which links production to consumption. Of course, not all ventures into the area of scanner-linked market surveillance have been unqualified successes. Indeed, a highly visible failure in an expensive start-up effort by Citicorp to develop its point-of-sale (POS) Information Services unit, suggests that much is still to be learned about diseconomies of scale and scope in the data business.[49]

Amex, like Sears, Roebuck and Company (Sears), has vast pools of data about its millions of customers. Amex has more than thirty-four million names in its international database of customers, and it has detailed knowledge of where they travel, where they eat, and, increasingly, what they buy.[50] Not only does Sears have a massive database of customers who have Sears cards, but also the company's recent entry into the competition for nonbank credit cards adds to the number of sources of transaction data from the corporation's subsidiaries involved in real estate and financial services. AT&T has joined this group with its offer of Visa and Mastercards and the transaction records it collects through its position as the dominant carrier of long distance and 800-number information calls.

Not even welfare recipients are excluded from this card-initiated system of transaction records. Experimental automatic teller machine (ATM) cards were issued in 1991 to welfare recipients in Baltimore, Maryland, and contracts with Affiliated Computer Systems promised the spread of computerized welfare payments to other states.[51] The card could be used at ATMs within the community to withdraw cash up to the amount of the monthly benefit, and it could also be used at participating stores in the community and charged against an equivalent in food stamps. Although the primary rationale for introducing the cards is a reduction in administrative costs, there is no reason to expect that the surveillance potential inherent in the transaction data will be ignored for long.[52]

The importance of telecommunications in the generation and routing of transaction information has led to the creation of an acronym to characterize this telephone transaction-generated information (TTGI).[53] Thomas McManus describes several classes or types of TTGI:

1. White pages information, which includes the alphabetical or address-based listings of telephone subscribers by name. Such a list is initiated through the application for service. In most service areas, subscribers are charged a fee *not* to be listed in such a directory.

2. New service order information, which includes the former number and address of subscribers who have obtained a new number or listing.

3. Calling detail records, which can be generated within organizations as well as by the telephone service organizations, include the date, time, and duration of calls from particular instruments to identifiable numbers. These records provide management with a means of controlling the use of the organization's telecommunications resources in the pursuit of efficiency, including restrictions on nonbusiness activities. Calling detail records also provided a powerful means of surveillance when corporate phones may have been used by whistle-blowers to contact the press or government agencies regarding questionable corporate activities. Telephone companies utilize calling detail records to identify customers who might be interested in special telephone services, such as long distance rates, or residential versions of 800-number service so that incoming calls from youngsters, friends, and distant relatives can be made more easily.

4. Billing and credit records, which add information about the customer's

history of payment and the variety of special services that might have been acquired to enhance the "plain old telephone service" (POTS).

5. Calling number identification, which refers to the controversial practice of forwarding the telephone number of the calling party through a residential or small business service called "Caller-ID," or to corporate users of 800 numbers or other specialized long distance services. By forwarding the number of the calling party, a record of the transaction can be generated at the receiving end, even if the telephone call has not been completed. Thus, a client calling an agent or his broker would leave a record that indicates not only that she called but how frequently and at what times the calls were made. Calls to 800 numbers for information or to issue complaints generate a transaction record. Calls to 900 numbers or premium information services generate a similar record, but one that can be quite precise in linking a calling party to a particular class of information.

McManus describes a complex and contentious struggle over the determination of who has what kinds of rights and responsibilities with regard to the use of these forms of TTGI. The issues involve the privacy interests of the consumers as well as the competitive interests of other telephone and information service providers who believe themselves to be disadvantaged by a monopoly firm's control over this information.

TTGI is not limited to that collected by telephone service providers. Increasingly the telephone or the telecommunications network is the critical link through which millions of transactions are accomplished each day between individuals and organizations in different areas of the globe. Many of these transactions are processed by third parties, which have no direct interest in the transaction but have access to the data generated by the transaction. The limitations on the uses to which this information may be put by these different parties have yet to be fully specified. These data have rapidly become an increasingly valuable addition to the panoptic sort.

Experiments

Each day, thousands of U.S. consumers participate in experiments without the benefit of having signed any informed consent forms. If we define an experiment broadly as a tightly controlled exercise in which individuals are provided with stimuli under varying circumstances to assess their response, then the thousands of market tests administered by the staffs of the nation's advertising and market research firms would qualify. These experiments, like those administered in the interest of science, vary in the extent of experimental control over the sample, the exposure, and the measurement of behavioral or attitudinal responses. Developments in communication technology have made important contributions to the reliability and validity of these field experiments, which come from increases in experimental control.

It may be the case that true experimental control—that which allows a researcher to claim the *ceteris paribus* condition, that all other things are equal—is not only beyond the reach but is perhaps outside the region of interest of the marketing community. The marketing researcher is interested not in basic human truths but in the response of particular classes of individuals to offers and appeals to buy a particular good or service. General insights about human nature, of the sort generated by scientific investigations, may inform the marketing research activity, but the market researcher in business has only limited interest in adding to science. Because marketing researchers are interested in responses of classes of individuals, the random assignment of individuals from a representative sample is far from the norm. Instead, we have seen and are more likely to see these researchers relying more heavily on an investigational paradigm that seeks to determine how persons of a particular group respond as circumstances change. Statistical control rather than random assignment will continue to rule the day.

For example, the rather sophisticated marketing studies, such as those offered by firms such as Information Resources (Behaviorscan), that utilize dual cable systems to test different commercials in different editorial contexts can determine in which programs their commercials will be seen. What they are unable to do most of the time is to increase the probability that individuals will see a desired *version* of the program, if they choose that program in the first place. Thus, part of the explanation for the response of particular consumers from particular demographic groups to particular versions of an advertisement for deodorant soap will be found in the unmeasured and perhaps unmeasurable reasons behind each viewer's choice to view program X rather than program Y. Information about why people choose and report liking certain programs is sketchy at best. Patrick Barwise and Andrew Ehrenberg suggest that it is in large part a function of circumstance that determines when a person is available to view.[54] However, large samples and the detailed information that is gathered about participants in scanning programs that link program viewing with shopping in participating supermarkets provide for quite remarkable analyses of the relationships among exposure, context, and consumer demographics and life-styles.[55]

An important technological advance that facilitates the linkage of media exposure to purchases of consumer goods is the laser optical scanning technology that reads the universal product codes assigned to the great majority of advertised commodities sold in supermarkets and variety stores. These stores utilize similarly coded cards to identify those customers who have requested the "privilege" of cashing a check or renting videotapes. Use of this coded card at the time of checkout provides a linkage of purchases, prices, and coupon usage that can be associated with information about the consumer that was supplied at the time of application or acquired from one of hundreds of competing list vendors.

Coupons are themselves an important resource in the analysis of consumer behavior. In 1988 more than 252 billion manufacturers' coupons were placed in print media alone, having increased dramatically in recent years.[56] A marketing service organization, the Advertising Checking Bureau, has a division, "Summary Scan," that is involved in the monitoring of coupons and promotions for consumer packaged goods. The bureau suggests that the increase in the use of coupons can only reduce their effectiveness in the short run as, on the average, less than 4 percent of all coupons are ever redeemed.

However, coupons are valuable as a tool in marketing research in that they can be issued in varying denominations and they can be sent to specific consumers or to target communities. Individuals may receive coupons by direct mail, they may be imprinted or inserted in periodicals to which individuals may subscribe, or different coupons may be inserted into the weekend newspaper that is delivered through subscription or for sale in neighborhood stores. Valuable marketing information is derived when and if coupons are redeemed.

Innovations in coupon technology have served to increase the information that such redemption provides when the coupon is personalized. "Personalization can be used to make variable offers. Since it is possible to create coupon offers with variable discount amounts, different offers can be used, which enables flexible testing and maximizes the opportunity for database-building."[57] One vendor of a proprietary technology called "Softstrip" claimed that it could be encoded with detailed information about the customer and printed on any form, including a manufacturer's coupon.[58] This information could then be revealed to participating vendors who would redeem the coupon or other token that carried the Softstrip code. In one example of its application, targeted consumers received a package announcing a contest in which the prize would be a trip for two to the Bahamas. A two-piece form served to distract consumers from the data gathering aspects of the "contest." One form, which included a space for consumers' names and addresses, also asked them to indicate whether they owned a video cassette recorder (VCR), where they shopped regularly, and on which day of the week they usually shopped. This form was to serve as their entry in the grand prize drawing. The second form, a tear off sheet, was supposed to serve as the token for an instant sweepstake prize of lesser value. This card had no clearly identifying marks; all the consumer would see was an arrow showing how to place the card into the reader to see which of several smaller instant prizes they had won. The Softstrip bar was described as the contest prize "key." In fact, the Softstrip contained detailed information about the customer: "head of household's name and occupation, total household income, number of children under 18 years old, number of employed people in the home and number of vehicles owned by household members."[59] The developers of the Softstrip technology also report that they have developed a set of printable colors that can be used to overlay, and make invisible, the Softstrip in case marketers are concerned that the public will react adversely to the presence of the unusual strip.[60]

DATA PROCESSING

Roger Clarke offers the term "dataveillance" as a device for characterizing the new forms of surveillance that have been occasioned by the increase in the distribution and use of computer-based technology.[61] His definition of dataveillance is indicative of its value: "Dataveillance is the systematic use of personal data systems in the investigation or monitoring of the actions or communications of one or more persons."[62] Clarke identifies two forms of dataveillance that have important distinctions and are worth considering in some detail. *Personal* dataveillance involves identifiable persons who by their actions have attracted the attention of the panoptic system; and *mass* dataveillance involves gathering data about groups of people with the intention of finding individuals in need of attention by the system. The techniques of personal dataveillance involve (1) the integration of data regarding an individual that might have been stored at different locations within the organization; (2) the screening or authentication of transactions by this person by comparison against internal norms or the prescreening or front-end verification of transactions that appear exceptional or problematic in comparison with available data, either on hand or gathered from other sources; and (3) the instigation of cross-system enforcement against individuals on behalf of other actors who claim to have been harmed.[63] Mass dataveillance techniques are similar to personal forms except for the fact that an individual's behavior need not appear to be exceptional; all individuals need to do is to be part of a subject population. Mass dataveillance also includes a form of "single-factor" file analysis of all available data against some norm, derived from other data or from law. Profiling is characterized as a form of multiple-factor file analysis, which might include a form of "aggregative profiling of transaction trails over time."[64]

Clarke suggests that the integration of seemingly different computer-based systems through telecommunications networks has generated a complex new form of information technology. New developments tend to strengthen the mutually supportive relations between the systems, which facilitate the management of production, travel, finance, security, and a host of administrative services. Enhancements in these systems are expected in storage; in the efficiency and user-friendliness of input and output devices (including advances in natural language comprehension); in the speed, efficiency, and reliability of communications between systems; and in the ability of systems to integrate different data formats (voice and image, symbols as well as numbers) and different processing logics (fuzzy logic and stochastic processes).

In the fall of 1991, Amex reported its plans to acquire two supercomputers noted for their ability to utilize thousands of processors operating in parallel. It is the nature of the information processing tasks that characterize the principal activity that explains the need for such machines. Although Amex was unwilling to reveal precisely how it would use the systems, expert opinion held that the machines would be used to "refine its analysis of cardholders' purchasing habits."[65]

Stewart Brand described a similar machine with 65,536 processors interconnected in a "sixteen-dimensional hypercube array," which was acquired by the Media Lab at the Massachusetts Institute of Technology (MIT).[66] Multiple processors allow large, complicated problems to be broken up into smaller chunks, each crunched by a single processor. The parallel processing approach is espcially important in pattern recognition and behavior modeling of the sort that facilitates the development and application of consumer profiles constructed from hundreds of different kinds of personal and environmental information.

Information Processing Technology

In 1983, the Institute for Computer Sciences and Technology of the National Bureau of Standards (NBS) published what it called an expert opinion forecast of what we might expect in developments in information processing technology through 1997.[67] It was clear then that increasing capacity and speed as well as declining cost would support expanded use of the computer in military, commercial, and consumer applications. It was also projected that advances in programming applied to the development of applications software would reduce the need for data processing professionals, in that the newer computers could be operated more easily by nonprofessionals. The success of the Apple Macintosh with image-oriented interface and point-and-click mouse seems to have justified its self-promotion as the "computer for the rest of us."

NBS reported the common view that important strides would be made between 1987 and 1992 as the "development of specialized processors in the area of database management and image processing areas will lead to major enhancements in query languages and image processing languages."[68] The experts predicted with remarkable accuracy that "relatively untrained users will become able to generate graphics (line charts, animation, maps, histograms, etc.) on-line with the systems in full color." These predictions included the ability of analysts to examine three-dimensional simulations of the behavior of models they were testing. Relatively inexpensive workstations have more than met that expectation. The experts at NBS were similarly correct in their projections that analysts would be able to perform many individualized analyses independent of the mainframes to which they might be connected. The accuracy of NBS projections into the future beyond 1993 will simply have to be awaited, but given the extent of analytical precision in their short-term projects, some confidence seems warranted.

NBS suggested widespread commercial availability of knowledge-based systems characterized by a high degree of interoperability.[69] They suggested that nonkeyboard interfaces will be commonplace and that knowledge-based systems will be used reliably in decision support systems.

As the number of transactions increases, firms have to develop ways to increase the rate of completion in order not to increase the waiting time for any customer in a queue. Increases for manual systems mean increasing the number of lines, the number of workstations, and the number of transaction processors. Account adjustments can add several minutes to a process that could conceivably take a matter of seconds. Automation of any subset of this process thus represents a potential savings, and automation has been pursued intensively.

Barbara Elazari describes the development of an on-line transaction processing (OLTP) system for Amex.[70] It became clear fairly early in the organization's modernization phase that Amex's impressive growth could not be sustained if it continued to rely on a manual authorization system. In 1976 Amex embarked on a modernization plan in which the goal was "to automate all the clerical work performed in support of customer accounts—activities such as account maintenance, ordering microfilm of statements and charges, writing letters, and financial adjustments."[71] Automation did not mean the replacement of clerical workers with robots, but rather the replacement of the paper records with a set of computer screens that could accommodate virtually all the transactions that required adjustments and that could not be performed entirely by software.

A variety of expert systems have been developed to increase the rate and efficiency with which information is processed to facilitate routine decision making. Amex developed an expert system called Authorizer's Assistant, which facilitates decision making about authorizing purchases for individuals who are at or beyond their approved charging limit.[72] The Amex system is a good example of the process of "knowledge engineering," which transfers the knowledge, primarily rules and a variable knowledge base, to a software system. In the case of Authorizer's Assistant, the expertise of five of the top authorizers at Amex was incorporated into the program. Even though since modernization the bulk of requests for authorization at Amex were handled automatically, the small percentage of cases that require the involvement of a human were still thought to be made more efficient with the assistance of an expert system:

> It evaluates credit authorisation requests in light of a cardholder's usual spending pattern. Its design reflects the problem that since the American Express card is not a typical credit card with a preset credit limit, the question of when to grant authorisation is not one of numbers, but one of judgement. ... Before this expert system was implemented, an authoriser would have to consult 12 to 14 data screens on a cardholder's history and patterns prior to authorising or denying a charge, or requesting confirmation of identification. Using the expert system to analyse the history and pattern, an authoriser now needs to look at only two to three screens to get a recommendation. *Though the system could make decisions on its own, American Express uses it only in an advisory capacity* [emphasis added].[73]

A similar process characterizes the credit card expert system developed for Mitsubishi by its research institute and Diamond Credit group. Here we find an expert system referred to as a Profile Analyser, which is used for scoring individual applicants in relation to their membership in certain theoretically constructed population groups. The 200 profile templates were developed through an analysis of data from a sample of 2,500 "good" cardholders, and 1,800 "failed" cardholders.

An original set of 340 patterns was reduced to the 200 "major profile factors." A credit level was then assigned to each profile. On the basis of information provided by individuals on their applications, they will be assigned to one of these profiles and will be denied or provided credit up to the limit specified by the profile.[74]

Expert systems have also been developed to assist credit card firms in detecting fraudulent uses of cards. Fraud detection is a complicated process that has to be completed rapidly and without costly error. A great many considerations must be made simultaneously: "the card user's track record, his or her ability to pay, any possibility of fraud detectable from past records, what the effect of denying the credit authorisation might have on the user's future use of the card: tear it up and switch to a competitor, what may be the aftermath for merchants."[75] This advanced system is designed so that it can use several different databases.

A similar system was reported to have been in the works for the IRS to facilitate automated tax examination. The efficiency rationale designed into this system is clear. As the system operates, it seeks to identify filers with the potential for a high payoff, and deductions are the principal focus. Ranges of deductions are compared against many hundreds of rules, and a final "integrator module" produces a result that can be compared against standards evolved through experimentation and analysis of past returns and investigations.[76]

Matching

On its face, matching seems to be a simple and obvious analytical approach to producing intelligence about individuals. Matches utilize a deductive logic, which suggests that if an individual's claim of rights to a particular status would assign her or him a place in list A, then that status might be validated by her or his appearance in another list B, which is causally or logically linked to either A or to a third variable that affects them both. A person applying for an automobile insurance policy (list A) is logically assumed to have a driver's license (list B). The negative or inverse model works in the same fashion. A person applying for a gun permit is presumably an adult over the age of eighteen (list A), but may not be a convicted felon (absent from list B). Persons who are claimants for unemployment compensation (list A), ought not to be found among the employed who are making contributions to their social security (list B). Matching is simply the comparison of lists to note the presence or absence of an identified individual in specified lists. The high-speed computer has made it possible for such matches to be made at costs that continue to decline at a rate that has made what was once a rare event a routine administrative requirement. Greater awareness of the possibility of savings associated with matches has created something of a challenge for bureaucrats to dream up innovative new matches, which might be used to identify individuals engaged in actitivies leading to waste, fraud, and abuse of resources. The social security number is the de facto universal identifier that facilitates the matching of such lists.

Matching has numerous uses as an aid to prescreening and qualifying applicants for bureaucratic services, whether from government or private firms. The logic is the same. The files of new applicants for public welfare numbering approximately 250,000 records might be matched against reported income and interest earning in the IRS files, covering nearly 180 million persons, to determine if the applicants are truly without resources as their application for assistance might suggest. Such record linkage is not limited to single organizations, because the failure to meet one's responsibilities with one member of the business community, such as paying one's rent, may result in the denial of access to other services, such as insurance. Matching has also demonstrated its potential as an aid in gaining compliance with bureaucratic regulations, especially those related to the payment of fees or fines. For example, in financially strapped Manhattan, new, portable computers called "mobile digital terminals" were put into service for sheriffs' deputies to allow the officers to match an automobile's registration against a file of unpaid parking tickets.

Increasingly, individuals are barred from enjoying one class of benefits or services because they have not met some requirement or obligation in some other area. At the University of Pennsylvania, students attempting to register through the campus telephone-based automated system (PARIS) were surprised to find that their registration was barred because they had not completed a required application with the student health service. Similar examples are easy to find and multiply with each passing day.

Federal and state governments utilize matching programs to identify and seek payment from individuals with outstanding student loans by restricting individuals' access to other government services. With loan defaults in 1990 exceeding $2.4 billion, and with persons in default representing some 17 percent of the borrowers, the Department of Education recommended a number of programs that would involve matching of the lists on which students and recent graduates would be likely to appear. The easiest targets were current or retired employees of the government. Because of the dependent relationship between numerous private organizations, including colleges and universities and the federal budget through contracts and grants, those private institutions find themselves under increasing pressure to perform such matches to demonstrate that their employees and clients have met all government requirements. The requirement that contractors assure the government that employees and clients are not scofflaws, deadbeats, or drug abusers can conceivably be expanded almost without limit to include other state interests in reproductive choice, traditional family values, and safe and responsible sexual practices. Employers already seem quite willing to pursue similar levels of control over nonwork-related aspects of their employees' lives without the compulsion of government regulation or contract limitations.

Although there is disagreement about the cost-effectiveness of matching programs, the Senate report on the Computer Matching and Privacy Protection Act of 1988 (S 496) described numerous matches that reportedly generated substantial savings for the governments that administered them. A match of social security files with the unearned income files of the IRS identified some $117 million in overpayments. Since the cost of the match and the follow-up was reported to be only $6.4 million, the economic savings were assumed to be substantial. Claims are also made that the use of matching in the form of "front-end verification" of eligibility has reduced the number of applications for government benefits, such as food stamps, presumably because fraudulent applications were eliminated.[77] The potential for matches to realize substantial savings generates a kind of competitive spirit among program analysts, who try to think up novel matches that might uncover actual or potential fraud, waste, or abuse of organizational resources. Once developed and tested, the ideas for these new matches spread like wildfire among organizations.

There are also "back-end" matches that serve as checks on the appropriateness of payments relative to the measured status of claimants. The Medicare program compares charges for medical services against the record of a patient's diagnosis to see if there have been inappropriate charges. Similar screening matches are likely to be pursued by private insurers.

Matching is routinely used for the verification of data about individuals, such as their addresses, telephone numbers, places of employment, and assertions they may have made about their income and indebtedness. There has been considerable controversy about commercial firms requesting that the federal government verify the social security numbers that individuals provide to those organizations. There has been even more vocal public concern expressed about reports that the IRS was considering matching its files against the estimates of personal income developed by the commercial firms that serve the marketing community.

Finally, in an era of increasing liability judgments for "negligent hiring," prescreening of applicants for employment against a variety of government and commercial files is becoming the rule.[78] Background checks against criminal history records, as well as credit files, is a commonplace screening match that enhances the data gathered from applications, paper-and-pencil tests, and medical examinations. Because the provision of medical benefits is such a substantial part of the compensation package of most large businesses, information about health status is particularly important. The demand for information about a potential employee's history of injury on the job has supported the emergence of several firms that provide matches against files of workers' compensation claims, injury-related lawsuits, and other indicators of risk.[79] Workers who appear on such lists may find themselves excluded from future employment even though their claims would be considered to have been legitimate by any legal standard. A person's appearance on a list is frequently sufficient grounds for rejection during periods of economic decline or stagnation when there is no shortage of available workers with unblemished records.

The possibility of matching applicants against federal and state databases of individuals with genetic characteristics considered problematic is also a problem that looms large on the horizon. Troy Duster notes that state and national registries for information received from newborn genetic screening programs are already in place, collecting data on the chromosome and genetic trait status of millions of infants. These data are collected for health and medical reasons, and often deal with whole populations, not just those at the greatest risk. ... These registries, now in their beginning stages, are part of the *machinery in place* (organizational, institutional, legal and physical) which will slowly, subtly, sometimes imperceptibly, help shift the refraction of human traits, characteristics, behaviors, disorders, and defects through a "genetic prism."[80]

Clustering and Segmentation

The simple comparisons of two lists for the presence or absence of identifiable individuals are multiplied in complexity when organizations seek to identify groups or segments of the population. The primary assumption underlying the pursuit of market segments as a competitive strategy is that "segments actually exist," and that all that remains for the analyst to do is to find the data and the analytical approach that reveals their underlying structural composition.[81] Because the collection of data is costly and time-consuming, the analyst is also concerned about the development of the most efficient ways to predict the responses of consumers. The assumption that segments actually exist is one that is easily satisfied by the realization that any market can be segmented in an almost unlimited number of ways, with the only limitations being those associated with the measurement of relevant attributes and those related to the power of the computer and computer software to handle a large number of variables and cases.

The selection of variables is guided by a continually evolving theory of consumer behavior. An early and still influential body of theory is centered on the stages of the life cycle through which an individual, family, or social unit is believed to pass. Individuals' needs, interests, and activities differ as they pass through adolescence and young adulthood, establish a household, become parents and grandparents, and enter retirement. Significant differences have been noted in the amount of recreational time that is spent viewing television as a function of age, marital status, and family size. The activities and opportunities that are characteristic of people at those stages also vary with race, gender, age, and membership in an identifiable subculture, perhaps associated with a neighborhood or geographical location.

Added to the traditional demographic identifiers are a number of personality or life-style characteristics. Ronald Frank and Marshall Greenberg utilized a combination of interests and activities to segment the television audience into fourteen groups, which added significant power to the ability of basic demographic measures to predict an individual's television program viewing.[82] Influenced by Patrick Barwise and Andrew Ehrenberg,[83] Ronald Simmons utilized a measure of cognitive style to predict television viewing preferences among African-American college students.[84] Finding such linkages between cognitive style and television program preferences within a relatively homogeneous population suggests that such measures may have some potential utility in other media segmentation schemes. The limitation of most of these approaches to segmentation is their reliance on voluntary responses from samples of the population. Economists have traditionally been wary of individuals' self-reports of their interests and opinions and have placed more confidence in indications of revealed preference—the actual behavior of individuals in the market. Transaction-generated information thereby increases the "ecological validity" of any segmentation scheme to the extent that it measures *behavior* rather than reported attitudes, perceptions, preferences, or intentions.

Although there are a dizzying variety of approaches to the segmentation of populations or markets, they share an underlying concern with maximizing the similarity within groups or clusters and maximizing the difference between those groups.[85] Within-group similarities may be based on a variety of measures of association between individuals. One measure of association is the correlation that expresses the similarity in the patterning of values among two or more individuals or cases. Jonathan Gutman reminds us that a correlation coefficient describes similarity in patterning, rather than similarity in attribute or behavior.[86] Thus, two persons may share strikingly similar relations in their height, weight, age, income, and education, and yet one can be substantially taller, heavier, older, wealthier, and more highly educated than the other. If the primary concern is the identification of group membership rather than the description of the characteristics of the segments or groups, then the preferred approach is one of clustering or multidimensional scaling.

Factor analysis is a popular approach for the identification of the similarities and differences between persons.[87] Factor analytic designs may explore the relationships between persons as determined by their comparison across a number of variables. Alternatively, analysts may examine the relationships between variables by comparing their values among a number of persons. The first and generally more popular application is called R-factor analysis. This approach allows the analyst to indicate which people are similar in terms of their similar responses to questions or in terms of their similarity in attributes and behaviors. Such an analysis can be used to produce factor scores, or a summary index for each theoretical complex that appears to differentiate between individuals in a sample.

Cluster analysis assigns individuals on the basis of the similarities between them in terms of their scores on some scale or measure, including a factor score generated by a factor analysis.[88] The example in a popular manual for statistical analysis by computer is the search for "relatively homogeneous groups" of beers, which are eventually grouped on the basis of commonality and difference in calories, sodium and alcohol content, and cost.[89]

An approach that reflects its instrumental purpose is called discriminant analysis. The analyst who has identified two or more different groups or types can utilize discriminant analysis to identify measures that are the most useful or reliable in assigning individuals to their nominal groups.[90] Such an analysis facilitates the design of experiments, surveys, or other data-gathering activities in which decisions have to be made about the tradeoff between cost and productivity of the information gathered about individuals in the sample. Discriminant analysis in its most direct application might be used to differentiate between those who will default and those who will not on the basis of historical data. Where such models have been developed on the basis of one set of data, they can be evaluated in terms of their success in predicting the histories of an alternative sample.

Multidimensional scaling (MDS) provides the analyst with the possibility of locating different products, including those of primary competitors in a multidimensional space (such as that described by considerations of cost, durability, safety, and style in automobiles).[91] Clusters of potential customers for the product can also be located in that same multidimensional space, thereby revealing which aspects of the product's "positioning" are most important to which segments of the population. The MDS approach, which uses consumer perceptions as well as their expressed preferences, is preferred to one that uses either one or the other. The perceptions are generated by asking consumers to indicate how similar or how different two attitude objects are from each other on particular dimensions. Frank, Massey, and Wind suggest that the MDS approach avoids the problem of asking people to be introspective and to give reasons for their choices in that it merely asks them to compare and to choose, leaving it up the the analyst to infer the rules that are operational.[92] Considerably more sophisticated approaches that seek a causal interpretation of consumer behavior include the increasingly popular structural equation models, which attempt to take into account the influence of the invariable errors in measurement that such research will involve.[93]

Market segmentation, then, utilizes the information derived from these statistical analyses to target messages to particular market segments. This segmentation has been demonstrated to work effectively even when the promotional message is delivered through mass media channels. As long as the message is directed to a particular audience segment and is designed to attract its attention, such as through the use of models and circumstances common to the target group, a requisite level of efficiency can be obtained. Of course, the most efficient approach would be one that identifies those programs for which the preferred consumers made up the majority of the audience.

The same analytical technology that produces the market segment is also utilized to generate conceptual profiles against which individuals may be compared. These profiles are used to identify individuals who represent a particularly high risk, or conversely, a particularly attractive marketing opportunity. A profile is an ideal type. Ideal types can be described statistically and confidence limits can be specified, which define the ranges for key variables that should be used to determine whether any particular individual should be labeled as a member of a particular group or not. Criminal profiles are common and familiar. The profiles are used by a variety of government agencies to determine which vehicles ought to be stopped, which suitcases ought to be inspected, and which tax returns ought to be investigated more closely. Similar profiles are used by commercial firms to indicate when credit authorizations are to be questioned, when bankruptcies seem likely, or when a particular offer might appear more reasonable.

A TECHNOLOGY OF POWER

The panoptic sort, which depends on ready access to personal information that can be used in combination with information about the relevant environment is, as I have suggested, a technology of power. It is a discriminatory technology, and it is guided by an instrumental rationalism. Like the content analysis procedure it imitates, the panoptic sort proceeds in stages and has component parts that vary in importance, depending on the purposes and interests of the controller. In the next section I will explore aspects of the panoptic sort including identification, classification, prediction, prevention and avoidance of risk, and allocation of life chances.

Identification

James Rule and his colleagues provide an analysis of the importance of a select number of items of documentary identification that have become necessities for an individual's successful negotiation of the bureaucratic maze.[94] They distinguish between the "documentary tokens," which individuals possess and frequently carry on their persons, and the data in files of organizations that issue those tokens or that require them to complete a given transaction. Moreover, they also note that both forms work together, the use of one depends on the existence and maintenance of the other. They suggest that personal documentation serves the social function of "generating certainty about people" and helps these organizations to "discriminate in their treatment of individuals."

The first, and perhaps most important, of such documents is that which reflects the creation of a record of a person's birth. Without a birth certificate, it is difficult to establish the long chain of documentary links that stretch from driver's license to credit card and passport. The driver's license, as a convenient picture ID card, is regularly demanded as a necessary adjunct to transactions involving the exchange of cash or commodities against personal or third-party checks, in addition to its role in the identification of a person presumed capable of driving an automobile. The document frequently contains information about sex, age, height, and eye and hair color, in addition to a signature, an address, and perhaps a social security number.

The social security card, possessed by "nearly every economically active adult in the United States," is rarely used as identification in the way that the driver's license might be. The social security number itself is the critical token used to verify or validate other claims of personhood. The credit card, which Rule and his colleagues discuss, has joined the driver's license as an item of personal identification, useful in other commercial transactions "because of the sophistication of surveillance and control achieved by the managers" of the most popular cards.[95]

At the core of their analysis is a question about the reliability of such documents when they are dependent on the individual to provide the evidence necessary to verify self-identification. They note the relative ease with which individuals are able to acquire false documents and then to use those documents as "breeders" to obtain a full complement of documentary tokens. They suggest that the primary factor that serves to limit the wholesale falsification of personal documents is the general uncertainty about the probability that organizations will bother to check or verify the claims. This is the same uncertainty about surveillance that made the operation of the Panopticon theoretically so efficient. Of course, the presumption of surveillance is not sufficient. Rule and his colleagues note that the commercial firms involved in authorizing credit transactions have developed sophisticated means of surveillance that they use to limit the unauthorized or inappropriate use of the token. What Rule et al. described in 1983 were the early developments of a technology of "self-checking," which is designed to reduce or eliminate organizational dependence on self-identification. Considerable progress has been made since then.

Among those items of identification that increase the extent and reliability of self-checking is the development of "smart card" technology. Early research had revealed that the debit cards that are used by individuals to withdraw cash and make other banking transactions through remote ATMs had losses that were twenty to thirty times lower than transactions with credit cards.[96] Use of the cards requires a personal identification number (PIN), and the transactions are generally conducted on-line, in real-time contact with the controlling records, thereby increasing the surveillance capacity of the system. The debit card does not qualify as a smart card because of its use of magnetic stripe technology. The stripe is limited in the information that it can carry, and, at least initially, it is limited in its ability to record information reflecting any change in the status of the user. Still, the 1987 estimates placed over one billion such cards in circulation. The smart card alternative would add integrated circuit chips, which would add important new functions, including "significant additional storage capacity, enhanced security, the ability to capture transaction amounts and characteristics, internally validated PINs, user-specified logic, and a permanently recorded transaction journal."[97] More sophisticated smart cards would replace the PIN with a biometric identifier such as a fingerprint, but that would require greater intelligence and storage capacity than is available at a reasonable price. Whatever the method, the smart card not only would help to establish the identity of the user, but also would contain the present balance or limit in the account. The smart card would combine identification with classification.

Similar cards have been proposed for access to the health care system. An experimental "Life Card" under development for Blue Cross/Blue Shield would contain some eight hundred pages of information about a person: their medical history, multiple identification checks, and perhaps even digitized copies of chest X-rays, scans, and other data that would facilitate the collection of medical histories in emergencies.[98] This development would take identification and classification into another sphere altogether.

Classification

Classification is a technology of control. It is driven by the purposes or interests of the actors who seek to take advantage of knowledge regarding the factors that produce or underlie the similarities and differences between people. Michel Foucault is not alone in characterizing classification as an activity that is linked intimately with the exercise of power.[99] Eugene Gallahue's discussion of the history of market standards provides a valuable insight into the means and justifications for the creation of classes, standards, and grades of marketable goods such as loaves of bread.[100] In the eighteenth century, Gallahue found, it was the responsibility of the monarch to protect the common interest by regulating the weight and quality of loaves of bread. Before the emergence of caveat emptor in the 1700s, grocers involved in the sorting of spices bagged and labeled these goods with their own marks as a guarantee of quality. These marks were very different from the brand name labeling, used by the National Biscuit Company's Uneeda Biscuit brand, which initiated an era of product differentiation in the early 1900s, serving purposes of market control and producers' interest.[101]

The process of sorting and grading produce has, of course, influenced the sorting and grading of humans in similar fashion, as we have noted with regard to the modern use of the term triage, which migrated from the sorting of coffee to the sorting of claimants for medical care.[102] Among the things that differ between the sorting and classification of produce and the sorting and classification of human beings is the fact that humans seem to have an interest in naming and sorting themselves. Paul Starr notes that a great many factors may be involved in determining whether the state (or the commercial system) accepts the self-definitions proffered by particular groups at critical moments in history.[103] The classification of people with African and Latin heritage remains a fluid and often contentious process at both official and social levels. The currency of the label African-American over the recently legitimized label "black" (whether capitalized or not), which replaced "Negro," "colored," the more offensive "nigger," and the regional variant "nigra," reflects a debate and struggle over self-definition that is far from completed. This struggle plays itself out in the continually changing category schemes for the census and other surveys that take note of racial and ethnic group membership.

The identification of an individual as being black or African-American is a particularly potent example of the arbitrary nature of many social classifications. It is almost laughable to consider that the genetic materials that would make someone black are such that they need only be present in one-sixty-fourth part, or the classical "one drop of Negro blood," to assign a person to that racial group. It is similarly absurd to classify the great variety of cultures represented in Europe and

Latin America under the bureaucratic label Hispanic. Yet, such classifications are common and bear the force of law.

Starr reminds us that the domains of social classification are social products, historically determined, reflecting in large part the exercise of economic and political power. Mary Douglas shares Starr's view in that she argues that "no superficial sameness of properties explains how items get assigned to classes. Everything depends on which properties are selected."[104] Starr suggests further that there is a process of "labeling" through which the same individuals would be "framed" quite differently for purposes of public policy if they are labeled as "homeless" rather than "vagrant." The comparisons are similarly clear when we note the differential response to the action of "terrorists" versus those of "freedom fighters." Douglas would add, however, the fact that the response of humans toward proffered labels is not always one of rejection:

> In the same way as sexual perverts, hysterics, or depressive maniacs, living creatures interacting with humans transform themselves to adapt to the new system represented by the labels. The real difference [between humans and bacteria reacting to injections] may be that life outside of human society transforms itself away from the labels in self-defense, while that within human society transforms itself towards them in hope of relief or expecting advantage.[105]

Classification generally involves some form of measurement or weighing. Differences not measured, for all intents and purposes, are differences that do not exist; clearly, they are differences that do not matter. Measurement is both a technical and a theoretical process that involves an ability to recognize similarity and difference. Foucault has suggested that classification is the "nomination of the visible."[106] I might add that the statistical technologies that describe the associations between hundreds of seemingly discrete variables, which would have been impossible without the high-speed computer, facilitate the naming of types that such analyses make visible in the same ways that the invention of the microscope made other classifications possible within the emerging natural sciences. Just as advances in technology make it possible to make distinctions between the visible more clear, advances in theory presumably make it possible to characterize that which is invisible (beyond vision), with more precision through inference from that which can be seen. A technology such as factor analysis explicitly seeks to link the relations between the visible and measured to the invisible (because unmeasured) variable or factor that those relations suggest.[107] The modern firm is actively involved in seeking to classify its present and potential customers through sophisticated analyses of the never-ending stream of data that electronic transactions produce.

James Anderson's discussion of the different ways in which one might conceptualize an audience attracted to (or produced by) a particular cultural product helps to emphasize the position of the analyst in determining the forms any classification might take.[108] He differentiates between formal audiences and empirical audiences. The formal audiences include what he calls the "encoded audience," which is evoked in frequently politicized discussions about an industry that is "serving the interests of the audience," or giving the audience "what it wants." This audience can be distinguished from the "analytical audience," which is conceptualized by scientists or critical theorists as the object of study or theorizing. Although potentially related, they are to be distinguished from the different "empirical audiences," which Anderson also defines. The aggregated audience is that which is represented by the Nielsen ratings. The categories (e.g., women, ages 18–49) are purely arbitrary and surely do not represent any purposeful self-identification by women who see a common purpose in their role as such an audience. That classification has, as Anderson notes, a clear purpose for the broadcasting executive who would like to charge advertisers for access to an audience with those characteristics. Anderson's "strategic audience" is one that has relevance to discussions of feminist consciousness, in that analysts may be interested in how such an audience, as a member of an interpretive community, would respond to a particular program or promotional appeal. The categories that are most prominent within the context of the panoptic sort are those that classify individuals in terms of their potential value. Potential value, however, is dependent on behavior at some time in the future. Thus, a major component of the panoptic sort is classification for the prediction of behavioral response.

Prediction

The panoptic sort is a predictive technology. It is even used to predict the likely behavior of jurors, and it serves as an aid to the preemptory challenges used by attorneys to improve their clients' chances of acquittal. In preparation for the high-profile trial of a member of the Kennedy family on the charge of rape, the representatives of a commercial firm, Trial Consultants, described the process of gathering data through extensive interviews and then correlating age, sex, education, and ethnic group membership with views on the guilt or innocence of a defendant. Questions that prove to have the greatest power to discriminate between those more or less likely to convict then become part of the voire dire. In advance of jury selection, one consultant suggested that the factor that would prove to be the best predictor was what she referred to as "the Kennedy love-hate factor."[109] Newton Minow and Fred Cate argue that the term "jury selection" is a misnomer in that what attorneys actually attempt to do is to "deselect," or select out, potential jurors in the interest of their clients. They suggest that this process, aided by social science, has the potential for serious distortion: "It is clear that if the membership of the panel is skewed by the selection process, then the fundamental guarantee of fairness—the diversity and breadth of experiences and views—is likely to be compromised."[110]

If the panoptic sort is a predictive technology concerned with deselecting rather than including and if the panoptic sort is based on probabilistic rather than exact predictions, then it is a technology concerned primarily with the assessment and avoidance of risk. Nancy Reichman focuses our attention on the assessment of risks as a conceptual marker underlying the identification, classification, and future interactions with individuals who engage the panoptic sort. She suggests that we ought to conceptualize "the growing reliance on probability, opportunity reduction, and loss prevention as part of a trend toward an insurance or actuarial model of social control."[111] The reduction of risk with regard to individuals involves the development of information that increases the ability of the actor to anticipate and thereby minimize losses by reducing contact with those who represent avoidable risk. The use of an insurance or risk avoidance strategy cannot be applied universally because its utility depends in part on the repetitive nature of the behaviors generating risk. The ability to predict a particular behavior depends on the similarities in the circumstances as well as a finite limitation on the number of relevant variables one can include in the predictive model. According to Reichman, "Insurance based techniques of control are largely mass produced and data dependent, and, thus, they require a level of routinization that has not been typical of social control in the past. Information that is used to screen, sort, classify, and exclude needs to be standard, and clearly defined so that it can be quickly evaluated."[112]

Yet, it is in that direction that we appear to be moving at high speed. A booming industry in risk assessment is emerging in the wake of increased corporate liability for catastrophic events such as airplane crashes, oil spills, hotel fires, and explosions in chemical plants. One company, appropriately named the Failure Group, is called into play after the fact to analyze what went wrong, assess responsibility, and make recommendations about ways to avoid repetition. Defensive risk assessment is in great demand in other less dramatic areas as well. Peter Huber describes the recent spiral in negative judgments that corporations receive in a variety of product liability suits.[113] The courts appear less willing to accept the claim that consumers ought to accept the risks inherent in the contract to buy. Instead, providers of goods and services must engage in poorly informed speculation about the kinds of uses to which some commodity might be put, which might entail some risk of harm. So informed, the firms attempt to warn consumers against such dangerous uses. And, in those instances in which the warnings are not sufficient, they seek to limit access to such goods by persons less likely to understand or heed such warnings. Each new judgment raises the level of uncertainty and the demand for more information about consumer behavior to exclude them from the risk pool.

Similar risk management techniques can be seen in the judgments being made by the courts regarding criminal recidivism. When serving as the director of the National Institute of Justice, James K. Stewart noted:

> To help avoid future crimes against innocent people, a judge or parole board necessarily assesses the likelihod of future dangerous behavior by an offender. Indeed,

laws in many jurisdictions require consideration of future danger to the community
as one factor in release decision. ... Predicting which offenders will be high-rate offenders remains as yet an inexact science. But continuing research is honing the accuracy and usefulness of prediction methods.[114]

Norval Morris and Marc Miller's review identifies three kinds of predictions that
are commonly made in the justice system: statistical predictions, based on the
comparisons of patterns of individual behavior with the behavior of others; an-
amnestic predictions, based on a person's repetitive pattern of behavior; and clini-
cal predictions, based on expert assessment of an individual's behavior.[115] They
suggest that "statistical predictions are the preferred method of prediction because they can be tested and are open to scientific challenge." They also note the
ethical concerns regarding questions of fairness and justice involved in using
group statistics to predict individual behavior: "The *meaning* of a prediction is
that the individual has a *condition*—membership in a group with certain behavioral probabilities—and not that the *individual* has that likelihood of the predicted behavior."[116] But they conclude that such considerations do not matter
when the person being assessed has already been convicted by a court. Outside the
criminal justice system, the questions of actuarial or statistical justice are not so
clear. Indeed, it may be noted that the criminal justice system itself may be challenged in terms of the apparent inequity with which it operates in charging, con-
victing, and sentencing to incarceration whites in comparison with persons of col-
or.[117]

Reichman notes that in "the insurance context, classification and exclusion
have been used to prevent individuals from joining risk pools. What insurers refer
to as 'selective discrimination' is the backbone of the industry."[118] She suggests
that the same selection principles have become central to the screening of prospective employees. Drug tests and honesty assessments are only part of the arse-
nal of devices that provide data for the assessment of risk.

The risk assessment/insurance model is also clearly at the heart of the credit
and financial services industry. James Rule noted in 1974 the importance of the
risk avoidance strategy for the consumer credit industry.[119] Because there was very
little in the way of collateral for much of consumer credit, the costs of default
would be relatively high. "Thus the art and science of credit management lie in determining, in advance, who will pay and who will not, and in screening credit applicants accordingly. This is, of course, a problem of social control."[120] Rule suggested that this form of social control would work through the "*prevention* of
default rather than the *coercion* of those who misbehave." In this way, the system
"acts to exclude the would-be delinquents from the opportunity to disobey the
rules."[121] What remained for the industry was the development of reliable techniques for the identification of those who were likely to default if given the chance.
The response was the development of increasingly sophisticated "credit scoring"
systems for estimating default risk.

Peter McAllister describes a form of "behavior scoring" that was being used by Citicorp Retail Services as an "early warning system," which reported "dramatic" results. The reduction of delinquencies by nearly 30 percent was projected to mean a 10 percent to 15 percent reduction in credit losses overall.[122] Early warning systems differ from credit scoring techniques only in that the points assigned are based on actual behavior rather than demographic information. Armed with the identification of customer accounts at the highest levels of risk, collections departments could focus their attention on them, rather than on those accounts of customers who would continue to pay without any intervention.

Proposals for the implementation of new smart cards would utilize a similar logic and would assess the risk of each transaction before it is completed because the intelligence in the card would allow it to generate a continuous assessment of the card and its user.

> This assessment opens a new and important facility. Does this cardholder have an "earned" credit line by paid performance? What is the "risk" as determined by the actual and current economic condition of the cardholder? How rapidly is the full credit line to be made available to this cardholder? Does the credit demand correlate with the combined balance of all account relations?[123]

The Target

It would be inaccurate to suggest that the panoptic sort has been restricted to the elimination of risk. After poor risks have been eliminated in marketing sorts, the classifications may then serve to guide specialized appeals to individuals or groups for whom the probability of success is highest. Very early on, data from the U.S. census were used to target commercial appeals to individuals on the basis of the character of the communities in which they lived. As early as 1973, the technology of "geocoding" had achieved a considerable degree of sophistication. Geocoding was defined as the assignment of geographical codes to records of events or other descriptive data. Geodemographic clustering was later to be assigned to the name of the procedure that linked extensive socioeconomic data to postal zip codes, which had been classified into one of forty different kinds of neighborhood types.[124] In 1973, however, the presentation of much more simple analyses of census data was held in some awe: "This same system, commercially applied, enables us to do penetration studies that will boggle your mind."[125] The author was describing the plans of a large circulation magazine publisher who wanted to send a special edition of the magazine to readers in high-income areas to collect a higher advertising rate. Apparently the IRS had made available income data by zip code. Using the zip code alone proved to be an imprecisely defined segment because there was considerable variability around the mean reported by the IRS. The census tract provided a more precise basis for targeting the distribution of the special edition because it revealed that the high-income households were tightly clustered together. The names and addresses of the people in the chosen tract were easy to obtain.

The same seminar presentation demonstrated the utility of linking computer graphics with the census tract file. Maps showing income, ethnic mix, and competitors were suggested as valuable aids to a hypothetical investor in pizza parlors in deciding where to build a store. This mapping capacity was developed for the 1970 census by the Census Bureau at a cost of $22 million. The project called Dual Integrated Map Encoding (DIME) was originally developed "to assist in the mailing of census forms, but private firms soon obtained it at the usual bargain rate— the cost of a copy of the computer tapes."[126] As an adjunct to the 1990 census, the Topologically Integrated Geographic Encoding and Referencing (TIGER) mapping service makes it even easier to generate readily interpretable maps of economic, social, and political geography at the level of census blocks, rather than at the metropolitan scale of previous Census Bureau services.[127] A promotional flyer from the Census Bureau referred to the database as "the Census Bureau's 200th anniversary present to the Nation."[128] Numerous actual and potential uses of the mapping capacity of the TIGER system were included in the pamphlet. Who could argue with the use of the system by police in Baltimore County, Maryland, to identify clusters of spousal abuse cases and to allow researchers to examine the linkages between this behavior and other indexes such as income, unemployment, and alcohol abuse?[129] More troublesome possibilities emerge when we consider the use of TIGER resources to make economic and political redlining more accurate and efficient.

Jonathan Robbin, the founder of Claritas Corporation, utilized a geographical logic to build a successful business devoted solely to targeting for commercial and political marketing. Early in his entrepreneurial career, Robbin identified some thirty-four descriptors that accounted for 87 percent of the variance in those measures across the neighborhoods in the United States defined by zip code.[130] These neighborhoods were then classified into forty different types or clusters and ranked according to an underlying index of quality. The names assigned to these clusters reflect the socioeconomic dimension that largely ruled the clustering scheme. The top cluster was called "Blue Blood Estates," and the lowest cluster was called "Public Assistance." The system was a roaring success:

> Magazines such as *Time, Newsweek* and *McCalls* were among the first clients, sorting their subscriber lists by cluster to publish upscale editions with ads hawking high-priced luxury cars and furs for the residents of Blue Blood Estates and Money & Brains. When Colgate-Palmolive wanted to test-market a new detergent for young families, it sent miniboxes to Blue Collar Nursery, characterized by starter-home neighborhoods teeming with young families.[131]

The political applications that began in 1978 were little different. By targeting the prolabor households that had been identified using the Claritas system at the census block level, it was possible to reverse an almost certain loss in a battle over "right to work." Public opinion surveys had indicated that the antiunion position was favored by an overwhelming majority. On election day, the results at the polls reflected a complete reversal resulting from the targeting of voters expected to oppose the measure.[132]

Naturally, a great many imitators emerged with their own versions of targeting methodologies based on census and other readily available data. One observer suggests that the "scope of file enhancements offered by some firms is astounding and, perhaps, a bit unnerving."[133] Kevin Kramer and Edward Schneider describe a trademarked approach called Custom Targeting, which proved to be especially useful in political campaigns.[134] They describe the technology as a "mechanism for ordering priorities—which segments of the electorate should get what kind of message, when, how and how often. Broadcast media buying, ad development, direct mail, phone banks, door to door canvassing, and candidate scheduling can all benefit from knowing *who to target and who to avoid* [emphasis added]."[135]

More sophisticated political targeting includes "life-style" data, enhanced with information derived from individuals' use of their credit cards. The comprehensive nature of this information research leads one analyst to remark that "geodemographic wizardry aside, computerized voter targeting is nearing a precision that suggests Orwellian individual monitoring and manipulation."[136] An advertisement in the trade publication for political consultants includes an almost bizarre image: four photographic portraits—two males, two females; two whites, two persons of color—each shown looking cross-eyed up toward their own foreheads, where the symbols of the Democratic or Republican parties have been printed. The ad copy reads: "If you need to know who's who on Election Day, you need to know about Conotabs. We'll locate your voters, check their addresses, find their phone numbers, *tell you all about them* and produce their names for calling and mailing [emphasis added]."[137]

Commercial and political targeting moves back and forth from high levels of aggregation to the identification of specific individuals based on an asssessment of how they will respond to a particular issue, opportunity, or challenge. The panoptic sort determines the extent to which individuals will be included or excluded from the flow of information about their environment. As applied to traditional print media, this approach is currently referred to as "target market publishing," in which both the advertising and editorial contents of the published magazines are targeted more directly to the perceived interests of individual consumers.[138] Magazines or catalogs are specially bound by printers such as the Kodak 4400, which is able to handle up to sixty-four different "signatures," or binding designs, for a single publication. An early innovator, *Farm Journal,* published using R. R. Donnelley's binding system, was able to print 8,896 different editions of that journal in 1984.[139] As applied to other communication forms, electronic media in particular, targeting is consistent with the notion of "narrowcasting," in which mass appeal messages are sent to increasingly homogeneous audiences.

Electronic systems promise the ultimate in narrowcasting or targeting, so it becomes possible to send an individualized message to each individual on the network.

Amex makes good use of the data it collects about its cardholders from their applications, and more important, from the transaction-based data Amex collects from its own sources and from commercial vendors. The segmentation within the community of Amex customers is not limited to the surface appearances indicated by the different colored cards (green, gold, and platinum), but "Amex card holders have been broken up into 15 distinct segments and each of them can be targeted with a high degree of precision."[140] This facility is expected to serve Amex well as it expands its publishing activities.

LIST VENDORS

The panoptic sort depends on ready access to information about the environment as well as about the individuals who make their way in their multiple and intersecting roles as citizens, consumers, and employees. The emerging market in personal information includes a growing independent sector of firms that supplies information that can be used in conjunction with data gathered internally. The following are just of few of the leading firms that are helping to define this sector.

Donnelly Marketing Information Services, a division of Dun and Bradstreet, offers a number of specialized database products and services. Conquest/Direct is described as a desktop marketing system that facilitates geodemographic market analysis. Clients are assured access to a database covering 90 percent of all U.S. households, which would allow clients to generate profiles of "customers" by demographics, life-styles, and retail sales expenditures. The software resources would allow them to generate customized color maps of target market areas. Related mailing list services include the possibility of making selections on the basis of "mail responsiveness, credit worthiness, vehicle information, ClusterPLUS lifestyles, contributors, financial investments, hobbies, occupations, census demographics and more."[141] An on-line service (Express) allows clients to perform the search and to order the mailing list resources by remote means.

In a letter to stockholders before the announcement of a merger agreement with Amex, Epsilon's president, Thomas Jones, described database marketing as a "household word among more knowledgeable marketers."[142] Epsilon Data Management counts not-for-profit organizations as among its more important customers for information services. At one time, its largest account was the National Rifle Association, providing nearly 25 percent of its income, but the list of clients also included the National Multiple Sclerosis Society. The approach to these customers reflects a view that social marketing is still *marketing*. In their offer of market analysis services, Epsilon's brochure asks "Who are your best customers? Where do they live? What charitable 'products' are they buying ... and why? We'll help you discover the answers through a comprehensive analysis of your marketplace."[143] The special services they promise their customers include the expansion of their donors list: "Our fully computerized Media Department analyzes more than 3,000 lists and 65 million prospect names every year—giving us firsthand knowledge of which lists are the best lists to help you acquire the most new donors."[144]

Some firms enter the telemarketing business as an adjunct of experiences that they have developed through the provision of services to their own organization. The Gannett Company, a dominant force in the newspaper business, announced the development of Gannett Telemarketing in 1989 as a spin-off of the telemarketing organization serving *USA Today*. The primary resource was the list of *USA Today* subscribers, but the lists were expected to continue to grow through the addition of names and addresses of entrants to the numerous sweepstakes run by the newspaper as an aid to circulation.[145] Early clients included firms selling sports videos, educational programs, and extended warrantee service plans.[146]

The American Student List Company, a subsidiary of American List Corporation, offered a variety of lists of college students in the United States. In 1990, lists by state were offered at $40 per thousand; adding zip code information would raise the cost by $5, as would sorting by class year. Field of study would add an additional $10 to the cost per thousand for the one-time-only use of these students' names and addresses. Another list vendor, Best Mailing Lists, offered hundreds of specialized mailing lists with prices ranging from $45 to $85 per thousand. Whereas space scientists were going for $45 per thousand in the 1992 catalog, sociology department heads were on the block at $60 per thousand, with teachers of high school mathematics priced at $65 per thousand. A number of the lists, such as those that identified political contributions by party or provided the home addresses of prominent men, were unpriced, suggesting that within this category, several lists of varying quality and price were offered and that the details would be supplied to customers who inquired further. An analysis based on new consumer lists published in the newsletter of the direct marketing industry, *Friday Report*, suggested that the most valuable names were white, middle-aged, high-income male consumers, especially when they have purchased high-cost consumer items such as computers or automobiles.[147]

Telesphere Communications (Telesphere) is a primary user of the geodemographic software and database of the Claritas Corporation. Among the more sophisticated services developed by Telesphere is its "Caller Profile Report," which would provide clients with an assessment of the character and "quality" of those persons who called a 900 number or other service that utilized automatic number identification (ANI) to capture the billing number identification of incoming calls. For advertisers using broadcast media, an analysis of penetration by area of dominant interest (ADI) represents one potentially useful product. Utilizing Claritas's PRIZM life-style clusters, Telesphere would allow an analysis of penetration among each of forty different life-styles linked to residential character. When combined with Telesphere's reverse telephone directory appending service, a caller can be identified by name and address, calling frequency, and broad life-style classification. The future of such linkage services will undoubtedly involve the classification of incoming calls before they are answered by a human operator.

A subsidiary of Equifax, National Decision Systems, offered what was called a higher level of precision in its MicroVISION targeting system because it was able to specify a zip + 4 level of geography involving ten to fifteen households, rather than the broader two hundred to three hundred households at the five-digit zip code level. The service claimed to have classified every single household in the United States into a market segment.[148] Computer-generated maps as well as current and projected demographic figures were theoretically available to customers on demand. Life-style information available to the firm allowed listing of individuals as members of segments defined in terms of price sensitivity, coupon use, brand loyalty, television use, and other characteristics of interest to consumer product marketers. Because it was a subsidiary of Equifax, a leading provider of credit bureau services, the personal information profiles offered by the firm also contained information about consumer credit activity—an activity that generated considerable negative response within the industry and in Congress.[149] National Data Systems also provided a comprehensive training program for users of their Infomark database management and marketing system, which would allow access to consumer databases, such as their proprietary list of some one hundred million employed individuals (Daytime Population), with only a desktop personal computer.

Responding to mounting criticism that resulted in legal actions initiated by more than a dozen states against TRW, the corporation announced the development of its own "privacy risk assessment" scoring system, which would allow the company and its clients to give due consideration to the sensitivity that certain data might hold for individuals, who might react by pressuring their legislators to take action.[150] The sensitivity scoring procedure developed by the company appeared to take a cue from the recommendations made by Raymond Wacks, who offered a classification of personal information sensitivity that was based on his assessment of the extent to which the collection and use of the data represented a risk of serious harm to the data subject.[151] The TRW list and that proposed by Wacks both placed information about health and race in the highest sensitivity categories. However, the recognition that certain data are sensitive and the refusal to sell that information to a buyer are quite different stories.

Ed Burnett Consultants' 1990 catalog included a number of special lists that could be acquired at rates higher than those usually charged for lists of business establishments and executives. In addition to the higher prices, several of the lists came with some rather uncommon restrictions, including the requirement that the Burnett organization be able to review the proposed mailing before the lists would be provided. This caution seemed particularly appropriate for lists of 23,000 subscribers to *Exceptional Parent Magazine,* a magazine "concerned with children's disabilities and impairments," or credit purchasers from Fashion Bug

Plus, serving women needing large-sized garments. This class of special lists also included some 60,000 paid members of the Smithsonian Institution who also attended the Smithsonian's seminars and tours.

The Database America (DBA) companies, of which Ed Burnett is a part, offer a variety of custom data enhancement services. A client would provide a customer file organized in a way that would facilitate its matching with DBA files of more than 84 million households, and a new enhanced file would be generated with information about purchasing behavior, estimated income, credit status (including credit cards), investments, and charitable and political contributions. Each enhancement would be provided at an additional one to two cents per record.

DBA claimed that the quality and completeness of their data about consumers exceeded that of their nearest competitors, except in the area of credit information. Whereas DBA's credit card data was limited to mail order records and questionnaire responses, credit agencies such as TRW had direct and privileged access to the actual credit records of the majority of individuals in the database.[152] A somewhat different kind of list is that provided by Nielsen Media Research, another Dun and Bradstreet organization, known most widely as the firm that produces ratings of media programs. Nielsen will provide random samples of working residential telephone numbers at costs ranging from six cents to twenty-six cents per number, depending on the size of the sample drawn.

One of the more well known efforts to introduce a consumer database product is the Lotus Development Corporation's product, Lotus Marketplace: Households. Developed jointly with Equifax and Apple Computers, the product was to have been a sophisticated compact disk-read only memory (CD-ROM) database of 80 million U.S. households and the 120 million adult consumers who reside there. For a fee of $695, a user with an Apple Macintosh could begin the process of customer "prospecting" through a specially tailored list of 5,000 names. Additional names could be acquired on the familiar cost-per-thousand basis. Available data would have included identification of the household's geographical location and zip code, the sex of adult consumers, an estimate of household income, buying behavior, and estimates of the revealed preferences of members of the household for more than one hundred product categories.[153] The product was designed for smaller businesses, which would presumably have a more limited need for consumer information than the larger businesses, which contracted with on-line services such as those offered by Dun and Bradstreet. Only a coordinated movement among advocates of privacy and among computer professionals prevented this project from being introduced.

On-line remote access to data represents a significant change in the nature of the market for personal information. Students and researchers are familiar with the bibliographic databases through which they may search for published and unpublished information on a variety of subjects. Journalists argue that the new databases and on-line searching capacity promise to transform the practice of journalism. Tom Koch identifies the professional journalist as the public's surrogate, who through the enhanced access to information that on-line searching provides is now able to offer an alternative vision to that which might be preferred by "flacks," or advocates, or other interested information sources.[154] Journalists pursuing corporate malfeasance can gain access to the financial reports that publicly held firms submit to the Securities and Exchange Commission (SEC), and to several other reports that the OMB still treats as allowable.

Highly profitable commercial services such as the DIALOG/Knowledge Index generally serve as brokers for information gathered by smaller firms. A second class of databases that may be searched through remote computers includes the growing number of statistical services and the associated services with "administrative registers," which are the files that contain information about identifiable individuals rather than aggregate statistics. The format of the data in some of these individually identifiable files makes it possible to generate aggregate statistics as well as to perform matches and sorts as part of the process of developing profiles.[155] Meredith Corporation, for example, claimed to have one of the largest of such databases in the fall of 1991. Their database of some 56 million customer profiles was reportedly constructed from 150 million different records, many of which were derived from Meredith's other communications and real estate operations.[156]

The growth in the number of firms competing in the market for on-line data has been nothing short of phenomenal. Starr and Corson suggest that the growing number of personal computers equipped with the modems necessary to access these services ensures continued growth in the industry supplying the data.[157] An increasing number of these personal computers are in private households, and government reports in 1988 projected strong growth for both computers and modems, reaching 23.9 percent penetration of U.S. households by 1992.[158] The launch of the consumer-oriented videotex service PRODIGY by Sears and International Business Machines (IBM) reflected this sense of optimism. For consumers unskilled or less sophisticated in the navigation of the hundreds of competing vendors, another group of brokers called "gateways" provides the nonspecialist with access and advice about gathering data. The approval in late 1991 for the entry of the Regional Bell Operating Companies (RBOCS) into the information business marked what is likely to become a watershed in consumer usage of these services.[159] What should be kept in mind is that use of these services by consumers will undoubtedly generate additional TTGI, which feeds back into the modification and correction of the panoptic technology.

4

CORPORATE PERSPECTIVES ON THE PANOPTIC SORT

IN PURSUIT OF THE CORPORATE VIEW

The panoptic sort is a technology that has been designed and is being continually revised to serve the interests of decision makers within the government and the corporate bureaucracies. The previous chapter focused attention on those organizations that utilize personal information to segment and target consumers through direct marketing. Of course, not all firms that are involved in direct marketing see the operation of the panoptic sort in quite the same way. This is due in part to the relative importance of database marketing to their overall income and in part to the extent to which their business involves direct contact with the public. Retail firms that provide services directly to the public are more sensitive to the goodwill dimensions of a public issue such as privacy, whereas service firms that deal with consumers only indirectly may feel less of a need to pay attention to public sentiment in this area. However, as the panoptic sort becomes an essential part of modern business practice, more firms will be forced to develop a corporate position on the underlying questions about the legitimacy of its use. To understand the dynamic process that underlies the evolution of a corporate posture, three firms were selected for a limited case study. This study served as a background for an analysis of a survey of business leaders.

I examined copies of the annual reports for 1984 through 1988 from three corporations that were active, or soon to be active, in the debates over personal privacy. My review of these corporate reports sought to characterize the different approaches to the issue of privacy and the panoptic sort as it was described to actual and potential shareholders. The corporation's letter to their shareholders is the primary instrument it uses to call attention to past successes and to problems on the horizon that the corporation is mobilizing its resources to address. Comments about information policy reflect the relative importance of these issues to different corporations in the information business. The three firms I selected for this study were the American Express Corporation (AMEX), TRW, and Equifax. Of the three, Amex has traditionally had the most direct contact with consumers and, therefore, it appeared to have made the greatest investment in generating goodwill through its involvement in privacy policy.

American Express

Amex has had extensive experience in dealing with the complexities of the privacy issue. This firm claimed leadership in the area of consumer privacy with its 1974 institution of a mailing list policy that would become a direct marketing industry standard. Through its Warner/Amex Cable Communications division, the corporation became the first cable operator to establish a privacy code in 1981, only to sell its share of the corporation in 1985.[1]

In its 1984 report, as a strategic accomplishment Amex presented a corporate policy that in the future will become a critical point in the public debate about privacy. This privacy sensitive year saw the introduction of Amex's One Enterprise concept: "Under the One Enterprise concept, we provide our businesses considerable autonomy but at the same time we expect them to work together as a single enterprise. At year end, approximately 140 One Enterprise projects were in operation or under development, including many where our companies 'cross market' products and services created by other members of the American Express family."[2] As such corporations as Amex become increasingly involved in seemingly unrelated lines of business, telecommunications facilitates the combination of customer data into a single marketing tool. Current restrictions on data sharing do not cover most of the internal uses of personal information outside the banking sector, but many observers recognize the potential conflicts that such practices may generate between what customers expect and what firms do as a matter of standard practice.

In 1985 Amex increased its involvement with the panoptic sort by consolidating its ownership of First Data Resources. In the view of Amex's management, "information processing has become more critical to all our businesses, in such areas as point-of-sale electronic services and telemarketing."[3] The 1986 report took note of the expansion in One Enterprise efforts to take advantage of the "opportunities inherent in their complementary strengths in markets, product lines and cultures" and looked ahead favorably on strategic efforts to "increase the precision with which we segment our markets—enhancing our ability to reach discrete groups while offering additional value matched to our particular needs."[4] As part of a corporate movement toward this strategic goal, Amex formed its Direct Marketing Group in 1986. One of its divisions, Merchandise Services, ranked as the fifth largest direct merchandiser, and First Data Resources continued to grow through acquisitions.[5]

Because 1987 had been a troublesome year for financial institutions in general, and especially for those with substantial stock market exposure, the Amex annual report focused more on the future than on the immediate past. Technological advances in artificial intelligence put the corporation's authorization and transaction processing business "ahead of the curve" in this growing industry. This expertise supported expansion into health care marketing, where they utilized simplified techniques for relational database analysis.[6] The 1988 annual report revealed even greater involvement of the corporation in privacy sensitive activities. The Data Based Services Group, already an industry leader in third-party authorization and transaction processing for bank cards and cable television systems, expanded further through two new projects. One project would join with Donnelley marketing "to access a database of more than 89 million households for marketing purposes"; the other, taking advantage of the possibilities of 900-number services, would "market services that may permit the simultaneous handling of up to 30,000 interactive telephone calls for marketing and entertainment purposes."[7]

Thus, we see that, over the years, Amex had become increasingly integrated into the direct marketing industry, not only as a direct marketer through mail and telecommunications but also as a dominant vendor of third-party authorization and processing services. This increased risk provided a clear rationale for the corporation's donation of an initial $50,000 grant to establish the Direct Marketing Association's (DMA) privacy task force[8] and its support for the adoption of standards of information practice, which would be considered progressive from nearly any position.[9] According to these standards:

1. The individual has a right to know that personal data about his life will not be rented or sold against his wishes and a right to know exactly what information a company makes available to others.
2. It is unethical for a company to collect information for one purpose and to rent or sell it for another purpose against the customer's wishes.
3. An individual has the right to know who is the sender of a direct mail piece.
4. The consumer should be clearly and frequently advised of his right to be excluded from any and all lists.[10]

Amex's long-term involvement with consumers through direct contact also provides an explanation for the appearance of more explicit discussions of corporate concern for the privacy issue in the company's annual reports.

In the context of discussions of public responsibility, the 1988 annual report described the expanded role of the company's Consumer Affairs Office. The office is responsible for "major initiatives in consumer protection and education," and it also "monitors the Company's Privacy Code of Conduct, which provides standards governing the collection, custody and use of customer information."[11] Because of the international scope of the corporation's business and the potential risks represented by the higher level of privacy protection in the European Community, participation by Amex's Consumer Affairs staff in public forums included many foreign sites in 1987.

In the corporation's report to the SEC, *Form 10-K,* there was a more explicit discussion of the potential regulatory restraints the corporation thought it might face in its privacy sensitive lines of business. Regulations linked to credit access, credit billing, and credit reporting were *not* thought to represent any particular threat to the company's card business, nor were there any specific regulatory risks associated with either the Data Based Service Group or the Direct Marketing Group.[12]

TRW

TRW, a major defense contractor and developer of sophisticated computer and information systems, began in 1984 to build on that experience to enter the information economy more directly.[13] The corporation's consumer credit reporting unit received only a slim paragraph's mention in 1985, but it was destined to become more visible each year.[14] In 1985, the information systems group, which included consumer information services, grew by more than 20 percent. The annual report claimed industry leadership for its credit reporting unit and announced the controversial new service, TRW Credentials, which was "developed to help consumers monitor and control the credit process"[15] but which was seen by critics as a means to gather even more information for credit files at the consumer's expense.[16]

In the 1986 annual report, TRW identified the information systems group as the most profitable and fastest growing part of the organization. Their market analysis suggested that the "growth of the information systems and services business reflects a fundamental change in the way people increasingly obtain the facts they need and want—from electronic databases."[17] The Credentials program was described more completely: "The service enables people to monitor requests for their credit histories and to apply for credit more easily by filling out a master credit application, which is then stored in a TRW data bank for authorized use by credit grantors."[18]

The report also noted the expansion of the credit reporting service to all fifty states and discussed TRW's controversial practices in which it "markets portions of its credit database to financial services firms that wish to target particular groups of prospective customers."[19] This same report underscored the integration of defense and commercial applications of advanced TRW information systems with significant implications for the enhancement of the panoptic sort. One such system was described: "Called the TRW Fast Data Finder System, it will enable users to scan raw data for nearly 600 different, complex search requests simultaneously at a rate of more than 7 million characters a second—the equivalent of six 500-page novels."[20]

In the 1987 report, information systems maintained its strategic importance for TRW, and major expansion was planned for those areas that utilized advanced information systems to collate intelligence derived from proprietary databases. By 1987, TRW claimed to provide more credit reports than any of its competitors, and its annual report noted practices that were later to make the corporation something of a pariah within the direct marketing community. The credit data in its files on more than 138 million consumers would be used by other clients to market financial products and services. This is a use of credit reports thought by many to be barred by the Fair Credit Reporting Act (FCRA), but no mention of these potential regulatory conflicts was mentioned in the annual report or in the *Form 10-K* report to the SEC.

Growth in the revenues and profits from the information systems group apparently stalled in 1988, but the annual report continued to identify it as "the key building-block business" likely to be enhanced through the acquisition of Chilton Corporation, establishing TRW as the unchallenged industry leader. Throughout the five years examined, none of the corporation's annual reports or *Forms 10-K* gave any indication of concern about the emerging privacy crisis.

It was not until spring 1989 that TRW began to take a more activist stance in response to growing criticism. It hired a social scientist as a vice president to help formulate its positions on information policy issues, and it funded a conference at Georgetown University in June to help focus debate on the issues surrounding technology and information policy.[21] It may be that TRW's decision to invest in a more visible public posture was the result of increasingly negative coverage in the press and negative comments from associates within the industry associated with a TRW mailing of names on a credit list to a reporter from *U.S. News and World Report*.[22] Reports that emerged in 1991 indicated that TRW was having second thoughts about its role in the information business after the attorneys general of several states had initiated suits against the corporation for its use of personal information from its credit files in ways these attorneys general considered to be barred by the FCRA.[23]

Equifax

Equifax has been intimately involved with the panoptic sort because its principal lines of business involve providing guidance to third parties about identifiable individuals. In the discussion of its corporate vision in 1985, the annual report reveals this centrality:

> With the emergence of the financial services industry in recent years has come a broader perception of Equifax's role as a provider of information for business decisions. This perception brings us closer to the consumer in the sense that the consumer's action creates the need for just about every service we perform. Stated another way, every financial transaction requires information, and the consumer, at the moment he or she initiates a transaction, triggers a process that can ultimately involve Equifax.[24]

The report notes that growth in recent years involved not only the expansion of their reporting network to owned and affiliated bureaus, but also the pursuit of new service options "in the areas of credit promotion, marketing, applicant prescreening and others."[25]

A special section in the report for 1984 focused on data protection, but the issue was approached from the position of a data manager concerned with guaranteeing the security of that data from access and tampering by computer criminals. Equifax indicated considerable corporate interest in and implied support for legislation that would levy substantial fines for unauthorized access or unauthorized use of information in a computer file. The extended discussion of the problem included the expression of concern that the press tended to present corporations as the criminals, rather than the victims of computer crime.

> The news media, which have an inestimable influence on the way people think about issues, can do a great deal to promote public understanding. In coverage of computer crime incidents, some media commentators have exhibited a disturbing tendency to portray the institution rather than the criminal as the villain. This is somewhat like blaming a bank for being robbed, simply because that's where the money was.[26]

Perhaps because the press coverage of computers in 1984 contained a considerable number of Orwellian references to corporate as well as governmental "big brotherism," this discussion in the annual report ended with an appeal for the development of a new coalition of interests, "a unified effort by the business information industry and its customers to arrive at solutions that protect data while allowing the unfettered use of technology necessary for the legitimate gathering, storage, transmission and use of business information."[27]

For Equifax, 1984 was a year in which the firm gained from increased corporate use of information in the panoptic sort as a means of risk avoidance. Equifax services were used to evaluate credit risks, as well as to aid in screening potential employees. The report noted that "marketers of goods and services increasingly relied upon selective information, especially demographic information targeted to population segments."[28]

The expansion of Equifax's involvement in the panoptic sort in 1985 included the addition of drug screening, as well as the highly specialized screening of potential employees that the company performed for organizations in the nuclear energy field. Its credit and marketing-related services were expanded to include sophisticated and largely automated routines for identifying potentially fraudulent applications or purchases. By 1987, Equifax claimed to be the "world's leading provider of information for consumer-initiated financial transactions," involving more than 1.5 million transactions each business day.[29] In a somewhat novel way of presenting the corporate position on policy issues, the 1986 annual report presented a panel discussion in which senior managers answered questions posed by a variety of interested parties, including a consumer-affairs specialist.

Richard Bullock, executive vice president of the National Council of Better Business Bureaus, asked the "privacy" question, presumably in the public interest: "With your increasing use of information, what are you doing to protect the public and maintain individual privacy?"[30] The published response was narrow and repeated the cloaking phrase, which excuses all and limits little: "There are Federal and state laws to protect privacy and to ensure that information is used properly and not released to anyone without a legitimate business purpose."[31] In addition, the response attributed to chairman W. L. Burge included notice of Equifax's efforts to increase computer security and emphasized the value of its automated systems, which provide the corporation with historical records of access to particular files. Equifax's corporate management saw no threats on the horizon arising from pending legislation that might have any adverse effect on the information industry or its role in the panoptic sort.

The rest of the annual report presented business sector reports that were glowing in their promise of continued growth in the information intensive aspects of the corporation's business. In its discussion of the consumer credit and marketing services, the report noted continued expansion of fraud detection and risk avoidance services: Through the use of "sophisticated statistical modeling, we help customers monitor credit portfolios to provide early warning of potential problem accounts."[32]

In 1987, Equifax continued to expand the number and variety of services to insurers and other bearers of risk. One new service with the informative acronym, CLUE, facilitates exchange of information, including motor vehicle records, to assist insurers in making underwriting decisions.[33] The corporation continued to claim a competitive advantage over other database management firms that were unable to enhance their target marketing profiles with credit information. This use of credit information for marketing purposes represents one of the more sensitive aspects of the practices of each of the three firms examined in this case study, yet Equifax gave no sign of recognizing this threat in its 1987 report. Equifax executives were heartened, perhaps, by their recent success in an appeal before the United States Court of Appeals for the Eleventh Circuit.[34] The court's analysis argued for a narrow definition of "consumer report," which would involve restrictions and penalties under the FCRA. Thus, market gains in that year, in the context of a judicial all-clear signal, led the firm to pursue an even more aggressive expansion in the following year.

The year 1988 saw the creation of a new division, the Marketing Services Sector, the acquisition of fourteen companies, and a significant common stock offering of nearly 2.9 million shares. Equifax's segmentation services were precisely the kind of profiling efforts that represented the leading edge of panoptic technology and were efforts about which privacy advocates had been complaining most vocally:

> Sophisticated models analyze various combinations of data using complicated mathematical equations and then construct indices to help predict consumer interest and buying potential for particular goods and services. The key to success in providing marketing information and services is to integrate all the relevant transaction activities and information available from Equifax to help businesses answer a variety of marketing questions.[35]

Equifax seemed apparently unconcerned about any kind of consumer backlash. Indeed, growing competition from other firms in the information industry seemed to be their prime concern. In a dedication to W. L. Burge, who retired as Equifax's chair in 1988, there was a clear sense that the troubled times associated with consumerism of the 1960s were past. Burge had become chief executive officer (CEO) in 1967, and the late 1960s presented substantial hurdles for the corporation because of the presumed influence of corporate practice on consumer well-being.

> During that period, which preceded what has now become the Information Age, Equifax, along with all who gathered and used essential information for decision making, came under serious challenge and examination by consumer groups and political activists. Some even questioned the right of business to evaluate risks. Mr. Burge led Equifax through it all with dignity and with calm assurance rooted in the knowledge that the Company was filling a vital role in society.[36]

However, by the end of 1989, Equifax had contracted with Louis Harris and Alan Westin to administer a national survey of public opinion regarding the kinds of business practices that many consider to be invasions of privacy. These Equifax surveys continue the series of such studies funded by Sentry Insurance and New England Telephone that not only inform industry public relations, but that also have been critical components of the public debate on privacy.[37]

Amex, TRW, and Equifax are three very different corporate "citizens." Their differences can be explained in part by the differences in the visibility that is created through their direct contact with consumers. Amex, the corporation with the most direct contact, appears to have been the organization most sensitive to consumer reaction about apparent threats to privacy or to abuses of personal information. Yet the need to expand sales, profits, and market share has led each of these firms to explore the instrumental use of personal information in ways that will continue to attract the harsh glare of publicity and the risk of sanction. For these and other firms like them, it is the use of personal information for the support of telemarketing that is most attractive and most risky.

THE TELEMARKETING VIEW

The telephone will increasingly become the focus of the debate about privacy and the panoptic sort. Not only is the telephone the instrument that provides an annoying intrusion into the privacy of the household, but, as has been noted, the use of the telephone for a variety of transactions is an important source of data that enhances a consumer's profile. This enhanced profile will generate still more annoying calls. Mark Nadel discusses the issues surrounding the threat that the telephone presents to "the right to be left alone."[38] The recognized privacy interest is seen to be the strongest in the home, yet the technology of the telephone allows for penetration of the barrier of the closed door and the pulled curtain. The insistent ringing of the phone is difficult to ignore, and even though devices such as answering machines or passive displays such as Caller-ID represent technological responses, they cannot completely protect against unsolicited and unwelcomed interruptions.

When the telemarketing industry introduced the automated technology that had the capacity to dial hundreds of numbers and play recorded messages (automated dialing recorded message players, or ADRMPs), many citizens and their legislative representatives argued that the invasion of privacy had gone too far. A variety of restrictive bills were introduced and passed in state legislatures across the United States. The patchwork nature of telephone regulation generates considerable difficulty for direct marketers and market researchers who utilize centralized phone pools to place calls around the country. Thus, the industry has had a powerful incentive to work toward uniform legislation at the federal level that would support unrestricted use of the telephone for "legitimate business purposes." Even when the congressional response to telemarketing reflects the general sense of public annoyance, the Federal Communications Commission (FCC) acts to protect the interests of the marketers.[39]

Limitation on the use of the telephone to gather information about consumers, generally without their informed consent, represents a second concern for the telecommunications industry and their primary clients in telemarketing. After divestiture and the seemingly interminable process of removing the competitive restraints on their participation in other areas of the information business, AT&T, the Bell operating companies, and their competitors in long distance have begun to offer a variety of information services that promise not only to expand revenue, but also to elevate the temperature of the privacy debate. The premium 900 numbers represent one such business venture with great business potential. The telephone company as carrier shares the fee collected on behalf of users of the service. As part of its service, the telephone company will forward the numbers and perhaps the names and addresses of the calling party. This information was recognized for its potential market value in that it could become part of a marketable list of persons demonstrably interested in a particular service. Arrayed against these corporate interests in the collection and sale of personal information are the claims made by privacy activists that individuals have substantial property rights in the information they generate through their transactions.[40]

Telephone companies see the provision of "privacy enhancing technologies," such as an option that would allow individual consumers to block the passage of their telephone numbers when they make specific calls, as a threat to the profit potential of an entire line of enhanced telecommunications services. One industry analyst suggested that the industry's expected income might be reduced by as much as 50 percent if blocking were allowed.[41] One AT&T vice president has been identified as linking these privacy questions to the entire future of what the phone companies call "the intelligent network." From the industry perspective, "that network relies on the ability to recognize and utilize the calling party's number.

And what effect some very broad, Luddite type of policy would have on the development of that network is of concern to us."[42]

Telephone-based services, such as the teletext service offered by Sears and IBM (PRODIGY), involve similar privacy issues. The PRODIGY system was designed from the start to be a marketing tool. After four years in development and some $300 million in investment, the service moved into test marketing with a number of hopeful vendors of shop-at-home services.[43] Advertisers, or "information providers" as they are called, are to be charged on the basis of the number of users that actually view their messages on the screens of their home computers. Thus, for the system to operate efficiently, it must provide a record of which "messages" have been viewed, although not necessarily by which consumers. That additional information is a valued enhancement that may or may not emerge as a separate product.[44] The PRODIGY service users are asked to provide demographic information at the time they initially "log on" to the system, and they add to that database each time they "jump" or "zip" or "look" or take some other action in response to a new screen. Item seven in the service agreement notes this fact: "One of the valuable and unique features of the PRODIGY service is its ability to personalize information and transaction services to each Member's interests. Personalization is based on data provided by the Member (or Membership Holder) to Prodigy, data derived from the Member's use of the PRODIGY service, and from the Member's responses to Prodigy's questions and surveys."[45]

The agreement indicates that aggregate information about members can be disclosed for any purpose the company chooses. Rules regarding the use of individually identifiable information about members seem to make it available for the marketing purposes of present or future "information providers." And thus, questions about the use of transaction-generated data are bound to emerge as privacy concerns for PRODIGY and its imitators.

DIRECT MARKETING ASSOCIATION

The DMA has the almost impossible task of bringing together the vastly different organizations (more than 3,500 in the United States) that share little in common beyond their use of a common marketing technology. The difficulties that these organizations have in finding a common policy stance that satisfies the needs of all of the members of business associations frequently serve as the basis for the formation of single-issue coalitions, which then contract with outside lobbyists to present their particular views on an issue.[46]

In support of its members, and as something of a foil against public outrage, the DMA sponsors mail and telephone preference services that allow consumers to indicate that they would prefer not to have their names included in national consumer lists. DMA officers participate actively in the policy process through their formal testimony in hearings and through their submission of language for proposed legislation. Their efforts to "educate" the public about direct marketing involves the publication and revision of pamphlets, booklets, and guides for good business practices. Their efforts to influence their membership include the establishment of numerous councils, task forces, and special seminars, which bring together industry leaders to discuss critical issues and concerns. The monthly newsletter, *Washington Report,* provides a regular update on regulatory and legislative activities.

The DMA is periodically forced to revise its "guidelines for ethical business practices," as technology and industry practices generate new problems. A recent version of the guidelines includes a policy statement regarding unlisted telephone numbers. The ethical position of the DMA is that "telephone marketers should not call telephone subscribers who have unlisted numbers unless a prior relationship exists."[47] Discussions within the DMA's Privacy Task Force, however, suggest that questions about automatic calling number identification, which threaten to reveal unlisted numbers and therefore make them available in published lists, may require revision of the guidelines.[48] Another association whose members are primarily in the business of providing "yellow pages" information services agreed that they would not release information about calls made to their services without prior consent. Some providers that would presumably be bound by the DMA policy seem determined to circumvent the policy by including the "electronic consent" (using the star button on a touch-tone phone) as part of the number unsuspecting customers would be asked to call.

The issue of transaction-generated data has the potential to stimulate considerable debate within the DMA as organizations such as TRW and Equifax pursue corporate strategies through activities likely to bring public wrath down on the shoulders of the industry. In one issue of the DMA's bimonthly newsletter, *Directions,* Ed Burnett, an active list vendor, discussed the privacy issue in the context of "problems and abuses." It seemed that different state legislatures had responded to growing public concern about privacy by placing restrictions on use of the public databases, such as automobile registrations.[49] Problems for direct marketers identified with the list industry arise most significantly when the commercial business of DMA's members becomes closely identified with the activities of government. In 1984, the association became alarmed when the IRS sought to use commercially available lists to identify persons who should have, but who apparently had not, filed tax returns.[50] In his testimony before a House committee, DMA chair Alexander Hoffman expressed the collective concerns quite clearly:

> They will come gradually to understand that the IRS is using census data to overlay on the basic mailing lists. And we believe that an inevitable consequence of such a chain of events carried out broadly and nationally would be a tendency of the people to view this as just one more invasion of privacy; just one more step in Government intrusion in our lives; and they would gradually tend to conclude that it is not a very good idea to have your name on a mailing list.[51]

In 1992, the direct marketing industry was threatened once again by the efforts of the FBI to acquire compiled lists from leading firms. The FBI was reported to be a steady customer of Metromail and used its MetroNet service to provide remote identification of individuals identified by telephone number, but the firm and its competitors claimed that they would oppose FBI requests for compiled lists.[52]

The government/industry link alone does not raise concern within the industry about its vulnerability to growing public concern about privacy and the consequences of the panoptic sort. In a forum organized for its readers, *Target Marketing* asked somewhat rhetorically, "What do you think is the most important issue direct marketers face today?" Katie Muldoon, a direct marketing CEO, answered very much on point:

> Privacy is my major concern because the consumer is becoming much more aware of the databases we are collecting—files of names of bankruptcies and the exact credit on individuals' charge cards and so forth. The consumer doesn't really understand how we use suppress files. They see this as a real invasion of their privacy. I believe this attitude will cause legislation. It is very frightening.[53]

Muldoon thought that the problem was exacerbated because it was not just consumers talking among themselves, but it was newspapers and other periodicals, and from her experience, "when publications talk about it, consumers talk about it more."[54]

TRW's business strategy produced many raised eyebrows and no small amount of concern within the DMA when it asked the IRS to validate the social security numbers of its more than 143 million data subjects. TRW would be likely to cause even greater concern if more people come to realize that it is a contractor with the U.S. Postal Service and it helps to process the millions of change-of-address forms that consumers submit when they move.[55] Members of the DMA have been openly critical of TRW in print and in industry seminars, but these do not exhaust the bases for disagreement. There are basic differences in philosophy and strategy that are still being ironed out within the DMA and within the corporations involved in direct marketing. TRW's response has been that much of the criticism that explodes periodically in the press is the result of competitive jealousy. "If I've got an airplane and you've only got a car, you don't want me to use the plane" was the reponse attributed to Dennis Benner, a vice president of TRW's Target Marketing Group.[56] Differences between firms in terms of their resources, their sophistication in the use of panoptic technology, and their understanding of the emerging privacy debate will be explored at a later point in this chapter.

ROBERT POSCH
AND CORPORATE OPINION LEADERSHIP

Robert Posch, vice president and counsel for the Book Clubs Group of Doubleday and Company, is a productive and highly visible defender of the interests of database marketers. Posch publishes a regular legal column in the trade magazine *Direct Marketing* and forcefully represents his views at conferences and seminars organized by the DMA. Posch's approach may be characterized as a frontal attack. He argues that there is no constitutional basis for a privacy claim. In addition, he minimizes the extent of the intrusion that telemarketing or direct mail represents. For Posch, "telephone marketing not only isn't an invasion of privacy but it isn't a nuisance either." Thus, he explains, "there can be liability for a nuisance only to those to whom it causes significant harm, of a kind that would be suffered by a *normal* person of ordinary sensibilities in a community."[57] Rather than respond to escalating claims for what he sees as a nonexistent right, Posch counsels the industry to push instead for its constitutionally guaranteed rights of free speech, which have been extended by the Supreme Court to include truthful commercial speech. "Free speech is the industry's public posture high ground and winning constitutional argument. Reliance on a 'cut our losses' argument on privacy means our opponents continue to define the issues and win the states."[58] Posch concludes by noting that "privacy is the Achilles' heel of database marketing law and consumer relations. How well we finesse this issue will determine whether non-store marketing prospers or follows other U.S. industries into decline as a result of their refusal to recognize changing public policy."[59] Posch has been especially vigilant with regard to the importance of lists to the direct marketing industry, suggesting that every list is important, and he has stated that to allow the state to restrict the industry's use of *any* list would eventually lead to their being restricted from using every list. "If we continue to lose non-commercial lists (e.g., motor vehicle, library, etc.) WE SHALL LOSE ALL LISTS," Posch emphasized, and then he warned, "already there are attempts to ban 'residence' and 'geographic discrimination.' This will increase as insurance companies unable to prescreen for AIDS will consider screening applicants by ZIP."[60]

Of course, not all sectors of the industry have been willing to adopt Posch's position. In a debate organized by the Long Island Direct Marketing Association, Posch argued his position against the more conciliatory, "corporate responsibility" views of Roy Schwedelson, CEO of WMI/Worldata.[61] Posch warned that recognition of any privacy claims in corporate data begins to take the industry down a slippery slope:

> There is no legal difference between a library list, a motor vehicle list or any other list. It's all one composite of information. If you believe we're right, and I do, then it's our free right to have this. But if you believe some lists are invasion of privacy, how do you distinguish them? We can be consistent for free speech, or we can get bogged down in privacy. If we get bogged down in privacy, we cannot win.[62]

Schwedelson's position is one that might be considered constrained rationality. He argues that privacy claims cannot be ignored or merely "wished away." From his analytical position, existing legislation restricting corporate activity under the FCRA will be brought to bear against the interests of direct marketing because of the behavior of several organizations, including TRW, that use credit data for marketing purposes in ways that generate public alarm. It is argued that because of their marginal position in the direct marketing industry, such credit reporting firms as TRW and Equifax do not share a full commitment to the industry's position regarding privacy. Schwedelson argues further: "If TRW loses on their database, they're going to go home [to their primary business] and leave us with the problem. Frankly, I don't think the DMA should have put Benner [vice president and general manager of TRW Target Marketing Services Division] on the Ethics Committee. That's like letting the fox run the hen house."[63]

Few question the fact that the privacy issue is destined to become a significant aspect of consumer affairs legislation in the 1990s. Attitudes toward business similar to those that characterized the turbulent 1960s might accompany the reemergence of ecological concerns on the national policy agenda. A lack of agreement on the issues within firms centrally or peripherally involved in the panoptic sort will continue to challenge associations such as the DMA quite severely. A survey of U.S. business leaders provides some evidence of cleavages within the corporate sector that may widen as the issue develops.

THE MAIL SURVEY

David Linowes reported on a survey of 126 Fortune 500 companies that sought to describe the nature and extent of corporate efforts to protect the privacy of their employees.[64] There had been no comparable surveys of corporate practices published with regard to corporate collection and use of consumer information, especially with regard to their use of such information for the purposes of marketing. This section describes the results of a survey that I designed to help erase part of this knowledge gap.[65]

Early in 1990, I sent letters to nearly one hundred corporate representatives who had been identified by the direct marketing newsletter *Friday Report* as having introduced some innovation in direct marketing. I was especially interested in those companies that had new products or services that developed, enhanced, or in some unique way, expanded the ways in which consumer lists could be used for marketing purposes. The letter of inquiry identified the sender as an academic interested in marketing technology, specifically in the use of customer data, and requested available material about the company's list products. About 25 percent of the companies responded, and their responses ranged from cursory to most generous. One secretary forwarded a copy of her employer's popular book on direct marketing.[66] Others provided marketing packages, with examples of list management and promotional services that the companies provide. These responses, in addition to the materials gathered from the academic and trade literatures, provided the basis for the questions that were pursued through a mail survey of corporate leaders.

The questionnaire reflected an attempt at classifying firms in terms of the organization's primary and secondary lines of business. Key variables included the size of the corporation, measured in terms of the number of employees. I had a particular interest in firms with multiple establishments, including separate divisions in quite different lines of business, because I thought that such firms were likely to move information across internal boundaries for the purpose of cross-marketing.[67] An establishment was defined as an economic unit, generally at a single physical location. With increasing conglomeration, mergers, and the expansion of the franchise as a form of business organization, definitional uncertainty about reporting level remains a serious analytical problem. Because an establishment may actually be identified as part of a division, an establishment is not necessarily the same as an enterprise or company, which may consist of one or more establishments.

Another measure linked to but not a substitute for any measure of size was an index of technological sophistication. In a survey by Lance Hoffman and Alan Westin, participants at a computer security conference in 1984 were asked to classify their organizations in terms of their sophistication in computing.[68] My survey followed that approach, and respondents were asked to classify their organization's general status as an information technology user. Related questions assessed the company's use of computers and telecommunications to store and access customer data.

A series of questions with ordinally scaled categories asked respondents to indicate the frequency with which they used customer information for marketing, used credit information to screen potential customers, or used customer information acquired from other internal units or from external vendors. A question related to the measure of the importance of customer information to the marketing function asked whether the organization had a special administrative unit or a particular individual assigned the primary function of managing the customer database. Another question inquired about the amount of attention that the organization paid to maintaining the security of their lists or files "to protect them against unauthorized use."

A checklist was used to allow respondents to indicate which of a variety of options they would consider to be a "fairly routine" technique that the organization used for marketing. The ten listed options included "use of a customer's name within a mailing"; use of "life-style lists to classify potential customers"; and customizing "catalogs to customer/prospect profiles."

A series of questions sought to characterize these corporations by their use of telecommunications, through outbound or inbound telemarketing. More important, I sought information about their use of the automatic number identification (ANI) service provided by long distance telephone carriers. Factual as well as hypothetical questions asked about the extent to which they used or might value services that could provide additional information about customers that might be gathered on the basis of their telephone numbers.

Several items asked about the nature of the corporation's policies regarding the release of customer information to third parties. These questions asked about whether customers were provided with the option of restricting the sharing of their names for use in mailing lists, and if there were such options, they were asked to indicate how frequently the customers were informed about such options and the manner in which customers might exercise them.

The final set of questions addressed the use of customer information as an issue of public policy. Respondents were asked to indicate the extent to which they believed that their business was being hampered by current restrictions on the sale or exchange of customer information. After indicating the extent to which they thought the use of customer information would emerge as a political issue in the next five years, respondents were presented a checklist that they could use to indicate what kinds of people would bear the greatest responsibility for the escalation of this issue. The list of nine potential actors included "antibusiness activists," "disreputable firms," "telemarketers," and "Congress."

Sample Selection

The source of businesses included in the sample was the Dun and Bradstreet Dun's Market Identifiers database, accessed through the DIALOG Information Retrieval Service. This particular database includes both private and public corporations with five or more employees, or companies with sales in excess of $1 million. The corporate files provide current addresses and financial and marketing information for nearly 2.4 million business establishments. In addition, the corporate record identifies all known businesses within the corporate family. For the purposes of this survey, I restricted this sample to the universe of listed corporate headquarters of public and private firms with more than fifty employees.

Standard Industrial Classification (SIC) coding was selected as the initial criterion used to define the relevant universe of firms. SIC codes are a uniform and commonly utilized system for classifying business establishments by their principal economic activities. For the purposes of this survey, "primary" was based on the value of corporate output associated with a particular activity, and outputs were defined as the value of receipts, sales, or revenue. If the company was an aggregate of several establishments, primary activities were defined on the basis of the relative value of aggregate outputs. Because of my interest in companies with major business activities in the marketing of consumer goods and services, I eliminated several SIC codes from the research population. With all exclusions based on size and SIC classification, a smaller population of some 97,172 organizations was initially identified in the search of the Dun and Bradstreet database.

A systematic sampling interval was utilized to select a more manageable group of 750 headquarters. Because of the ratio of small to large firms, the initial sample was thought to contain too few representatives of the larger firms involved in consumer sales. A subsidiary sample of 109 of these large firms was included in the group to which surveys were mailed.

Of the 859 establishments included in the sample, responses of some sort were received from 238. Seventeen were returned as undeliverable by the U.S. Postal Service. Some 26 were either blank or the executives indicated that they had no consumer sales and were not eligible. Only 181 questionnaires were received that could be qualified as complete or partial responses. Although the covering letter promised anonymity, there was evidence of considerable mistrust of the project within the target community. Identification numbers on the return envelopes that had been assigned to facilitate record keeping were obliterated by more than a dozen respondents. The sample was further reduced by the elimination of any questionnaires with a substantial number of missing responses. The sample used for the analysis that follows totaled 139 cases.

CORPORATE POLICY AND PRACTICE

Because of the relatively small sample and high rate of nonresponse, descriptive statistics are relatively meaningless as anything other than a description of the tabulated sample. That is, we can have no real confidence that they accurately represent the broad segment of U.S. business most directly involved in the collection and use of personal information for marketing purposes. As with any survey of the general public, we expect that those firms most sensitive about the privacy issue were more reluctant to respond. However, information about the nature of the sample provides some background against which to assess our analysis of the associations between characteristics, orientations, and the information practices of those who did respond.

The twenty-six different SIC categories were combined into six comprehensive classes: Retail Sales; Banking/Insurance/Real Estate; a Services group including Transportation/Lodging/Recreation/Restaurants; Automobile Sales and Services/Personal Services/Miscellaneous Repair; Telecommunication Services/Mass Media; and finally, Health/Legal/Social Services. The largest group was Retail Sales, containing approximately 30 percent of the sample. The smallest groups were Telecommunication Services/Mass Media, with less than 7 percent, and Health/Legal/Social services, with approximately 10 percent.

Although there is a tendency to treat corporations as fictional persons and further to consider that the organization has a personality, or a corporate style, it is important to keep in mind the fact that corporate practices reflect decisions made by individuals. To the extent that chief executives can impose their opinions on others in the organizations they direct, one might argue that the executive speaks for the company. That relationship is never perfect, and, in any event, is rarely apparent to an outsider. Still, I felt it was important to question the executive at the top about the firm and its relationship to the panoptic sort. Sixty percent of the respondents indicated that they were the CEOs of their establishment. Another 23 percent of the surveys were completed by executives in general managerial posi-

TABLE 4.1   Corporate Tendencies (in percentages)

| | Low | | | | High | No |
	1	2	3	4	5	Response
Technological sophistication	5.0	20.1	40.3	26.6	7.9	0.0
Use customer information						
to market	5.8	17.3	42.4	25.2	7.9	1.4
Use internal sources	27.3	19.4	25.9	14.4	2.2	10.9
Enhance with purchased						
data about customers	45.3	28.8	12.2	7.9	4.3	1.4
Depend on vendors for						
customer information	23.7	43.9	16.5	8.6	2.9	1.4
Get customer information						
electronically	57.6	17.3	9.4	5.0	5.8	5.0
Use outbound telemarketing	57.6	15.8	17.3	3.6	0.7	5.8
Use inbound telemarketing	45.3	15.9	16.5	10.0	4.3	7.2
Would find added						
demographics useful	41.9	23.7	20.9	7.2	0.0	7.2
Add data to phone #s	54.7	21.6	15.1	5.0	0.0	3.6
Estimate of customer's						
concern about data use	8.6	8.6	19.7	23.7	19.4	20.9
Attention to list security	7.9	6.5	15.1	19.4	34.5	16.5
Limited by laws	39.6	23.7	7.9	0.7	3.6	24.5
See lists as an						
emerging issue	4.3	14.4	39.5	26.6	9.4	5.9

tions. Less than 3 percent of the forms used in the analysis were completed by employees in public relations, although nearly 7 percent were from sales or marketing.

We note a nearly normal distribution of responses describing the corporation's status as an information technology user (Table 4.1). The greatest number of responses identified the organization as being mainstream, with slightly more than 30 percent identifying themselves as advanced users or even trendsetters in some areas. A similar proportion indicated that they kept customer data in a centralized database, which could be accessed remotely through a corporate network. With regard to the use of customer information for marketing, the tendency within this group was toward more rather than less frequent use of data in this way. Approximately 40 percent of the respondents reported that they used credit or financial information in selecting new customers. As many of the firms were small, single-unit establishments, it might be expected that nearly a fourth never utilized customer information from other units, divisions, or affiliates in their marketing efforts. Less than 20 percent of those responding to this question indicated that they used such information very much or extensively.

Neither outbound nor inbound telemarketing was a method relied on by many of these respondents, and outbound was slightly less popular than inbound as a marketing tool. Given the relatively limited use of the telephone for marketing purposes, it was also not surprising that respondents tended to see little value in a

TABLE 4.2 Marketing Techniques (percentage using routinely)

Practice		Practice	
Use customer's name in a mailing	56.9	Use customer profile for mailing	33.8
Classify customers demographically	34.5	Use zip code–based profile	40.3
Use surveys to gather customer data	28.1	Target marketing with statistical models	19.4
Classify prospects by life-style indicators	9.4	Classify prospects by psychological profiles	3.6
Prescreen customers with credit lists	20.1	Customize catalogs to match customer profiles	5.0

service that might provide demographic information with incoming calls (Table 4.1).

With regard to the attention they paid to the security of their customer lists, respondents tended to claim that security was a very high priority. On a five-point scale, five being the highest, the mean was 3.8, with 5 as the modal (or most common) response (34.5 percent). Respondents tended not to think that their business practices were currently being limited by laws governing the sale of lists. The mean on the same five-point scale was 1.7, with 1.0 as the modal response (39.6 percent).

With regard to marketing techniques that respondents believed were used "routinely" within their firms (Table 4.2), the use of the customer's name within a mailing was the most popular, used by more than 56 percent of the respondents. The most sophisticated techniques, those facilitated by computer processing of customer transaction information, were used by only a few firms. Psychological (3.6 percent) and life-style (9.4 percent) profiles were used routinely by less than 10 percent of the respondents. Although it was not the most popular technique, zip code–based profiles were used routinely by more than 40 percent of the respondents' organizations.

The responses to a question about customer lists as an emerging public issue were almost normally distributed, with a mean of 3.2, although only six respondents (4.3 percent) indicated that it would not emerge as an issue at all.

A series of questions asked respondents to indicate which individuals or groups would be most responsible for the escalation of the use of customer records into a public issue. The questions were coded so that responsibility could be assigned values, ranging from none to major, in three steps, with three indicating major (Table 4.3). On the basis of the mean ratings, list vendors are seen as the most likely culprits, followed by telemarketers and disreputable firms. Antibusiness activists were assigned major responsibility by approximately 28 percent of the respondents, whereas list vendors were so labeled by nearly 63 percent. Disreputable firms were assigned major responsibility by more than 56 percent of the respondents, but aggressive competitors were generally seen as blameless.

TABLE 4.3   Actors Seen as Responsible for the Escalation of the Customer Information Issue (percentage identified as major, N=139)

List vendors	62.6
Telemarketers	57.6
Disreputable firms	56.1
Complaining customers	54.0
Federal regulators	48.9
Congress	46.8
State legislators	43.9
Aggressive competitors	23.0
Antibusiness activists	27.3

Underlying Patterns in Corporate Responses

In the next section, I examine the corporate orientation to the panoptic sort through the use of a simple method for differentiating between types of firms. This differentiation is made not only on the basis of their characteristics such as size and technological advancement, but in terms of corporate orientations toward customers' claims of privacy interests in the company records that identify them. What is sought here is evidence of some patterns or relationships that might suggest that there is an underlying linkage between the nature of the firm and the postures of management toward its customers. Three primary variables are explored: the size of the establishment; its sophistication with regard to information technology; and its primary line of business. A nonparametric correlational approach is used as a first step in estimating the relations between these variables.

Table 4.4 presents the correlations between eight predictors and thirteen types of corporate practices. To facilitate interpretation of the coefficients, a superscript *a* is used to indicate a relatively conservative criterion of significance. Coefficients so marked may be interpreted as indicative of a genuine, even if weak, association between these variables.

The size of the corporation is seen to be positively linked to five of the thirteen comparisons. The strongest association ($r = .52$) is with a measure of the extent to which the firm gathers information about customers from vendors electronically (Electron). Recall that more than half of the respondents indicated that they never gathered information in that way. Thus, the association of this behavior with the size of the corporation seems reasonable on the face of it. The somewhat lower correlation ($r = .39$) with a variable indicating that the firm enhances customer files with information purchased externally (Exacquir) underscores the distinction between the technologies perceived to be available and those deemed appropriate to different sorts of firms. Somewhat lower still, but in the same direction ($r = .29$), is the tendency of the larger firms to depend on vendors for customer data (Depend). Although the number of respondents actively involved with inbound telemarketing (Inbound) is small, there is still a positive, or direct, relationship between company size and such an approach to sales.

TABLE 4.4 Correlates of Business Practices

Practice	Correlations with Predictors							
	1	2	3	4	5	6	7	8
Usemktg: Extent of use of customer information for marketing purposes	.14	.33[a]	−.07	.15	.02	−.01	.02	−.13
Inacquir: Extent of use of customer information acquired internally	.20	.41[a]	−.12	.02	.04	.03	−.02	−.01
Exacquir: Extent of use of customer information acquired externally	.39[a]	.42[a]	−.06	.02	.10	−.02	.09	−11
Depend: Extent of dependence on commercial vendors for customer information	.29[a]	.27[a]	−.12	.10	−.10	.02	.05	.05
Electron: Extent of electronic means to acquire customer information	.52[a]	.34[a]	−.18	−.10	.05	.06	.24[a]	.00
Outbound: Extent of use of outbound telemarketing	.31[a]	.31[a]	−.16	−.09	.16	−.01	.36[a]	−.15
Inbound: Extent of use of inbound telemarketing	.25[a]	.18	.04	−.16	.16	−.09	.23[a]	−.12
Callinfo: Extent of use of information about callers	.20	.17	−.22	−.07	.04	.17	.16	.01
Telnos: Uses information based on telephone numbers of callers	.05	.03	−.03	−.08	−.05	.11	.13	−.10
Concern: Extent of customer concern about sale of name	.14	.08	−.01	.16	−.19	−.21	−.01	.33[a]
Security: Extent of attention paid to customer name security	.14	.13	−.20	.26[a]	−.26[a]	−.18	.04	.33[a]
Lawlimit: Extent of legal limitations on sale of customer names	.11	.10	−.12	.09	−.11	.00	.03	.16
Issues: Belief that customer information will escalate as an issue	−.09	.07	.07	.04	−.09	−.15	−.08	.20

TABLE 4.4 (cont.)

Predictors
1. Size (number of employees)
2. Technological sophistication
3. Retail Sales SICs
4. Banking/Insurance/Real Estate SICs
5. Services/Transportation/Lodging/Recreation/Restaurant SICs
6. Automobile Sales and Service/Personal Services/Miscellaneous Repair SICs
7. Telecommunications Services/Mass Media SICs
8. Health/Legal/Social Services SICs

^{a}p = .05, or less, two=tailed

Technological sophistication with regard to information technology emerged as the most important correlate of the business practices explored. Although this was statistically significant in six of the comparisons, there are some departures from the associations with size worthy of comment. Technological sophistication appears to be more strongly associated (r = .33) with the use of customer information for marketing (Usemktg) than may be explained by corporate size. Although one would think that the more technically sophisticated firms would be more likely to have the capacity to gather and process information received electronically from external sources (Electron), the association is not as strong as it is with regard to corporate size. Instead, there is a more consistent association with the tendency to utilize internal (Inacquir, r = .41) and externally purchased (Exacquir, r = .42) data.

When we examine the associations in Table 4.5, it appears that company size is the primary characteristic that explains the use of particular analytical techniques or different classes of data or information. The use of surveys (Survey), targeting with statistical models (Targstat), life-style (Life-style), and psychological profiles (Psych) is positively associated with the size of the firm as measured by number of employees. The only significant association with technological sophistication is with the use of surveys, which suggests that computerization is an aid and perhaps a necessity for interpreting survey data.

Overall, the identification of the firm's SIC group failed to provide any reliable indications of the likely orientations or practices of firms within that group, including the use of marketing techniques. This may be due, in part, to the substantial diversity within the groups as constructed for this analysis. Only a larger sample, utilizing the two-digit SIC code, will allow us to answer this question more conclusively. Membership in the group representing firms involved in telecommunications services and mass media is significantly associated with three tendencies, all logical correlates (Table 4.4). These firms tend to gather customer information electronically (r = .24) and to engage in outbound (r = .36) as well as inbound (r = .23) telemarketing.

TABLE 4.5　The Association Between Organizational Characteristics and Marketing Techniques (N = 139)

Practice	Correlations with Predictors							
	1	2	3	4	5	6	7	8
Custname:								
Uses customer's name in a mailing	.02	.18	−.09	.15	−.10	.07	.11	−.09
Custprof:								
Uses customer profile for mailing	.16	.07	−.27[a]	.13	.04	.02	.12	.01
Demograp:								
Classifies customers demographically	.11	.07	−.02	.09	−.05	−.18	−.01	.21
Zipprof:								
Uses zip code–based profile for customers	.10	.18	−.16	.10	−.01	−.00	.02	.12
Survey:								
Uses surveys to gather customer data	.35[a]	.24[a]	−.10	−.11	.05	.08	.16	.00
Targstat:								
Pursues targeted marketing with statistical models	.37[a]	.08	−.09	.07	.08	−.23	.09	.14
Life-style:								
Classifies prospects by life-style indicators	.40[a]	.11	−.05	−.10	.10	−.15	.12	.06
Psych:								
Classifies prospects by psychological profiles	.34[a]	.11	.04	−.10	.04	−.09	.11	.06
Screen:								
Prescreens customers with credit lists	.05	.21	−.02	.11	−.14	−.00	.09	−.11
Catalog:								
Customizes catalogs to match customer profiles	−.01	.20	.14	−.03	−.09	−.02	.07	−.07

Predictors

1. Size (number of employees)
2. Technological sophistication
3. Retail Sales SICs
4. Banking/Insurance/Real Estate SICs
5. Services/Transportation/Lodging/Recreation/Restaurant SICs
6. Automobile Sales and Service/Personal Services/Miscellaneous Repair SICs
7. Telecommunications Services/Mass Media SICs
8. Health/Legal/Social Services SICs

[a]$p = .01$, or less, two-tailed

TABLE 4.6   Rotated Factor Matrix (varimax) Business Information Orientations
(N = 121 cases, loadings > .35)

				Loadings for Factors				
Variables	1	2	3	4	5	6	7	8
Fedreg:								
Federal regulators would be responsible if customer records become an issue	.93							
Stateleg:								
State legislators would be responsible	.91							
Congress								
Congress would be responsible	.79							
Activist:								
Activists would be responsible	.56							
Compet:								
Aggressive competitors would be responsible	.55	.55					.36	
Telemkt:								
Telemarketers would be responsible		.81						
Disrep:								
Disreputable firms would be responsible		.76						
Listvend:								
List vendors would be responsible		.72						
Catalog:								
Customizes catalogs via customer profiles			.75					
Usemktg:								
Use of customer information for marketing			.71					
Exaquir:								
Enhancement of files with externally purchased information			.63					.39
Zipprof:								
Use of zip code–based customer profiles				.81				
Demograp:								
Classification of customers demographically				.80				
Psych:								
Classification of prospects by psychological profile					.80			
Life-style								
Classification of prospects by life-style					.72			
Targstat:								
Use of statistical models for target marketing				.36	.55			

TABLE 4.6   (Cont.)

| | Loadings for Factors | | | | | | | |
Variables	1	2	3	4	5	6	7	8
Custname: Use of customer name in mailings						.79		
Survey: Use of surveys to collect customer data						.60		
Custprof: Use of customer profile for custom mailing				.40		.57		
Telnos: Add customer data to telephone numbers			.36				.71	
Issues: Belief that customer information will grow as an issue							−.68	
Screen: Uses credit-based prescreening of customers								
Customer: Complaining customers would be responsible if customer records become an issue								.75

With regard to the extent that the organizations pay attention to the security of their customer records (Security), the strongest link is with membership in the Health/Legal/Social Services group ($r = .33$), followed by the Banking/Insurance/Real Estate group ($r = .26$), and there is a striking reversal ($r = −.26$) with regard to the Services group, for whom customer records are of only limited concern.

None of these measures of corporation type are reliable predictors of the respondent's identification of the individuals or groups that their leaders believe to bear the greatest responsibility for any escalation in concerns about the panoptic sort.

An Alternative View

In an attempt to reduce the number of variables, while exploring the underlying structure of information practices that characterizes these firms, a factor analysis was performed with the twenty-three variables with the highest response rate. Table 4.6 presents the eight factors that account for 65 percent of the measured variance. Only variables with factor loadings greater than .35 are included in the table. The first two factors, explaining 16.6 and 13.0 percent of the variance, respectively, reflect the loading of eight of the nine actors identified as being responsible for the

TABLE 4.7   Multivariate Analysis of Variance
Factor Scores with Three Independent Variables (significance of F, N = 121)

Dependent Variables	Level of Significance for Interactions and Univariate Sources						
	1	2	3	4	5	6	7
Multivariate (8 Factor Scores)	.65	.28	.15	.02[a]	.32	.02[a]	.16
Factor 1	.86	.60	.74	.52	.71	.16	.47
Factor 2	.49	.70	.95	.81	.90	.95	.92
Factor 3	.07	.16	.87	.68	.48	.32	.73
Factor 4	.79	.18	.38	.09	.68	.23	.71
Factor 5	.87	.91	.03[a]	.01[a]	.07	.31	11.
Factor 6	.50	.59	.07	.22	.50	.04[a]	.74
Factor 7	.98	.46	.20	.76	.18	.44	.29
Factor 8	.29	.04[a]	.05[a]	.01[a]	.03[a]	.01[a]	.01[a]

Pillais test of significance ([a]$p<.05$)
Employ = Number of employees
Usetech = Technological sophistication
Indgroup = Industrial group membership
Interactions and univariate sources:
1. Interaction of Employ, Usetech, and Indgroup
2. Interaction of Usetech and Indgroup
3. Interaction of Employ and Indgroup
4. Interaction of Employ and Usetech
5. Indgroup
6. Usetech
7. Employ

escalation of the privacy issue. The variable representing aggressive competitors loads substantially on three factors and is therefore not particularly useful as an aid to defining the factors. With the elimination of this variable, factor 1 appears to be a political factor, whereas factor 2 is a business or corporate factor.

Factor 3, its clarity marred by the loading of Exaquir on factor 8 as well as factor 3, reflects a common tendency for those that use customer information, including that acquired externally for marketing, also to use that information in specially tailored catalogs. Factor 4 has high face validity, linking the use of zip code profiles with the use of demographic classification. Factor 5, which shares the tendency toward using statistical models with factor 4, includes a further tendency toward the use of life-style and psychological measures.

Factor 7 is somewhat difficult to interpret. It suggests a tendency to blame aggressive competitors for an issue respondents do not see as likely to escalate in the near future. Both of these tendencies are associated with fairly extensive use of data to enhance corporate files based on captured telephone numbers. Perhaps this factor reflects a bit of wishful thinking, rather than being an accurate reflection of current corporate practices. The final factor (8) reflects a tendency to use information acquired externally to enhance customer files, and to fear that if these practices escalate into a major issue in the future, it will be because of the actions of these disgruntled customers.

Table 4.7 presents the results of a multivariate analysis of variance approach, which takes into account the linkages between the underlying tendencies that these factors represent. Factor scores for 121 cases were used to estimate eight different dependent variables (factor 1 to factor 8). The table presents an evaluation of the importance of the explanatory variables, singly or in interaction with other predictors, as the source of different patterns in the distribution of factor scores. The multivariate scores reflect the contributions of the predictor variables to the variance of the eight dependent variables taken as a group, whereas the eight univariate scores reflect the contribution of the predictors to the variance in each of the factors independently.

With regard to the explanation of the variance in the set of factors, only two measures appear to have any demonstrated explanatory power: technological sophistication (Usetech) and company size (Employ). The interaction between size and sophistication is a significant factor (p = .02). At the same time, company size is not a significant factor by itself (p = .16), although technological sophistication is (p = .02). Whatever influence corporate size has with regard to the multivariate question, the univariate analysis suggests that it is limited almost entirely to factor 8. The distinction between these two influences may be pursued further by examining the univariate analyses associated with factor 6. Where technical sophistication is a source of influence with regard to variance in the use of customer names, profiles, and survey methodology (p = .04), company size seems to matter not at all (p = .74).

With regard to factor 5, reflecting the tendency to utilize sophisticated modeling, including the relatively less popular psychological and life-style profiles, the interaction of corporate size and technological sophistication is the most important source of measured variance (p = .01). There is a significant interaction effect (p = .03) of company size and industry group (Indgroup) membership, by which the larger firms in particular groups are more likely to use computer profiles.

Factor 8, which reflects the peculiar tendency of some firms to rely on external sources for customer information but to fear that disgruntled customers will be a major source of the escalation of public concern about marketing practices, is seen to be affected by every measure except the most complex interaction of all three variables. Examination of the univariate alphas would suggest that industry group identification is the least useful in regard to this measure. Size, sophistication, and their interaction are all significant sources of influence. The correlation data suggest that, especially for those in the Health/Legal/Social Services sector, the relationship between bigness and anxiety about customer complaints is positive. Unfortunately, at least for the purposes of interpretation, firms in this sector are less likely to be dependent on externally acquired customer information. One interpretation that solves the apparent paradox in the data is the suggestion that firms in this sector expect the problems to emerge not because they acquire customer information, but because someone might release this information without proper authorization.

Some support for this explanation can be found in the tendency of these firms to have customers who are very much concerned about personal information (r = .33) and for the firms themselves to report paying considerable attention to the security of their customer data (r = .33) while also maintaining a substantial belief that customer information will emerge as a major policy issue (r = .20). Support for this interpretation is also found in the Equifax (1990) survey of business leaders in "privacy intensive industries." Respondents from the human resources and insurance sectors were most likely to believe that their customers were genuinely concerned about the practices associated with the compilation and use of mailing lists.[69]

BUSINESS PERSPECTIVES ON
THE PANOPTIC SORT

These data suggest that the use of panoptic technology is just beginning to make its way into the pool of organizational resources. The association with corporate size and technological sophistication is not surprising, but it underscores the influence of dominant firms in the establishment of the corporate culture. Linowes's claim that "major corporations are standard setters of business practices"[70] deserves to be taken seriously, although my analysis suggests that there are important differences between organizations, many of which are reflections of the orientations of their chief executives as individuals, rather than strictly a function of structural demands.[71]

These data also suggest considerable awareness of and concern about the potential consequences of a consumer backlash. Business executives seem to share a common tendency to see problems as being caused by others outside their own organization. Because of this, less attention is paid to their own corporate practices. Similarly, as we will see in the next two chapters, individuals *have* an awareness of the existence and operation of the panoptic sort but they tend to see it as affecting the lives of others, rather than themselves.

5

RELATIONSHIPS AND EXPECTATIONS

IN SEARCH OF PUBLIC PERCEPTIONS

The development and implementation of the panoptic system are conditioned by the level of awareness and acceptance of practices and consequences as normal, legitimate, and consistent with the broadly held public understanding of the rights and responsibilities of institutional actors with regard to the collection and use of personal information. The dynamic interaction among technology, market, and nonmarket relations governing the exchange of value and the laws and social customs that condition their development defies any simple categorization. The materialist view generally holds that the laws and customs of a society—the superstructural realm of culture—are determined in the final analysis by the changes in the realm of production and exchange. Although it is difficult to establish the primacy of the technical over the exchange relations, because technological innovation is generally understood to have been a response to stagnation or constraint in the operation of the market or government sector, we tend to accept the view that sees changes in attitudes and opinions about information practices as having been occasioned by changes in technology and its application.

What people feel about a particular social practice depends on what they know about it and how they understand its use, its justification, and its consequences for them or for others. The relationships among the cognitive, affective, and behavioral spheres of social opinion are more closely linked in theoretical models than they are in empirical social research.[1] Not all of the difficulties have to do with problems of measurement. Almost insurmountable difficulties lie in the contextual or situational variety that qualifies opinion and constrains action. Thus, confidence in what people say they believe and intend to do has to be tempered by a recognition that circumstances always intervene.

Anthony Giddens's exploration of practical and discursive consciousness underscores the methodological difficulties that speak for caution as we approach the assessment of social opinion.[2] Giddens distinguishes three levels of consciousness, which bears an unfortunate association with the Freudian levels of id, ego, and superego. The unconscious is presumed to be simply unavailable to researchers and analysts because it is also unavailable to Giddens's knowledgeable actor.

The connections and distinctions between the levels of practical and discursive consciousness matter most to our ability to access and understand social opinion. Practical consciousness refers to the knowledge, insights, logical structures, schemas, rules, and cognitive resources that individuals have access to while they are engaged in their social routines. Yet, not all of this knowledge is available to an individual at the level of discursive consciousness, where they might report or discuss their reasons or rationales for taking a particular action. Tacit knowledge is a resource at the level of practical consciousness. Giddens suggests that there may be something of a "negative bar," or restriction on an individual's ability to monitor actions reflexively or to represent the complex logics that underlie seemingly contradictory preferences and values. People simply cannot tell you all they know, especially with regard to their reasons for the actions they take.

These difficulties raise, or at least should raise, a number of red flags when social scientists claim to be able to represent individuals' mental structures or schemas, their value systems, or their preferences for goods, services, or social outcomes and policies. Amos Tversky and Daniel Kahneman have used creative experiments to provide devastating critiques of rationalist assumptions about consumer behavior.[3] Their examples have great force because of the gaps they reveal between what people say they value and what they demonstrate they actually value when they are forced to make a choice. This difficulty is complicated further when the forced choices required by a standardized questionnaire or survey instrument bear only a limited but probably unmeasurable relationship to the complex attitudes, opinions, or preferences that individuals may actually hold.

Social researchers are not unaware of the problems of reactivity that complicate their efforts to measure knowledge and social opinion.[4] Questions asked in the early part of an interview help to prime or establish a frame or orientation that is likely to constrain or limit the range of responses to questions asked later in the interview. Understanding that a survey has something to do with "privacy" is bound to color a person's responses to questions about personal attributes, such as income and educational attainment, in much the same way as such a recognizable frame might influence responses to other questions about views on genetic screening, drug tests, wiretapping, or surreptitious monitoring. Efforts to modify the influence of question order through randomization can make only a modest contribution to solving these and related problems of reactive bias.

An additional problem is found in the nature of sampling and in the untenable assumptions that have to be made about samples as representatives of attitudes and opinions that matter. Clearly, it is impossible to ask everyone about everything. Yet each step we take away from this conceptual ideal widens the hole through which bias, distortion, and misrepresentation creep into models of social opinion. The truly random sample has never been taken because a complete sampling frame does not and cannot exist. Approximations of randomness depend on the quality of the sampling frames that are available. Even sophisticated approaches such as Random Digit Dialing, which is thought to overcome the difficulties represented by nonpublished numbers, are unable to overcome the fact that telephone service itself is not randomly distributed to all households.[5] Universal telephone service is a fiction, and there are significant differences associated with gender, age, race, and marital and employment status reflected in the distribution of households without telephones.[6]

As noted in the discussion of the expanding market in personal information, the increasing pressure on individuals to provide information about tastes, preferences, and opinions has resulted in a growing reluctance to participate in surveys or to complete questionnaires. It is also likely that persons who are particularly concerned about privacy are even less likely to agree to participate in such surveys. Thus, any survey that is concerned about opinions related to privacy and personal information will be nonrandom and systematically biased.

Even if a truly random, and thereby representative, sample of individuals could be constructed, it would still be necessary to sample opinions and the experiences on which they are constructed. And, because this sampling is ultimately done by the participants in the survey, its scope thereby depends on their memories, their interests, or their motivations, and a variety of other factors beyond the researcher's control. The fact that these distortions are themselves nonrandom, but may be linked systematically to the question at hand, opens the hole still wider.

All this suggests the need for great caution in interpreting the results of surveys and interviews as reflections of what people understand, believe, feel, or intend to do with regard to the panoptic sort. One response to the problem of measurement has been the attempt to utilize multiple measures and a variety of means through which to assess social opinion. Focus group interviews are frequently cited as a means through which researchers can begin to appreciate the great range of responses and constructions of the subjects of concern. These groups help the researchers to recognize the variety of ways in which individuals have come to label or talk about events, relationships, and emotional reactions. Of course, focus groups are not without their own problems. Because groups are rarely naturally occurring, much of the time and energy of group participants may be spent in coming together as a group, and the chemistry of a particular group may simply not be conducive to exploring a particular issue.

Before a national telephone survey was developed and administered in January and February 1989, a set of five group interviews was conducted in summer 1988.[7] Each of the two-hour sessions was tightly formatted so that the experiences of the five groups would be directly comparable in terms of the questions that were asked and the procedures that the participants were to follow in moving toward what they saw as the best expression of the group's thinking about privacy and the panoptic sort.[8]

THE GROUP INTERVIEWS

After explaining the purpose of the group, the interviewers elicited personal intro-
ductions by having participants talk about their favorite food, favorite color, favorite subject in school, favorite teacher, and the like. Next, the interviewers introduced the subject of privacy by asking participants to indicate how much
attention they had paid to the issue of privacy before they had been contacted by
the members of the project. The subjects were next asked to name an invasion of
privacy and to indicate why they thought it was an invasion.

To focus the group's attention more directly on the nature of surveillance in everyday life, the interviewers showed a five-minute videotape that was produced
especially for the project. The tape, conceived as a "day in the life" of an ordinary
person, provided examples of the ways in which transaction-generated information might be combined to create a detailed image or profile of an individual. Examples included use of a credit card to purchase a train ticket, employment application forms, computer monitoring on the job, monitoring cameras in the
supermarket, automatic teller machines, and even a videotape kiosk that made a
record of a rental transaction. The connection between transaction information
and targeted communication was made through references to direct mail presumed to have come from lists generated by magazine subscriptions. On the videotape shown to the group, a closing image appeared on the television screen that
was being viewed by the principal actress as she relaxed at the end of her busy day.
The picture was of herself as she had appeared at the beginning of her day, just as
she had entered the train station.

The questions that the project interviewers pursued in the remaining time were
directed toward the gathering of assessments of three key components of an orientation toward informational privacy: (1) what participants knew about the technologies that are used to gather information to create profiles of consumers; (2)
who they thought was likely to use such techniques and what they saw as the
boundaries of legitimate use of these techniques or the information that they produced; and (3) what they thought about the sharing of information produced
through these surveillance methods.

As a final opportunity for the groups to organize their thinking about these issues in the context of this highly focused discussion, they were asked to act as
though a representative of the news media was waiting outside the room to record
their thoughts. Each person was asked to compose a statement for the television
cameras on "privacy as the issue of the 1990s." All sessions were tape recorded and tran-
scribed, and those transcriptions provided the basis for the analysis that follows.

THINKING ABOUT PRIVACY

Our uncertainty about the nature of public concerns about privacy is due in part
to the limitations inherent in the questions asked in public opinion surveys. Sur-

vey evidence suggests that there are no universal definitions of privacy, and individuals are likely to be responding to quite different things when they indicate the presence or absence of concerns. I thought that it was important to understand the salience of privacy as an issue by understanding both the level of concern and the basis for that concern. Participants in each group were asked to indicate the extent to which they had given much thought to the privacy issue before being contacted.

The general response was that privacy per se was not something most participants had given any thought to. In every group, one or more individuals suggested that the questionnaire had really forced them to think about privacy in ways they never had before. Some indicated that what they understood to be the domain of privacy concerns was quite different from the broad range of issues addressed in the questionnaire.

For some, an external event, highlighted in the media and usually concerned with a politician, had caused them to think about privacy in the recent past. For others, there were personal experiences, usually related to work and often triggered by questions they encountered on an application form. And for others, concern about drug testing was the stimulus for their beginning to think about privacy. One man worked in a shipyard that had recently instituted a drug-testing policy. As he understood the new policy, any accidental injury would make him subject to a drug test: "Like you just cut your finger or bang your finger, or fall, ... you go to the dispensary for an aspirin or bandaid, [and] you have to take a urine test. They got 60-year-old men down there taking a urine test for drugs."

One participant decried the lack of privacy on the job because of the constant press of people in a cramped office. This example was countered by someone with the opposite concern—the isolation felt by a newcomer to a community where people rushed home in the evenings and, in the pursuit of their privacy, closed their automatic garage doors, not to be seen again until the next day.

Another person reported having been sensitized to the issue by discussions with friends who also worked with computer databases. She shared their concern about the amount of "garbage and misinformation there was" in those files. This concern with privacy, linked to the inaccuracy of data in files, was heightened for one participant whose own credit records had been confused with those of his parents because they shared the same last names and had similar addresses.

One group was composed of persons who had recently been called to serve on a jury. Perhaps because the members of this group were all registered voters (that was the basis on which they were selected for jury duty), they expressed considerable concern about the role of government in invasions of privacy. The examples they provided began with an expressed concern about banks sending the government information about their personal savings and the fact that they were linking that information with social security numbers. Another example described experiences with FBI surveillance in the 1960s. One man's wife had sought access to her file through the Freedom of Information Act, and when the report was received, he was alarmed by the nature of information and the variety of methods that had been used by the FBI to gather information for his wife's file. Another member of this group expressed concern about the potential impact of information in his own FBI files, which indicated that he had led a demonstration some eighteen years ago. He had been told that this information could not be erased from his file, and he was thus worried that he might be barred from future employment or might otherwise suffer because he would be perceived as a threat to national security.

DEFINING PRIVACY INVASIONS

A follow-up question asked participants to provide explicit justifications for calling something an invasion of privacy. Very few of the responses had actually identified the reasons underlying their selection of particular examples as invasions of privacy. Television programs and recent news stories were a ready source of examples that defined a privacy invasion as an act that stepped outside of some zone of legitimate action that participants had drawn in their personal conceptual scheme. This zone was frequently drawn on the basis of an assessment of the presumed relevance of the information being collected. For one participant, the limits were clearly drawn: "I know when I was going to school, ... they would always emphasize family orientations, such as marriage, legitimacy, things of that nature. They always wanted to know whether your parents was married or what ... just didn't have anything to do with being helpful to go to school." A similar response reflected a concern with the structural conditions of disclosure that might involve embarrassment. There was an apparent distinction between being asked an irrelevant question on a form and being asked the same question in a personal interview: "I was once asked face to face in an interview if I was married, and I felt the implication was that it was a question of whether or not I was stable. I felt that it didn't have much to do with my qualifications for the job."

One person thought it "outrageous" that something someone did while they were in college should be relevant to their consideration for high office. This oblique reference to the charges of marijuana use by nominees to the Supreme Court reflected a widely held belief that public figures deserved more privacy than the media seemed willing to allow. One participant's comments suggested that the victim was not merely the public figure, but the members of the audience who were continually being subjected to these stories: "It seems like once they get a hold of something, you know, that happens in their life ... you know they drag it all out, and I don't want to know every time they go to the doctor, I don't want to know every time they go to the bathroom. You know, some part of their life is private." Another continued the critique of the press: "They're taking things that are not crucial to the issues or your judgement of the individual. They're blowing it all over the place as if implying it should be."

Participants frequently mentioned negative consequences as the criterion on which a determination of an inquiry as an invasion of privacy could be made.

Some participants highlighted the loss of control that is involved in invasions of privacy. The consequences that might flow from a loss of control over personal information were frequently linked to the use of derogatory information in personal credit histories. Individuals were seen frequently to have to suffer the negative consequences that flowed from the use of false, or at least contestable, information in their credit files—information that they did not even know existed but that, nevertheless, was being treated as factual by lenders.

The practice of sharing personal information for marketing purposes was also seen as an invasion of privacy. One participant noted that the act of getting married generated telephone calls from insurance agencies; visits to an obstetrician generated calls from diaper services. There was general agreement among the groups that the widespread practice of sharing subscriber lists was an invasion of privacy, but it was the consequence of receiving unwanted solicitations, rather than any inherent unfairness or impropriety, that seemed to be the primary basis for concern among the participants.

PROFILES

The interviewers determined the extent to which participants were familiar with the concept of profiling. After the participants had focused their thinking by means of the "day in the life" videotape, the interviewers asked the members of each group to help identify some terms that might describe the "pictures of ourselves" that are formed through the records or traces we leave as we go about our daily lives. The notion of a profile was familiar to most members of the groups. More sophisticated observers included other technical language, describing the method as one of modeling, a relational database, or a computerized biography. One creative member offered a suggestion that described the profile as an autopsy " 'cause it could be death by the examiner depending on whether you filled an interest." One observer's critical response labeled profiles as "preconceptions based on circumstantial evidence."

A matter of interest was to determine whether people could identify the different circumstances in which these profiles could be used in ways that would help make a person's life easier or, alternatively, could harm a person or make his or her life more difficult. Some participants readily assumed the perspective of business or industry users of personal data. Information about customers or potential customers was seen as a potential source of savings or a means to avoid wasted effort: "I think it probably saves money. Like those stores can calibrate their orders of milk or cheese or other perishables depending on how much exactly they sold from those bar codes and there's less waste ... then the prices, in theory, could be lowered somewhat."

The business or organizational purpose in acquiring lists of potential clients or donors was readily identified as a legitimate use of personal transaction data. As one participant suggested:

I was about to say that the obverse of your, what you object to [is] ... buying a book and getting notice of other books. That probably does make it easier for cultural, maybe valuable cultural enterprises and undertakings to get started. ... If you're starting a book club or a dance group or a theater subscription series, you want to buy a list of people who go to the theater, and those are likely to be of value to the community and possibly even to you, so it seems to me that there are some legitimate areas where this is useful.

Participants agreed that consumer profiles might actually serve to reduce the number of telephone solicitations or the amount of junk mail they receive if the senders actually knew more about them—for example, that they did not like to receive telephone solicitations: "I was thinking if people knew what type, ... that you don't like those kind of calls ... the phone company could maybe filter out those kinds of calls, if they knew. You see, if they could get to that extent, the phone company could ... [be] monitoring your phone calls." Another suggested that "maybe the junk mail would become only junk mail of things that you would be interested in, rather than a thousand things you're not interested in."

People tended not to include the government in their set of compilers who might gather data in a way that would make life better for the individual. One participant did include the census as "patterning the country to see where we're going, so they can plan for the future." In general, however, the government, especially the police and the IRS, were more readily identified when it came to the participants' suggestions of compilers of data who may cause some negative consequences of profiling.

When asked to think about the problems that might be associated with profiles, the overwhelming tendency was to focus on the consequences that would flow from having false, inaccurate, or outdated information in the profile. Several participants suggested that this problem was made even worse with the use of the computer because data takes on a kind of permanence, and data managers are slow, if not actually resistant, to make corrections. Computers are seen to malfunction, automatic teller machines to run out of money, and "computer error" becomes a ready excuse for poor service or carelessness: "It's ineptitude which we've always had with us and we always will, but the computer makes it so much more difficult because people go ... well, the computer says so. You can't argue with the computer. And, the idea that the computer could be wrong is completely alien to these peoples' culture."

Several participants identified the negative consequences that would flow from the development and use of a profile or model to discriminate against individuals because they shared characteristics with others who might be credit risks or who might have a lower estimated potential as customers. One participant identified the practice of redlining as an abuse of profiles. "This has a self-fulfilling prophecy because it is impossible to get home repair loans and then all the houses go ... turn into slums and then obviously people live there who are not middle class because that's all they can afford."

To pursue participants' understanding of the problems associated with faulty profiles or decision models, the moderators relayed the story of a young woman who had applied for a credit card, responding just like the thousands of others who had been solicited as the dates of their college graduations approached.[9] This English major was notified that her application had been rejected, and after submitting a request for the reason, she received a note indicating that her "area of study (literature)" disqualified her. As anticipated, the general response in the groups was one of incredulity. Many consumers assume that credit decisions are based entirely on an assessment of one's honesty, reliability, or record of prompt payments in the past. Few considered that the selection criteria might also include some estimate of a person's economic potential—the kind of life-style, including the use of other banking services, that an engineering graduate might eventually purchase, but that an English major was seen to be unlikely to choose.

"I don't agree with it. Just because he's an English teacher doesn't mean he's ... you could make $5 an hour and still pay your bills on time, or you could make $70,000 a year and not pay the bills." Many simply refused to believe that such a thing really happened. They knew of youngsters who were just graduating from high school who were given credit cards for an upscale department store. Others thought that it was simply a case of a poor decision made by an individual, rather than a reflection of company policy: "Well, some low-level person made a bad decision. In my opinion anyway. Because I don't believe a higher-level person would have done that. It's just too absurd."

A rather sophisticated critique of the use of profiles was presented in the jurors' group. The intelligent consumer of news and entertainment was seen to be increasingly denied a vital information service by the the mass media because of a marketing logic that pursues the largest possible audience. This "least common denominator tendency toward most marketing and entertainment decisions" means that quality content disappears. And "you lose the freedom of choice. ... They're dictating what you're going to watch, so you lose the freedom."

The participants' criticisms of profiling also emphasized the extent to which it was impersonal. Decisions were not based on the particular circumstances of the individual; instead, a person is merely a statistic. Insurance companies were frequently criticized for their dependence on actuarial statistics and probabilistic models in making decisions about coverage or rates: "Insurance is a big one. I mean they have statistics, just built up on guesses. ... They know that ... most males under the age of 25 drive recklessly, so they boost their insurance premiums ... it makes you seem like you're not really a person, you know, because they base everything in statistics."

TECHNOLOGY OF SURVEILLANCE & LIMITS ON DATA GATHERING

The interviewers asked a series of questions to determine the extent to which participants could identify people who collect personal information, the variety of methods used to acquire this information, and the range of uses to which the information is put. The "day in the life" tape and the discussions to this point had introduced a great variety of examples of information gathering, but group participants continued to add examples of data-gathering activities. Surveys, questionnaires, and applications were combined with transaction records—a category in which some participants included the records generated by people who read the gas and electric meters. The fact that most applications for insurance, especially medical insurance, involve a blanket provision of consent to the provider to gather information about your present health and past claims was taken by some participants to be common knowledge. Credit reporting agencies such as TRW were also identified as active gatherers of personal data. These responses together would compose a thick catalog of legitimate business or government purposes justifying the collection of personal information.

As a way of triggering further discussion to more clearly identify what participants saw as limits—the boundaries beyond which the legitimacy of the collection of information would be questioned—the interviewers offered the groups a somewhat embellished representation of hair analysis techniques. Around the time of these interviews, hair analysis was being promoted as a reliable way of testing for drug use.[10] There had also been considerable speculation that other information about the individual could be gained from an examination of the genetic material in the hair follicle. Genetic analysis was described as able to provide information about potential susceptibility to illness, stress, or workplace hazards, and thus such information might be useful as a job screening aid.

Again, a great many participants accepted the blanket justification of data gathering associated with a legitimate business need to know. For them, almost any information could be justified if the organization could demonstrate that it was relevant to a business decision. Others sought to find the limits in the consequences of ignorance. That is, some kinds of jobs or decisions have what some participants considered to be serious consequences, which served to outweigh the interests of the individuals in their privacy. "Things to do with like public safety type jobs, you know, I'm definitely against ... drug testing and lie detector tests, but you know, if somebody's going to be flying an airplane, they gotta be straight."

A few participants sought to establish limits based on the invasive nature of the technology that would be used to collect the information. It was clear that many participants identified the body as being the ultimate dividing line between the private and the public realms. In the words of one participant: "Bodily information. Your hair, your drug test. I mean that is absolutely absurd to me, and to me there's just no cause. If they're hiring you to type all day long, let's say, what does it matter about all that stuff? They can find out your health records from your references. They don't need your bodily info, the way you were describing."

Participants offered other, related responses: "I don't think anything having to do with your physical self should be available"; "on the form they asked me to fill out, they asked my height, my weight . . and all I did was put a question mark next to it and didn't answer it, because I was applying for a job in the skill areas. What do you need my height and weight for?"

An important variant on the concern for relevance in data gathering was the concern that only negative information be retained. Such a view gives the individual the benefit of the doubt. It presumes innocence, rather than assuming that every employee is a thief or every applicant is a high risk:

> In other words, they shouldn't record every little thing that you do, only if you do wrong. If you take a loan, and you pay a loan, it shouldn't be recorded. Nothing should come up. If you mispay a loan, then it should go on your record. ... In other words, when you look into a person's record, if you want to look for a credit check and you find nothing, that means he didn't do anything wrong. ... I should not be a risk because I never had a chance to do something. I should only be a risk if I did something wrong.

For this participant, anything other than negative information is irrelevant and ought not to be recorded in anyone's file. Such a policy would have made life much simpler for a participant in another group. It seems that, within a short period, she had made three different credit applications related to the purchase of a house that needed remodeling. Her application for an additional credit card was rejected because there had been "an excessive amount of investigation into my credit, which of course I initiated." Her attempts to correct this situation only added to her frustration: "And of course, I wrote this furious letter. You know, to these anonymous people. What you do is then you write a letter and then you wait 30 days, in order for them to check it out. And you can't yell at anybody, because they don't answer the phone, and so you're left with this tremendous frustration of the total irrationality of this."

When the interviewers probed people's views about what restrictions should be applied to data gathering by government agencies, there was considerable uncertainty about these limits. The consensus was that the IRS should be able to gather any financial information that would help it to decide whether one was paying one's "fair share of taxes." At the same time, the respondents felt that FBI investigations of library records to identify foreign spies were a threat to the freedoms that characterized U.S. democracy. Again, the jurors' group offered some of the more detailed justifications for their concern:

> There's kind of an inverse ratio ... between power and offensiveness. That the government and the FBI in particular ... any form of the government being very powerful (and if you don't like this government you can't pick another government), they should be most severely restricted because you don't know where to go ... except into exile. ... Only just slightly less [restricted] ... should be those places like TRW, computer banks, and the insurance companies that share files. There should be a hedging of inquisitorial rights of individuals and firms with whom you can either choose to do business or not ... or [those] whose findings you can challenge or not.

Similarly, a person might not even know the criteria being used for an evaluation: "You know ... you don't even know what to tell them. You don't have no excuse. You can't even defend yourself. I think it's areas of not being able to defend yourself ... in an employer's situation, that's interviewing you. ... That's basically it, you're not able to defend yourself."

DATA SHARING LIMITS

Although the relevance criteria within the limits of invasiveness associated with an individual's body might apply with regard to the initial gatherer of information, the interviewers asked the participants if they would use a different set of criteria to establish limits on the sharing of personal information.

Whereas one participant would limit the collection and storage of anything other than negative information in response to the question of sharing, another participant suggested that any data that would help the data subject should be included. Several respondents suggested that organizations should seek a person's permission before they share any information about that person with others. At the very least, the participants thought that those who gathered or provided any data from a person's files to others had a responsibility to inform that individual that the sharing had taken place.

Several participants distinguished between public and private, or corporate, rationales for the sharing of personal information. There was greater latitude expressed for the gathering of data for collective or public purposes, as well as an expression of a greater willingness to restrict sharing by private concerns. One participant expressed it in terms of individual differences in tolerance for the appeals from commercial or nonprofit organizations that come from the sharing of information about purchases or economic status.

Underlying these responses is the instrumental concern ultimately with the benefit or harm that might flow from the sharing of personal information. People would like to restrict the sharing of harmful information and facilitate the sharing of beneficial information. In one view, "I don't care about what people know about me personally, unless it's used against me, in some negative fashion. Then it becomes a problem." In the view of some, sensitive information is information that, if released or shared, could cause some harm to the subject of the information:[11]

> When I think of the census and what they collect, it's not harmful information. How many people live in your house, what sex they are, what your income is. That's not harmful. Harmful is when you start getting into what diseases they have, or what's their psychological orientation or sexual orientation. What the hell you gonna do with that? ... The law could define this type of information before it is used ... [They] must have some clearances; [with] this kind of information, you don't need clearances.

Participants, however, noted the difficulties in differentiating between what is genuine harm and what is simply an annoyance. The general sense was that information shared for marketing purposes was not harmful; it merely had the potential to increase the extent to which a person would be annoyed by solicitations. There were very few hard-liners, or privacy fundamentalists, who took the position that no unsolicited material should be sent to the home: "If I want insurance, I'll ask for it."

THE CAPSULE VIEW

At the end of nearly two hours of talk about privacy, the interviewers asked the members of each group to formulate a personal statement for a local television station that summed up their feelings about privacy as an issue. Most of the participants were quite reflective in their summary statements. Several returned to points they had attempted to make earlier but apparently thought that a particular aspect had not been given its due weight. Among the jurors, two responses stand out. One participant sought to bring attention to what he saw as a critical aspect of Western social philosophy—the high value we place on individual autonomy. The loss of privacy means the loss of the "space in which to be an individual." The source of the threat to this space was found in the immediately following response: "It occurred to me that as long as people can make a living on invasion of privacy, then privacy is going to be invaded. It's money in the back of it. As long as they can make money from it, or gain power, then, they'll use it."

The relevance criterion was summed up best by a statement that suggested that "every person should have access to information on a need to know basis. No information should ever be used to restrict or limit one's pursuits, happiness, or joy of life as long as this doesn't impinge on others." One participant offered a rather elegant statement of the complexity of the issue, suggesting that "information used to inform and protect can also be used to invade, discriminate and harass. The questions of who should know, what should be known, and why they should know it are questions that must be answered either by a consensus or a majority of the people involved." Another person gave a more terse ultimatum: "If I haven't applied for a loan, if I don't affect national security, and I'm not a criminal element, then stay out of my business."

It was clear from this survey that there are several different levels of meaning that are called into play when people are asked to think about privacy. Also, different realms of activity are involved. Participants apparently utilized quite distinct schema when thinking about privacy in relation to the government as compared to their employers, to organizations providing them with goods and services, or to their friends, neighbors, or coworkers. These differences have to do, in part, with their recognition and their acceptance of the relative power of the actors in each of those relationships and their faith or trust that such power will not be used for illegitimate ends. The overall tendency within the group as a whole was to trust organizations not to gather more information than they need to make necessary business decisions. This tendency to trust was reinforced by a belief that there was a fairly reliable body of law that restricted serious invasions of privacy; or, if there were no laws, it was felt that it was only a matter of time before such protective legislation would be passed.

For this group, personal experiences apparently played a critical role in helping to crystallize a person's orientation to a particular aspect of privacy. Readily produced examples of problems with government files or credit files or mailing lists support the view that personal experience tends to make certain attitudes more salient and more stable than others. The assumption that persons of a certain race, gender, level of education, or work status will share orientations toward privacy as a result of their shared experiences appears to have been supported in the discussions and in the written responses to the questions.

In general, the members of these focus groups had a high degree of awareness of the techniques of marketing that are already in widespread use. A substantial majority found such uses appropriate and, therefore, not a serious invasion of their privacy. Only a small minority expressed strong criticism of such approaches toward the rationalization of the marketing function.

The next chapter explores the issues that were raised in the focus groups through primary and secondary analysis of data from several national surveys.

6

THE SOCIAL ORIGINS
OF VIEWS ON PRIVACY

INTRODUCTION

The purpose of this chapter is to explore the insights into the nature of social opinion that can be derived from an analysis of survey data. The data used for this analysis have been collected from a variety of sources, and they differ considerably in the extent to which I have been able to look behind the numbers and search for the underlying meaning of the responses captured by the questionnaires. The primary and most valuable sources of data have been three datasets that I have acquired from the Louis Harris Data Center. These files contain data from the public samples of surveys administered by the Harris organization for which Alan Westin served as faculty adviser. Each survey was financed by a company that was involved in some way with the insurance industry, and many of the questions reflect that corporate/institutional interest.[1] The surveys also reflect Westin's long-standing interest in privacy and computer technology. The 1983 survey focused on public perceptions of the computer and computer-based technology and their influences on the quality of life. Privacy was a subset of that larger area of interest. Primary survey data come from a study I conducted with support from a grant from AT&T.[2] These data include questionnaires completed by participants in five focus groups and 1,250 adults interviewed by phone through AT&T's prime contractor, Maritz Marketing, in 1988 and 1989, respectively.[3] Each of these surveys will be referred to primarily by their dates of administration, 1978, 1983, 1988, 1989, and 1990. Additional data about the nature of social opinion come from published studies or from searches on the subject of privacy through the Roper Center.[4]

THE PENUMBRA OF FEAR

One of the first considerations that must be addressed is the potential confusion that is introduced when the complex of opinions relevant to the panoptic sort are compressed under the single rubric of concerns about privacy. There are a great many definitions of privacy, and one can never be clear about which aspects of that construct are being evoked when an individual is asked to express an opinion. The sustained publicity surrounding the Senate hearings to confirm the nomination of Judge Robert Bork to the Supreme Court heightened public awareness of privacy as a right that was not mentioned specifically in the Constitution but that can be seen as emanating from a penumbra reflecting interests protected by the First, Fourth, Fifth, Ninth, and Fourteenth Amendments. Questions of reproductive rights, sexual relations, and a variety of other activities that might be questioned or even forbidden by law have become attached to the overly broad concept of privacy through its association with constitutional protection of fundamental liberties.

The notion of "informational privacy" associated with the formative contributions of Alan Westin refers to the "claim of individuals or groups or institutions to determine for themselves when, how, and to what extent information about them is communicated to others."[5] This definition, although central to my interests here, is rather strictly limited to the sharing or distribution of information and does not address the related questions about the collection of that information. There has been much said and written about the indignities involved in the collection of information about drug use. Concerns about the invasiveness of surveillance techniques, the impropriety of involving male officers in the search of female suspects or prisoners, or the use of mass screening and random testing are all linked to conflicts about the legitimacy of an inquiry into particular spheres of personhood, which are complicated by aspects of manner and place. The point I wish to make here, however, is that we are never quite sure about the underlying dimension of this complex that is being tapped when individuals are asked to respond to a question about privacy per se.

Concern About Privacy

When we inquire about the public's concern about privacy, we operate from an assumption that privacy is something that is universally valued and, more important, is perceived to be at risk. Privacy in this regard refers to some attainable status, generally discussed in the context of an individual's control over the access that others might have to regions, including regions of personality, that the person holds as private. Thus, in the area of informational privacy, the concern about a potential loss is based on the fear that individuals will no longer be able to exercise control over access by others to information that defines them. In a variety of relationships with others, and especially through interaction with representatives of institutions, individuals may provide access to information about themselves voluntarily to facilitate interaction, in exchange for information of presumably equal value, or more reluctantly, as part of a nonnegotiable requirement for access to other desired goods or services. Each of these circumstances or relationships is marked by a particular set of expectations or assumptions about the uses to which the information will be put, including the extent to which the information will be shared with others. Increased concern about privacy can reflect a declining confidence that others, especially institutional others, will maintain personal information as confidential. Increased concern about the loss of privacy can also reflect a common perception that interactions with organizations increasingly involve less than voluntary surrender of personal information of varying degrees of sensitivity.

The concept of sensitivity is one that has been explored with great effect by Raymond Wacks, who has attempted to classify broad categories of personal information in terms of its sensitivity.[6] For Wacks, sensitivity has two related dimensions: the personal, as distinguished from the public aspects of being, and the consequential, which implies the potential of harm to the individual that might result if unauthorized access or unauthorized use is made of that information. Sensitivity might be thought of in terms of the "information value" of the "bits" or "chunks" or insights that are gained, and the linkage of that information to other complex chains. Sensitive information is highly linked to other critical aspects of a person's economic and political status. Thus, sensitivity is a continually evolving, socially constructed sphere of consequentiality. Its points are not fixed, but must change as behavior, interests, orientations, tendencies, and the like move in and out of favor within different spheres of activity in a society. Individuals may differ markedly in terms of what they consider to be personal and consequential. And, as I will discuss in the next chapter, these differences make the formation of a legal regime quite difficult because the standard of a "reasonable person" as a component of an "expectation of privacy" necessarily reflects dominant cultural norms. Thus, information about what a young man thinks about sports cars would not be considered highly sensitive; however, information about what that young man thinks about young women would be sensitive, because information about sexual orientation and identification is highly linked in contemporary discourse and culture to considerations of health status, intimacy, and even suitability for employment and training.

Increased concern about information privacy also reflects the belief that the sophisticated approaches to matching and profiling, which facilitate the use of personal information stored in unrelated files, are being used to produce sensitive information from that which was not sensitive in its original form. Such a concern is not simply paranoid fantasy, as some would have us believe, but has found a place at the highest levels of government. At one point, the Reagan administration proposed to create a category of sensitive information and to ban the use of database-searching software by foreign intellectuals because such software would facilitate the production of intelligence that might be damaging to the national security interests of the United States. Use of the *technology*, not the basic information, was to be banned because the searching algorithms were too efficient. It previously had been thought that it would have been too costly to produce an equivalent level of useful information by processing the data in published reports manually.[7]

Changes over Time

As technology changes, as its applications in the panoptic sort expand, and as scholars and the press report on the consequences of its use, concerns about privacy are likely to change. James Katz and Annette Tassone provide one of the few analyses of trends in public concerns about privacy.[8] Although the trends are not clear, reflecting in part the differences in the formulation of the questions and the constructs they tap, Katz and Tassone identify several studies that suggest that the proportion of the public that is very concerned about "threats to, or invasions of, their privacy" has increased substantially. In addition, people seem to believe that the loss of privacy will become an even greater problem in the future than it was in the 1980s. In the Appendix to their report, Katz and Tassone include data from several Harris and Roper surveys regarding privacy, and it can be seen that the proportions fluctuate from year to year. It is not clear whether these fluctuations are reflections of variability in the samples, or whether they reflect the salience of the privacy issue in the public discourse at the time. Public policy deliberations about privacy in Congress, or the spectre of the much feared "1984" and the domination by "big brother," can be seen to be linked closely to increases in the numbers of citizens who are concerned about privacy. A question that asked respondents to indicate how close we had come to the society that George Orwell had described in his book *1984* found the proportion who thought that we had already arrived at such a society to have more than doubled between 1983 and 1988 and to have tripled between 1983 and 1989 (from 6 percent to 19 percent).[9] The Harris survey published in 1979 reported that 31 percent of the public was "very concerned" about "threats to ... [their] personal privacy"; the Equifax survey in 1990 found that the proportion had increased to 46 percent.

A QUESTION OF TRUST

A key dimension underlying the levels of concern that individuals might have about threats to their privacy is the relationship of trust they may have developed with individuals or organizations with whom they interact and on whom they may depend for access to goods and services. The more we trust an individual or an organization, the less concerned we are likely to be that they will abuse that trust and use the information to cause us harm or be careless in their sharing of that information with others who might cause some harm. A number of surveys over the years have asked respondents to indicate the extent to which they trusted or had confidence in the information practices of public and private organizations.

One can compare the rankings that respondents assigned to institutions that are deeply involved in the collection and use of personal information (Table 6.1). In the 1978 data, rankings are based on the proportion that agreed with the statement that the organizations or individuals were "doing enough to keep the personal information they have on individuals confidential." In the 1990 data, rankings are based on the mean ratings of trust in a scale ranging from 1 (no trust) to 10 (complete trust) when trust means that they will "collect and use information about people like you in a responsible way."[10]

TABLE 6.1 Organizational Rankings by Trustworthiness

	1978	1990
Least	Credit bureaus	Credit bureaus
	Internal Revenue Service	Insurers
	Insurers	Internal Revenue Service
	Social Security Administration	Telephone companies
	Census Bureau	Employers
	Employers	Social Security Administration
	Telephone companies	Hospitals
Most	Hospitals	Census Bureau

Perhaps most notable are the decline in the trustworthiness of the telephone companies and the improved status of the Census Bureau. In response to a question about their confidence that the Census Bureau was not sharing personal information with other government agencies, only about 13 percent of the respondents indicated great confidence in this agency in 1978.

Of course, the 1990 survey was taken at a high point in the national debate about Caller-ID, as well as during the administration of the 1990 census. Both were the subject of considerable press coverage; that for the Census Bureau was quite a bit more laudatory than that for the telephone companies. A similar question asked in 1983 allowed for a ranking of some of these institutions in terms of their perceived tendency to maintain the confidentiality of the personal information they had gathered. The order, from most to least trustworthy in this regard, was the IRS, telephone companies, the Census Bureau, insurers, and credit bureaus. In 1983, the loss in public confidence that accompanied the breakup of the AT&T monopoly had only just begun to emerge. All of the rankings computed from these national surveys identify the credit bureaus as the least trustworthy of the information intensive organizations, although by 1990 a newcomer had been added to the list. Companies that were involved in direct mail or telemarketing sales anchored the least trustworthy end of the scale with a mean rating of 2.9, with their nearest competitor, the credit bureaus, earning a mean rating of 4.5 in a scale that reached to 10.

HOW DID YOU GET MY NAME?

I have suggested that the level of public opposition to direct mail and telemarketing is considerably below that which would emerge if respondents to surveys actually understood the countless ways by which their names, addresses, and other personal information were added to the files of the list brokers. Not even people we might expect to be aware of such practices have an understanding of the extent to which personal information from transactions becomes part of the panoptic sort. One colleague, a business school professor, reports that she expanded her professional interests from management information systems to questions of privacy and personal information after she began receiving direct mail solicitations after her purchase of gifts for a baby shower.[11] Another colleague (who asked to remain anonymous) related the story of an invitation he had received to speak before an organization. On asking about compensation or an honorarium, he was told that the organization had not yet decided. Their decision was to be based in part on his record of donations to certain Jewish charities. He had given to some, and not to others, and they were as yet undecided how this record was to be evaluated. He was first shocked and surprised that they had access to information about his charitable contributions, and furthermore, he was annoyed that his record of giving should in any way determine whether he should be compensated for his lectures. Of course, his experience suggests that there are probably a considerable number of other scholars whose records of donations would have disqualified them from speaking at all!

In the 1990 survey, respondents were asked three questions that reflected different levels of awareness and concern about organizations' data gathering and use that might affect them through the marketing of personal information. Nearly 58 percent of the respondents suggested that it was a major problem that consumers were being asked to provide "excessively personal information" by organizations that gathered information about consumers. A slightly smaller proportion (55 percent) felt that "inaccuracy and mistakes" were similarly problematic. However, a considerably smaller proportion thought that the sharing of personal information between companies in the same industry was something to be concerned about (39.8 percent). Yet, in the same survey, 97 percent of the respondents indicated that they thought it was a "bad thing" that companies could "buy from mailing list companies information about your consumer characteristics." When asked further about how concerned they actually were about this, a relatively small percentage (28.2 percent) indicated that they were very concerned. It is perhaps this level of response that convinced Equifax, the survey's sponsor, to move forward with its partners on the development of the disastrous Lotus Marketplace CD-ROM project. A decade earlier, Equifax representatives had indicated to Congress in testimony regarding a Fair Financial Information Practices Act that they placed more confidence in their contacts with the subjects of their files through disclosure interviews than they did in the results of "highly touted opinion surveys."[12] It is especially ironic that the survey criticized in 1980 was administered by the same team that produced the analysis for Equifax in 1990.

The fact that there is widespread agreement that a particular business practice is wrong on the face of it but is not at the same time apparently worthy of great concern, points to the underlying sense of faith that people have in the operation of the marketing system. That a corporation would share information without first gaining permission is seen as an indication of poor manners, an abuse of the trust that is at the heart of the relationship between a customer and the organizations that individuals may come to depend on. However, businesses' use of information about their purchases and transactions does not represent a particular threat or an identifiable risk to a great many adults.

In a factor analysis of responses by focus group members to questions about the technology of surveillance, the strongest factor identified was one termed Mybusiness.[13] This factor reflected a general feeling that what people read, the films they viewed, the numbers they called for information, and, more generally, how they spent their money were their business and no one else's. Another factor (Trust) served as an index of the confidence people had that organizations would use information appropriately. This factor included agreement with the following: "The more organizations know about me, the better they can meet my needs"; "organizations have to have the best workers, and testing helps them to choose"; and, "you simply have to give up some privacy to enjoy the conveniences of the modern world."

In 1989, however, 61.3 percent of the respondents indicated strong agreement with the statement that "companies should seek your permission before they tell anyone else about the products you buy or the services you use." Yet, when asked if they believed that "the more businesses know about me, the better they can meet my individual needs," nearly 25 percent agreed strongly and another 43.1 percent agreed somewhat. Presumably, it should not really matter how businesses gather this information as long as they are gathering it to meet the consumers' needs rather than to exclude them from markets and opportunities. When the correlation between these two measures is examined, the relationship is near zero and tending toward the inverse ($r = -.05$, $p = .09$). That is, people who think that a business ought to seek permission before sharing information about its customers are somewhat less likely to believe that having such information helps the business to serve its customers any better. This correlation suggests that there is more than courtesy at issue.

CAN THEY REALLY DO THAT?

Part of the construction of social opinion is linked to the public's understanding of the technologies that are used to generate intelligence through various forms of surveillance. The literature of alarm that is thought to have stimulated public concern about privacy highlighted the role of the computer as a device that made it possible to collect and store tremendous amounts of personal information in files that people knew little about but that could be used to control their lives. When asked in 1983 if they believed the statement that "personal information about yourself is being kept in some files somewhere for purposes not known to you," some 66 percent indicated that they believed that it was. When asked in 1989 if having a social security number makes it easy for organizations to gather personal information from different sources, nearly half of the respondents (49.6 percent) were confident that this was true, and an additional 32 percent tended to agree. The use of information stored in unknown files and the use of a social security number as a reliable token for matching those files are the ingredients necessary for the production of detailed profiles of consumers.

One aspect of profiling is the assumption that past behavior can be used to predict future behavior. Indeed, the assumptions underlying predictive models are relaxed considerably in that predictions need not be made on the basis of information about the past behavior of any *particular* individual, but on the basis of the behavior of other individuals in the class or group to which a person may be assigned on the basis of one or more of that individual's attributes. The 1989 survey asked respondents to indicate the extent to which they agreed with the statement that "how a person behaved in the past is a good indicator of how they'll act in the future." More than 60 percent of the respondents indicated at least some agreement with that statement, although only about 20 percent indicated that they agreed strongly. A related question asked if they agreed that "psychological testing helps employers to select the best workers for the job." A somewhat smaller proportion agreed (52.2 percent), with only about 14 percent agreeing strongly. If the correlation between these two measures is examined, a relatively strong association ($r = .16$) is found, which indicates that those who have faith in tests also have faith in projections based on the historical record. Thus a substantial proportion of the public believes that profiles represent meaningful intelligence about individuals, and information in such profiles, therefore, can rise to the level of "sensitive" and thereby become the basis for concern.

THERE OUGHT TO BE A LAW!

There is a distinction to be made between what people believe is technologically possible and what they feel is justified, either morally or under the law. These perceptions are susceptible to change as conditions change. John Detweiler's analyses of changing perceptions of social entitlements provided an index of changing expectations regarding "legal protection from unauthorized use of confidential information." In 1979, 88 percent of respondents indicated that they felt so entitled, with 70 percent expressing optimism regarding that status. By 1984 only 69 percent felt so entitled, although slightly more expressed some optimism about an improvement (72 percent).[14] One interpretation of the change is based on the increased level of surveillance initiated by the Reagan administration's war on "fraud, waste, and abuse" in the provision of government services and a generalized policy toward creating "downward expectations" about social entitlements.

There are also differences that emerge in terms of comparative legitimacy. In a Harris survey in 1978, respondents were asked to indicate whether they thought that the maintenance of certain files by public and private organizations was justified. Observed differences reflected confidence in the organizations as well as evaluations of the sorts of persons who might find themselves in particular files. Whereas more than 87 percent of the respondents thought that the government was justified in using matching to compare welfare rolls against employment records to "identify people claiming benefits they are not entitled to," only about 47 percent thought that the IRS was justified in comparing "tax records against credit card records." Nearly 52 percent thought that it was acceptable for the insurance industry to maintain a central file of individuals who were *suspected* of making fraudulent claims, but only 22.8 percent thought that it was similarly appropriate for a central file to be maintained for the use of employers that would contain the names of individuals who had been "treated for mental health problems."

Questions asked of the participants in the 1988 focus groups provide some insights into the underlying dimensions that help to organize the public's highly differentiated sense of justice regarding data collection.[15] Respondents were asked to indicate the extent to which they believed a list of persons "should be entitled to privacy rights as you understand them." They were asked to assign scores ranging from 1 (no rights at all) to 10 (absolute rights). Factor analysis was used to identify the underlying constructs with which the scores for particular classes of persons were most highly correlated.[16] Not surprisingly, one factor that emerged was composed of three measures linked to crime (Criminals): criminals, persons who have been convicted of violent crimes, and persons who have been convicted of nonviolent crimes. There is some comfort, perhaps, to be taken in the fact that persons who had only been arrested and not yet convicted were evaluated differently from the convicted criminals. Persons who were only suspected of crimes but who had not been arrested were classified as having rights similar to government workers, political activists, politicians, minors, and workers responsible for the safety of others (Politicos). A third class of individuals seen to have similar privacy rights was composed of people who deal with the public, persons who apply for credit, workers who handle large sums of money or sensitive data, and people who travel by air (Risks). The fourth group included people who might knock on your door or who might call your home telephone number (Sales). One way to assess the benefit of the doubt that these respondents assigned to these groups is to compare their average scores. On the basis of the means, or average scores, for the groups defined by the factor analysis, the members of the focus groups would assign privacy rights, from greatest to least, to members of the following conceptual groups: Politicos (mean = 7.76), Risks (mean = 7.08), Sales (mean = 6.21), and Criminals (mean = 4.01).

There is a distinction to be made between the regulation of information gathering and the regulation of its sharing or exchange. Katz and Tassone report a Cambridge Reports question regarding whether respondents favored "laws that would restrict the exchange of information between government and private institutions." The proportion favoring such laws increased from 56 percent to 69 percent between 1986 and 1988.[17] The increase in concern may reflect the level of publicity that followed reports of government use of commercial data to enhance the efforts of the IRS. But it is also this aspect of information sharing that makes the panoptic web so difficult for individuals to escape. The extent to which individuals are concerned about sharing by one organization and not by another is an indication of their understanding of the risks that such sharing might entail. In

TABLE 6.2   Orientation Toward a Legislative Response

Policy Area	1989 Mean (S.D.)	1978 (%)
Medicine and health	7.3 (2.6)	63.7
Social security numbers	7.3 (2.8)	–
Credit cards	7.1 (2.7)	60.8
Mailing lists	6.9 (3.0)	60.9
Telephone call records	6.9 (3.0)	51.1
Insurance	6.8 (2.6)	64.9
Employment	6.8 (2.6)	61.4
Political activity	6.6 (3.0)	–
Consumer purchases	6.0 (2.9)	–

the 1989 survey, respondents were asked to indicate the extent to which they thought that there was a need for strong laws to "control the sharing of personal information." The scores ranged from 1 (no need) to 10 (very great need). Table 6.2 presents the areas ranked in terms of the mean ratings assigned by respondents for particular classes of information.

The range of responses was quite narrow, as indicated by the means and standard deviations. The estimated need for a regulatory shield suggests that respondents seem little concerned with the use of most transaction-generated information. By ranking information about consumer purchases at the bottom of an ordered list, well below the positions assigned to mailing lists, telephone call records, and credit cards, respondents appear to see less of a relationship among the four areas than my analyses would suggest.[18]

It is clear, however, that this concern is continually evolving. In 1978, interviewers assessing the perceived need for regulation of some of the same organizations asked respondents to indicate how important it was "that Congress pass legislation" to control their information practices. The second column of figures in Table 6.2 indicates the proportion of respondents in 1978 who thought that it was important for Congress to act regarding these information spheres. Telephone call records were clearly seen as the least problematic area.

A somewhat different approach was taken in the 1983 survey. Interviewers asked respondents about whether or not they would favor specific forms of regulation governing particular kinds of offenses. By 1983 the public's orientation toward regulatory or legal action appeared to have grown more aggressive and punitive. In none of six regulatory areas identified did less than 66 percent of the respondents indicate that they favored regulation. The least popular regulation was that which would have specified "just what kind of information about an individual could be combined with other information about the same individual"—in other words, rules governing the construction of profiles (66.5 percent). The most popular legislative option was a law requiring "that any information from a computer that might be damaging to people or organizations ... be double-checked thoroughly before being used" (90.6 percent).

The overwhelming majority of respondents in a survey performed for the National Consumers League in 1989 indicated that they thought that it was inappropriate for employers to base hiring or firing decisions on the basis of information about "off-the-job" activities, especially those activities that might reflect lifestyle.[19] This region of privacy included several behaviors, such as smoking or poor diet, as well as status considerations, such as obesity, which could easily be demonstrated to be relevant to job performance or to employee expenses in the sphere of health insurance or medical costs. Yet adults fairly consistently wish to deny employers the right to even inquire about these matters.

OPPOSITIONAL TENDENCIES

There is a distinction to be made among what individuals report they understand, how they feel about practices and the need for a regulatory response, and what they report they do on their own to protect their interests. During the focus group discussions, several participants discussed the ways in which they responded to what they thought was an improper invasion of their privacy or the ways in which they acted to disturb the operation of the panoptic sort. Options ranged from the active refusal to supply the information or the provision of false information to the rather passive avoidance of situations in which the request for personal information would be likely.

Individuals have to be extremely confident about their rights, their value to the institution, or the availability of suitable options before they resist the panoptic sort by refusing to provide requested information. When asked in 1989 if respondents had ever refused to provide information or had left questions blank that they thought were inappropriate, nearly 35 percent indicated that they had. When asked a similar question in 1990, 46 percent indicated that they had refused inappropriate information requests from business, but only 15 percent had refused such requests from government.

Several studies have reported the increasing resistance of people to requests for them to participate in public opinion surveys. Some of this resistance is their understandable reaction to what the industry calls "sugging"—sales efforts made under the guise of research. When asked in 1989 if they had ever been asked but had refused to participate in a survey, 28 percent indicated that they had. This response was from a sample in which approximately half had never before participated in a survey.

A more passive response is the simple withdrawal from or avoidance of situations or circumstances when one might be required to provide information that might conceivably be disqualifying or embarrassing or might threaten the loss of other relationships currently enjoyed. That is, an individual might not apply for welfare or insurance benefits because completing the application might require updating information about one's status in an agency file, providing information about living arrangements, or transforming extremely complex circumstances into a simple yes or no answer—any of which might serve to alter the status quo in a negative way. There has been a rather dramatic increase in the number of persons who report that, at one time or another, they did not apply for something because they did not want to provide information. The proportion increased from 14 percent in 1978 to 30 percent in 1990.[20] Curiously, only 11 percent of the respondents to the 1989 survey indicated that they had "failed to apply" for something for the same reason.

It is always difficult to assess the extent to which individuals will attempt to circumvent or oppose the operation of the panoptic system by the introduction of false or misleading information. Lying is not a socially acceptable activity, and individuals hesitate to admit to lying, even to an anonymous telephone interviewer. It is not clear that a projective measure is always more accurate than a direct inquiry in this regard either. When interviewers asked people directly in 1989: Have you ever "provided false or misleading information on an application that you felt they had no right to ask?" only 8.5 percent of the respondents indicated that they had. Yet, when asked in 1990 if they thought that "most people" were likely to misrepresent the facts often or "a lot, " 33 percent agreed with regard to employment qualifications, 35 percent agreed with regard to health insurance applications, nearly 42 percent agreed with regard to income taxes, and another 35 percent agreed there was frequent misrepresentation on loan applications.

In the 1990 survey, interviewers asked about several items that related to specific concerns linked to the introduction of new technologies. There was an ongoing public debate surrounding the introduction of Caller-ID. This technology would enable a device to display the telephone number of incoming calls *before* the first ring. Opponents claimed that the device represented an invasion of the privacy of the calling party. The telephone companies argued that it potentially increased the privacy of the called party because it would allow them to screen incoming calls. The *Equifax Report* indicated that 43 percent of the respondents thought that the service should not be allowed to be sold. When interviewers asked respondents a follow-up question, which included an efficiency and privacy enhancing rationale for the service, 25 percent of the respondents suggested that it should be banned completely and another 55 percent thought that if it were offered it should be regulated by law. When they were asked a third time, with the notice of a potential added benefit in the form of a reduction in obscene and harassing telephone calls, 27 percent of respondents still favored banning the technology, indicating it as too intrusive, and another 48 percent would allow the service to be offered only if individuals could block the display of their numbers. The Commonwealth of Pennsylvania intervened by ruling that the Caller-ID technology was barred by Pennsylvania's wiretapping statutes. Yet, in the context of the increasing press coverage of the "war against crime" or the "war on drugs," national survey data suggested a significant increase in public acceptance of wiretapping, from a low of 16 percent in 1975 to a high of 26 percent in 1989.[21] Thus, again, an increasing share of the public seems to feel that it is appropriate to use a privacy invasive technology in pursuit or control of criminals, as long as its use is restricted in its reach into their personal lives.

In the 1989 survey Caller-ID was not described by name. Instead, interviewers asked respondents to indicate the extent to which they agreed with the statement: "It would be good to know who is calling before I answered the phone." Some 38 percent agreed strongly, and 35 percent agreed somewhat. Thus an overwhelming majority liked the *advantage* of knowing the identity of callers in advance, but a substantial majority also believed that such a technology needs to be limited or controlled.

There is a clear ends/means justification underlying the public response to this technology and its use. There is also an issue of reciprocity and fairness that has been raised in the debates about Caller-ID, which will be explored more fully in the next chapter. Because information about another brings advantage and power, it is understandable that individuals would like to know who is calling, would like to know what is on their mind, and, if it is a sales call, they would be pleased to know in advance whether the first offer the caller makes will be their final or best offer. At the same time, these respondents would *not* like to reveal any information about themselves, especially any information that might change the balance of power against them. The value of such a technology as a bar against the annoyance of sales calls is reflected in the fairly high level of interest in a potential application of a fictional enhanced Caller-ID service. Approximately 72 percent of the respondents to the 1989 survey agreed that "someone should invent a telephone that would automatically screen out calls from people trying to sell you things."

It should be noted that Caller-ID as proposed, and then as offered in several markets, does not fully meet the informational requirements of this majority, in that only the number of the calling party is delivered. Supplemental services might display additional information about the calling number, but it is only when the personal calling number, such as the PIN or the social security number, is delivered that the called party will really be confident in knowing who is calling and the likely nature of the call.

STRUCTURATION, OR THE SOCIAL ORIGINS
OF SOCIAL OPINION

It is important from a critical perspective to identify the social origins of the views on the panoptic sort that come to characterize identifiable groups in society. Social origins matter from a materialist theoretical position. Social origins also matter from a social policy perspective. If we understand how it comes to be that individuals accept what some of us may recognize as an oppressive and limiting relation of power, we stand a greater chance of intervening to change those relations. This orientation resists the common analytical tendency to explain attitudes and perspectives by using other attitudes and perspectives. Although the correlations or predictive ability of such models may be high, there is very little contribution to our understanding of the processes that may have given rise to both sets of opinions. Those involved in marketing research are less interested in explanations than they are in reliable predictions of consumer behavior. If an attitude will predict an opinion, that is more than enough. If that attitude can predict a behavior with any degree of confidence, that is an insight worth some money! The critical scholar, however, is interested in understanding the social processes that underlie both attitudes and behaviors.

One broadly identifiable approach toward the development of explanatory models is referred to as the social categories approach. It suggests that members of identifiable social groups will share common attitudes, opinions, and reactions to novel circumstances because they have had similar experiences and have been subject to similar socializing influences during formative periods. The underlying assumption behind the classification of respondents by race, class, and gender is based on the expectation that the socialization of African-Americans differs from that of whites; that young women have different experiences than young men, and that they have those experiences interpreted to them in ways that differ substan-tially from those of young men. The same logic applies to differences that reflect the variance in social experience among persons from different social classes.

IN SEARCH OF SOCIAL EXPLANATIONS

A secondary analysis of the 1978 Harris dataset provides our first broad look at the social basis for privacy orientations (Table 6.3). This database, with more than 1,500 cases and more than 200 variables, provided an opportunity to examine the influence of race, gender, employment, political ideology, age, and education on a multitude of constructions of the panoptic sort. Variables were all dummy coded so that agreement with a privacy enhancing view would equal one; otherwise, the variable would be coded as zero. Factor analysis[22] was used for the purpose of data reduction; estimates of reliability[23] are provided as an index of the additivity of scales suggested by factor solutions, and one-way analyses of variance were conducted for an assessment of the magnitude of the differences among groups identified by the social categories as measured.

Of the seven predictor variables, only political ideology can be characterized as an attitudinal construct that might be specified as a *result* of a complex of social experiences, rather than as a contributing cause of a person's orientation toward the panoptic sort. It is an important variable in this secondary analysis in that it is a significant discriminant in each of the eight factors presented in the table. However, it is not directly causal, even though it appears to be highly correlated with other measured views.[24]

Factors 4, 6, and 8 appear to reflect the most substantial differences among the social typologies identified by race, gender, employment status, nature of employment, political ideology, and education. For factor 6, the categories described by each of the variables are associated with highly significant mean differences. All of

TABLE 6.3   Social Origins of Orientations Toward the Panoptic Sort (1978)

Factor 1. Practices (Use of psychological tests, lie detectors, eavesdropping, monitoring via television, monitoring of speed, and so forth; 5 variables, alpha = .6942)

1.	Race	Sex	Job	Jobcat	Polview	Age	Educat
2.	p>.05	p<.01	p<.01	p>.05	p<.01	p<.01	p<.01
3.		W/M	S/R		R/N	25/65	AA/O

Factor 2. Autoinsur (Automobile insurance companies should not have the right to obtain information about applicants' drinking, credit, health, criminal record, and the like; 6 variables, alpha = .755)

1.	Race	Sex	Job	Jobcat	Polview	Age	Educat
2.	p<.01	p>.05	p<.01	p<.01	p<.01	p<.01	p<.01
3.	W/O		SA/R	PF/F	L/N	21/65	G/7

Factor 3. Finances/1 (Banks, finance companies, insurance companies, credit card companies, and credit bureaus should do more to keep information confidential; 5 variables, alpha = .895)

1.	Race	Sex	Job	Jobcat	Polview	Age	Educat
2.	p>.05	p<.01	p<.01	p<.05	p<.01	p<.01	p<.01
3.		M/W	S/R		R/N	25/65	AA/12

Factor 4. Government (e.g., IRS, CIA, FBI, government, SSA, Congress should do more to keep personal information confidential; 6 variables, alpha = .839)

1.	Race	Sex	Job	Jobcat	Polview	Age	Educat
2.	p<.05	p<.01	p<.01	p<.05	p<.01	p<.01	p<.01
3.	W/H	M/W	SA/R	PF/O	L/N	40/65	G/12

Factor 5. Finances/2 (Banks and other financial institutions ask for too much information; 5 variables, alpha = .843).

1.	Race	Sex	Job	Jobcat	Polview	Age	Educat
2.	p>.05	p<.01	p<.01	p>.05	p<.01	p<.01	p<.01
3		M/W	S/R		R/N	18/65	12/7

Factor 6. Employers (Employers should not be allowed to ask personal information, such as questions about race, age, marital status; 5 variables, alpha = .798).

1.	Race	Sex	Job	Jobcat	Polview	Age	Educat
2.	p<.001	p<.001	p<.001	p<.001	p<.001	p<.001	p>.001
3.	W/B	W/M	SA/R	PF/SL	L/N	25/65	G/7

Factor 7. Passivity (Failed to apply for job, credit, or insurance because respondent did not want to give information; 2 questions, alpha = .972)

1.	Race	Sex	Job	Jobcat	Polview	Age	Educat
2.	p>.05	p>.05	p<.01	p>.05	p<.01	p<.01	p<.01
3.			SA/R		L/N	25/65	BA/7

Factor 8. Matching (Computer used to predict fraud, drug use, mental patients, government files, identity cards, and so on; 5 variables, alpha = .697)

1.	Race	Sex	Job	Jobcat	Polview	Age	Educat
2.	p<.01	p<.05	p<.01	p<.01	p<.01	p<.01	p<.01
3.	W/O	M/W	SA/R	PF/F	R/N	30/65	G/0

Key: 1=variable name; 2=significance level; 3=highest over lowest group mean, Scheffe test of difference

Race: W=white; B=black; O=Oriental; H=Hispanic

Job: HR=hourly; SA=salaried; SE=self-employed; R=retired; U=unemployed; S=student; H=housewife; D=disabled

Jobcat: PF=professional; M=manager, official; PP=proprietor; C=clerical; SL=sales worker; SK=skilled crafts; O=operative; SE=service; F=farmer

Polview: C=conservative; M=middle-of-the-road; L=liberal; R=radical; N=not sure

Educat: 0=no formal schooling; 7=1–7 years completed; 8=8 years completed; 11=9–11 years completed; 12=12 years completed; C=1–3 years of college; AA=AA degree; BA=BA degree; G=one year or more of graduate school the differences are significant at the 99.9 percent level of confidence. With regard to the differences among groups evaluated by the Scheffe test, whites more than blacks wish to restrict the employer's collection of irrelevant personal information. They may think that this information is irrelevant because information about marital status, race, height, and the like is thought to have no meaningful link to job performance. Women were more adamant than men, salaried and professional workers more so than other employees. This appeared to be a liberal position. Indeed, in all eight factors, self-proclaimed liberals or radicals were found to anchor the most extreme privacy seeking end of the distributions. Age was also a significant component in each of the factors, with the oldest cohorts anchoring the most conservative, or least concerned, position on the scale. Education was also a significant influence in each of the factors, and the general tendency was for those with the most education, frequently those with some graduate training, to be the most concerned with the preservation of their control over their personal information.

Gender, Race, and Ethnicity

Being female is a relatively important influence on the way one comes to understand, accept, or reject particular aspects of the panoptic sort. When the correlations between being female and holding privacy related attitudes as measured in 1989 are examined, several significant relationships emerge. By using a conservative standard of greater than 99 percent confidence, it was found that women reject the statement: "The more people know about you, the more control they have over your life" ($r = -.11$). This is consistent with a tendency for women to reject the statement: "How a person behaved in the past is a good indicator of how they'll act in the future" ($r = .09$). These data suggest that women are less likely than men to be selective users of the media in that they view more hours of general television ($r = .11$) than they attend to public affairs on television ($-.08$) or in the press ($-.10$). This greater exposure and the presumed dependence on mainstream television would suggest that women are more likely to be subject to the hegemonic rather than the oppositional influences of the medium.

Race and ethnicity influence individuals through the same kinds of socializing experiences that generate differences between men and women. In the 1989 survey, the strongest association with minority ethnic status, being African-American or Hispanic, is revealed in the tendency to agree that corporations gather only what they need in order to make good business decisions.[25] African-Americans and Hispanics apparently also share a tendency to accept the narrow specification of privacy interests as being linked to having something to hide. Being African-American ($r = .14$) is more closely associated with this view than is being Hispanic ($r = .05$) with regard to one's estimate of the extent of public concern about privacy. The data indicate a greater tendency for Hispanic respondents to want to know who is calling before they answer the phone. One executive at AT&T suggested that this preference among Hispanic individuals may be related to the greater commonality in surnames, which results in more unwanted calls from people with "wrong numbers" that they gathered from directories or from directory assistance. African-American respondents tended to reject the view that past behavior was a reliable predictor of the future ($r = .11$), a perspective that, as we have seen, was apparently shared by a large number of the female respondents ($r = .09$). Overall, the number of differences linked to gender and ethnicity was not large, and many do not survive statistical controls designed to remove the influence of social class.

Income and Social Class

Increasingly, respondents to surveys appear unwilling to indicate their household income. Twelve percent failed to answer the household income question in 1989, with nearly 10 percent refusing outright. A similar proportion (10.9 percent) did not provide the information when requested by Harris interviewers in 1990. It is not unreasonable to assume that those who refused to answer this question are more protective of the financial aspects of their personal identification. If those respondents are excluded from analyses that utilize income as an explanatory variable, the influence of that particular sensitivity is underestimated. By dividing the respondents in the 1990 survey into those who did and those who did not provide an estimate of household income, it is possible to compare the means of those two groups on core questions. For example, there was no significant difference between the two groups in terms of the proportions of persons who said they were very concerned about threats to their personal privacy. There was no difference between the groups in terms of their belief that consumers had lost control over how information about them was circulated. There was only a marginal difference between the two groups in terms of the proportions of persons who reported a great deal of exposure to information about the potential misuse of personal information. However, there was a highly significant ($p = .005$) difference between the two groups in terms of the proportions of persons who reported being very concerned about the sale of personal information to mailing list firms. Consistent with our assumptions about sensitivity, those who did not report their income were more likely to report such concerns.

Alternative measures of social class included the level of education attained and the nature of work performed by the respondent or the principal wage earner. The 1990 survey included a measure of social class that introduced an ideological spin that is difficult to untangle in that the categories included the labels "lower class" and "working class," which may have served as representational or affiliative categories rather than as more objective indicators of status.

By using the nature of the work of the principal wage earner as an index of class, an ordinal scale was constructed that ran from hourly, to salaried, to self-employed. This measure was positively correlated with education ($r = .21$). Several weak correlations emerged when ranks on this scale were compared with the ranks on the twenty-five constructs in the 1989 survey. The strongest association noted is with regard to what might be called a victimization measure. The higher one's social class, the less likely respondents were to feel that people with power try to take advantage of people like them (r = −.10). Those in the lower classes were also more likely to report an interest in knowing who was calling before they answered the phone (r = −.09), perhaps to avoid the pressure of creditors seeking payment. Class, as measured, was also a factor in explaining the preference of some respondents for policies that might limit the kinds of information that employers might gather about job applicants. Curiously, those in the lower classes tended to be more accepting and trusting of business, as evidenced by the correlation of class with the beliefs that businesses rarely gather more information than they need and that the more information they gather, the better businesses can meet their individual needs (r = −.08).

Education

Education has always been a powerful factor in the explanation of social and behavioral differences. It has been seen to produce differences in two ways: first, through common experience or socialization; and second, through the transformation of an individual's capacity to process information and ideas. Education is the door through which individuals enter into experiences that further broaden and condition their existences. Education is part of a process that helps to determine the social contacts that a person will find enjoyable and beneficial in work and in recreation. It is usually thought to be a liberalizing influence, but, as discussed later, not all aspects of one's concerns about the panoptic sort can be understood as a reflection of a political continuum.

Educational attainment, such as that associated with the completion of specific stages—high school, college, and graduate degree programs—represents a mark of personal achievement. On the one hand, it is not surprising to note that those with more education had the strong tendency to reject the view that "there is very little that an individual can do to improve the quality of their life" (r = −.18). We noticed that there was an even stronger tendency toward the denial of power as indicated in the statement: "Most people with power try to take advantage of people like me" (r = −.24) . There was a similar rejection of the suggestion that "computers give big organizations an unfair advantage over the average person" (r = −.15).

On the other hand, those with more education appeared to be more accepting of the logic and rationales behind the panoptic sort. For instance, there was a tendency for those with more education to agree with the statement: "How a person behaved in the past is a good indication of how they'll act in the future" (r = −.15). However, their acceptance of the logic of the models does not mean that they found such business use legitimate. Those with more education were found to be more willing to restrict data gathering by insurance companies (r = .11), in part because they apparently do not believe that "companies rarely gather more information than they need to make good business decisions" (r = .11). And they tended to reject the view that "the more businesses know about me, the better they can meet my individual needs" (r = .09).

Overall, those with more education tended to share a much lower estimate of the general public's concern about privacy than did those with less education (r = −.21). Significantly, their view of the public's concern was less cynical in that the more highly educated tended to reject the view that "the only people who are concerned about their privacy are people with something to hide" (r = .15).

Age Cohort Analysis

In nearly every analysis of each available dataset, age has emerged as an important source of variance in opinions. There are several ways to think about the influence of age on one's policy orientations. We might consider age to be an index of maturation. In general, we have come to characterize a particularly liberal or progressive social and political orientation as youthful—revolution is sparked by the youth. It is generally accepted that we grow increasingly more conservative as we age, as our liberal ideals repeatedly confront the cold hard realities of economic and social responsibility. Thus we might expect political, economic, and social conservativism (even though they are clearly different concepts) to increase with age. This view might be labeled a life cycle model of value change to the extent that different roles and requirements influence changing attitudes and orientations. Such a structurational view suggests that there are common demands on people that characterize particular life stages, which explains the greater similarity within, rather than between, broad age cohorts.

There is a second approach to understanding the influence of age that does not see it as a continuously occurring process of maturation. This approach suggests that certain orientations, political and social values in particular, are established fairly early in life and tend to reflect the dominant values being expressed within the cohort when such values are formed (between eight and twelve years of age). With this theoretical position, we would expect to see age cohorts remaining relatively homogeneous and, more important, relatively stable in orientation as they age. Thus adults who reached political maturity during the Roosevelt period of state activism should be quite different from those who matured during the height of McCarthyism or the U.S. cultural revolution of the 1960s. Ronald Inglehart argues that the most powerful influences on cohorts are economic, and among the economic influences the most powerful are changes in educational attainment. [26] He notes that in the United States, the rate of access to higher education doubled from 1950 to 1965. [27] He suggests that education, especially college, changes students dramatically, making them more liberal, less authoritarian, less ethnocentric, less dogmatic in their views, and more interested in political matters. He notes that, although the U.S. population almost doubled between 1920 and 1970, "more than sixteen times as many college degrees were awarded in 1970 as in 1920."[28] Inglehart's "post-materialist values" are the result of changes in the economic resources available to individuals in different industrial countries, which are enhanced through education and the expansionary vista provided by television.

Inglehart's approach has much in common with that developed by Milton Rokeach.[29] Rokeach focuses on human values as relatively stable core constructs, which have been demonstrated to have predictable links to attitudes and opinions about various things, including automobiles and political candidates and television programs.[30] Whereas Inglehart's approach seeks to identify the common core values of a nation as a reflection of its level of economic development, Rokeach's approach involves the pursuit of difference. It is the differences in the core values that predict and explain the observable differences in attitudes, opinions, and behaviors. Unlike Inglehart, Rokeach makes no effort to specify the complex of "cultural, societal and personal experiences" that contribute to an individual's value structure. However, his analytical framework pursues a social categories approach and demonstrates significant differences in structure between whites and blacks, men and women, and social classes defined by income and education. He concludes that "the many value differences found between the very poor and rich almost suggest that they come from different cultures."[31] At least thirty of the thirty-six values Rokeach uses reveal significant age differences. "The general impression gained from inspection of the data is one of continuous value change from early adolescence through old age with the presence of several generation gaps rather than just one."[32] The differences between Inglehart and Rokeach at one level have to do with the different values measured. Inglehart's postmaterialist index represents only a small subset of the complex of values that are measured in relation to each other in the Rokeach scheme. The second problem is in the unit of analysis. Inglehart seeks to make comparisons among nations; Rokeach's analysis seeks comparisons among groups.

The third approach is one that suggests that there are important differences within cohorts that are associated with the concrete experiences individuals may have, experiences that might be common to a group based on race, gender, or class but that may also represent orientations based on cumulative experience that is not predicted or explained by the other influences, independently or in combination. This view recognizes the complex nature of influences on social orientations but assumes that these influences are dynamic, rather than stable, and reflect learning to accept or to resent and resist institutional demands.

The first two positions are incompatible with each other, and the third risks the frustration of unmanageable complexity. Longitudinal data would be required to answer the question with any confidence. Such data are not readily available, and questions about the panoptic sort were certainly not on the research agenda early enough to make such comparisons possible. Two less satisfactory alternatives involve the comparison of samples taken at different points in time while making a generally untenable assumption that the samples are truly representative of the same populations, just separated by a given number of years. Such an approach is also troubled by the nature of cohort measurement and the irregularity of survey administration. Not all surveys ask for age in years, in part because some respondents refuse to provide a precise answer. Instead, respondents are asked to indicate if their ages fall within a given range. The differences in the size of the cohorts so described and the length of time between surveys make it impossible to assume that the same cohort has simply become five years older, that is, merely shifted from one cohort to another. The third difficulty is common to all cross-sectional analyses: the need to assume part of what you seek to discover—that personal attributes indicating group membership allow the assumption of similarity in experience within group or cohort.

Because of all of these difficulties, no single approach is satisfactory, but if the evidence from multiple approaches points in the same direction or toward the same conclusion, our confidence should increase. For example, if we examine the distribution of ideological self-identification by age and focus on the proportion of the samples in 1978 and 1990 who claim to be conservative, there is a curvilinear pattern (Figure 6.1). In the 1990 survey, the low point is reached by age twenty-five, whereas the low point was not reached until age thirty-five in the 1978 assessment. The younger cohorts are considerably more conservative in 1990 than their counterparts were in 1978. Thus, although there is evidence of a traditional "maturational" move toward greater conservatism with age, the increasing conservatism of political discourse may have had a direct effect as well. [33] The challenge of separating the complex of influences called maturational from the common experiences that are associated with the life cycle but that vary with race, class, and gender is confronted in this section.

A similar but potentially troubling pattern is seen in the curves (Figure 6.2) reflecting the relationship between age and political cynicism. Although the pattern is similar to that of a growing conservatism, overall the level of cynicism has declined in 1990 in comparison with that in 1978. Because the measure of cynicism is the proportion of the cohort who agree that how one votes bears little relationship to what government does, the fact of increasing conservatism in the whole population, linked with a declining cynicism, suggests a greater confidence in the political process associated with the Reagan and post-Reagan era. Such a conclusion is clearly not warranted as a general model because there are different responses in different cohorts. For the three oldest cohorts, there has been a substantial decline in trust in government (to look out for one's interests), but a substantial increase for the younger cohorts, which may reflect a changing structure of reward in the society (Figure 6.3).

What is most striking about the public's trust in institutions is the great shift in the level of trust in business (Figure 6.4). Although respondents in the older cohorts are more satisfied with business, the gap between the 1978 and 1990 cohorts increases dramatically and suggests that a considerable improvement in business

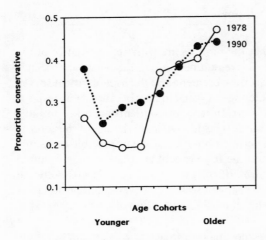

FIGURE 6.1 Conservatism and age

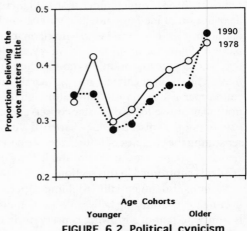

FIGURE 6.2 Political cynicism

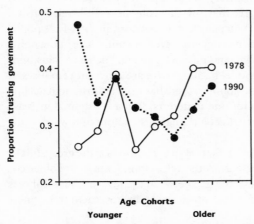

FIGURE 6.3 Trust in government by age

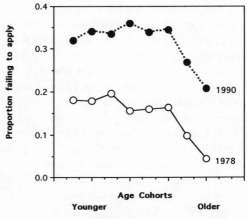

FIGURE 6.4 Trust in business by age

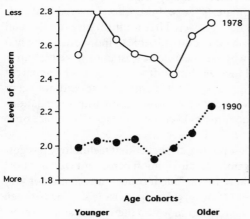

FIGURE 6.5 Extent of concern by age

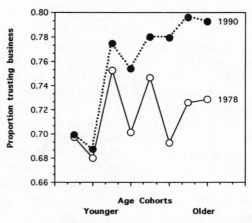

FIGURE 6.6 Failed to apply by age

practices (or in public relations) had occurred in twelve years. This pattern suggests that there has been a dramatic improvement in the interactions between businesses and older adults. It may also mean that the level of expectation has also changed, which may contribute to a higher level of annoyance when particular businesses step out of line.

As is clear from Figure 6.5, the level of public concern about privacy had increased dramatically between 1978 and 1990. The shapes of the age distributions change most noticeably in the younger cohorts, in whom the level of concern increased more dramatically than with any other cohorts. Also, the greatest level of concern occurred in an earlier cohort in 1990 than in 1980—the opposite of what we would have seen if those with the greatest concern had merely gotten older in twelve years.

An upward shift in the proportion of age cohorts who have decided not to apply for something needs to be interpreted cautiously (Figure 6.6). The form of the question produces a cumulative estimate. That is, those who answered in the affirmative in 1978 would presumably have answered in the affirmative in 1990, and thus any increase in the proportions would be attributable to individuals who had never been passive before 1978, but who had been so at least once since that time. As a cumulative measure, it should increase but shift to the right. The apparent failure of the curve to shift to the right suggests that the increases did not occur equally across all cohorts. Indeed, we would have to suggest an inverse relationship with age: As people get older, they are less likely either to face the choice or to take a passive response.

Alternatively, the measure of technophobia, the belief that technology has gotten out of hand, reflects a relatively gentle shift in opinion consistent with a cohort aging interpretation (Figure 6.7). Those in the fourth cohort in 1990 are not very different from those in the third cohort in 1979. The pattern is similar between other lagged cohorts except for the final cohort in whom there is a dramatic reversal. Such a reversal must indicate a changed perception in that cohort. Both static and lagged comparisons would be statistically significant with samples of this size.

A different approach has been taken in the exploration of the influence of age in the 1989 survey. In a factor analysis of the unweighted cases, the twenty-four attitudinal variables produced eight factors accounting for nearly 50 percent of the variance (47.8 percent).[34] Factor scores were generated for each factor, and the factor scores were subject to multivariate analysis of variance with gender and age cohort as variates. Gender emerged as a significant main effect on the set of factor scores. Univariate tests revealed that gender mattered most with factors 3, 7, and 8. Factor 3 might be characterized as an antilist factor. Three measures loading most heavily on this factor were: (1) a belief that individuals had "a right to have their name removed from any mailing list," (2) agreement with the statement that there "should be a way to keep your name off certain mailing lists," and (3) agreement with the statement that companies should "seek your permission before they tell anyone else about the products you buy or the services you use."

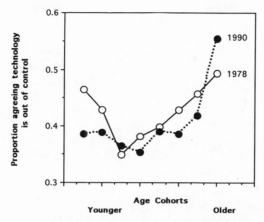

FIGURE 6.7 Fear of technology by age

Factor 7 was primarily concerned with technology and the predictive utility of data. Three measures loading heavily on this factor were: (1) the belief that past behavior was an indicator of the future, (2) the belief that psychological tests would be helpful for employers involved in choosing the best employees, and (3) a tendency to reject the associated belief that companies rarely gather more information than they need to make good business decisions. Respondents with high scores on this factor believed corporations could gain useful intelligence from personal information, although they did not believe its use was always justified. The third factor (8) for which gender-linked differences were the strongest, involved agreement with the statement that you "have to give up your privacy to enjoy the convenience of the modern world" and rejection of the claim that "information provided to the Census Bureau is held strictly confidential." None of the tests of the gender/age interaction were statistically significant.

However, the classification of respondents into five age cohorts reveals age to be a highly significant main effect. The univariate tests identify age as a significant factor in seven of the eight comparisons. The only factor in which age did not play a major part was factor 4, which involved the desire for a device like Caller-ID that would identify the calling party but would also serve to screen out calls from sales people. These two measures are highly correlated $(r = .32)$.

Trust in business and government data handlers also varied significantly with age in the 1990 survey. An analysis of variance using the means of the trust scores for each of eight cohorts reveals a highly significant relationship $(F = 8.487, p < .001)$. The relationship was significantly linear, with a negative correlation $(r = -.08)$. However, it is also clear that the curve is U-shaped, with the greatest trust among the youngest cohorts, the least trust within the middle groups, and the seniors reflecting a somewhat greater degree of trust than the middle group (Figure

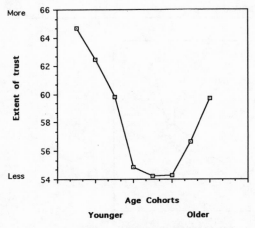

FIGURE 6.8 Trust index by age

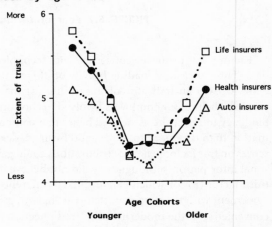

FIGURE 6.9 Trust of insurers by age

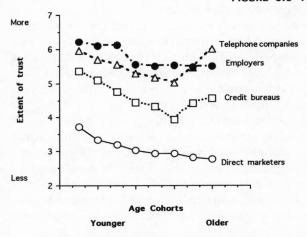

FIGURE 6.10 Trust of data handlers by age

6.8). However, by examining the age-linked distributions of trust for a subset of the organizations, an experience-based interpretation of this relationship presents itself.

The most consistent curvilinear pattern is with the insurers (Figure 6.9). The decline in trust reverses or levels off at the fourth cohort, involving respondents thirty to thirty-four years of age. The younger cohorts' trust in these insurers is a reflection of their level of interaction with these organizations that require forms, tests, and blanket permission for investigations into their background and status. The continuing need for new automobile insurance subjects persons of this age group to the full weight of surveillance and the risk that something in their files will operate to deny them this service. This analysis, of course, assumes that, on balance, all interactions with insurance providers are negative experiences. The improvement in trust is not related to any change in insurer practice but is rather a tendency of respondents to forgive and forget negative experiences further in their past.

The same is not true for most of the other data handlers identified in Figure 6.10. The level of trust of direct marketers declines steadily with age, reflecting increased marketing pressure organized in pursuit of the increased wealth of the older cohorts. The explanation for the results for the telephone companies and credit bureaus is similar to that offered for the insurance providers. The older cohorts have limited experience with making applications for telephone service or seeking credit for major purchases.

The Media and the Information Environment

One of the most powerful sources of explanatory power in the 1990 dataset is to be found in the response of individuals to a question about their exposure to information about the panoptic sort. The Harris/Equifax survey asked respondents to indicate how much they had "heard or read during the last year about the use and potential misuse of computerized information about consumers." Responses were coded into five categories ranging from 1 (a great deal) to 4 (nothing at all). A fractional proportion of respondents (eight people) indicated that they were not sure, and, for the purposes of this secondary analysis, the responses were recoded to assign those eight cases to a middle category of uncertainty or indifference. Then responses were reverse coded so that greater exposure received the higher score.

The relationship between exposure and a generalized concern about personal privacy is highly significant, linear, and direct. The more people have heard or read about the use and potential misuse of computerized information about consumers, the more concerned they are about threats to their privacy ($r = .13$, $p < .001$). The relationship is even stronger ($r = .15$) with regard to concern about the sale of personal information by the list industry for use by businesses marketing goods and services. A similar relationship appears with regard to the summary index of trust discussed earlier, except that the relationship is inverse: the less you have heard or read, the more you trust organizations that collect and use information about consumers ($r = -.14$).

Alan Westin proposed an index measure that combined responses to four questions: extreme concern about threats to privacy; a belief that businesses seek excessively personal information from consumers; a belief that the federal government still invades its citizens' privacy, even after Watergate; and a belief that consumers have lost all control over the circulation of their personal information.[35] This measure is even more strongly linked to exposure ($r = .18$). There was no apparent relationship between being exposed to stories about information use and abuse and respondents' opinions regarding Caller-ID. This suggests that the relatively high level of opposition must have been based on an opposition to the technology more than an understanding or acceptance of the claims made by privacy activists that the technology would be used to gather TTGI in the same way that ANI services gather information generated by calls to 800- and 900-number services.

There is a tendency for those with the greatest exposure to information about the panoptic sort to also be more likely to work with computers on their jobs. Along these same lines, those who have the greatest exposure to this information also tend to agree that privacy activists play an important role through their "work to protect people's privacy by exposing abuses, bringing lawsuits, and sponsoring legislation."

In the 1989 survey, several questions were asked that allow us to conduct an investigation of the influence of exposure in somewhat more detail. George Gerbner and his colleagues, working within the tradition of cultivation analysis, have tended to focus on television as the primary source of media influence.[36] The cultural indicators perspective, which underlies much of this work, assumes that a common representation of social reality pervades all that television presents. Thus it matters very little what particular programs a person views; it matters only how much television is viewed. Interviewers gathered a measure of overall exposure to television in response to a question that asked: "What is the average number of hours that you watch television on a typical weekday?" Responses were measured to the quarter hour, with the mean response computed as 3.01 hours.[37]

Because there remain good logical and empirical reasons to believe that differences in people's understanding of some of the complex issues related to the panoptic sort will be derived from, or at least associated with, their exposure to discussions of issues not common to entertainment fare, interviewers asked additional questions about more specific viewing. They asked respondents to indicate how often in the last six months they had watched "programs on television having to do with politics, government, or public affairs." Responses were placed into one of four categories from 1 (never) to 4 (frequently). Interviewers asked a similar question with regard to newspapers.[38]

An analysis of the correlations suggests that, although there is little media-related difference in respondent positions on the need for banks, finance companies, and credit bureaus to do "more to keep personal information confidential," the tendency between the selective and nonselective measures is diametrically opposed with regard to respondent beliefs about business practices.[39] These data would appear to support an assessment of television's hegemonic role in that greater exposure is associated with greater agreement with the statement: "The more businesses know about me, the better they can meet my individual needs." Those who pay more attention to public affairs on television and in the press are more likely to reject that view. Similarly, the influence of general television viewing is even stronger with regard to agreement with the statement that "companies rarely gather more information than they need to make good business decisions." Those reading more about public affairs tend to reject that view.

A similar divergence is seen with regard to the claim that "the only people who are concerned about their privacy are people with something to hide." Apparently, the more people watch television in general, the more they are likely to accept such a view; the opposite is true for those who pay more attention to public affairs in the press, or even on television. At the same time, it should be noted that those who view more television estimate the extent of public concern about privacy to be higher than those who watch less, and this tendency is opposite to that which characterizes those who watch public affairs programs.[40]

A causal interpretation of these data associates general television exposure with a hegemonic view of business as good, efficient, and fair. Recognition of a widespread public concern about privacy is modified by an interpretation of that concern as being unjustified—a reflection of guilt. The only association that is inconsistent with such a business-oriented view is the tendency among the heavier viewers of television to express an interest in a device that would screen out telemarketing calls. One interpretation, of course, is that heavy viewers resent the interruptions that such calls produce in their viewing, rather than reject business or marketing in general.

Political Interest, Involvement, and Ideology

The literature in recent years has begun to question the utility of traditional measures of ideological self-identification.[41] A bipolar scale ranging from radical to conservative may be seen to have been influenced by long-term trends in the overall political climate, which reflect an increasingly conservative tendency, as well as by particularly salient assaults on one pole or the other.[42] The attack on "liberal ideas," which characterized the Bush/Dukakis campaign, may have influenced the willingness of respondents to identify themselves as liberal, despite John Fleishman's finding that such influences were difficult to demonstrate.[43] In the 1989 survey, responses to the question that asked for the identification of the respondent's political orientation indicated that the current tendency was indeed a movement toward conservatism. On a 10-point scale, in which 1 was conservative and 10 was liberal, the mean was 4.8, with nearly 70 percent scoring 5 or below.

Three measures, derived from the terminal values inventory developed by Milton Rokeach, were included in the 1989 survey as an alternative index of political orientation.[44] Interviewers asked respondents to indicate how important they thought each of three values was to them; 1 was equal to being not at all important and 10 was equal to being very important. The most important of the three for the persons in this "conservative" sample was Freedom, with a mean of 9.6. Not surprisingly, Equality was less important, with a mean of 8.7. Equality is a traditionally liberal value, and it continues to provide a basis for distinguishing respondents in terms of their privacy preferences—especially with regard to their views on the need for legislative action.

Interviewers measured people's interest in politics and public affairs by a question utilizing a simple 1–10 scale, in which 10 represented very great interest. The interviewers asked respondents to "rate your interest in politics, government, or public affairs." The mean of 7.1 suggests a moderately high interest in politics in this sample. By the use of two additional questions interviewers sought to determine if that interest was reflected in the use of the mass media for information about politics. One question asked about the frequency with which people watched "programs on television having to do with politics, government, or public affairs" in the past six months. Somewhat less than 25 percent indicated that they never or rarely watched such programs, whereas nearly 40 percent indicated that they did so frequently. When asked to indicate how much "attention they pay to stories about politics, government, or public affairs" when they read the papers, 21 percent indicated that they paid little or no attention to such stories.

Interviewers asked questions about seven different items, each reflecting a different form of involvement or commitment to a "social problem, political issue, or political candidate." These items were: marched or demonstrated; signed a petition; wrote a letter; attended a meeting; joined an organization; donated money; and sought additional information. Interviewers asked respondents to indicate whether they had or had not taken each of these actions. The activity reported most frequently was the seeking of additional information. But only 55.1 percent of the respondents indicated that they ever made such an explicitly purposeful search. The signing of petitions and the donation of money in support of causes appeared to be the next most popular form of involvement. Only 4.4 percent of the respondents indicated that they recently marched or demonstrated, and only 18.7 percent indicated that they had joined an organization. Only eleven respondents, on the one hand, could be identified as very active, in that they indicated that they took each of the seven actions in the past year. On the other hand, 198, or nearly 20 percent of the sample, indicated complete inaction, in that they had not taken even one of those actions in recent memory. An activism score, computed as the simple sum of the activities reported, will be discussed as an important correlate of privacy perspectives.

Table 6.4 presents the relationships between the explanatory variables I have discussed in terms of their bivariate relations with particular orientations toward

TABLE 6.4 Correlations Between Explanatory Factors

Variable	2	3	4	5	6	7	8	9
1. Watchpol	.48[a]	.01	.30[a]	.14[a]	.20[a]	−.08	−.05	.01
2. Readpoli		−.11[a]	.41[a]	.21[a]	.23[a]	−.09[a]	−.04	.10[a]
3. Avghrstv			−.17[a]	−.27[a]	.07	.11[a]	.12[a]	−.03
4. Activist				.36[a]	.06	−.06	−.05	.09[a]
5. Education					−.06	−.09[a]	−.06	.01
6. Cohort						.04	−.08[a]	.01
7. Female							.04	.12[a]
8. Black								.04
9. Equality								

[a] $p < .01$

Key:
1. Watch politics and public affairs on television
2. Read politics and public affairs in newspapers
3. Average hours of television viewing
4. Index measure of activism
5. Educational attainment
6. Age cohorts, younger to older
7. Being female, dichotomous variable
8. Being black or African-American, dichotomous variable
9. Rating of importance for equality, low to high

TABLE 6.5 Multivariate Influences on Privacy Orientations (hierarchical regression)

Predictors	Criterion Variables		
	Public Concern	Privacy Laws	Privacy and Guilt
1. Class	−.016	.004	.016
2. Gender	.070[a]	.063[a]	.098[b]
3. Age	.004	.084[b]	−.041
R-sq change	.022[c]	.018[c]	.010[a]
4. Education	−.145[c]	−.073[a]	.066[a]
R-sq change	.028[c]	.002	.017[c]
5. Rokeach	−.073[a]	−.041	−.082[b]
6. Ideology	−.004	.033	−.025
R-sq change	.005	.003	.011[b]
7. Interest	.017	.028	−.033
8. Involved	.022	−.038	−.109[b]
R-sq change	.001	.009[b]	.019[c]
9. TV hours	.080[a]	.005	−.079[a]
R-sq change	.005[a]	.000	.006[a]
10. Watch pol TV	−.067	−.008	.061
11. Read politics	.033	.122[b]	.065
R-sq change	.003	.010[b]	.008[b]
R-squared (adjusted)	.045[c]	.033[c]	.061[c]

Beta = Standardized betas, all variables in the equation
[a] $p < .05$, [b] $p < .01$, [c] $p < .001$

the panoptic sort. The relatively high correlations within the table help to identify structures of similarity and difference within the sample. For example, those who tend to watch political or public affairs programs on television are also more likely to pay attention to political issues in the press ($r = .48$). However, while there is no clear relationship between watching public affairs and watching television in general, those who do attend to politics in the press would appear to limit their television viewing to politics as well, as the relationship between such reading and general television viewing is negative ($r = -.11$). Those who watch political television also tend to be relatively more involved, or activist, than others ($r = .30$), but the relationship between media use and activism is considerably stronger with regard to print ($r = .41$). The finding that this selective media use also characterizes the older and more highly educated cohorts is consistent with the contemporary literature. It is also unfortunately the case that women and African-Americans are less closely attuned to politics and public affairs and tend to spend more of their spare time with general television fare. The value placed on equality was generally quite high, and the variance was slight. There is, however, a solid basis for understanding the tendency for women, activists, and avid readers of politics to favor equality. The absence of an association with being African-American is a bit more problematic.

Multivariate Analysis: 1989 Survey

Table 6.5 presents the results of an effort to examine the combined influence of variables that had been demonstrated to be related to several different orientations toward the panoptic sort. A hierarchical regression design allows an analyst to enter variables into an equation in an order reflecting underlying theoretical assumptions about causal order. Variables may be entered singly or in groups representing a class of variables or influences. The coefficients labeled "R-sq change" estimate the proportion of the variance in the criterion variables (ranging from 0 to 100 percent) that is "explained by" or statistically associated with the variables just entered. At each step, the change in the R-squared value indicates an addition to explanatory power beyond that provided by variables already in the equation.

Of particular importance in such an approach is the fact that the presence of variables in the equation statistically removes or partials their influence from that of other variables in the model. That is, such an approach, for example, allows an estimate of the importance of educational attainment, after the common influence of gender on both the criterion variable and education has been removed statistically. Although this is not an explicit estimation of the importance of the interaction between education and gender, it increases our confidence in the R-squared value as a measure of explained variance.

In using the regression model, in which the influence of gender can be statistically controlled, we can more confidently utilize all 1,250 cases without weights. This is especially important when meaningful interpretation would require the elimination of all cases that did not have complete data for all variables used in the analysis.

The following were selected for use as independent, or predictor variables:

1. Class: An ordinal measure, treated as interval, based on the employment status of the main wage earner. Work for hourly wages was coded 1, salaried compensation was coded 2, and self-employment was coded 3.
2. Gender: A dichotomous variable; male = 1, female = 2.
3. Age: A continuous measure, the respondent's reported age at last birthday.
4. Education: An ordinal measure, treated as interval, ranging from "no formal school" = 1 to "postgraduate education" = 8.
5. Rokeach: A computed ratio score, expressed as the value of Freedom divided by the value of Equality.
6. Ideology: An interval measure, ranging from 1 to 10; 1 = conservative, 10 = liberal.
7. Interest: An interval scale, measuring reported interest in politics; 1 = not at all interested and 10 = very great interest.
8. Involved: A computed factor score. The output of a factor analysis of the seven variables utilized earlier in the simple additive index of Activism. The initial variables were dichotomous, with 1 = having taken the action and 2 = not having taken the action. Thus, in this analysis, utilizing factor scores, lower scores represent greater involvement, or activism.
9. TV hours: An interval scale, measuring average daily television viewing to the nearest quarter hour.
10. Watch political TV: An ordinal scale, treated as interval, measuring viewing of public affairs programs on television; 1 = never and 4 = frequently.
11. Read Politics: An ordinal scale, treated as interval, measuring the attention paid to public affairs material in the newspaper; 1 = none and 4 = quite a bit.

Three variables were selected for use as criterion (dependent) variables:

1. Public Concern: This interval measure is the projective index of respondents' concern, reflected in their estimation of the extent of concern among average Americans about "threats to their privacy." Although this, as with the other measures, is highly skewed, with 33 percent of the respondents choosing 10 as their response, there *is* substantial variance to be explained, as is suggested by a mean of 7.56 and a standard deviation of 2.42.
2. Privacy Laws: This is a simple additive index composed of the sum of the scores for each of the nine areas in which respondents could indicate the

extent to which they thought that there was a need for more strong laws to control the sharing of personal information (alpha = .85).

3. Guilt: This is an ordinal measure, treated as interval, that reflects respondents' agreement with the view that privacy concerns are limited to people with something to hide. As the responses are coded, 6 = strong agreement and 10 = strong disagreement. This measure is also severely skewed toward rejection, with only 15 percent of the respondents reporting agreement.

In each of the three models in Table 6.5, the equations are statistically significant, but the amount of variance explained is quite small. Because there is less variance in the criterion variable, it is not surprising that more of the variance in Guilt is explained than is one's estimate of Public Concern or one's preference for Privacy Laws. What is more important at this point is the importance of the predictor variables in each of these models.

In each model, the coefficient for gender is statistically significant. This can be interpreted to suggest that after we control for age, education, political interest, involvement, and even television exposure, there remains an independent contribution of gendered experience to an individual's orientation toward privacy as it has been measured.

Age, so important in many of the bivariate relationships discussed previously, remains a significant factor only with regard to the preference for a regulatory response. Because the variables are not independent but are significantly correlated with each other, caution is needed in interpreting the magnitudes of the beta coefficients as indicating their relative importance as explanatory factors. This is even more of a problem when the low R-squared measure suggests that the model is underspecified. Still, the sign of the coefficient for Education suggests that less rather than more education leads one to seek protection of one's privacy interests in the legislature. The larger, positive coefficient for Read Politics can be interpreted to mean that in general, exposure to press coverage of political issues lends support to a view that the legal system can meet the public's needs in this area.

The negative sign for Education emerges again in the model with estimates of Public Concern about privacy. When all the measured influences are controlled, those with less education tend to estimate the level of public concern to be higher than those with more education. Thus, those with less education are more likely to see privacy as a widespread concern and to see regulation as a viable option. The smaller but positive coefficient for television hours suggests that a representation of the life of the average American as one in which privacy is of great concern may be provided by exposure to television in general. Thus, with all other measured variables considered equal, including Education and Class, the more time respondents spend watching television, the greater is their estimate of the threat to privacy.

The importance of television viewing is also reflected in the model evaluating acceptance of the claim that privacy reflects Guilt. The negative sign for the coefficient reflects the wording of the question and therefore should be interpreted to mean that the more one watches television, the more one accepts the limiting view. Whereas more education is associated with rejecting that view, when education and other measured variables are held constant statistically, increased television viewing is associated with the acceptance of guilt. How might this relationship be interpreted?

In both the Concern and the Guilt models, the Rokeach variable is statistically significant. Recall that the Rokeach variable is the ratio of Freedom to Equality. Thus the higher the value of the Rokeach variable, the more freedom is valued relative to equality. The negative sign of the coefficient for Rokeach in both equations should be interpreted to mean that those favoring freedom more than equality tend to see that privacy is less of a problem than those who value equality somewhat more, and that those favoring freedom also tend to agree that the pursuit of privacy is an attempt to keep others from knowing about activities that are, at the very least, not in public favor. The political involvement factor suggests that those less involved in political activities are also more likely to accept the narrow view. Thus television viewing is associated with a socially conservative posture, but it may also be seen to contribute to a view that so many people are concerned about their privacy because they are doing so many things about which they share a sense of guilt. These are things that they would not be doing if others could easily find out about them. This is a powerful indication that the lower social classes have agreed to play according to the rules of the game as long as this game is being played under the watchful gaze of a panoptic system. And, noted earlier, heavy television exposure is associated with a mistrust of power ($r = -.12$) and a sense of powerlessness ($r = -.08$). The heavy viewers are in a "mean world"—they perceive that their personal freedom is limited, and they apparently have little hope of doing anything about it.

Although the previous analyses make some assumptions about the nature of the experiences that individuals have in their interactions with various organizations, the data gathered in 1990 allow examination of the relationship between negative experiences and measures of trust or concern. Interviewers asked three questions about respondents' experience with automobile insurers, health insurers, and credit bureaus. One question asked whether respondents had ever "been refused health insurance or been told that you had to pay a higher rate because of your health or the amount of your medical bills." Both refusal and being asked to pay a higher rate were coded as 1; otherwise, the response was coded as 0. A similar question asked if the person had "ever been refused auto insurance or been told that you had to pay a higher rate because of your accident and claims record." Again, refusal and higher rate experiences were coded as 1. The final question was a simple indication of whether the respondent had ever been refused credit. This variable, called History, was then used in combination with other predictors. Only thirty-eight respondents reported having had all three kinds of negative experiences. Some 261 reported having two, and 714, or approximately 32 percent of the respondents, reported having had at least one such experience.

Analyses of variance indicate that History is a significant factor in explaining differences in Trust, with the least trust expressed by those with the most negative history ($r = -.10$). It is also the case that those with the most negative experiences express the greatest general concern about the panoptic sort. Indeed, the data suggest that those who have been "burned" most frequently are also most likely to try to avoid further rejection, as is indicated by their greater tendency to report having failed to apply because they did not want to be asked more questions ($r = .15$).

When the differences in level of trust among members of different social classes are examined, there is a critical difference between the influence of knowledge from third parties and knowledge from direct experience. The cultivation hypothesis associated with George Gerbner contains a variant called "mainstreaming," which suggests that although concrete social experience may set people apart in terms of their understanding of the world, sharing the common experience of television brings them together in the mainstream.[45] The data in support of this hypothesis reveal that groups, such as whites and African-Americans who differ about perceptions of crime in the low television condition, will share a similar view of crime in the high television condition. This similarity is usually the result of one group's reducing the extremism of its views.

Exposure to information as measured in the 1990 survey is not precisely a measure of media exposure. We cannot assume that respondents were exposed to the same information in the same way that we can if we ask about their viewing of television. Contrary to the expectations of the mainstreaming hypothesis, the four social classes are not brought together through increased exposure to information about the panoptic sort (Figure 6.11). Greater exposure is associated with a lower level of trust for all social classes, but convergence does not apparently occur. Concrete social experience appears to be operating more forcefully, as is indicated in Figure 6.12. Where the classes are relatively close together in the condition of no negative experiences, there emerges a dramatic class division as negative experiences cumulate. First, no one from the lowest class was counted among the thirty-eight respondents who were so privileged as to have had three negative experiences. For the poorest of the poor, two strikes are all one is entitled to. However, the class divisions are dramatic, which may indicate that the absence of ready alternatives suggests that the actual costs of rejection as experienced by the poorer respondents are much higher than we find in the simple measure of History as event.

Figures 6.13 and 6.14 show that neither exposure nor direct experience serves to bring together groups differentiated by life cycle stage. Three age groups, young adults (ages 18–29), economically active adults (ages 30–49), and mature adults (ages 50+) respond to different levels of exposure as well as to their negative experiences with service providers. For all groups, exposure and experience are associ-

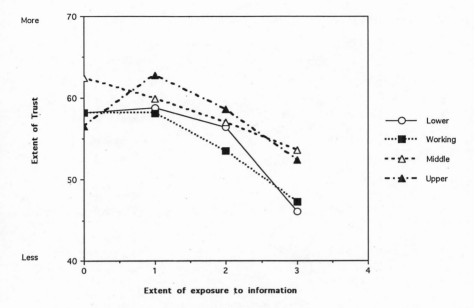

FIGURE 6.11 Trust, class, and exposure

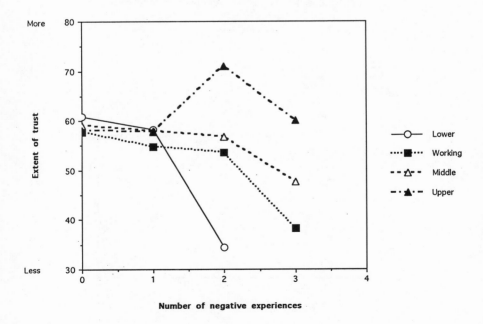

FIGURE 6.12 Trust, class, and history

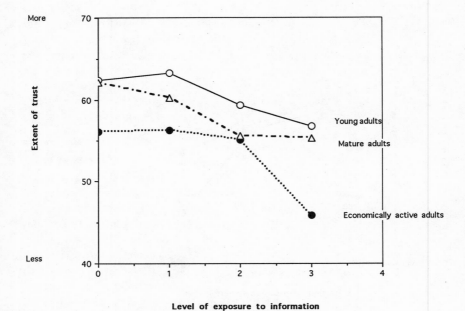

Level of exposure to information

FIGURE 6.13 Trust, life cycle, and exposure

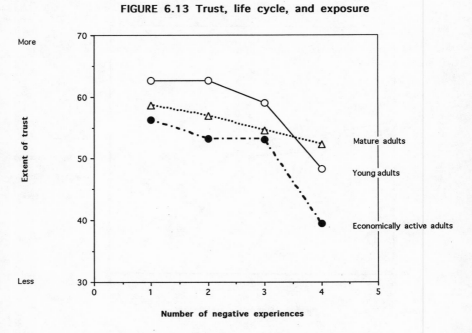

Number of negative experiences

FIGURE 6.14 Trust, life cycle, and history

ated with declining trust in institutions. The anomalous behavior of the mature adults, in whom the extremes of experience and exposure are not associated with the same loss of trust as the other cohorts, might be explained in two ways. The first, as noted earlier, is that class position provides some security and access to alternatives. The second, which is difficult to test with the data as measured, is that the qualifying experiences occurred earlier in their economic lives; this influence has dissipated, and the exposure to the horror stories in the press has less weight because they are no longer subject to the risks so described.

SUMMARY

The factors that are involved in the development of an individual's response to the panoptic sort are many, and their relationships are complex. The data analyzed in this chapter describe a dramatic increase in the public's awareness and concern about what are considered to be invasions of privacy. The differences among groups of people identified on the basis of their race, gender, age, or social class position appears to be related to the differences in relative power with regard to organizations that those positions represent. These differences appear to change dramatically with the relationships that become most salient at particular stages in an individual's life cycle. Yet not all of the attitudes seem to reflect direct personal experience. The mass media play a critical role in informing people about the risks and dangers that people like themselves face in their relations with the institutions of business and government. A critical role played by the mass media, especially television, is the reinforcing of a compliance with the dominant values that legitimate the operation of the panoptic sort.

7

A DATA PROTECTION REGIME

NEED WE INVOLVE THE LAW AT ALL?

It is important to recognize the difference between the law as an ideal, a moral structure, and the law as a weapon, a resource. It is the strategic use of the law and the legal system by goal-oriented actors that introduces contradictory forces, which is part of the structuration to which Giddens refers with regard to social systems in general. Far too frequently, we tend to talk about the law as the even-handed instrumentality that ensures that the universal values claimed for any society are protected and guaranteed. This idealized system is no less an illusion than the ideal of the competitive marketplace, which is thought to operate autonomously to produce optimal social results. It is important to understand those circumstances in which assumptions about the law cannot stand. Many of the problems with the law as a system are similar to the problems that have been identified with regard to the market. They are problems rooted in the vast inequality in power and influence that operates in a system that depends on the assumption of equality.

The law can be, and has been, used as a weapon, a machete with which to hack away enough brush to provide some breathing room, a protected space within which to pursue personal interests. This use of the law is to be distinguished from a notion of the law as an expression of a basic moral vision, a set of guiding principles that serve as foundations supporting relations among persons. The adversarial nature of legal practice and the resultant ends-means rationale have contributed to the disruptive, contradictory, and nearly unmanageable morass of theory, regulation, and case law that applies to the definition and preservation of an individual's rights in relation to the operation of the panoptic sort.

Understanding the dialectical evolution of the law requires a recognition that the process of structuration always reflects the actions of persons acting in pursuit of their interests, and it always reflects the significant differences in power among these actors as they act and react to the unexpected and unintended consequences of actions taken or restricted in the past.

Argumentation in the context of the pursuit of tort relief and compensation must be understood as strategic communication. As Habermas reminds us, strategic communication is not pursued in the interest of understanding, but rather in the interest of private gain.

However useful the pursuit of private gain might be in explaining the behavior of individuals and their associations, it does not provide a sufficient explanation of the behavior of judges, legislators, and administrative bureaucrats whose daily decisions are also involved in the reproduction and transformation of a legal regime. Ongoing debates about the relative autonomy of the state and the pursuit of self-interest by policy actors provide more questions than answers about the forces that determine the structure of laws and regulations that define privacy.[1] Explanations of the development of the legal regime with regard to personal information and privacy are made even more difficult because of the specific nature of the issues to be addressed. It is hoped that this chapter contributes to our understanding of these issues by breaking them into parts that reflect the competing and contradictory interests involved.

PERSONAL PRIVACY AND DATA PROTECTION: A TANGLED WEB

According to Richard Hixon, "privacy, in concept and by tradition, is a basic human right; as a legal entity based in social reality, however, it is ambiguous at best. The concept is important, yet it has acquired different, at times contradictory meanings."[2] In this chapter, my emphasis will be on the development of law and regulation with regard to informational privacy, and within that general category, I will pursue an interest in the regulation of the behavior of private firms. It is in the area of private corporate action that the law is most in need of attention.

The interests that are evoked by the concept of privacy are many and confused. The challenge in understanding how particular forms of social practice have developed to protect these competing and perhaps contradictory interests involves an attempt to represent the similarities and differences between the underlying factors in ways that are most helpful in understanding the laws, the machines, and the bureaucratic systems that have emerged to protect those interests. The analytical challenge and logic are similar to those leading to the use of factor analysis. I seek to identify the underlying factors that define a conceptual structure in which these factors relate to each other and to the ideas, actions, and technologies that help to define them. Just as with factor analysis, there are different rationales for choosing different solutions, based on assumptions about the underlying structure, such as whether they are correlated with each other or are orthogonal. These assumptions force a certain kind of thinking about the construct.

One line of tension that emerges clearly in this conceptual factor analysis is that between the individual and the collectivity, between the public and the private. Let us ask ourselves if all the rationales for providing or guaranteeing the private are antagonistic or opposed to the public or collective interest; or, can we find in the rationale for the protection of privacy the same underlying assumptions and instrumental rationality that justify the protection of individual interests in intellectual property. With regard to copyright, patent, and other forms of protection for individual rights to intellectual property, a contribution to public knowledge is the underlying goal. For the public interest in knowledge and creative works to be served, it is argued, individuals must believe that they will receive just compensation for their efforts at invention and creative expression. Similarly, the operation and survival of a vibrant democracy may be specified as a goal that defines active, informed participation by its citizens as a necessary prerequisite. The autonomous development of that citizenry can be argued to depend on the protections of personhood and individuality that privacy describes.

Alan F. Westin has been credited with making the most comprehensive analysis of the variety of interests that are part of the complex generally referred to as privacy. The most central concerns about what has been called informational privacy were explored in his *Privacy and Freedom*.[3] Essential to Westin's definition is the emphasis on the desire, claim, or right of individuals to decide for themselves the extent to which they will be exposed to others. This exposure includes their physical person, their attitudes, their opinions, and their activities. Since 1967, literally hundreds of commentators have sought to amplify, extend, and explain the complex of rights that form this cluster. David Flaherty offers a list of thirteen different privacy interests, which I suggest would form two identifiable but correlated factors. Factor 1, the control of access, would involve the right to be let alone; the right to a private life; the right to limit accessibility; the right of exclusive control of access to private realms; the right to minimize intrusiveness; the right to enjoy solitude; the right to enjoy intimacy; the right to enjoy anonymity (the right to limit identification); the right to enjoy reserve; and the right to secrecy. Factor 2, the right to control disclosure or representation, would involve the right to control information about oneself and the right to expect confidentiality.[4] The challenge in understanding the importance of these rights is to explore the contributions that control over *access* and *representation* make to the development of an autonomous individual.

Autonomy

Hixon's discussion of the long-term evolutionary changes in the meaning of the term privacy places special attention on the changes that emerged between the sixteenth and nineteenth centuries.[5] In this period, privacy came to be associated most clearly with a sense of individual, personal privilege, not altogether unrelated to the privileges associated with class position. The importance of this privilege in relation to the demands or requirements of the state on an emerging bourgeoisie is a distinction that ought not be lost. Barrington Moore, Jr., suggests that the desire for privacy emerges fundamentally when society places obligations on a person that this person cannot or does not want to meet. He suggests that until the end of the nineteenth century, only the propertied and employing classes were able to claim and enjoy any measure of privacy.[6]

Part of our understanding of the meaning of autonomy involves an individual's freedom to determine how she or he will respond to options and challenges. Autonomy is an ideal. There are always limitations and constraints. Many of these limitations are sociocultural. The extent to which an individual conforms to the expectations of others is the extent to which she or he has given up some autonomy. The panoptic sort threatens the autonomy of the individual by increasing the range of activities that may be brought under the watchful eye of significant others. If every action generates a record and if this record is available to a wider and wider sphere of interested, or potentially interested, others with the power to make decisions about a person's options, the freedom of action becomes self-limiting. The limitation on autonomy that derives from the belief that one is being watched is not restricted to formally illegal behaviors. Depending on the individual, the constraint spreads to include behaviors that may be merely questionable or out of fashion. The limitations on autonomy that characterize the panoptic sort are evermore broad because it is unclear just who is watching and what their interests and standards might be.

Individual autonomy may be realized in part through the maintenance of distinguishable personae that a person may adopt as the situation may require. These varying personae will be reflected by differences in dress, language, posture, and dynamism that are understood to be appropriate to a setting or an interaction. We can find a basis for understanding the importance, for an individual, of the ability to keep spheres and personae relatively independent of each other by considering the concept of cognitive dissonance.[7] The anxiety that people feel when they are forced to confront conflicting or incompatible beliefs, values, or opinions operates to restrict their effective functioning. Yet it is clear that individuals have developed complex mental structures or schemas that allow logically incompatible understandings to coexist, primarily because they are rarely called into play at the same time.

The operation of the panoptic sort threatens the ability of the individual to maintain these structures of personality independent of each other. Their representation in profiles is structured externally by others according to the others' interests rather than their own; any apparent incompatibility within the structure is resolved through a process of classification, which is necessarily limiting because it cannot approach the flexibility with which individuals can shift between their operational selves. Restrictions on the freedom of individuals to make these shifts, to adopt the personae they believe to be appropriate to the circumstance, are thus linked to a loss of control over information about themselves.

Frequently, the level of autonomy in the postmodern age is compared with that which was available in preindustrial times or in isolated rural communities. It is not that the extent of constraint is necessarily any greater than it has been at any point in the past, but that it is very different in terms of the visibility of constraint. The power is diffused invisibly, and is often exercised without the knowledge of the persons so constrained. It is this diffused, distanced, and semiautomatic quality of panopticism that makes it so difficult for individuals to challenge power on the basis of an analysis of its operation.

It is also important to recognize that limitations on individual autonomy are not entirely imposed from without. The efficacy of control is determined in part by the extent to which it has been internalized. It is a deeply vexing issue that surrounds the difference between external and internal constraint. A constraint is no less limiting if people apply it to themselves. If we truly believe that autonomy— freedom of action and freedom of choice—is a primary value, even *internalized* restrictions on the range of options must be seen as a limitation on that value, if the process through which the internalization took place was one in which options have been limited by the exercise of power. As noted, differential awareness of the panoptic system will be reflected in different responses to its constraint. The growing number of persons who have decided not to apply for some product or service to avoid revealing information about themselves represents only one of many forms of response that reflect an internalized constraint.

Related Interests

All of us are not equally proud of all that defines us as a person. Our evaluation of ourselves is based in part on comparisons with externally developed standards. We are able to enter into interaction with others to the extent that we can believe that those aspects of our person that would not be looked on with favor may be held in reserve, away from the public gaze. For many of us, the display of our bodies represents the potential risk of embarrassment. No less is true of our thoughts. Elisabeth Noelle-Neumann has identified a construct that suggests that people are less willing to express their opinions in a manner reflecting the extent to which they perceive their opinions to be at variance with the majority of those around them.[8] We are concerned that we not reveal weakness to actual or potential enemies. Access by others to those things we hold in reserve involves the potential loss of control and the transfer of power to the other. Part of the definition of privacy interests includes the ability to limit access by others to areas that we would prefer to hold in reserve, protected perhaps as in "sanctuary."

David Bazelon, echoing the comments by Alan Westin made ten years earlier, identified the nurturing of individuality, expressed as the right to be different, as an aspect of autonomy.[9] This individuality is realized through experimental self-discovery, which cannot operate when a person is always under surveillance, always being evaluated, always at risk. The pursuit of autonomous self-determination, therefore, requires a zone of privacy, which frequently means an actual physical space wherein experimentation might take place. This developmental process depends on some degree of seclusion, or isolation, areas in which a person can retire with some confidence that her or his privacy will be respected. Gary Bostwick defines repose as "freedom from anything which disturbs or excites."[10]

Another aspect of this process of autonomous development involves the expression of emotions and opinions and the exploration of intimate relationships without the pressure of having to consider the opinions and assessments of others. This space for relatively unhindered release is believed to be essential for human survivability—part of the reproduction of the individual's capacity for labor and interaction in the public sphere. It is, perhaps, the identification of the sexual with this intimacy that privacy allows that has occasioned the problematic definition of reproductive rights as privacy rights per se.

Reproductive rights, as part of the realm of sexual behavior, may be seen to be part of the "zone of intimate decision," which is currently protected under the expansionary interpretations of the Fourteenth Amendment, which suggest that only due process can restrict the right of individuals to make intimate decisions. The decision of the U.S. Supreme Court in *Roe v. Wade* has fundamentally altered how we think about privacy.[11] The sexual arena is clearly an area in which there are greater, and perhaps more legitimate, "expectations of privacy, " although there is danger in establishing orders of priority that are susceptible to change and are responsive to influence. The issue of information privacy, however, should not be focused on the limitations exercised by the state on what one might legitimately *do* within this zone of intimacy, but on how the state, or other uninvited party, would come to *know* what is or is not being done.[12]

THE HERITAGE OF WARREN AND BRANDEIS

Samuel D. Warren and Louis D. Brandeis are credited with having published the seminal law review article in 1890 that began the chain of theoretical agglomerations that make up the privacy regime in the United States today. Entitled "The Right to Privacy," this article proposed an addition to the body of laws that protected person and property. As they argued, developments in the law involve a continued expansion through the identification and specification of new rights, such as the right to "enjoy life" as enabled by the "right to be let alone." They argued that the process of expanding the coverage of a regime of rights was inevitable and was part and parcel of the expansion of civilization. Indeed, they suggested that "the elasticity of our law, its adaptability to new conditions, the capacity for growth, which has enabled it to meet the wants of an ever changing society and to apply immediate relief for every recognized wrong, have been its greatest boast."[13]

One environmental force demanding expansion of the law was thought to be intellectual reasoning, which compelled recognition that protections for property needed to be extended beyond the physical to the intangible—hence, the development of rights to intellectual property through copyright, patent, and trade secret protections. An opposite force was associated with the emergence of needs occasioned by the development of technologies that threatened to limit the private enjoyment of personal pursuits. In the circumstance at hand, it was the popularization of instant photography and its use by photojournalists that Warren and

Brandeis saw as pressing for the expansion of intangible property rights to include this new right of privacy.

Warren and Brandeis did not limit their criticism to journalism per se, but they clearly sought to challenge the commercialization of the private sphere of the individual: "Modern enterprise and invention have, through invasions on his privacy, subjected him to mental pain and distress, far greater than could have been inflicted by mere bodily injury."[14] This hyperbolic claim was made in the context of a discussion of the transformation of gossip into a trade "which is pursued with industry as well as effrontery."

In their argument that developed their position on this new right, we can find the seeds of the narrower right of information privacy developed by Alan Westin. Warren and Brandeis reached to the record of common law for the right of an individual to determine "to what extent his thoughts, sentiments, and emotions shall be communicated to others."[15] This right of publicity thus formed the core of their newly formed right of privacy. But unlike the exploitative rights that are inherent in the copyright and are realized on publication, the rights envisioned by Warren and Brandeis were negative rights: the value of which lay in the ability of the individual to *prevent* publication. It is the distinction between the economic value derived from the exploitation of personal information and the personal, sentimental, emotional, or other less pecuniary dimensions of value that is at risk of being lost in contemporary discussions of a market for personal information with compulsory licensure akin to that in the area of broadcast retransmission. But more about that later. It is sufficient to make it clear that Warren and Brandeis thought that "the protection afforded by the common law to the author of any writing is entirely independent of its pecuniary value, its intrinsic merits, or of any intention to publish the same."[16] The right, they argued, is therefore not a right of property but a right of "inviolate personality."

Warren and Brandeis also suggested a distinction between the protections and property interests that might inhere in intellectual property by virtue of the amount of labor expended in its production. This distinction would privilege the products of artistic and intellectual labor. They suggested that if forced, one might argue so as to demonstrate that the effort involved in conducting oneself properly is at least as substantial as that involved in creating a work of art. Thus the claim of substantial labor should also be set aside as making little contribution to a theory of difference between claims of a right to restrain publication of information *about* an individual from information *produced by* that individual.

They suggested that a photographer who makes additional copies of pictures taken of a client from a glass negative that she or he has is guilty of a breach of an implied contract.[17] Although the courts have moved far from this view since 1890, the argument still rings true—the photographer may have performed the labor to produce the negative and may have come to possess the negative, but she or he has done so only in the context of providing a service to the client. Subsequent use of the image ought to be limited by law as well as by courtesy to those uses explicitly noted or unambiguously implied by the initial contract. The same, it might be argued, should apply to any records (akin to negatives) that are generated by transactions involving long- or short-term contracts. It cannot even be argued that the client need specify the nature of the records kept. The subject of a portrait need not know how glass negatives are to be made or even that creation of a photograph requires a negative at all. The contract is for an image, the choice of the technology is that of the professional, but the fact that one process produces a potentially useful artifact should not by itself assign any rights to the professional to use the aspect of personality captured therein.

The cases of photographic invasion by journalists identified by Warren and Brandeis differed from those in the case of portraiture, in that there is no longer any necessity of participation, contractual or not, between the photographer and the unwilling, and increasingly unknowing, subject. It was the ability of this technology to capture images at will that required, in their view, the entry of a raised legal fence or the threat of successful tort action.

It should not be forgotten that Warren and Brandeis did not propose a right without limit. Indeed, several limitations were suggested in the analogies they discussed in the common law of slander, libel, and intellectual property. They included a broad exclusion for matters of "public or general interest," which on the face of it seems an opening large enough to drive a carriage through. If the distinction comes down to a definition of what it means to report or make public in the interest of the general welfare, it could be argued quite easily today that the public, which is the community of credit granters or health insurers or automobile insurers or perhaps the community of employers, has a legitimate interest in knowing about potential customers or employers. Thus the only restrictions that would be appropriate would be on knowledge or information that is unrelated to their activities as members of that particular "interested public."

The core distinction that is noted but not fully developed by Warren and Brandeis is the interest in protecting the privacy of "private life."[18] The realm of private life includes things that "all men alike are entitled to keep from popular curiosity," and this realm is to be distinguished from the more public aspects of life that are not the subject of publicity because the individual is not worthy of public attention.

The underlying emphasis on publicity of the sort accomplished by the press and other media of mass communication implied a multiplication of images—if not tangible images, then images in the minds of the observers or readers of the published report. Because of the technical limitation on the reach of the oral representation of those same facts and impressions, Warren and Brandeis would not find a cause for action if the publication were made through unaided speech. The injury from oral gossip was thought to be so slight as to be unworthy of concern.

Some eighty-nine years after Warren and Brandeis made their historic contribution, James Barron wrote to explain why the legal protections against the presumed excesses of the press never developed as the authors had intended.[19] Rather than developing as a limitation on the "public disclosure of embarrassing private facts" by the mass media, the tort of privacy had developed so as to emphasize three other torts: (1) intrusion into a person's seclusion or private affairs, (2) publicity that places a person in a "false light in the public eye," and (3) the appropriation of the person's name or likeness for commercial or other advantage. After noting the preference of the courts for the guarantee of a "free press" capable of defining newsworthiness as broadly as it wished, Barron turned his attention to a demonstration that Warren and Brandeis's initial representation of the severity of the harm was a broad overstatement, reflecting not a principled defense against a ruthless press but a hostile response of a hypersensitive individual (Warren) who enjoyed the benefits of a skillful and willing second in the person of Brandeis (who had actually written the article out of friendship and indebtedness).[20] Barron may have succeeded in finding, in pique and petulance, a reason for the original article and its emphasis on the press, but he left for others the task of explaining how other aspects of the privacy regime have evolved so expansively over the years.

A QUESTION OF DIGNITY
AND OTHER INTANGIBLE INJURIES

In a gallant, if only partially successful, effort to "put the straws back into the haystack," which the law of privacy had become by the mid-1960s, Edward J. Bloustein seeks to find the core rationale for the legal defense of privacy.[21] In the process, Bloustein turns the authoritative statement of torts from Dean William Prosser inside out, by picking up the thread of theoretical difference that most had dropped or missed entirely in their reading of Warren and Brandeis. Bloustein reminds us that the "concept of 'property' was put forward by the courts as a fiction to rationalize a form of legal relief which was really founded on other grounds of policy."[22] As we are just beginning to learn with regard to the problem of corporate speech, legal fictions such as "corporate personhood" take on a life of their own and do great damage to the underlying values, which at one point seemed to require such a fiction for their preservation.[23] Unlike the courts and scholars who must have seen the point as incidental, Bloustein argues that the starting point for the explication of a privacy interest was to be found in Warren and Brandeis's reference to "inviolate personality," which deals with "the individual's independence, dignity and integrity; it defines man's essence as a unique and self-determining being."[24]

Now defining the essence of humankind is heady stuff. But that is indeed Bloustein's self-imposed charge. He understands Warren and Brandeis's motivation to be derived from a fear that "a rampant press feeding on the stuff of private life would destroy individual dignity and integrity and emasculate individual freedom and independence."[25] On his way toward the explication of this interest, Bloustein mounts an assault on Prosser and the received wisdom of the American

Law Institute by finding the dignity interest in each of the torts that have come to define privacy since 1890.

With regard to intrusion, Bloustein argues that the injury is not mental or emotional distress, but rather the fact that intrusions are "demeaning to individuality ... an affront to personal dignity." If a person is not able to determine who does and does not have access to the realms that they define as their own, they are by definition less than whole. Another individual who is able to enter unbidden must be seen to have superior power, and if the entry is pursued with apparent legitimacy, they must also be assumed to be of higher status and worth. In Bloustein's words, "He who may intrude on another at will is the master of the other."[26] Bloustein also suggests that there is a distinction without a difference when the intruder is an agent of the state rather than another private citizen—the wrong, a challenge to the liberty of the individual, is still the same even though the power of the actors may differ substantially.

With regard to the disclosure of private facts, Bloustein rejects the distillation by Prosser of the privacy interest into a concern with reputation. An injury to reputation evaporates if the public response is sympathetic and understanding. Yet Bloustein argues that the affront to dignity remains. The essence of the affront is to be found in the fact that publication allows not one but perhaps thousands to join the intruder at the window peering in on the private experience of either joy or suffering. Both are intrusions; only the means are different. "The wrong is in replacing personal anonymity by notoriety, in turning a private life into a public spectacle."[27] A public figure loses much independence and becomes subject to the claims and demands of the public. People on the street address movie stars and demand the attention of public figures as if they knew them personally. The kind of face-to-face intimacy that films and television provide explains this forwardness, in part. The majority of public figures may be understood to have exchanged part of their individuality for what they believe to be greater financial rewards. However, public disclosure, by mass communication or networked virtual memory, creates a public person without the benefit of prior consent; indeed, such transformations of personhood frequently involve coercion.

Commercial exploitation, the third tort identified by Prosser, has been the most damaging point of departure from the underlying thesis of Warren and Brandeis. When one's image, profile, or personality is appropriated and used by another without warrant, it is the victim's liberty or freedom to decide that it has been abridged. Rather than focus on the negligible proprietary interest that might inhere to such a threat, Bloustein argues that commercial exploitation represents the same insult embodied in the disclosure of private facts. "In the public disclosure cases what is demeaning to individuality is being made a public spectacle by disclosure of private intimacies. In these cases what is demeaning and humiliating is the commercialization of an aspect of personality."[28] The threat to liberty that is at the heart of this insult is that some part (intangible though it may be) of a person is *taken* and then *used* by another without permission. To focus the tort on pecuniary value essentially eliminates the possibility of pursuing successful claims on behalf of average citizens because the value of their images in the market is insignificant—they have no market power. The cases of public figures, in which there may be identifiable, measurable, indeed substantial, economic rents associated with their claims of proprietary interest, should not be allowed to distort or distract attention from the primary concern with misappropriations that generate harm in the taking.

Jonathan Graham cites the case of *Shilbey v. Time, Inc.* as an example of a case in which the tort of appropriation was inadequately pursued, but he concludes that its impact would have been minor in any event because the definition of the tort had been limited to commercial exploitation in relation to product endorsement.[29] In *Shilbey,* the petitioner claimed that the sale of subscription lists constituted an invasion of privacy because the information about the plaintiff's personality that might be inferred from such a list was the equivalent of an image, or likeness, not unlike that provided by a photograph or an artist's rendering. The fact that it was transferred to another party without permission made it an actionable appropriation. Unfortunately, the argument in the case clouded the issue by suggesting that the harm came by way of resultant appeals and solicitations from others interested in reaching a consumer with such apparent qualities. An earlier decision in *Lamont v. Commissioner of Motor Vehicles* had introduced this distraction by arguing that the solicitations that flowed from the sale (by New York state) of information from automobile registrations represented the privacy loss (seclusion), rather than the loss of control over personal information (appropriation and transfer), which is at the heart of the issue.[30] Although subsequent harms *may* flow from an unauthorized disclosure of private facts, the courts have erred by focusing on this, rather than on the initial action, which is the primary breach.

In a most insightful passage, Bloustein argues that the "right of publicity," which has emerged to respond to the proprietary interests of those with saleable images, is itself dependent on a prior recognition of a right of privacy. In his view, "Name and likeness can only begin to command a commercial price in a society which recognizes that there is a ... right to control the conditions under which name and likeness may be used. Property becomes a commodity subject to be bought and sold only where the community will enforce an individual's right to maintain use and possession of it against the world."[31]

Thus, following Bloustein's argument, there is truly no right of publicity, but only the right to demand a fee for not enforcing one's right to privacy.[32] Just as the disclosure of private facts may bring sympathy rather than scorn, Bloustein notes that commercial use may bring fame, compensation, and other benefits that the subject may actually value and enjoy. Many drivers who have been convicted of driving while under the influence of alcohol actually appear to have been pleased that a firm that makes portable "breathalyzers" was able to identify them through court records and sell them a device that would help them to determine when the alcohol in their system exceeds the legal limit.[33] Yet, this arguably positive outcome does not overcome Bloustein's objection that, however beneficent the motive or successful the result, the "touching" is considered wrongful because without consent, it represents a threat to the freedom of the individual to decide.

Perhaps we have been led to consider with amusement the fears of native peoples that a camera would steal their spirit, yet there is much here to treat seriously. It is a peculiarity of information that I have discussed, that one can *take* or possess information from someone without denying that person further use of that information. There is still a *taking* that has to be considered and evaluated. The emphasis on exploitation is focused on how that which was taken has been used. The presumption is that some "takings" do not give rise to injury unless the harm is to reputation. Yet I join Bloustein in arguing that that which is taken by the "peeping Tom" or the intruder is inherent in the taking itself. This theft of personal dignity inheres in the right to decide, the right to control access to the person.

Clearly, such taking is commonplace in the perception and apperception of others whenever we encounter or observe them in public spaces. Such taking moves to an invasion of privacy when the observation occurs in a space defined as private by the individual. Yet developments in technology that allow the experience of such taking to be repeated, to be reviewed at leisure, and perhaps to be extended to others change the nature of the contract that is implied when individuals enter and pursue their interests in a public space. What is suggested here is that if people thought that more than fleeting and imperfect memory might be involved in the taking of their image through the unaided glance, then greater reserve would characterize behavior in so-called public spaces.

The "false light" cases represent the fourth and perhaps most easily disposed class of torts that Bloustein recasts through the lens of individual dignity. It is simply the case that the use of *any* representation of a person without consent is an abuse of personality, whether the representation is accurate or distorted. Bloustein rejects Prosser's economistic emphasis on the assumption of a proprietary interest that is threatened by distortion. As noted, the economic value of the interests of the broad mass of the public is treated as *individually* insignificant by the market, and because of this, its force in the regime of tort injury is negligible. Here, as with commercial use, the law of defamation is seen to benefit from the law of privacy once it is understood to be based on an interest in human dignity.

After dispensing with the distortions inherent in the limitation of privacy to torts, Bloustein turns his attention to the substantial area of privacy law that is found in state constitutions, statutes, and nontort decisions under common law. He notes the statutory prohibitions against peeping Tomism, including the use of more sophisticated technical means, and the prohibitions on the disclosure of confidential information. In noting that the very collection of personal information that is required for access to the benefits of government represents an impairment of privacy, Bloustein concludes, perhaps a bit too hastily, that "most of us have agreed, however, that the social benefits to be gained ... are worth the price of diminished privacy."[34] He seeks to retrieve part of his lost ground, in my estimation, by suggesting that the expectation in such exchanges of information is that the use of the information will be limited to the purposes for which it was gathered. Although a popular demand, this is a naive hope. We recognize that the purpose of the state is comprehensive, and therefore, all information becomes relevant if it can somehow, now or in the future, be used to further a legitimate state interest. The corporate interest is no less expansive.

To conclude Bloustein's contribution to our understanding of informational privacy, I note his emphasis on the question of means. If the fundamental value that is to be preserved is captured by the concepts of dignity and individuality, what makes privacy different from other actions that threaten those values are the *means* that are used to gain access or weaken control. The "character of the interference" with individual liberty helps to define invasions of privacy.[35]

ALL OF THIS AND DEMOCRACY TOO?

Spiros Simitis makes it clear that the pursuit of privacy as an index of individual autonomy is incompatible with egalitarian or communitarian forms of democracy.[36] In his view, the claims made for a legally guaranteed protection of privacy, at least with regard to protection from the state, are of a kind with the liberal pursuit of personal, private benefit, without concern or responsibility to any collectivity. "The more, therefore, that privacy is equated with a deliberate and legally protected seclusion of the individual, the more the right to be let alone develops into an impediment to the transparency necessary for a democratic decisionmaking process. As long as the data required to understand and evaluate the political and economic process are withheld, suppressed, or falsified, participation remains a pure fiction."[37] Yet Simitis is fully aware that the routinized systems of bureaucratic surveillance operate not to produce a kind of transparency that facilitates democratic participation, but instead to produce a *legitimate* demand for more privacy. The rational desire of individuals to avoid disclosure is based in part on the limitations they face in gaining the information *they* need to evaluate the relevant environment, including the environment in which they are expected to provide informed consent for the collection and use of personal information. In this environment, a privacy regime does not guarantee participatory democracy but rather enhanced protection of the interests of the elites who are better able to negotiate the panoptic maze.

A COMPLEX OF INFORMATIONAL RIGHTS

One way in which the goals of autonomous self-development may be realized in the context of a formal social structure is through the development of a regime of rights that establishes the limitations on freedom that are necessary so that the exercise of one person's freedom does not unjustly limit the freedom of another.

This emphasis on informational privacy leads quite naturally to a consideration of a regime of informational rights as guaranteed by a democratic state.

Anne Branscomb has made an important contribution to understanding the competing claims and rationales that complicate efforts to establish such a regime of rights.[38] Each of ten broad rights she identifies can be seen to involve a matter of "balancing equities and sensibilities that often defy codification."[39] The "right to know" may be seen as primary, beginning with the right to know oneself. The right to know about one's environment includes the right to know about the risks and opportunities one faces and the qualities of goods and services that one might acquire. This right to know is believed to be essential for the smooth and efficient operation of the market and the political system as well. However, this right is clearly limited.

One limitation is to be found in the procedural limitations on a "right to collect information." In order to know, *someone* must have a right to collect information. Yet Branscomb suggests that the right to collect information is reserved primarily to government, although we would do well to follow Foucault and note that a great many professionals have also been "qualified" and privileged by the state to collect information. The distinction that clarifies this right is related to the extent to which coercion or force can be used to compel disclosure. By withholding services until approval is given for a particular investigation or search, organizations restrict individual liberty to some degree. The difference between public and private investigations is that agencies of government exercise those access rights by means of the rule of law and the ultimate threat of force, rather than through the mechanism of an explicit or implied contract governing the exchange of value in the market. Private actors exercise these investigational rights through the exercise of economic or social power—the same power involved in shaping, defining, and extending or limiting rights as circumstances change.

Branscomb's distinction between the right to collect and the right to acquire information is subtle but is worth noting. The right to acquire information is the right of equal access to information that has been collected by others authorized to do so. The right to education might be interpreted as a right of access to accumulated knowledge as information. Underlying her conception of access as a right is a specification of a certain class of information as a public resource. The public nature of this information derives in part from the use of public funds or legislated advantage in some stage of its production or in the protection of its producer's market position.[40] The privatization of government information represents a reduction in the public's right to demand access to information that may have been produced at public expense.[41]

Branscomb defines a "personal right to privacy" as a right of individuals to withhold information about themselves, that is, to restrict access to personal information. This right is a limitation on the right of others to collect or even to gain access to information. Thus the right to privacy may be seen to limit the right to know when knowledge of the other is necessary if one is to pursue an interaction or relationship with that person. Although Branscomb indicates some doubt that this right is an expression of some long-standing and fundamental instinct, its position as a right with both moral and legal status cannot be denied. In Branscomb's view, the creation of formal rights or limitations on inquiry follows very closely the changing assessments of the sensitivity or the potential for harm that would follow from disclosure. Presumably, restrictions would evaporate as soon as consequentiality was diminished beyond some socially determined level of tolerance. It might be argued, for example, that questions about the nature of one's sexual preference would no longer be restricted once society achieves some level of tolerance of homosexuality and gay life-styles.[42]

Branscomb notes that businesses are able to protect their trade secrets under a broad blanket of legislative and judge-made law. I agree with those who suggest that corporations are not truly persons and thus ought not to be considered to have rights of privacy. Yet similar instrumental concern with the consequentiality of disclosure is at the heart of trade secret protections. Branscomb includes within this category of trade-related protections the shield laws, which allow journalists to resist attempts by others to learn their sources. Yet we also should note the growing exceptions to corporate privacy that are inherent in the privileging of the public's right to know about the dangers that corporate operations represent.[43]

If individuals exercise a right to prevent access to personal information, they may also choose to provide access but reserve the right to limit the sharing or disclosure of that information to others. Branscomb includes in this specification of rights the problematic sharing of personal information that is produced through commercial transactions. Another right, the "right to protect information," is more directly linked to an effort to define and classify different kinds of information and the limitations that might be placed on disclosure. Government documents provide a model in that they can be stamped or classified as sensitive, confidential, secret, top secret, and so on, and their distribution can be restricted to persons qualified through classification as well as by "need to know." Similar classifications of personal information are made within organizations that handle information of varying sensitivity.

However, it is not until she begins to define a "right to control the release of information" that we begin to see the emergence of the concept of information as property. In *United States v. Miller,* the U.S. Supreme Court held that individuals had no legitimate interest in their bank records, which were required of the banks by the Bank Secrecy Act.[44] The government's interest in identifying criminal activity, including tax avoidance through its examination of bank transaction records, had resulted in the passage of a federal record-keeping requirement. Because the bank was keeping the records to meet the requirements of the government and not at the request of the depositor, the court argued that, without an interest, there could be no expectation of privacy in those records. Individuals were put on notice that they place themselves at risk when they enter into a business relationship that involves the surrender of personal information, that this information might be shared with the government. The dissent by Justice William O. Douglas in a related case is notable for its prescience, if not for its utility in limiting access to information. Douglas recognized that "a person is defined by the checks he writes. By examining them the agents get to know his doctors, lawyers, creditors, political allies, social connections, religious affiliation, educational interests, the papers and magazines he reads, and so on *ad infinitum*."[45] Persons are similarly known by their telephone call records, their videotape rentals, their magazine subscriptions, and their accumulated and detailed credit card transactions. Demonstrating a legitimate interest and a privacy expectation in such data pools is the goal that *Miller* helped to frustrate.

Branscomb's recognition of a commercial property interest emerges primarily through her notice that actors who have been given the right to collect personal information for one purpose have sought to transform the informational products of that transaction into marketable goods in a way that exceeds the rights of access. She extends the definition of this right of control to include a corollary right to "release information at a time or place of one's choosing."[46] Presumably the exercise of this right involves a legally binding constraint on any agent that has been given the right to make the information public. The timing of the release of information can be seen to have significant economic consequences. The successful exploitation of property interests in entertainment products such as theatrical films depends in part on the ability of distributors to control and coordinate their release in theaters, via cable, via videotape, and finally through broadcast television.

The property interest in personal information is made explicit in the right she defines as "the right to profit from information." However, her discussion in this area is almost entirely limited to questions of intellectual property, except for the novel discussion of the commercialization of personal histories or memoirs. The fact that exceptions have emerged to limit the realization of profit from popularization of illegality suggests a variety of social interest rationales on which such limitations might be based.[47]

Concerns about personal information emerge again in Branscomb's discussion of "the right to destroy or expunge information" in the records or files of others. Concerns about "freeze dried" criminal records that provide a representation of individuals as they were, not as they are today or as they might become in the future, are at the basis of this claim. It is similar to the claim of a "right to correct or alter information" in the files or records of others.

Finally, the right to know is linked to the right to speak, or in her words, the "right to disseminate information." The right of access to information about oneself and one's environment is argued to be limited if there is not also a right of access to the means through which that understanding can be communicated to others. Making this link between the right to know and the right to speak links all the informational rights into a system of governance that we have come to call democratic. Conflicts about the extent to which these rights are to be limited to natural persons and citizens or will extend to fictional persons and others granted rights of national treatment remain the source of conflict with regard to informational privacy in ways similar to conflicts about intellectual property.[48]

INFORMATION PRIVACY AND CORPORATE SPEECH

As Branscomb's review of rights suggests, there are a number of tensions between rights that have no inherent priority, except those that might privilege the rights of individuals over the rights of corporations. Robert Posch, as a representative of the interests of the direct marketing industry, claims that the industry's most powerful legal stance in the debate over informational rights is one that argues that the primary constitutional issue is one of free speech, rather than one of individual privacy.[49] Posch takes as a given that which is still controversial in some admittedly limited circles, that corporations have First Amendment rights. Limitations on corporate speech are seen in any restriction imposed by state action on a firm's ability to sell customer lists, which these firms wish to define as speech. Given that the information in lists is primarily factual, First Amendment claims represent a powerful argument, as Posch and his colleagues have come to recognize. Tort restrictions on the commercial disclosure of private facts have been limited in practice by both extent and public interest exceptions. It is also the case that the distribution of lists may not be seen as publication, limited as they are to a select group with a legitimate business interest. It might be seen as a different matter, however, if feminists, for example, rented space on a bulletin board and published a list of local citizens, public figures, and "average Joes" who had subscriptions to *Penthouse* or were frequent callers to a sexually oriented phone service.[50]

At the moment, the courts still have not erased *all* distinctions between commercial and other forms of protected speech. C. Edwin Baker discusses commercial speech as a problem in the theory of freedom that helps us to understand the remaining gaps.[51] Although we might wish to make a distinction between commercial speech that seeks to inform or influence consumers with regard to a product or service and the forms of speech involved in the sale of personal information in the form of lists, it is not a distinction that serves well. Baker argues that commercial speech, as it relates to advertising, is at least as important as other forms of speech in terms of its influence on how we understand and act in the world. Such a position with regard to commercial and other forms of speech makes sense, he argues, in the context of a marketplace logic where ideas are allowed to "compete," and superior ideas, like superior products, win in the long run. If, however, commercial speech is viewed through the lens of a "liberty theory" of the sort he prefers, a rather different conclusion is seen to emerge.

The liberty theory, as Baker presents it, focuses on the interests of the speaker and her or his choice to speak, rather than on some assessment of the usefulness of the content of the speech to a listener or to listeners in general. Whereas usefulness is relative and broadly conditioned, individual liberty is more broadly absolute.

Because the pursuit of profit is a purpose imposed by the market, commercial speech within the marketplace is distinguishable from the speech of individuals, which is used for expressing an almost unlimited variety of perspectives on individuality and self. The expression of self is, of course, preferred to the pursuit of profit within markets.[52]

Baker's posture on human liberty thus finds commercial speech wanting because of its limited instrumental purpose. Commercial speech seeks to influence the realization of profit by modifying individual preferences. This purpose is in conflict and is perhaps even incompatible with the value of self-determination. Therefore, the "very values of respect for human autonomy and self-determination that require the first amendment necessitate that commercial speech be subject to collective, political control."[53] He argues, further, that when a given activity is subject to regulation and the conduct of business is clearly and necessarily regulated, it follows that speech that is an integral part of that activity should also be subject to regulation in pursuit of the same public interests.[54] Thus the regulation of lists as commercial speech might reasonably be pursued on behalf of the legitimate and demonstrated state interest in preserving individual privacy.

WHO'S THE ENEMY HERE?

Privacy, rather than being seen as a state that one might seek to attain, may be seen as a protection *against* unwarranted access or disclosure. We invest in protections against threats. The character of the protections must reflect in some way the character of the threats. The nature of the defense is determined in part by the nature of the attack. The nature of the attack, although about this I am less certain, may reflect the nature of the attacker and the means that are chosen. The choice of means may reflect the power and the power differential between the actor who seeks access and the individual who seeks to limit it. Kenneth Laudon suggests that "privacy is a value which describes a power relationship between individuals and organizations. This relationship can be seen as a continuum marked on one side by complete informational moral supremacy of the individual, and on the other by complete supremacy of the organization and its needs for efficiency and survival."[55] I cannot, however, envision a single continuum, because organizations differ from each other in important ways in terms of the nature of their threats to privacy. Comparisons of industrial nations suggest that aspects of their people's history have influenced how the citizenry of different nations depart from each other in terms of their fear of the state, rather than of the private firm, with regard to personal information.

Priscilla Regan suggests that ordinarily we might expect that a distinction would be made between public and private bureaucracies and that private bureaucracies would be regulated more severely because these actors would not enjoy the same level of legitimacy that agencies of the state are assumed to command.[56] She notes that, instead, the exact converse is true—the bureaucracies of the state have been constrained more completely in most Western democracies.

John Bennett suggests that part of the difficulty that characterizes the development of a privacy policy in Western democracies is the fact that there is "no identifiable external group which receives a cost or benefit from the production of the policy"; because of this, there is no clientele or constituency for such a policy.[57] No politician sees her or his long-term future to be dependent on satisfying a demand that is so poorly articulated. Flaherty also sees this problem of the identifiability of interests at the base of legislative confusion and inactivity because it "is very difficult to demonstrate need in the commonsense way that Congress requires. This is the particular bane of the sectoral approach to sectoral protection, since it is too hard to document the necessary horror stories without holding full-scale investigations of a particular sector."[58] The problem of "identifying the culprit," on the one hand, is reflected in the development of legislative protections against excesses, rather than an affirmative effort to protect fundamental rights and freedoms. On the other hand, the bureaucracies of the modern state, both public and private, find that privacy, however defined, represents an obstacle to the pursuit of their organizational missions.

Protections Against the State

The passage of the Privacy Act of 1974, the primary instrument for regulating the information practices of federal government agencies in the United States, is thought to have been a response to the excesses linked to President Richard Nixon after Watergate. David Linowes reports that there were some 3.5 million personal files that federal agencies maintained on U.S. citizens,[59] and he cites a National Bureau of Standards report that outlined the informational abuses that would shock the nation further when the extent of the abuses was revealed in the Senate intelligence hearings coordinated by Frank Church.[60]

Political surveillance is a readily understandable concern. Much has been written about the need to limit such uses of state power. The administrative use of surveillance by the state is less closely studied, although the interests of the state are barely distinguishable from the interests of corporate bureaucracies in this regard. Flaherty finds it ironic that the Reagan administration paid so little attention to privacy, in that "the protection of the individual from various forms of government intrusion is surely a conservative issue."[61] What Flaherty misses in this ironic glance is that conservative concerns about privacy were easily subordinated to concerns about efficiency and the administration's program to "eliminate waste, fraud, and abuse" in government through the use of matching, profiling, and a host of other privacy-threatening technologies that would be focused on the poor and at the lower reaches of the middle class.

The ability of the government to avoid the restrictive intent of the Privacy Act through its use of administrative exceptions, such as those that defined restricted data sharing as "routine," simply exemplifies the problems inherent in self-regulation.[62] As Flaherty noted in 1984 with regard to the OMB, the executive branch organization charged with oversight of the Privacy Act: "OMB is doing nothing on the policy side of privacy. It would not be unfair to say that OMB is and has been essentially uninterested in privacy issues. It views its role under the Privacy Act as one of balancing interests, not on behalf of privacy but in favor of the needs of government. This is a very limiting factor from a privacy perspective, since OMB is hardly an impartial arm of the executive branch."[63]

The potential threats to privacy that were inherent in the administrative use of matching were identified early in their history.[64] Eventually these issues made their way through a series of congressional hearings only to result in the legitimation of the very practices that early critics had claimed were barred by the Privacy Act. In her testimony before the House committee hearings on matching, ACLU staff attorney Janlori Goldman noted that the bill "does not impose any subtantive limits on matching programs."[65] Yet she expressed support for the proposed bill because it would "enhance privacy and due process rights of citizens who are the subject of matching and verification programs." Thus a program of questionable efficiency in terms of dollars saved for dollars expended, but of unquestionable (although unmeasurable) costs in terms of the loss of privacy to the millions who would be matched routinely, was supported by one of the chief advocates for consumer privacy rights. It seems naive to believe that the hundreds of thousands of citizens subject to surveillance through matching of their records would be regularly scanning the Federal Register to note that a match was about to occur. That they could do little about it anyway would make the awareness of an impending match even more costly. To compound the error, the ACLU recommendations sought to further define as a legitimate *justification* for a match, "evidence" from a benefit/cost study that only *projects* likely outcomes. That is like expecting investor-seeking producers to project next year's earnings. Referring to this testimony in particular, Flaherty appears to share its logic and its measure of the legislative pulse: "The new law emphasizes due process and administrative goals, including analysis of costs and benefits, rather than concentrating on privacy and surveillance issues. This reflects a shrewd political assessment of how best to persuade Congress to act."[66] As we shall see, this second best solution is replicated time and time again as privacy advocates have attempted to control private bureaucracies.

Protections Against the Corporation

The critical and perhaps most problematic aspects of the balancing of interests that set the interests of the individual against the interests of the organization are to be found in the expression and development of the concept of a "legitimate business interest." As discussed in the previous chapter, there is a general willingness within the population to allow business to gather the information it needs in order to make business-related decisions. There is considerable variance, however, in the belief that business will limit its information gathering to that which is truly necessary. Differences begin to emerge when inquiries are made about whether employers, insurers, vendors, or government agencies should be limited in the kinds of information they can ask for directly. Researchers have yet to fully explore what people see as limitations on the kinds of investigations that these organizations might pursue to collect information from third parties. It is clear, as I have noted, that the relative ease and marginal expense that allow organizations to search, sort, match, and acquire information from discrete, independent, and remote databases serve to increase the amount of such information demanded. The only constraint appears to be the definition of what is a legitimate business interest.

The development of rights and privileges for corporations, including the development of the fiction of the corporate person, can be seen to have had a justification in the broader common, or public, interest. For society to enjoy the economic benefits that the corporate form could provide, it was believed that incentives had to be provided to individuals to encourage the use of the corporate form. Herbert Hovenkamp suggests that a concern with growth was a dominant force in the early days in U.S. history, and this concern can be seen in the development of laws involving contracts, debts, and eventually the rights associated with the corporate form.[67] The American model, which Hovenkamp refers to as classical political economy, was vintage trickle-down theory: Make the society wealthy, and the wealth of individuals will thereby be achieved in due course.

Hovenkamp suggests that the ideological position of the leadership in the U.S. government changed from the preclassical federalist orientation of Alexander Hamilton, which supported an active role for the state in the development of the economy, to the classical laissez faire vision of Andrew Jackson, which warned of the dangers of monopoly power. The government might avoid such dangers at the same time it realized the benefits of incorporation through an emphasis on "the public purpose" as a rationale for whatever privileges a monopoly grant might entail.

Some of these advantages included the privilege of limited liability. Morton J. Horwitz suggests that a tension between the logic of the law and the logic of the natural sciences with regard to causation and responsibility was at its height around the turn of the century. The challenge for the law was to establish a basis for understanding the extent to which a chain of causality could indicate a line of responsibility for injuries. Entrepreneurial energies might be diminished if there was an absence of "foreseeability" in the limits of liability.[68] Contemporary risk analysis can be seen to be a further response to these issues, and such analyses increase the demand for information.[69]

Although the U.S. Supreme Court in *Tureen v. Equifax* suggested that there might be abuses of privacy through unreasonable intrusion by corporations, it was still believed that "in order to make informed judgements in these matters, it may be necessary for the decision maker to have information which normally would be considered private, provided the information is legitimately related to a legitimate purpose of the decision maker. In such a case, the public interest provides the defendant a shield which is similar in principle to qualified privilege in libel."[70] Neither this court nor others have fully considered the tension between business interests and what might be claimed as more basic individual interests in privacy.

Susan Gardner[71] explored the privacy interests inherent in the use of a variety of techniques, many of them of questionable reliability, to assess the honesty of employees or persons who were candidates for employment.[72] Such examinations are criticized because they are intrusive and because they are an affront to the dignity of an individual. The definition of "honesty" is categorical rather than empirical. That is, a score is assigned to an individual on the basis of a test or measurement exercise, whether an electronic analog, such as provided by a polygraph, or a more theoretical abstraction of the sort generated by a paper and pencil test. An individual's score is then compared with the distribution of some normative scale, and the location of that score is the basis of an employment decision. Individuals who want a job or who want to keep the one they have are without a meaningful option. Their refusal to take a requested but voluntary test may be interpreted as evidence of dishonesty or disloyalty. They are, therefore, compelled to surrender their privacy. They are made to suffer an indignity at the same time that they are compelled to answer questions that frequently bear no identifiable relationship to their ability to perform a job.

Restrictions on the use of polygraphs or other tests of employees raise critical questions about the possibility of establishing general standards that would specify which questions and which means of gaining access to personal information ought to be barred as a matter of policy. If we accept, as a matter of course, that employers have a right to know the qualities of persons whom they consider for employment (and indeed, we may have imposed on employers a requirement to know to avoid legal liability for irresponsible hiring), then we face a contradiction.[73] By restricting the collection of information that employers consider to be relevant by form or content, we increase their need for information that reveals these qualities only indirectly but may in consequence provide insights into other, previously uninteresting aspects of personhood.

SENSITIVE INFORMATION

Raymond Wacks's contribution to this problem is to identify what he calls "sensitive information." From his position, the general failure of the law of privacy is a failure to identify the types of information that are most in need of protection.[74] Thus, Wacks's emphasis is on content rather than means. He notes that the definitions of these areas of sensitivity are culturally determined and therefore vary significantly within and between nations. For example, income appears to be much less sensitive in the Scandinavian countries than it would be in Great Britain or in the United States.[75]

The notion of sensitivity has great value if we consider the concern about linkage. Identification by itself is usually not problematic. It is the linkage of reliable identification with a sensitive measure, such as sexual orientation or political affiliation, that raises privacy concerns. The most difficult aspect involved in developing a measure of sensitivity is a recognition that there are also individual differences in sensitivity or concern about aspects of personhood.

Even though Wacks claims that his scalar is based on an assessment of the "potential for serious harm to the subject," it must be recognized that even this is a relative measure.[76] Standards of reasonableness, or average person standards, are inadequate by definition because no person can be precisely average; they must be at least fractionally more or less than average. It is not at all clear what kind of rules of thumb, or even empirically validated standards, we might develop. It should be clear, however, that an explicit, socially developed standard would be more democratic than standards that currently evolve in the narrow vision of elite jurists.

Wacks uses the kinds of data normally held by public and private agencies in Great Britain to create twelve different categories of information. The categories include: biographical information and data about the home, family relationships, employment, finances, health, education, ideology, police, habits, leisure activities and travel, and communication. Within each of these categories, Wacks then assigns ratings indicating one of three levels of sensitivity: low, medium, or high. Although Wacks is to be applauded for the diligence with which he developed his list, I am sure that many will find much to argue with in his ratings. For example, none of the travel and communication categories receive a rating of high sensitivity. Telephone numbers contacted, newspaper subscriptions, periodical subscriptions, and books borrowed from libraries or purchased from book clubs are all classified as being similarly sensitive, and all of them less sensitive than information about the "frequency of sexual intercourse with spouse." If the basis for such a sensitivity rating is the potential for harm to the data subject, the nature of the harm in this category escapes me, at least when compared with the potential harm from inferences drawn from reading records. Similarly, data about past voting behavior are identified as being highly sensitive, as are sixteen out of thirty items listed under medical information.

In addition to the problems in assigning ratings to individual items of information, which Wacks recognizes as problematic, the use of such a scale would also need to explore the possibility that empirical sensitivity would vary as information from different categories is combined.[77] Thus an image of an individual that might be generated from information about communication, address, and employment could easily exceed the sensitivity level of a single item of information about the regularity of sexual activity with one's spouse. Furthermore, the correlations between measures suggest the very real possibility that limitations on access to one source of information do not truly limit access to the knowledge or intelligence that information would provide. Consider the following argument.

Richard Posner's analysis of privacy rights emphasizes the interests of individuals in concealing "information about themselves which others might use to their disadvantage."[78] On the face of it, this is a concern with sensitive information as Wacks defines it. The neoclassical posture that Posner reflects seems to assume the absence of any moral or social limits on the pursuit of those interests.[79] Thus Posner assumes that "people want privacy in order to manipulate other people by concealing from them aspects of their character, prospects, or past that would if known reduce their opportunities to engage in advantageous market or nonmarket transactions."[80] He claims that discrimination on the basis of race and gender reflects little more than a rational response to the costs of acquiring more reliable information about performance. Because the mean of a population is the best estimate of any individual's score, selection among groups is thought to be made on estimates of mean group performance.[81]

As the association between disadvantageous information and life chances is explored further, Posner's analysis leads him to conclude that privacy legislation is designed primarily to limit discrimination against identifiable groups who share in common several disqualifying attributes or qualities. Privacy legislation, as he sees it, forbids the use of such information in specific economic decisions. Privacy legislation limits the panoptic sort and is therefore inefficient on its face. Posner reports finding a correlation between a state's presumed interest in limiting racial discrimination and the number of statutes in that state that protect individual privacy.[82] Posner concludes, with some insight, that the ban on discrimination by race or gender will have little effect so long as those who wish to discriminate can identify correlates of race and gender that predict mean performance just as well. It is this insight, that the panoptic sort is capable of finding analogues or indexes that serve the same function as more politically or socially sensitive indicators, that weakens the long-term utility of any definition of classes of information as being more or less sensitive. Robert Posch actually defines efforts to restrict the use of credit histories as being contrary to the interests of historic civil rights legislation, precisely because it would force the industry back to a policy of geographical redlining.[83] When barred from using one form of information, decision makers will pursue the second best solution, which might involve using additional information sources.

However, when the socially conditioned association between indicators is quite strong, barring the use of a particular indicator may, in the short run, increase the benefits enjoyed by a particular group. That is, barring the use of information about bankruptcies or prison records may allow more African-Americans to gain employment and credit because of the high proportion of black people with such problems.[84] However, Posner concludes further that *any* restrictions on the nature and amount of information that employers or creditors might gather represents a negative-sum game for society as a whole because "the effect of such statutes on the public as a whole is to increase the amount of fraud in society, raise interest rates, and reduce business productivity."[85]

This final analysis of Posner's ignores the social costs that result from the real discrimination that is allowed to continue, even in the face of restrictions on the use of some categories of personal information. Empirical evidence of racial discrimination continues to mount, yet analysts claim to be unable to identify which inputs into the panoptic sort are responsible for the resultant pattern. An examination by the Federal Reserve Board of the limited success that African-Americans and other minorities experienced in obtaining home mortgages in 1991 revealed a striking pattern of discrimination.[86] Minorities were denied mortgages two and three times more often than whites. The logical assumption that differences were explained by income did not stand up to scrutiny. In fact, when income was held constant, the apparent discrimination actually increased, producing even greater disparities at the upper-income levels. Not even creditworthiness might explain the differences, because credit reports are being used increasingly as prescreening tools, and therefore applicants with poor records are not even shown a home in the first place. Because utilities and other service providers have begun making reports to credit agencies as soon as bills become delinquent, a great number of African-Americans find themselves shut out of the housing market even before they begin. Thus, something other than income or creditworthiness predicts or explains the failure of African-American consumers to acquire mortgages. It is clear for any who would care to look that race, or an index of race, whatever its form, was being used to disqualify any but the most exceptional applicants for loans.

REASONABLE EXPECTATIONS
AND THE DESTRUCTIVE GALES OF TECHNOLOGY

Among the many insights that Spiros Simitis has provided, one of the most influential and troubling is his linkage of privacy to the realization of an active democratic state. "Neither freedom of speech nor freedom of association nor freedom of assembly can be fully exercised as long as it remains uncertain whether, under what circumstances, and for what purposes, personal information is collected and processed."[87] The realization that such uncertainty might be resolved through the recognition that there may be no limits, because there are no longer any reasonable expectations of privacy, does not, of course, engender great joy. Yet, as will be seen, the U.S. Supreme Court has moved actively and aggressively to narrow the limits of reasonableness.

Laurence Benner suggests that the decline in the scope of reasonableness in recent years has been dramatic in comparison with most of the years that have passed since the ratification of the Fourth Amendment.[88] Although the Fourth Amendment was concerned fundamentally with the control of the federal government, the right formalized a principle that might apply to each and every institution with the power to impose its will on individuals. The amendment defined a right of security against unreasonable search and seizure and specified further that warrants governing such searches must be specific and demonstrate probable cause. However, the reasonableness clause soon became separated from the warrant clause, and each became weakened on its own.[89] In its early stages of demise, the reasonableness clause became balanced against an indication of state interest. "If the government's need to intrude outweighed the citizen's privacy interest infringed by the intrusion, then the instrusion was 'reasonable' and did not violate the Fourth Amendment."[90]

Benner charges the Rehnquist Court with making the most far-reaching excursions into the privacy realm through its rulings on the appropriateness of drug and alcohol tests of employees without the requirement of an assumption of probable cause. All that was necessary for the search of persons or property was the successful claim that there was a legitimate public interest, such as the safety of rail passengers or the smooth operation of public agencies. Furthermore, it appeared that little more than the concern with "efficiency" and "convenience" was needed to justify a search. If this same court allows the search of one's trash, when a truly reasonable expectation would be that it becomes mixed with the trash of hundreds of others and that the link to a particular household is forever lost, then there is little basis for expecting that such a court would keep the government from searching through the residue or "trash" that is the computerized record of the hundreds and thousands of transactions we make as we go about our daily lives.[91]

In the case of *Skinner v. Railway Labor Executive's Association*[92] this hardening court suggests that even the most invasive of techniques, involving the taking of blood or the supervised collection of urine, raised privacy interests that could be subordinated to "the government's 'special interest' in ensuring rail safety."[93] But invasiveness as a test does not hold against the assault of reasonableness of expectations, which crumbles in the wake of technological advance.

Benner credits the ruling in the case of *Katz v. United States* with developing the line of argument that he believes has resulted in the total loss of Fourth Amendment protection.[94] If it is possible to argue that no "search" actually took place, then there can be no claim of a Fourth Amendment issue. No search under the Fourth Amendment has occurred if the court determines that no reasonable citizen could have expected privacy interests to survive inspection. In *Katz*, the court concluded that an individual had no reasonable expectation of privacy in a public telephone booth, aware as he or she must be that the police have access to and are likely to utilize surveillance devices that would allow them to listen in on at least one side of a conversation made from a public telephone. Similarly, a California court would follow this logic and rule that a citizen could not have a reasonable expectation of privacy in his backyard, 10-foot fence or not, because it was clear that airplanes and helicopters fly overhead and could take pictures of things, like marijuana plants, growing in a backyard.[95] By leaving it up to the judges to determine the reasonableness of expectations and by placing the burden on the defendant to convince them otherwise, the requirements of the Fourth Amendment simply evaporate. Thus, Benner argues, "The Court's refusal to conceptualize privacy as a power to control who has access to information about ourselves has led to diminishing expectations of privacy, and thus to diminished protection under the Fourth Amendment."[96] Benner is joined by James Tomkovicz, who suggests that we ought to determine the need for Fourth Amendment protections not on the basis of reasonable expectations, but on the basis of an individual's need for informational privacy. For him, "courts should attempt to ascertain whether the government's actions deprived an individual of informational privacy and whether the individual's freedom to exercise and enjoy constitutional rights required some degree of informational privacy vis-à-vis the government."[97]

As the technological means to gain or facilitate access to personal information about individuals continue to develop and to become all the more broadly available as the cost, complexity, and skill requirements necessary to use them are all diminished, it will soon be the case that no expectation of privacy at all could be reasonable. Just because the courts have based the erosion of this constitutional right on the need to reduce crime, it would be *unreasonable* to expect that it will not spread on the basis of some pressing need to eliminate waste, inefficiency, or even bad taste.

FIGHTING BACK

One response to this assault against civil rights that has come to characterize the U.S. Supreme Court is the creation of a statutory right through legislation at the federal and state levels. Loretta Murdock argues that a "statutory approach would provide both certainty and a clear legal basis from which individual and organizational rights and obligations could be determined."[98] Murdock has a national policy in mind, and her recommendation echoes a common call for the creation of a national agency with the responsibility for protecting privacy interests. Preemption of state options in this regard is based on a recognition of the high level of integration of commerce in the United States, which is facilitated by telecommunications. The likelihood that states would develop inconsistent or even conflicting legislation can be inferred with confidence on the basis of a glance at any of the recent compilations of privacy laws published by Privacy Journal.[99] As will be discussed further on, attempts at federal preemption in the area of Caller-ID underscore the consequences of piecemeal legislation, which does not involve a clear definition of the underlying privacy interests.

Colin Bennett asks us to consider the distinction between an approach that emphasizes technology as compared with one that emphasizes civil rights.[100] Failure to recognize the interests and imperatives of private and public bureaucracies has led technologically oriented scholars to suggest technological solutions. David Chaum's proposal for a "public key/private key" solution, which would allow individuals to adopt different personae and identities as they interact with different bureaucracies, fails to recognize the pressures that would deny individuals the right to use such personae in their economic and political lives.[101]

If the problem with information privacy is simply one of the inappropriate use of technology, then Bennett suggests that specific restrictions can be developed that might control the use of computers for the matching of independent databases. However, it is also recognized that the problem of data linkage emerged as a result of an independent change in the nature of technology. Previously, privacy advocates were concerned about the threat inherent in the creation of a single, massive database, which would contain information about every citizen and would perhaps be subject to the control of some enemy or to an unexpected shift in the democratic orientation of the government. Today, however, the technological reality is one in which there is not any single computer, but hundreds and thousands of computers that can be accessed remotely and linked on demand for searches enabled by use of a common identifier like the social security number. It seems unlikely that a policy response will forbid the development or use of a technology with a demonstrated value. By the same token, efforts to regulate and limit the use of technologies seem fine in the abstract, but in the light of experience have been demonstrated to be ineffective.

The civil rights approach focuses on the rights of the individual, and the "concern is essentially to protect or promote the individuality, dignity, or integrity of each and every one of us."[102] The result of this approach would be the development of a set of "fair information practices," which supposedly would guide information handlers. The difficulties inherent in the coexistence and differential commitment to both of these approaches are based on the recognition that the actors who, on the one hand, have an interest in utilizing the most efficient technologies and may only begrudgingly respect the claims of individual rights must, on the other hand, also be trusted to guarantee those rights. As David Flaherty suggests, "It cannot be emphasized too strongly that the incentives for the government and the bureaucracy are in the direction of invading, or at least ignoring or neglecting, privacy interests rather than protecting them."[103] Flaherty concludes that "without a privacy protection commission, it will be of dubious utility to continue to rely on individuals protecting their privacy through their own initiative in the courts and on shaping data protection legislation on a sector-by-sector basis. The processes are simply too expensive and complicated to be accomplished without continuing input by the specialists working for a data protection agency."[104]

We should have no illusions, however, about the chances of success that a national policy and a national agency would enjoy. Flaherty's exploration of the differential success and common difficulties faced by data protection officials in Europe and North America suggest that the problems are inherent in an underlying conflict of interests. For example, one essential requirement of any data protection agency if it is to actively pursue the goal of privacy protection is independence from the political process. The OMB, which is responsible for the administration of the Privacy Act, has historically been unconcerned about privacy and did not feel any pressure from the Reagan administration, because privacy was not to be found on its agenda. It is only the occasional hearings and investigations organized by Congress, such as the investigation of matching programs in 1982, that have forced the OMB to pay any attention to questions of privacy.

THE MARKETPLACE SOLUTION

The problems involved in maintaining appropriate control over personal information are little different from any other social problems that are on the national policy agenda in that we are likely to hear the same response: Let the market decide. As the argument goes, the state is incapable of determining rules that should govern the allocation of goods and resources; that is the role of the market. Personal information, to the extent that it has a value to more than the individual it describes, can be controlled by the operation of the marketplace, with the involvement of the state limited to providing an assurance that contracts will be honored. Even Alan Westin, whose earlier work underscored the linkage between control over personal information and individual autonomy, has come to extend that logic to suggest that individual freedom is best served when property rights are determined and individuals can sell this information to the highest bidder.[105] At one level, this marketplace approach appears to be consistent with a notion of individual liberty—individuals choose the level of privacy with which they are most comfortable. But not all those who support a liberty theory equate freedom in markets with other expressive freedoms.

In an interesting and instructive discussion of the differences between the rationales behind exchange or market activities, which should be regulated, and the private uses of property, which are expressive of freedom and individuality and should not be regulated, C. Edwin Baker links market exchange with the exercise of power, one actor over another. Because this exchange takes place in the context of power relations and involves attempts to produce influence, regulation in the public interest is justified. Baker is explicit about this. "In an exchange, each party conditions the availability of a resource on the other party doing something he or she would otherwise not choose to do. … This exercise of power is inherent in exchange."[106] The compulsion need not be complete or absolute for us to recognize that there is some degree of power or influence. Recall, if you can, any experience you have had in bargaining with another over the price you will pay for some craft. Replay the dialogue. "Sorry, I just can't take any less than that." You respond, "Well, this is my last offer." He sighs, and says, "All right, I don't want to carry all this stuff back home with me, but you are getting a real bargain here, and I am not making a cent!" This example is not about truth, but about a struggle, in which each negotiator is reluctant to give up value freely. This is the nature of exchange. Depending on the nature of the market, some are price makers and others are price takers—a point to which I will return.

For Baker, these power-seeking, instrumental uses of property would thereby include the sale or exchange of rights in personal information. Because it is exchange, rather than expression, a liberty theory does not require that it be privileged. Furthermore, Baker's assessment of the allocative function of exchange suggests that the society can and should evaluate and presumably choose between systems of allocation "in terms of fairness, general welfare, and societal self-definition."[107] It is under such a model that questions would be raised about the development of a market in personal information and the need for regulatory oversight of such a market.

What Westin and other proponents of the marketplace solution (and their numbers are legion) seem to forget, or choose to ignore, is that *all* markets for information are characterized by substantial inefficiency and inequity. These markets fail almost by definition because of the nature of information as a commodity.[108]

Contract Problems
in the Market for Personal Information

Meheroo Jussawalla and Chee-Wah Cheah discuss the substantial inequalities that lead to market failure.[109] They define privacy invasions as externalities that are the products of other transactions involving individuals and corporations. An externality may be positive or negative, seen as a cost or a benefit, but its critical character is that it is not the primary focus of production, consumption, or exchange, but is incidental. We are most familiar with pollution as an externality that is associated with the manufacture of industrial products. The loss of privacy can be seen in the same way as an external consequence of the sale of those products. If we consider, for example, a man who wishes to buy a suit to attend a wedding, to be properly fitted, he must disclose information about his height and, perhaps, his girth. If he is overweight, he may not wish to make such a disclosure, but it is a requirement of the transaction. He may even have to submit to the "touch" of the tailor, who in her or his own self-interest, wants to ensure that the measurement is accurate. Paying for the suit will involve other requests for information that would not ordinarily be disclosed. These losses of privacy are externalities, incidental to the purchase of a suit.

Rohan Samarajiva and Roopali Mukherjee provide additional examples of such external costs in their discussion of the requirements of personal information that was thought to be necessary to limit access by minors to sexually explicit communications.[110] The loss of privacy that would occur if an individual were forced to use a credit card or to provide a telephone number for a return call because carriers no longer wanted to provide billing services for sexually explicit material is unquestionably an externality. The difficulties with externalities, which underscore their importance as signs of market failure, are to be seen in the limitations on the ability of parties to control them.

An additional problem in the functioning of markets in which privacy losses are involved is the notion of transaction costs. Jussawalla and Cheah suggest that because the number of "potential 'providers' of privacy invasions" is so large and "it is too costly for a data subject to engage in private contracting with all those who might violate his privacy, the collective enforcement of privacy rights appears warranted on grounds of economic efficiency."[111]

An even more important contribution to understanding the problems inherent in market solutions is the recognition that individuals are contract takers rather than contract makers. Unlike formal contracts and regulations governing intellectual property, many of the contracts that involve the transfer of personal information are implicit, and these standard forms "tend to place data subjects in an unfavorable position" in relation to the data gatherer. Although individuals may see the cost (in terms of value foregone) of not providing the information as substantially higher than the cost of providing it, individuals frequently do not realize that the costs associated with the loss of control over personal information occur long after the initial transaction has taken place. The individual is not able to monitor or control the use of that information after it is disclosed. The problem with standard forms and implicit contracts is that the average consumer does not have the time, knowledge, or skill needed to engage in negotiation of the contracts governing each transaction with privacy implications.

Jussawalla and Cheah recognize that the bureaucracies or data users might find or claim that it is too costly to gain the consent of individuals. Indeed, the courts have acted on the side of commerce in assuming that consumers' rights have been waived, rather than subjecting corporations to the expense of gaining consent through formal contracts. The challenge, which would have to be faced if either a market or an administrative solution were sought, would be to develop a more explicit recognition of the problems inherent in gaining meaningful consent.

Informed Consent

It is unlikely that individuals fully consider the consequences that might flow from their disclosure of personal information, their agreements to permit background and status investigations, and their implicit consent for an organization to share or exchange this information with other organizations that claim "legitimate business or government" interests in such information. It is or it should be clear that no one can be fully informed about the consequences that might result from such blanket authorizations. Similarly, there is a question about whether consent is ever freely given if the alternatives are far too costly. The costs of alternatives rise dramatically in the face of monopoly supply. But the essence of monopoly supply is realized in the context of a virtual network in which information known to one is known to all who have access and have a "need to know." In such an environment of informational transparency, such as that which characterizes the market for health insurance, refusal by one insurer is a reliable predictor of refusal by most others because each shares access to the same information.

There is no right to informed consent comparable to the right that has been recognized for privacy in the U.S. Constitution. However, to the extent that we recognize the right to privacy as a right that enables the development of an autonomous individual and involves freedom of choice, then informed consent is directly linked to the exercise of such choice. It is argued that "to respect an autonomous agent is to recognize with due appreciation that person's capacities and perspective, including his or her right to hold certain views, to make certain choices, and to take certain actions based on personal values and beliefs."[112]

If the right to privacy involves the right to control access to aspects of the person, then the right to informed consent has similar roots. Edward Bloustein argues that the tort in privacy is more appropriately considered to be akin to that developed for battery, in that it involves access to the personality without permission. Informed consent has similar roots in that "the battery theory of liability protects the right to choose whether to permit others to invade one's physical integrity, and thus is based on the general right of self-determination in the law."[113] The injury is not dependent on any physical harm that might ensue, but it is the touch itself that is the affront. Justice Benjamin Cardoza is credited with the first formal expression of the right in the context of a physician's responsibility, which emphasized the liability a physician would face. "Every human being of adult years and sound mind has a right to determine what shall be done with his own body; and a surgeon who performs an operation without his patient's consent commits an assault, for which he is liable in damages."[114] Although there is room to debate which standards ought to be followed in determining the sufficiency of the explanation—those standards of professional convention, or those that recognize the differences between individuals in terms of their knowledge, situation, and responsiveness to authority—the parallels between the claims are striking.

There is, however, little room for optimism that fully informed consent will ever become the rule governing interactions between individuals and corporate bureaucracies, any more than it is the rule with regard to the state. Martin Gardner describes the variety of ways in which the courts have acted to fictionalize consent, including the rise in the standard of police reasonableness, which finds sufficient consent when no actual consent was received.[115] This reasonableness standard even extends to consent that is given in response to deception. Gary Marx describes the elevation of deception to the level of high art. Deception is justified by some as being ethical on the basis of an ends-means rationale. "If the intent is noble, then the action is justified, even if it has some bad effects."[116] Marx's comments reflect the difficulty that is inherent in the balancing of social and moral values: "In dealing with such moral dilemmas, the problem is not only whether we can find an acceptable utilitarian calculus, but that the choice always involves competing wrongs. The danger of automatically applied technical, bureaucratic, or occupational subcultural formulas lies in their potential for generating the self-deluding and morally numbing conclusion that a costfree solution is possible."[117]

PUBLIC POLICY AND THE PANOPTIC SORT

As I suggested at the beginning of this chapter, the law is both a product and a process that reflects substantial differences in power. Most of the time, the development of rights under the law must be seen as a zero-sum game; in order for someone to win, to improve her or his lot in life, someone else must lose. This view of the law is far removed from the naive assumptions about the operation of an efficient market, in which trades are not made that worsen any trader's condition. The negotiation of rights under the law is an adversarial process because rights are in conflict. All too often, when the regime of rights is changed, many who lose in the process have no way to make their voices heard. This problem is most severe when those changes are made in the courts and the process involves a kind of accretion or disintegration without a focal point or critical event.

The negotiation of statutory rights is no less characterized by distortions of power and influence. Edward Laumann and David Knoke suggest that organizations differ significantly from individuals in their ability to mobilize resources, including informational resources, to achieve goals in influencing public policy.[118] Industry lobbyists attempt to convince legislators that their interests, linked as they are to the interests of powerful funders, depend on forging a legislative response that does the least harm while at the same time giving the impression of ensuring the greatest good. The power of the Direct Marketing Association (DMA), representing the combined interests of retailers dependent on mail and telephone access to customers identified by computerized prospect lists, is revealed as substantial in the example of the Video Privacy Protection Act of 1988 and the continuing debate over telephone caller identification.

The Video Privacy Protection Act of 1988

In the record speed with which this legislation was passed there is a bitter lesson about power and influence in the outcome of this policy debate about personal information. Policy activists increasingly find themselves taking solace in what they see as small victories snatched from a sea of almost certain defeat. I would suggest that instead of victory, these measured retreats actually have served to reify and legitimate practices that were previously carried on behind a screen of uncertainty. I recall asking Janlori Goldman, a privacy specialist with the ACLU, to explain her apparent change of heart with regard to a fundamental issue of privacy rights. It appeared from her comments that she now accepted the institutionalization of the DMA's negative option as the norm for information practice. She indicated that no other option was politically feasible. In the realm of necessity, in which the ACLU would have to face the DMA on bill after bill that threatened privacy interests, Goldman felt that some ground had been gained, instead of a major battle having been lost.[119] You may be the judge.

In June 1988, Robert Kastenmeir, citing the release of U.S. Supreme Court nominee Robert Bork's video store rental records to the local press, introduced the Video and Library Protection Act of 1988. The bill, as initially introduced, would have prohibited the release of individually identifiable information about patrons of video stores and libraries (library related issues would later be separated from this bill). It would permit disclosure of information about these patrons under rather limited circumstances, such as a court order or the "specific and informed consent" of the user.[120]

The hearings provided the occasion for the expression of strong public advocacy positions from the American Library Association and the ACLU. A representative from the Video Software Dealers' Association also testified in support of the bill and underscored the need for limitations on government access to rental data and apparently accepted the need for "clearly expressed written, informed consent" on the part of the consumer.[121] However, Richard Barton, senior vice president of the DMA, took a somewhat different position. First, he argued that mailing lists or the use of mailing lists per se was not an invasion of privacy. The wording of the proposed legislation, which required an affirmative consent on the part of the consumer, would, in the eyes of the direct marketing industry, guarantee that such lists could never develop. That is, in his view, requiring affirmative consent is "frankly tantamount to prohibition for use of these lists."[122] Questioners did not pursue Barton to determine whether this effective prohibition would occur because individuals valued their privacy or because they were generally suspicious of business and would not give their consent voluntarily. Industry representatives regularly claimed that the failure of people to make use of mail and phone preference options was evidence that they were not concerned about privacy.

As part of his formal testimony, Barton included numerous examples of consumer options that the direct marketing industry would prefer to see instituted. In effect, Barton was suggesting that the legislation formalize and provide a legislative justification for the negative option as the standard form of implied consent. If consumers would prefer that their names not be included on a list and sold to list vendors and other direct marketers or perhaps to government agencies or political consultants, the consumers would have to exercise the option of indicating that preference. Otherwise, the firm would assume that such sharing of rental information had been agreed to through informal consent.

Two days after Barton's testimony, the lead article in an industry newsletter, *Friday Report,* highlighted the industry's position on the proposed legislation and criticized the Congress for introducing a potentially harmful distinction between mail order and retail purchasing lists. In the view of the editors,

the real distinction should be the release of categories of purchase behavior for legitimate marketing purposes versus the disclosure of any consumer information re-

quested on an individual for non-credit authorization purposes. Unless the re-
questor is a potential credit grantor, strict fines are warranted for release of
information on an individual. But if this legislation passes, will magazine subscription lists be next?[123]

The DMA was making a distinction between economic or financial information
and information about consumption patterns, as though this difference reflected
a fundamental specification of a privacy zone as beginning at the point of financial information. There was also a distinction being drawn between marketing as
a legitimate business purpose and credit authorization as a legitimate but different purpose. It was at the very least disingenuous for Barton to suggest that financial information was not a highly valued component in the marketing mix. His attempt at distancing is understandable, perhaps, in the light of an emerging debate
about just this issue that involved mounting public complaints against the sale of
credit information as a part of the services being offered to marketers by TRW.

On October 3, the day before the bill was scheduled for mark up, the president
and chairperson of the People for the American Way wrote to Kastenmeir to express the organization's strong support for the requirement for informed affirmative consent. Yet, on November 11, *Friday Report* claimed a "great win" for the industry in that the bill that had just been signed by President Reagan was one that
would stand as "a congressional endorsement and trade-off which should carry us
into the next century." What could this be? With the leadership of Ronald Plesser,
former general counsel of the U.S. Privacy Protection Study Commission, the
DMA's Privacy Group was apparently able to engineer the insertion of two crucial
paragraphs into the bill.[124] Under the law as signed, video operators *could* disclose
the names and addresses of consumers as long as they had "provided the consumers with the opportunity, in a clear and conspicuous manner, to prohibit such dis-
closures"; and equally important in terms of the practices it legitimated and reified, the bill specified that "the subject matter of such materials may be disclosed
if the disclosure is for the exclusive use of marketing goods and services directly to
the consumer."[125] Two years later, representatives of Blockbuster Video, one of the
nation's largest providers of video rentals, indicated that they had not even discussed the inclusion of the negative option in their membership forms, even as
they were reportedly about to embark on a program to sell their customers lists to
direct marketers.[126]

Calling Number Identification

The debate over the introduction of calling number identification services provides another example through which to examine the relations between technology, market, and culture that are being reproduced over and over as the panoptic
sort develops into its intermediate forms. Calling number identification is just
one name for a complex of related technologies and services that provide automatic delivery of calling party identification (CPI). Potentially, there are no tech-

nological limits on the identification of the calling party. Initial proposals for a Caller-ID service involved the fowarding by a central office of the billing or account number for the calling party to a device, owned or rented by a residential or small businesss consumer, that would capture and display this incoming number. Because the calling party number was delivered during the first silent interval of the signaling cycle, it would be possible for a person to identify an incoming call before the first ring was heard. Differences in the sophistication of the devices that subscribers might use in conjunction with such a service ranged from the simple units capable of display, capture, and storage of a limited number of calls into a record that included the time of the call to sophisticated systems integrated into home computers that could trigger a display of the caller's profile. It soon became clear that an associated market of caller identification services and system enhancements was likely to develop. These services might supply names, addresses, and different amounts of the information about the calling parties that were currently available through the hundreds of database vendors marketing personal information. Telephone companies or their competitors in the enhanced services market promised to develop and maintain files, reverse directories, and call management systems to meet the needs of small and large businesses.

As will be discussed, a related service escaped much of the initial controversy generated by Caller-ID. Perhaps because it had been presented as a business-to-business offering, it had somehow avoided the watchful gaze of privacy activists. ANI refers to the delivery of the calling party identification to businesses that have contracted for long distance 800- or premium 900-number services. The numbers, gathered initially for billing purposes, remain as a transaction record, and their delivery to the receiving or called party makes them different only in form, rather than in kind, from the delivery of the number through a Caller-ID service.[127] AT&T's INFO-2 service, an early use of the company's integrated services digital network (ISDN), delivered the incoming number in a way that promised to facilitate the handling of incoming calls, as well as to contribute to the development of telemarketing databases. As the debate over Caller-ID matured, several observers asked a critical question: "Why should ANI, which already is used by 'non-telephone companies' for purposes other than billing, be granted even a 'temporary' exemption from the blocking requirements imposed on Caller-ID? Is there really a significant difference between the fact that Caller-ID is marketed as a residential/small business service, while ANI generally is sold as a pure business offering?"[128]

The Public Service Commission of the state of New York, responding to an initiative of Commissioner Eli Noam, issued a call for comments on the general issue of privacy in telecommunications that helped to identify several of the core issues in the calling number identification (CNI) debates.[129] One contribution that Noam thought an investigation by New York state might make was the establishment of "reasonable expectations" of privacy in telecommunications. The hope that *discussions* organized under the administrative gaze of an activist state commission would establish the bounds of reasonableness and thereby help to define the limits of legal protection moves to a point just short of hubris. However, the arrogance of the claim is tempered only by the recognition that the telephone companies favored a policy of establishment by publicity.[130] That is, if the public could be made aware that a technology exists and is in widespread use, then reasonable persons could no longer have any expectation of privacy regarding their identification whenever they made a call. The trade and privacy press provided numerous examples that suggested that the telephone companies were not above creating fictional public demand for Caller-ID by requiring their employees to write letters to the Public Utilities Commission.[131]

For Noam, the complex of privacy concerns could be reduced to two interests: (1) the interests of the called party in controlling unwanted intrusions into the private spaces individuals have defined for themselves, and (2) the interests of the calling party in maintaining control over information about themselves. Both interests are potentially affected by the technology of caller identification, and both interests can be seen to be inextricably linked but contradictory at the point at which commercial interests emerge. The interests of the called party in controlling intrusion are recognized as a part of a broader privacy interest in seclusion; the interests of the calling party are recognized more directly as the interests in autonomy that I have joined Westin in calling information privacy, or the right of determination.

In addition to discussing the privacy interests of calling and called parties, Noam's memorandum identified the economic interests of the complex of businesses that utilize CNI to coordinate sales and marketing and the telecommunication service providers themselves who are interested in the income from CNI delivery as well as the profits to be derived from related enhancements. In addition, interested parties include the police and emergency service providers that find their activities both enhanced and threatened by the widespread adoption of CNI technologies.[132] Indeed, even the growth of international businesses that depend on telecommunications is seen to depend on CNI and an absence of regulatory barriers to the flow of information. Thomas McManus examines the competing interests in the information generated by telephone-based transactions in a way that reveals the tension between the interests of individuals and the interests of commercial firms.[133] The importance of transaction processing for comparative advantage in business is also explored in some detail by the U.S. Office of Technology Assessment.[134] The primary focus in this section, however, will be on what has been misrepresented as an opposition between individuals rather than between individuals and organizations.

Called Party

As already noted, the interest in seclusion does not demand an absolute prohibition but involves exercise of the right of self-determination in that individuals claim the right to determine which informational stimuli they will receive and which they will deny access. CNI, as a technology, can be seen to be privacy enhancing in this regard in that it provides information that people can use to decide if a caller should or should not be granted access. Developments in the control of signaling information by digital telecommunications networks allow telephone companies to offer a variety of enhanced services, some of which can be seen to support privacy interests.[135] Bell Communications Research refers to this category of services as CLASS, and Bell Atlantic markets its offerings as IQ Services. Many of the proposed services promise to facilitate the identification of the caller. For example, calls from family members or for particular members of the household could be given a distinctive ring. Most of these services involve some measure of consent, or at least prior knowledge, of the calling number of persons to be so identified. Caller-ID differs significantly in its method and in its proposed use.

In their promotion of Caller-ID, representatives of the telephone companies have emphasized the uninvited "intrusions" into the private sphere by individuals making obscene or similarly harassing calls. The technology would serve a *screening* function by allowing the consumer to identify an incoming call by name, number, or other means of identification and thereby avoid these unwanted messages. Opponents of Caller-ID have suggested that alternative techniques are available that would allow screening but that would not require the same level of identification. In several ways, the alternative technologies are considered to be superior to Caller-ID in that they are potentially more efficient, and do not raise competing privacy claims. For example, a blocking feature (Call Block) would allow a residential user to notify the telephone company, through the use of a simple procedure, which numbers the central office should bar from ringing through. By itself, the Caller-ID feature would not eliminate the disturbance represented by the ringing of an unwanted call. Unless that number could be blocked or barred from ringing through, a form of harassment could continue in a manner that is clearly disturbing of solitude and repose, especially if the calls were placed late at night. An individual's knowing the number of the incoming call would not, by itself, eliminate such harassing calls.

Still another available service would allow the person being harassed to forward the number of the last incoming call to a special unit of the telephone company or authorized agency (Call Trace). This forwarding would provide documentation of the call, and, in addition, harassment specialists would be able to counsel the consumer about how to proceed to take formal legal action against the harasser. For parties willing to confront harassing callers directly, another available feature (Call Return) would cause the number of the last incoming call to be redialed and a warning of legal action or some other threat might be delivered. None of these particular alternatives would require that the harassed party actually see a display of the number or other identifying information about the alleged harasser, although some proposed services would allow consumers to record the incoming number for future use.[136]

A different kind of harassment, generally not mentioned by the telephone companies in their promotion of Caller-ID, is that which describes the annoyance and distraction that accompanies calls from telemarketers or organizations seeking contributions. The level of annoyance from such calls increased dramatically with the use of automated systems that are capable of calling hundreds of numbers, delivering a scripted appeal, and collecting order information, all without the requirement of a live caller. Those systems that would not disconnect, and that would thereby bar outgoing calls until the prerecorded message was completed, generated several state and federal initiatives seeking to outlaw automatic dialers.[137] Caller-ID could provide only limited control to the individual because the thousands of numbers from which such calls might be made were unlikely to be known to the called party.

Options that have been explored to increase the ability of individuals to control access via telephone have been limited in part by concerns about the protections afforded to commercial speech under recent interpretations of the First Amendment.[138] Whereas a telephone preference service, such as that offered by the DMA, that would allow individuals to indicate that they did not want to receive any telemarketing calls at their homes would support industry self-regulation, any regulations that barred an entire class of callers because of the presumed content of their messages immediately raise objections on constitutional grounds.[139]

The alternative some courts have taken is to argue that they are regulating conduct rather than speech. Such an approach is pursued in the regulation of automated calls as a class and in limitations as to times at which unsolicited calls might be barred. The primary concern is to increase the ability of the individual to determine which calls they welcome and which they would prefer to avoid.[140] The problem is one of the gathering of information that the caller may not wish or may not be able to provide in advance of gaining entry via the telephone. A key aspect of this desirable information is concerned with intent. A salesperson presumably calls with the intention of making a sale, not with the intention of invading privacy and disturbing the peace of each home entered electronically. Attempts to distinguish between commercial and noncommercial or charitable solicitations raise the similar problem of establishing any form of blanket specification of the kinds of calls that might be limited by law.

Of course, enhancements and more sophisticated telephones might display more detail about the incoming call, such as that derived from reverse directories, but the cost of such enhancements would severely limit the usefulness of the screen for the average consumer. Easily imaginable are technological options that could identify the level of privacy desired by the called party, issue warnings about that person's own definition of intrusion or harassment, and then finally leave it up to the calling party to choose if, when, and in what manner information will be exchanged to gain entry. The same options that lead callers with touch-tone phones through branches and chains of automated call routing systems installed by several large organizations might allow calling parties to identify themselves and the nature of their call before they could make any progress through various levels of access. This interactive screening might approximate the kind of control in the home that executives traditionally realize through their secretaries who frequently ask for name, organization, and the nature of the call before telling you that Ms. Highpower is unavailable at the moment. Of course, all of these options represent substantial costs that individuals must bear if they wish to maintain whatever level of privacy they enjoyed before the electronic roadway increased access to their homes.[141]

Calling Party

The connection between the interests of the calling party and those of the called party is simple. The parties are often the same. When making a call to a business or government office, individuals may, or perhaps should, have an interest in controlling their identification or, at the very least, in limiting the extent to which that information can be shared with other parties. Generally, a person calling a doctor would have no hesitation in providing the doctor with information about where she or he can be reached. The doctor's office might need to call back if, for some reason, an appointment had to be changed. There are any number of other imaginable reasons for the doctor or other service provider to have ready access to a customer's telephone number. Emergency service providers have an easily justifiable reason for knowing the number (and address through a reverse directory) of an incoming call. Any number of circumstances may prevent the caller from providing this information. There is no expectation, however, that the doctor would supply that number without explicit permission to a number of vendors who might offer the caller additional goods and services.

Many of the discussions of Caller-ID have introduced a distraction by suggesting that callers have no privacy interest in their telephone number. [142] In approving the offering of Caller-ID in South Carolina, Judge Thomas Hughston argued that if there were any interest in the number, it rested with the telephone company. Consumers do not ordinarily select their own telephone number but have one assigned for the convenience of the telephone company. [143] By itself, the telephone number is of little interest to anyone. It is only the fact that it provides a means of access to a person identified with it that makes its disclosure to others a matter of privacy interest. The large number of individuals who pay a fee for ensuring that their numbers are not published or revealed by directory assistance suggests that the level of privacy interest in the number as a means of access is quite high for a great many individuals. Estimates published by the Library of Congress put the proportion in California at 55 percent,[144] with the prize going to Las Vegas with more than 62 percent of telephone subscribers opting out of the telephone directory.[145]

But the number itself is not the concern. The concern arises when the number is associated with an address and, through the address, with additional information that serves to define an individual.[146] There were apparently enough consum-

ers who wished to avoid leaving an audit trail that a firm charging $2 per minute
for domestic calls and $5 per minute for international calls opened for business
with great fanfare in 1990. By calling a central number before completing the intended call, all records of the telephone contact between the calling and the called
party would be eliminated.[147] Furthermore, when the name, address, and telephone number are associated with a particular activity, the concerns about the
panoptic sort reach a more serious level. Finally, when the telephone call itself
serves to add to the profile of the citizen or consumer, the call for a legislative response begins to be heard. Although residential users of Caller-ID are unlikely to
collect and share information about persons who call their homes, it is not so
clear that small businesses will be similarly disinterested, and there is overwhelming evidence that larger businesses are making use of ANI information to develop
marketing databases that aid the panoptic sort.

It is possible to think of telephone transaction-generated consumer lists as
guides to the homes of the stars. Persons who would be included on a prospect list
for a telemarketer because they either made purchases by phone or made an inquiry about some product they saw advertised on television have not acted know-
ingly to invite these calls. Although, as a matter of policy, the providers of some
lists might not include persons with unlisted telephone numbers, a great many
others are not so constrained. But focusing on whether the phone number is unlisted or not misses the point. The fact that the telephone number has been listed
at all does not mean that it has been listed in relation to a particular call or class of
calls the subscriber might make. It is the association of the number called with the
calling party identification that produces an indication of interest or orientation
that an individual may or may not be willing to disclose or have disclosed to a
third party.

With an answering machine, the calling party has the option of heeding the
usual request and leaving information about the date, time, and purpose of the
call. The cajoling creativity you hear in many of those recorded messages suggests
that only a proportion well short of 100 percent of the callers willingly comply. The
Caller-ID technology automatically leaves a record of each call and the time at
which it was made unless the callers have been allowed to block the forwarding of
their calling number or have placed the call from a public telephone. Although we
might not expect the courts or the legislatures to actively support the privacy interests involved in the social lie that is threatened by Caller-ID—no more calls to
one's spouse claiming to be working late in the office or no more calls to the office
claiming to be in bed with the flu—other privacy interests are very much at risk in
an era of CNI.[148]

There is little doubt that real-time CNI can be used by business to improve the
efficiency and quality of the services delivered. Automated billing for premium cable television services could be facilitated by some form of CNI; billing for other
services facilitated through telecommunication seems to be a natural gain in efficiency. The identification/authorization link represents potentially valuable sav-

ings of time and effort. The number of potential enhancements in the efficient provision of service to customers grows with every passing moment. According to one source, "an inbound telemarketer can pull up a customer record based on a telephone number, personalize the greeting to the calling party and associate the calling number with an existing account record, such as ordering information."[149] The improvement of relationships with existing customers through this use of CNI by businesses provides little room for complaint.[150]

However, critics of CNI have suggested that there are other uses of this technical capacity that are more problematic. In addition to providing information that adds to a consumer profile, the involuntary identification of the calling party can facilitate economic redlining or the provision of differential quality service based on an assessment of the quality of the neighborhood from which the call was placed. Economic discrimination on the basis of race is a fact of life that we cannot simply wish away. African-Americans who do not "sound black" on the telephone when they call to ask about a job but who find all the jobs have miraculously been filled when they come in to apply in person might see the number of such disappointments decline in an era of CNI. CNI increases the possibility that callers from communities identified as likely to be poor and African-American may be routed to long queues or to messages indicating that loans, insurance, apartments, or jobs of interest are no longer available. They will save a trip downtown or out to the suburbs, but they still will not get that job.

Innovative suppliers of information services are already providing a broad array of caller information to add to the billing number passed by AT&T and other carriers. Although not initially available in real time, Infomedia Corporation provided "800 ID" services, which included "complete name and address, with up to 24 demographic characteristics about the caller."[151] A representative from MCI described a variety of justifications for using real-time CNI functions that included security and custom answering; a variety of database "lookup" activities; specialized routing options that would forward calls to specialized locations, such as to operators able to provide special skills needed by customers; and a form of triage or prioritization, in which the "platinum" customers could receive the highest standard of service.[152] James Rule and Paul Attewell have described the use of computerized systems to discriminate among incoming telephone calls to a taxi service. The possibilities for applying this form of the panoptic sort are almost unlimited:

> Previously, the approximately ten telephone operators/dispatchers on duty would perform these discriminations themselves, answering each call and then deciding how rapidly to dispatch a cab. Now this process is computerized. The computer classifies each incoming call according to its potential profitability; lowest priority calls from the general public and ascending priorities to corporate subscribers according to the fees they pay.[153]

With enhanced CNI, some consumers from "low profit/high risk" neighborhoods will find that they have great difficulty in "getting through" when they call for taxies, pizza, or other services.

The Need for Caller-ID

The carriers who have made substantial investments in the installation of Signalling System Seven (SS7) enhancements believe that much of the expected value to be derived from its advanced digital signaling features are placed at substantial risk if consumers are provided with free blocking. According to one analyst, "With blocking, the take rate is expected to be reduced by 50 percent, which would make the billion dollar investment much more risky and therefore much more prolonged and delayed in terms of its rollout."[154] Pacific Bell estimated that expected revenue from Caller-ID with blocking would be as much as 30 percent lower than if the service were offered without blocking.[155]

In his testimony before the Pennsylvania Public Utility Commission, Gary Marx raised a critical issue regarding limitations on the lines of business that telephone companies might profitably pursue. "If Bell can establish the right to give out now private information about a caller—their telephone number—the precedent may very well permit the Telephone Company to transmit with a call all sorts of other data. ... If the calling party gives up all rights when they make a call, as the Telephone Company appears to argue, then there would not appear to be any logical restraint on the transmission of such data."[156] Rohan Samarajiva, in his comments submitted to the New York Public Service Commission, called attention to evidence that the FCC had been concerned about the telephone companies' use of their privileged access to customer network proprietary information (CNPI), which would place them at a competitive advantage over other providers and vendors.[157]

A year later, the American Newspaper Publishers' Association (ANPA) raised a similar cry of alarm under the banner of privacy concerns following the removal of restrictions on telephone company entry into information businesses from which they had been previously barred. Cathleen Black, CEO and president of the ANPA, argued that "up until now, the Bells have had no incentive to fully exploit this information ... but the very second they get into the content end of the information business, you can bet that they'll take advantage of every fact they know. If you call an auto repair shop, the Bells will have that information in a computer. They'll be free to sell that information to local car dealers. ... Call a marriage counselor, and the next thing you know a divorce lawyer may call you. ... I hate to even think about what they might try to sell you after you call that '976-LUST' line."[158]

Negative Versus Positive Option

To date, the DMA has been rather successful in convincing policymakers that the negative option is the most efficient and socially responsible way to regulate business information practices. The negative option assumes that reasonableness is defined by openness to commercial, charitable, and political speech. The only time that limits on such speech should come into play is when individuals have indicated that they are not interested in receiving such information. Individuals are expected to indicate this status by choosing the negative option, indicating, for example, that they do not wish to receive any direct mail solicitations. The negative option is a highly inefficient technology: It is all-or-nothing, it is relatively nonselective, and it is fairly nonresponsive. That is, by notifying the DMA, you have presumably notified those of its members who will invest in the added cost of purging their lists of all such individuals that you do not wish to receive any solicitations from organizations with which you do not already have a relationship. This is not a status that changes without action on your part, and to the extent that its operation depends on routine checking by all telemarketers, it is likely that calling lists will be out of date if you change your status periodically. It is nonselective because it is a blanket denial. There are few opportunities for the individual to specify the class of solicitations that might, under certain circumstances, be acceptable. It is nonresponsive in that it is time-consuming for the consumer as well as for the DMA to maintain the up-to-date status of the system.

An alternative approach would be based on the assumption that individuals generally prefer solitude. When they wish information or an information-based service, they will seek it out. It is not unreasonable to assume that individuals would be the best judge of when they are the most interested and therefore most receptive to information of a particular kind. Others with information to provide ought to assume that, unless requested, no information is desired. This would be the positive option. Through a variety of means, individuals would provide a positive indication that yes, I want to learn, hear, see more about this subject at this time. Individuals should be free to choose when they are ready to enter the market for information.

There may be an implied contract in which it is assumed that individuals accept, as that part of the cost they must pay for access to information and entertainment, having to sit through advertisements between segments of a television program.[159] People also have apparently come to accept, perhaps begrudgingly, that the price they must pay for information through "talking yellow pages" or other advertiser-supported audio-text services is exposure to a brief message. But there is also considerable evidence that people pay less attention to messages of limited interest, which adds to the inflationary spiral as advertisers attempt to find new ways to attract and maintain the potential consumer's attention. It simply is not the case that we assume that the price we pay for having a telephone is a blanket invitation to a commercial appeal.

Segmentation and targeting is a marketing strategy pursued by business to reduce the likelihood that a message is received by an individual who has a near zero chance of responding affirmatively to a particular appeal. In reality, by allowing individuals to choose messages in which they are interested, the probability of a successful relationship is much higher. This aspect of interest-determining information seeking explains the value of the yellow pages as an information service. The options are alphabetized and indexed or are searchable by subject of interest.

The value in the positive option is its preservation of the individual's right to choose. Information about past purchases of chocolate, combined with information that the person is a repeat buyer of "clothing for the big woman," might provide the marketer of chocolate (or other vendor of sweets) with a basis for betting that there may be an interest in their product. Information that indicates that this person has also been a customer of several diet and exercise programs and has enrolled in these programs in the late spring of most years may also suggest that her power to resist an appeal is not great. Information from coupon promotions may even provide data about her price elasticity of demand for chocolate at different times of the year. All this information suggests vulnerability. But if this woman is trying to get through this particular winter with her weight under control, she is not likely to seek out this information on her own. With unhindered telemarketing, fed with information generated from caller-identified transactions, the positive option is not hers to choose.

The fact that so few people call or write to have their names included on a no-call list is not an indication that people enjoy receiving telemarketing calls, any more than the small number on the mail preference list is proof that direct mail is a response to consumer demand. Processing the reams of direct mail many people receive is less intrusive and less annoying than a telemarketing call. However, if the technology of mail delivery were such that a person would have to answer the door for each piece of mailed appeal, the public response would surely be at least as hostile, if not even more so, than the reponse to telephone solicitations.

Full line blocking is the telephonic equivalent of the positive option. It assumes that the normal state of telephone calls is that which obtains at the present time, anonymity with regard to the incoming call. It should be up to individuals to determine if and to what extent they are willing to identify themselves in response to requests from those on the other end. However, success in defining the positive option as the preferred option, more consistent with my vision of individual autonomy and the privacy that protects and nurtures it, seems unlikely.

FAIR INFORMATION PRACTICES

It is not that there is no legal safety net that limits the operation of the panoptic sort. The ACLU has published a second edition of their handbook, *Your Right to Privacy,* which is quite comprehensive in its coverage of constitutional, statutory, and common law protections.[160] An impressive review that focuses on computer-based information systems has been provided by Meredith Mendes.[161] What we have is a safety net full of holes, one in need of maintenance and repair, yet all we see on the horizon are signs of a storm, a tsunami with the potential for tearing the net to shreds. Numerous sources describe the principal areas in which there has been success and identify those areas in which technology and common practice have eroded gains seemingly overnight.

Critical events theorists like Laumann and Knoke[162] would have us emphasize key decisions by the U.S. Supreme Court, such as that in *U.S. v. Miller,* which serve to accelerate change through the establishment of some new standard or principle.[163] Others would have us look more closely at the power of interest groups in limiting the reach of privacy supports at the point at which they threatened collective interests.

Although success by privacy advocates in the legislative arena has been difficult to claim, the threat of adverse publicity remains a potent weapon. The Lotus Marketplace case represented an example of a grass-roots (if elite) mobilization that received timely and supportive press coverage.[164] The *Wall Street Journal* has continued to play a curious role in publicizing challenges to the legitimacy of the information practices of the credit and direct marketing industry. In December 1990, Michael Miller, who has been the source of a number of articles critical of business information practices, adopted an alarmist stance in reporting on alleged plans by Blockbuster Entertainment to market customer data. The article began with an unvarnished threat: "The next time you pick up a James Bond movie at the world's biggest video chain, the spying may start long before you turn on the television."[165] The article continued to describe the potential threat that was inherent in the corporation's plan to sell information to direct marketers and reported the similarities between Blockbuster's plans and practices already common to other retail chains. Within days, the press published denials from Blockbuster's management that they had ever made any such plans.

Although the press has played an important role from time to time in raising public awareness and calling attention to particularly egregious departures from the ideals that we maintain regarding privacy and the autonomous individual, David Flaherty has been clear in his warning that the press is an unreliable guardian of those values because its attention is so easily distracted. I have already provided a daunting amount of evidence to suggest that the judicial system is incapable of holding on to the thread that runs through the various pieces of the puzzle of torts. There is evidence that the U.S. Supreme Court has done all in its power to strip away what remained of the thin veneer of protections that could be claimed within the shrinking domain of reasonable expectations. It is also clear that those legislators who might pick up the mantle of privacy in defense of constituent interests would find themselves immediately under attack from a rapidly mobilized and fully armed phalanx of corporate lobbyists, in a coordinated assault made easy by the narrowness of any single bill's reach. This same fear of corporate revolt has left the FCC all but powerless to do more than to form advisory committees, announce investigations, and schedule proposed rule-makings, all the while secretly hoping that Congress would act on its own.

A great many commentators on the question of privacy and the law have suggested the need for a comprehensive privacy initiative,[166] an appeal made almost annually since the publication of the report from the U.S. Privacy Protection Study Commission.[167] They have recommended the establishment of a code of fair information practices that would govern the collection, use, and exchange of personal information, and most have called for an independent body with the power to ensure their effectiveness. The European response to privacy concerns has been seen to be enormously threatening to those businesses in the United States that have come to depend on the control and the revenue that an unfettered panoptic sort has meant. In 1990, after the publication of a draft proposal to govern the collection and sale of consumer information within the European Community, members of the DMA and their counterparts within the European advertising community began to mobilize to oppose the restrictions that such a compact would put into place. What is striking is the fact that the proposed rules would do no more than make explicit the data protection guidelines that had been established in the Council of Europe in 1980, and the Organization for Economic Cooperation and Development (OECD) in 1982.[168]

David Flaherty identifies twelve principles that he suggests should apply to all personal information systems under government control.[169] I see no compelling reason to limit these principles to agencies of the state. The first principle calls for openness, or transparency, in the sense that there should be no files containing information about individuals that are secret. This principle of openness might be reasonably expanded to include a responsibility of notification, which informs individuals that they have become the subject of a file. Although this might seem, on the face of it, to represent an administrative burden and expense, it should serve the second and third principles well.

The second, third, and fourth principles—necessity, minimization, and finality—call for limitations on the collection, storage, and use of personal information to the maximum extent possible, primarily through limiting such collection to that which is necessary and relevant. Simitis has suggested making the data collectors responsible for demonstrating the necessity for all the information they collect, and Flaherty's principle requires that the purposes need to be established in advance of their collection.[170] The rationale underlying this principle appears to be linked to Flaherty's sixth principle involving the control of linkages, transfers, and interconnections that involve personal information. In that further information or intelligence about individuals is produced through such linkages, which clearly were not specified in advance, each linkage represents, at least conceptually, a new collection of personal information.

The fifth principle would require the identification of persons who would be responsible for ensuring that personal information is maintained consistent with these principles. Presumably this principle would also require the provision of resources and the necessary autonomy that would allow this person or persons to pursue the interests of privacy without fear.

The seventh principle, that requiring informed consent, is absolutely fundamental to the understanding of privacy as an aspect of individual autonomy, yet it is a principle that is rarely honored in practice. We must assume that informed consent means consent freely given, by which an individual has meaningful options. This principle of informed consent is an expressed preference for the positive rather than the negative option. Consent cannot be assumed in the absence of an expressed denial. Instead, the assumption ought to be that of reserve, until such time as panopticism no longer represents the risks that are so apparent today. Consent is especially important with regard to the sixth principle, controlling linkage and exchange. The rationale and the risks that flow from consent, as well as the costs of refusal, ought to be made clear before any transfers or linkages proceed.

The eighth principle, that requiring accuracy and completeness in personal information systems, is potentially contradictory. To ensure accuracy and completeness, a bureaucracy will demand more information, more often. It is not clear that the principles of limitation and finality will overcome this contradiction. To realize the benefits that these principles promise, Flaherty's ninth and tenth principles call for the establishment of special rules and regulations governing access to and use of personal information. They also call for the specification of appropriate civil and criminal penalties for their abuse. As has been the historical lament, "laws are meant to be broken," and "the exceptions make the rule"; the realization of the goals that these principles are meant to support depends on the collective will of the people to enforce the rules and to punish offenders if necessary. The protection of individual privacy requires a level of vigilance and commitment to these principles that simply does not exist. As Barrington Moore suggests, "It is about as plain as anything can be that big bureaucracies are here to stay and that attempts to restore privacy and individual autonomy by dismantling bureaucracies as such are doomed to failure."[171] The only alternative appears to be another bureaucracy; yet the level of resistance in the United States to the idea of a data protection agency has not diminished despite the continuing increase in public concerns about privacy.

The eleventh principle, that which ensures individuals of the right to have access to records in order to evaluate, challenge, and correct inaccuracies, places too great a burden on individuals. There is little doubt that information about individuals exists in some detail in hundreds of files, most of which these individuals are probably unaware of. It is only when there is a problem that they can trace to the use of a particular list, such as a credit report or an insurance file, that they might be led to request access to their files. It was only in the heat of publicity about government "dirty tricks" that members of the public began to request access to the files held on them by the FBI. Yet it should certainly be clear by now that a great many other files contain inaccuracies that serve to limit or constrain a person's options. Perhaps it is not too far-fetched to imagine that people will come to check up on their informational health in the same way that they make periodic visits to their physicians and take periodic note of their own physical health status. A list of preventive screenings of classes of files may come to be as important and as routine as periodic checks of weight, blood pressure, and cholesterol levels.

Flaherty's twelfth principle, the right to be forgotten, to become anonymous, and to make a fresh start by destroying almost all personal information, is as intriguing as it is extreme. It should be possible to call for and to develop relationships in which identification is not required and in which records are not generated. For a variety of reasons, people have left home, changed their identities, and begun their lives again. If the purpose is nonfraudulent, is not an attempt to escape legitimate debts and responsibilities, then the formation of new identities is perfectly consistent with the notions of autonomy I have discussed. The courts and the legislatures have developed ways to make it possible for corporations to even reduce their obligations through the declaration of bankruptcy. Corporations, unlike individuals, can be rather easily dissolved and formed anew on action of their boards of directors. Why should corportions as fictional persons already have rights that natural persons still long to enjoy?

8

CONCLUSION

AND SO TO CONCLUDE

In Majid Tehranian's book, *Technologies of Power,* we are left with two options, totalitarianism or communitarian democracy.[1] Realist to the end, Tehranian also suggests that the communitarian option might be opposed by two second-best alternatives: limited success or co-optation. The future is indeterminant, and the trajectory remains hidden because the past is never, ever, truly repeated. Some form of rehabilitated democracy is a common theme in the final pages of most works that offer comment on contemporary society. Samuel Bowles and Herbert Gintis suggest that our future lies in the direction of a "post-liberal democracy."[2] This future is also uncertain, dependent as it is on a revolutionary expansion of personal rights against the competing expansionary claims of property. These more democratic futures depend on the successful conversion of liberal individualism into a collective awareness of common interests, which will transform the discourse of rights into a discourse of radical empowerment. These visions are steadfastly idealist and resist the pessimism that flows from a more structuralist theory of domination.

Can we agree with Tehranian that there is no *telos,* or essential purpose or end, that is inherent in the technology that we have defined as the panoptic sort? Can the technologies developed during the control revolution in late capitalism be transformed to serve a democratic purpose, or is such a system of control *inherently* antidemocratic?[3] Does workplace democracy need a system of disciplinary surveillance? Does a democratic public sphere need political strategists armed with sharply focused citizen profiles? Does an efficient market need consumer research? Advertising and promotion? Segmentation and targeting? Or are these activities incompatible, mutually inconsistent, contradictory, and antagonistic to the notion of free acting, fully informed rational producers and consumers?

It has been and remains my view that the panoptic sort is an antidemocratic system of control that cannot be transformed because it can serve no purpose other than that for which it was designed—the rationalization and control of human existence. This is a different vision from that which I once held as a youth. Then, social engineering was a good thing. Social engineers would operate the panoptic system in the interests of the "World Community." Social engineers would correct problems in people just as surely as civil, chemical, and electrical engineers and aerospace technicians corrected problems in the flow of rivers, the fertility of the soil, and the time it took to get from here to there. Yet today, environmentalists are not alone in their assessment of the consequences of allowing these engineers and their employers a free hand in bringing nature under the control of science. We are seriously at risk. Estimates vary widely, but the ranges between ten and one hundred years do not speak well for the changes in the quality of life we may experience anywhere along the road to an almost certain global catastrophe.

We have little reason to rejoice about the success of social engineering either. The insanity of the urban core reflects a hopelessness that is reproduced by the operation of the panopic sort—a discriminatory technology that selects out and rewards self-identification as deviant and dysfunctional and increases the sharpness of distinctions that are then reified and institutionalized. Panopticism identifies, breeds, cultivates, and reproduces failure.

Robert Entman's book, *Democracy Without Citizens,* talks about the emergence of an American democracy in decline. This political environment, which Entman describes as a "spiral of demagoguery, diminished rationality in policymaking, heightened tendency toward symbolic reassurance and nostalgic evasion of concrete choices, and ultimately misrepresentation of the public," is a joint product of two institutions, the government and the press, independently pursuing strategic rather than democratic goals.[4] Entman's solutions for the problems of American democracy do not give one hope: government financing of national news organizations run by the major political parties is a solution that moves as close to disaster as anything I could imagine.[5] But if not this, by what means *are* we to realize participatory economic democracy? Is the development of a movement, a U.S. Green party, for example, of the sort which Tehranian seems to suggest, something that we will approach with the aid of specialists, professionals, or strategists? Will we mount a direct mail campaign? Is this a process that involves leadership? Another vanguard perhaps? Will the state stand by? How will the corporate giant, Culture, Inc., respond to our "please, hold" while we get our new political act together so we can take it on the road?[6]

How is it that the emancipatory and critical project of Jürgen Habermas is to be realized when the the actors in the period of transition to democracy believe they must act strategically rather than democratically?

If actors are interested solely in the *success,* i.e., the *consequences* or *outcomes* of their actions, they will try to reach their objectives by influencing their opponent's definition of the situation, and thus his decisions or motives, through external means by using weapons or goods, threats or enticements. Such actors treat each other strategically. In such cases, coordination of the subjects' actions depends on the extent to which their egocentric utility calculations mesh.[7]

Habermas argues that "agreement in the communicative practice of everyday life rests simultaneously on intersubjectively shared propositional knowledge, on normative accord, and on mutual trust."[8] None of these requirements obtains at any scale that could be called substantive, and the operation of the panoptic sort, which is a strategic rather than a communicative technology, does not require nor support their attainment. The panoptic sort reduces the need for communicative understanding by increasing the isolation of individuals. At its ultimate level of development, each individual might have contact only with the network (after all, what needs can we imagine that cannot eventually be met more efficiently through an automated panoptic system?). Although *trust* might be valued instrumentally, in the absence of viable alternatives trust becomes a luxury, rather than a structural requirement.

The ethical principles that must be shared before communicative action can leave strategic communication to history cannot be infused in the same way that stannous fluoride can be introduced into the water supply. Moral development is a process of learning, one that takes historical time. Habermas cites assessments of the level of moral consciousness in the United States that place more than half of the population below the "postconventional" target, and others have shown people to be quite capable of regression to prior stages of moral development.[9] To subject this process of moral development to *la technique*, perhaps even using the panoptic sort to facilitate the identification of those in need of remedial work, cannot serve the desired ends.

The privacy agenda, which includes the creation of an independent bureaucracy that would have the responsibility for ensuring the survival of privacy interests, is similarly problematic. David Flaherty is quite sober in his recognition of the difficulties that privacy commissioners face.

> The harsh reality is that data protectors run the risk of being only a tiny force of irregulars equipped with pitchforks and hoes waging battle against large technocratic and bureaucratic forces equipped with lasers and nuclear weapons. This is especially true for their essential work in the public sector, where they are not simply a part of the government, but the primary protector of citizens in their relations with the government itself.
>
> The issue is essentially one of power. ... In terms of external conflicts over power relations, data protection agencies are squeezed between power holders and the powerless in trying to foster public support for their goals.[10]

Flaherty also recognizes the inherent tension that keeps the state from acting aggressively to restrict the development and use of any technology, especially new forms of information technology that are seen to be the wave of the future, which might carry a troubled economy into the next Kondratieff upswing. Because of these pressures, and his self-proclaimed status as an optimist, Flaherty holds on to the hope that a data protection agency, which will articulate and pursue privacy interests on a continuous basis, might keep the panoptic system under control. He is entitled to his dreams. But because he fails to pay sufficient attention to the importance of disciplinary surveillance to the survival of corporate capital, Flaherty's analysis ignores a critical dynamic that makes the assumption of government control unrealistic.

The panoptic sort does not engender trust and a sense of community. Quite the opposite is the result. And, as we understand the notion of deviation amplifying, positive feedback loops in the general theory of systems, growing mistrust leads to expanded surveillance, and each cycle pushes us further from the democratic ideal.

WHAT IS TO BE DONE?

Jacques Ellul describes a future in which the technological system has reached its highest level of integration. It is an image of the future that leads one to ask "What's wrong with this picture?"

> It will not be a universal concentration camp, for it will be guilty of no atrocity. It will not seem insane, for everything will be ordered, and the stains of human passion will be lost amid the chromium gleam. We shall have nothing more to lose, and nothing to win. Our deepest instincts and our most secret passions will be analyzed, published and exploited. We shall be rewarded with everything our hearts ever desired. And the supreme luxury of the society of technical necessity will be to grant the bonus of useless revolt and of an acquiescent smile.[11]

My sense is that this is not the kind of future that any of us would design.[12] It is not the future of our dreams and fantasies. But it is the future that is promised by the panoptic sort, and it is a future that we can see in faint outline.

We are, as Stewart Brand suggests, engaged in the work of "inventing the future," but this future, as Marx reminds us, is never faithful to our design. This is true in large part because each of us has our own incomplete versions of the more complete design. Indeed, because the design process is ongoing, many of us are working with versions that are obsolete, that have been replaced or superseded, but somehow we missed the notice or discarded the mailing. Whether through forgetfulness, carelessness, or childlike stubbornness, some of us refuse to join the project and climb aboard this train as it begins to pick up speed.

It is the work of critical scholarship to raise doubts in the minds of the other passengers, to give voice to their unspoken concerns about the competence of the engineers, to validate their mistrust of the digitized voices that announce the next station or the final destination. It is the work of critical scholarship to speak to the engineers, to wonder aloud with them about whether the tracks will carry a train this long, this fast, that far.

In L. Frank Baum's great story, *The Wonderful Wizard of Oz*, we are provided a vantage point from which to see great trickery and illusion. When Dorothy and her friends came before the Wizard, each saw a different representation. Dorothy saw Oz as a great head, the scarecrow saw a lovely lady, the tin woodman beheld a terrible beast, and the lion envisioned a ball of fire—all illusion. Within the panoptic future, addressability and verifiability mean that it is much more likely that each of us will be exposed to a different, customized, administratively tailored image of our immediate environment, our risks, our options, and the opportunities for the realization of our dreams. In the *Wizard of Oz*, it was Toto, scared by the lion's roar, that knocked over the screen and revealed the Wizard as a "little, old man, with a bald head, and a wrinkled face," rather than an all-knowing, all-seeing, and all-powerful granter of wishes (who always demanded something in exchange). Perhaps because it takes more energy than one can, or perhaps should, bring to bear to knock down the screens around the panoptic machine, critical scholarship should be focused on generating small holes or tears in the screen that will allow others to see more clearly how the illusion is produced.

My project is not the lion's roar, just a tiny rent in the screen. There is much more to be seen. Make a hole for yourself, or help me to widen the one that I have already begun.

NOTES

CHAPTER 1

1. Henry L. Wells was the director of Credit Research, Spiegel, Incorporated. The pointing system was described in a seminar paper entitled "New customer credit reporting system," pp. 4–21. In a photocopied collection entitled *Numerical Pointing Plans for Evaluating Consumer Risks.* The Second Consumer Credit Symposium. University of Pennsylvania, January 10, 1963.

2. Kevin Robins and Frank Webster, "Cybernetic capitalism: Information, technology, everyday life," pp. 44–75. In V. Mosco and J. Wasko [eds], *The Political Economy of Information.* Madison: University of Wisconsin Press, 1988.

3. *Webster's New Collegiate Dictionary.* Springfield, MA: G. & C. Merriam, 1974.

4. A similar definition from the *Oxford English Dictionary* is provided in Gerald R. Winslow's *Triage and Justice,* Berkeley: University of California Press, 1982, which provides a detailed exploration of the inequities and moral dilemmas involved in medical triage.

5. *Webster's Third New International Dictionary* (unabridged). Springfield, MA: G. & C. Merriam, 1976.

6. The notion of information subsidies suggests that actors with the reasons and the resources necessary to produce influence over the actions of others will do so in part through the provision of information that favors one option over another. This information is seen as a subsidy because it reduces the costs an individual would face if she had to gather the information on her own. See Oscar H. Gandy, Jr., *Beyond Agenda Setting: Information Subsidies and Public Policy.* Norwood, NJ: Ablex, 1982.

7. Jürgen Habermas, *The Structural Transformation of the Public Sphere: An Inquiry into a Category of Bourgeois Society.* Cambridge, MA: MIT Press, 1989.

8. Stephen K. White, *The Recent Work of Jürgen Habermas: Reason, Justice and Modernity.* New York: Cambridge University Press, 1988.

9. Oscar H. Gandy, Jr., "The political economy of communications competence," pp. 108–124. In V. Mosco and J. Wasko [eds], 1988, op. cit.

10. Randall Bartlett, *Economics and Power: An Inquiry into Human Relationships and Markets.* New York: Cambridge University Press, 1989, pp. 3–8.

11. T. B. Bottomore, *Karl Marx: Selected Writings in Sociology and Social Philosophy.* New York: McGraw-Hill, 1964.

12. David J. Sholle, "Critical Studies: From the Theory of Ideology to Power/Knowledge." *Critical Studies in Mass Communication* 5 (March 1988):16–41.

13. Nicholas Garnham, "A political economy of mass communication," pp. 24–30. In *Capitalism and Communication: Global Culture and the Economics of Information.* London: Sage Publications, 1990.

14. Robert Horwitz, *The Irony of Regulatory Reform: The Deregulation of American Telecommunications.* New York: Oxford University Press, 1989.

15. Anne Branscomb, "Property rights in information," pp. 603–642. In M. Gurevitch and M. Levy [eds], *Mass Communication Review Yearbook.* Vol 6. Newbury Park, CA: Sage, 1987; Anne W. Branscomb, *Who Owns Information?* Occasional Paper No. 2. New York: Gannett Center for Media Studies, May 1986.

16. Amitai Etzioni, *Genetic Fix.* New York: Macmillan, 1973; Troy Duster, *Backdoor to Eugenics.* New York: Routledge, 1990.

17. Karl Marx, from the preface of his *Contribution to the Critique of Political Economy* [1859] excerpted in Bottomore, 1964, op. cit., p. 52.

18. Dan Schiller, "How to think about information," pp. 27–43. In V. Mosco and J. Wasko [eds], *The Political Economy of Information.* Madison: University of Wisconsin Press, 1988.

19. Brian Burkitt, *Radical Political Economy: An Introduction to the Alternative Economics.* New York: New York University Press, 1984; Howard J. Sherman, *Foundations of Radical Political Economy.* Armonk, NY: M. E. Sharpe, 1987; Richard D. Wolff and Stephen A. Resnick, *Economics: Marxian Versus Neoclassical.* Baltimore, MD: Johns Hopkins University Press, 1987.

20. Joseph A. Schumpeter, *Capitalism, Socialism and Democracy.* 4th ed., 11th impression. London: Unwin University Books, 1966, p. 28.

21. Arun Bose, "Modern Marxian political economy," pp. 90–115. In David K. Whynes [ed], *What is Political Economy? Eight Perspectives.* New York: Basil Blackwell, 1984. Bose suggests the emphasis was in the original, but the reference did not include the citation from Marx, referring instead to his 1980 volume *Marx on Exploitation and Inequality.*

22. Dan Schiller, 1988, op. cit., p. 36.

23. Jacques Ellul, *What I Believe* (trans. Geoffrey W. Bromiley). Grand Rapids, MI: Eerdmans Publishing, 1989, p. 135.

24. Ibid., p. 137.

25. Ellul might have derived this from the orientation of Marx, who envisioned the realization of man's potential as the essence of liberty, which could only be obtained after the development of productive capacity made such personal development possible.

26. William Julius Wilson, *The Truly Disadvantaged: The Inner City, The Underclass, and Public Policy.* Chicago: University of Chicago Press, 1987.

27. Ellul, 1989, op. cit., pp. 138–139.

28. C. George Benello, "Technology and Power: Technique as a Mode of Understanding Modernity," pp. 91–107. In C. Christians and J. Van Hook [eds], *Jacques Ellul: interpretive essays.* Champaign, IL: University of Illinois Press, 1981.

29. Jacques Ellul, *The Technological Society* (trans. John Wilkinson). New York: Vintage Books, 1964, p. viii.

30. Similar criticisms have been lodged against the otherwise impressive analysis of information technology published by James Beniger, *The Control Revolution: Technological and Economic Origins of the Information Society.* Cambridge, MA: Harvard University Press, 1986. See, for example, G. J. Mulgan, *Communication and Control: Networks and the New Economics of Communication.* New York: Guilford Press, 1991.

31. Joseph A. Schumpeter, 1966, op. cit., pp. 81–86.

32. Rogers Brubaker, *The Limits of Rationality: An Essay on the Social and Moral Thought of Max Weber.* London: Allen and Unwin, 1984.

33. David Beetham, *Max Weber and the Theory of Modern Politics*. London: Allen and Unwin, 1974, p. 65.

34. Reinhard Bendix, *Max Weber. An Intellectual Portrait*. Garden City, NY: Doubleday (Anchor), 1962, pp. 458–459.

35. Beetham, 1974, op. cit., p. 242.

36. Frank Webster and Kevin Robins, *Information Technology: A Luddite Analysis*. Norwood, NJ: Ablex, 1986, p. 73.

37. Robert G. Meadow, "Political campaigns, new technologies and political competition," pp. 5–16. In R. Meadow [ed], *New Communication Technologies in Politics*. Washington, D.C.: Washington Program of the Annenberg School of Communications, 1985.

38. Christopher Dandeker, *Surveillance, Power and Modernity: Bureaucracy and Discipline from* 1700 to the Present Day. New York: St. Martin's Press, 1990, p. 9.

39. Robert J. Holton and Bryan S. Turner, *Max Weber on Economy and Society*. New York: Routledge, 1989, p. 66.

40. Brubaker, 1984, op. cit., p. 19.

41. Meheroo Jussawalla and Chee-Wah Cheah, "Economic analysis of the legal and policy aspects of information privacy," pp. 75–102. In M. Jussawalla and C. Cheah [eds], *The Calculus of International Communications*. Littleton, CO: Libraries Unlimited, 1987.

42. Brubaker, 1984, op. cit., p. 42.

43. Randall Bartlett, *Economics and Power: An Inquiry into Human Relations and Markets*. New York: Cambridge University Press, 1989.

44. Michel Foucault, *Discipline and Punish: The Birth of the Prison* (trans. Alan Sheridan). New York: Vintage Books, 1979; especially Chapter 3, "Panopticism," pp. 195–230.

45. Ibid., p. 201.

46. Ibid., p. 203

47. Oscar H. Gandy, Jr., and Charles Simmons, "Technology, privacy and the democratic process." *Critical Studies in Mass Communication* 3 (June 1986):155–168.

48. Kevin Robins and Frank Webster, 1988, op. cit.

49. Michel Foucault, "Classifying," pp. 125–165. In *The Order of Things: An Archeology of the Human Sciences*. New York: Vintage Books, 1973.

50. Paul Rabinow, "Introduction," in P. Rabinow [ed], *The Foucault Reader*. New York: Pantheon, 1984.

51. Mary Tew Douglas, *How Institutions Think*. New York: Syracuse University Press, 1986, p. 100.

52. Ibid., p. 20.

53. Jelena Grcic-Polic and Oscar H. Gandy, Jr., "The emergence of the marketplace standard." *Media Law and Practice* (1991):55–64.

54. Peter G. Moore, *The Business of Risk*. Cambridge: Cambridge University Press, 1983.

55. Stanley Cohen, *Visions of Social Control: Crime, Punishment and Classification*. Cambridge: Polity Press, 1985, p. 196.

56. Ibid., p. 267.

57. Rick Roderick, *Habermas and the Foundations of Critical Theory*. New York: St. Martin's Press, 1986.

58. Stephen A. Resnick and Richard D. Wolff, *Knowledge and Class: A Marxian Critique of Political Economy*. Chicago: University of Chicago Press, 1987.

59. Anthony Giddens, *The Constitution of Society: Outline of the Theory of Structuration.* Cambridge: Polity Press, 1984.

60. David Held and John B. Thompson [eds], *Social Theory of Modern Societies: Anthony Giddens and His Critics.* Cambridge: Cambridge University Press, 1989.

61. Ann Showstack Sassoon [ed], *Approaches to Gramsci.* London: Writers and Readers, 1982.

62. George Gerbner, Larry Gross, Michael Morgan, and Nancy Signorielli, "Living with television: The dynamics of the cultivation process," pp. 17–40. In J. Bryant and D. Zillman [eds], *Perspectives on Media Effects.* Hillsdale, NJ: Lawrence Erlbaum, 1986.

63. Anthony Giddens, *The Nation State and Violence.* Berkeley: University of California Press, 1985.

64. Ibid., p. 309.

CHAPTER 2

1. By this I am referring to the prescreening requirements, or "front-end verification," that is required if an individual applies for federally supported social welfare benefits. It also includes the growing number of biological and genetic screens that are now required of newborns.

2. Reference is made here to Foucault's notion of power as being based in relations and where power does not truly exist unless the agent is free to act in more than one way. Power is demonstrated when the choice is limited according to the wishes of power. Power is also demonstrated when choices freely made limit future choices. See Michel Foucault, "Afterward. The Subject and Power," pp. 208–226. In Hubert Dreyfus and Paul Rabinow, *Michel Foucault: Beyond Structuralism and Hermaneutics.* 2d ed. Chicago: University of Chicago Press, 1983.

3. Michel Foucault, *The Order of Things: An Archeology of the Human Sciences.* New York: Vintage Books, 1973, p. 136.

4. Troy Duster, *Back Door to Eugenics.* New York: Routledge, 1990, p. 97.

5. Daniel Hahneman and Amos Tversky provide a detailed and elegant discussion of the nature of risk aversion and the absence in linearity that characterizes the valuation of losses and gains. "Choices, values and frames," pp. 153–172. In N. Smelser and D. Gerstein [eds], *Behavioral and Social Science: Fifty Years of Discovery.* Washington, D.C.: National Academy Press, 1986.

6. Randall Bartlett, *Economics and Power: An Inquiry into Human Relations and Markets.* New York: Cambridge University Press, 1989, p. 30.

7. Ibid., p. 46.

8. Amitai Etzioni, *The Moral Dimension.* New York: Free Press, 1988, pp. 246–247.

9. C. Edwin Baker, "Posner's privacy mystery." *Georgia Law Review* 12 (1978):476. Baker argues that because existing preferences are subject to influence in that laws not only affect the realization of preferences but also affect what preferences we have, and further, because the influence of existing preferences is likely to be conservative rather than progressive, the existing preferences ought not to be given as justifications for restrictions on liberty.

10. Bartlett, 1989, p. 101.

11. Samuel Bowles and Herbert Gintis, *Democracy and Capitalism.* New York: Basic Books, 1987.

12. Ibid., p. 77.

13. This is a point made quite forcefully by Mark Hepworth and Michael Waterson, "Information technology and the spatial dynamics of capital." *Information Economics and Policy*, 3 (1988):143–163.

14. Bartlett, 1989, pp. 127–128.

15. Several of these approaches to policy formation are explored in Oscar H. Gandy, Jr., "Public relations and public policy: The structuration of dominance in the information age," pp. 131–163. In E. Toth and R. Heath [eds], *Rhetorical and Critical Approaches to Public Relations*. Hillsdale, NJ: Lawrence Erlbaum, 1992.

16. G. William Domhoff, *The Power Elite and the State: How Policy is Made in America*. New York: Walter de Gruyter, 1990.

17. Michael Schwartz [ed], *The Structure of Power in America*. New York: Holmes and Meier, 1987, p. x.

18. Edward Laumann and David Knoke, *The Organization State: Social Choice in National Policy Domains*. Madison: University of Wisconsin Press, 1987.

19. Michel Foucault, *Discipline and Punish: The Birth of the Prison*. (trans. Alan Sheridan). New York: Vintage Books, 1979. This is Foucault's core work in this regard, although later comments and expansions are noted in Hubert Dreyfus and Paul Rabinow, *Michel Foucault. Beyond Structuralism and Hermaneutics*. 2d ed. Chicago: University of Chicago Press, 1983; and Paul Rabinow [ed], *The Foucault Reader*. New York: Pantheon, 1984; Graham Burchell, Colin Gordon, and Peter Miller [eds], *The Foucault Effect: Studies in Governmentality*. Chicago: University of Chicago Press, 1991.

20. Michel Foucault, "Questions of method," p. 84. In Graham Burchell, Colin Gordon, and Peter Miller [eds], *The Foucault Effect: Studies in Governmentality*. Chicago: University of Chicago Press, 1991.

21. Foucault identifies other common dichotomies: mad/sane, dangerous/harmless, normal/abnormal, which are common to systems of coordination and control.

22. Michel Foucault, 1979, op. cit., p. 197.

23. We wish to avoid the error of some critics of Foucault who seem to have focused on the Panopticon as a structure and lost sight of panopticism as an administrative technique.

24. John Dinwiddy, *Bentham*. Oxford: Oxford University Press, 1989, p. 8.

25. Foucault, 1979, op. cit., p. 202.

26. Ibid., p. 205.

27. Ibid.

28. Frank Webster and Kevin Robins, *Information Technology: A Luddite Analysis*. Norwood, NJ: Ablex, 1986; Kevin Robins and Frank Webster, "Cybernetic capitalism: Information, technology, everyday life," pp. 44–75. In V. Mosco and J. Wasko [eds], *The Political Economy of Information*. Madison: University of Wisconsin Press, 1988; Kevin Robins and Frank Webster, "Information as capital: A critique of Daniel Bell," pp. 95–117. In J. Slack and F. Fejes [eds], *The Ideology of the Information Age*. Norwood, NJ: Ablex, 1987.

29. Dreyfus and Rabinow, 1983, op. cit., p. 160.

30. Foucault describes a system of classificatory codes that distinguished the very good from the mediocre, the bad, and the "shameful" classes. Foucault, *Discipline and Punish*, pp. 181–182.

31. Michael Lewis, "Leave home without it." *New Republic* (September 4, 1989):19–22.

32. Ibid., p. 183.

33. Foucault, *Discipline and Punish*, p. 189.

34. Giddens's criticism of functionalism in general and of creeping functionalism in Marxist theory is discussed in his *The Constitution of Society*. Cambridge: Polity Press, 1986, pp. 15–19, and in his *A Contemporary Critique of Historical Materialism*. Berkeley: University of California Press, 1981, pp. 293–297.

35. Giddens, 1981, p. 26.

36. Giddens, 1981, p. 46.

37. Giddens, 1981, p. 47.

38. John B. Thompson, "The theory of structuration," pp. 56–76. In D. Held and J. Thompson [eds], *Social Theory of Modern Societies: Anthony Giddens and His Critics*. Cambridge: Cambridge University Press, 1989.

39. Thompson, 1989, p. 63.

40. Giddens, 1986, op. cit., p. xxx.

41. Giddens, 1981, op. cit., p. 36.

42. Bartlett, 1989, op. cit., pp. 43–44.

43. The concept of hegemony, associated with Antonio Gramsci, and the critical theory of the Frankfurt School and its revisionist emanations in the work of Jürgen Habermas, stand as the dominant exemplars of a Marxian response to this problem.

44. Erik Olin Wright, "Rethinking, once again, the concept of class structure," pp. 269–348. In Erik Olin Wright [ed], *The Debate on Classes*. London: Verso, 1989; Erik Olin Wright, "Class boundaries and contradictory class locations," pp. 112–129. In A. Giddens and D. Held [eds], *Classes, Power and Conflict*. Berkeley: University of California Press, 1982.

45. Wright, 1989, p. 276.

46. Erik Olin Wright, "Models of historical trajectory: An assessment of Giddens's critique of Marxism," pp. 77–102. In Held and Thompson, 1989, op. cit.

47. Wright, 1989, p. 89.

48. Selections from Max Weber, "Economy and Society," pp. 60–73. In A. Giddens and D. Held [eds], *Classes, Power and Conflict*. Berkeley: University of California Press, 1982; "Classes, Status Groups and Parties," pp. 43–61. In W. G. Runciman, *Weber: Selections in Translation* (trans. Eric Matthews). Cambridge: Cambridge University Press, 1978.

49. This was a style of life which Thorsten Veblen had subjected to such unremitting criticism in his *Theory of the Leisure Class*. New York: New American Library, 1953.

50. Giddens and Held, p. 67.

51. Arthur L. Stinchcombe, *Information and Organizations*. Berkeley: University of California Press, 1990, p. 274.

52. Ibid., p. 292.

53. Ibid., p. 294.

54. The nature of the dual labor market and the problems of the urban ghetto have been explored in some detail by William Julius Wilson in *The Truly Disadvantaged*. Chicago: University of Chicago Press, 1987; see also: Richard M. Cyert and David Mowery [eds], *Technology and Employment: Innovation and Growth in the U.S. Economy*. Washington, D.C.: National Academy of Science Press, 1987; and John D. Kasarda, "Urban industrial transition and the underclass." *Annals: AAPSS* 501 (January 1989):26–47.

55. Stinchcombe, 1990, p. 303.

56. The mainstreaming hypothesis, as a specification of the cultivation hypothesis, suggests that people whose concrete social experience would generally produce quite different social perceptions tend to have more similar perceptions if they share the common cultivating experience of televiewing. The movement of those in the upper classes is the opposite of that of those in the lower classes, but both groups move toward a common mainstream. A discussion of mainstreaming and other aspects of the cultivation hypothesis can be found in George Gerbner, Larry Gross, Michael Morgan, "Living with television: The dynamics of the cultivation process," pp. 17–40. In J. Bryant and D. Zillman [eds], *Perspectives on Media Effects*. Hillsdale, NJ: Lawrence Erlbaum Associates, 1986; and Nancy Signorielli and Michael Morgan [eds], *Cultivation Analysis*. Newbury Park, CA: Sage, 1990.

57. Stinchcombe, op. cit., p. 303.

58. Geoff Mulgan, *Communication and Control: Networks and the New Economics of Communication*. New York: Guilford, 1991, p. 53.

59. Giddens, 1986, op. cit., p. 171.

60. Ibid., p. 261.

61. Oscar H. Gandy, Jr., "The political economy of communications competence," pp. 108–124. In V. Mosco and J. Wasko [eds], *The Political Economy of Information*. Madison: University of Wisconsin Press, 1988.

62. Derek Gregory, "Presences and absences: Time-space relations and structuration theory," pp. 185–214. In Held and Thompson, 1989, op. cit.

63. Gregory, 1989, p. 208.

64. These perspectives on technology are discussed in a recent book by Majid Tehranian, *Technologies of Power: Information Machines and Democratic Prospects*. Norwood, NJ: Ablex, 1990. Tehranian offers what he calls a "contextualist" perspective, by which the use of technologies depends primarily on the existing structures of power into which they are introduced.

65. Jacques Ellul, *The Technological Society* (trans. John Wilkinson). New York: Vintage Books, 1964.

66. Jacques Ellul, *Propaganda: The Formation of Men's Attitudes* (trans. Konrad Lellen and Jean Lerner). New York: Vintage Books, 1973.

67. Ellul, 1973, p. x.

68. Ibid., p. xvii.

69. Clifford G. Christians, "Hegemony and the technological system: Gramsci versus Ellul." Conference paper. Annual meeting of the Association for Education in Journalism and Mass Communication, Boston, MA, August 1991.

70. See especially, Antonio Gramsci, *Selections from the Prison Notebooks*. London: Lawrence and Wishart, 1973; Anne S. Sassoon [ed], *Approaches to Gramsci*. London: Writers and Readers, 1982; and selections in A. Mattelart and S. Siegelaub [eds], *Communication and Class Struggle*. Vol. 1, *Capitalism, Imperialism*. New York: International General, 1979.

71. Jürgen Habermas's emphasis on the influence of commercialization in the transformation of the role of the press as an aspect of the traditional public sphere and the site of opinion formation does not reach Ellul's level of attention to questions of technique. See his *The Structural Transformation of the Public Sphere: An Inquiry into a Category of Bourgeois Society* (trans. Thomas Burger). Cambridge, MA: MIT Press, 1989.

72. John Wilkinson, "Translator's Introduction" to Ellul, *The Technological Society*, 1973, p. xv.

73. Ellul, 1973, p. 134.

74. C. George Benello, "Technology and power: Technique as a mode of understanding modernity," pp. 91–107. In C. Christians and J. Van Hook [eds], *Jacques Ellul: interpretive essays*. Champaign, IL: University of Illinois Press, 1981.

75. Ellul, 1973, p. 135.

76. David Lovekin, *Technique, Discourse and Consciousness: An Introduction to the Philosophy of Jacques Ellul*. Bethlehem, PA: Lehigh University Press, 1991, p. 143.

77. Ellul, 1973, op. cit.

78. Ellul, 1964, p. 43.

79. Ibid., p. 47.

80. Ibid., p. 54.

81. Ellul, 1964, p. 171. This development of a planning role for economics and economists is at the heart of John Kenneth Galbraith's enfolding of technique and propaganda in his work on the management of demand. See his *The New Industrial State*. New York: Signet, 1968; and especially his *Economics and the Public Purpose*. Boston: Houghton Mifflin Co., 1973. Not even the subversive economics of E. F. Schumacher, as expressed in his *Small Is Beautiful: Economics As If People Mattered* (New York: Harper and Row, 1973) managed to avoid the pursuit of technology and planning, as though calling it "appropriate" somehow hid the fact that the concern was with efficiency and productivity.

82. I recall, and not without some pleasure, taking courses in a department at Stanford called Engineering-Economic Systems, which was involved with assessing the technological efficiency of engineering systems designed to solve social as well as material problems. There were also courses in the Food Research Institute concerned with economics, development, and national planning clearly not limited to agriculture; another school offered courses in the economics of education, which mused about "investments in human capital" and "educational production functions." In association with the medical school, Victor Fuchs offered a popular course on the economics of health, which focused on the choices made by individuals following Gary Becker's notions of household production, which conceptualized invidivduals as "producing" their own health or illness. The introduction of economic concepts and efficiency rationales into the logic of the courts has been seen by several commentators to have pushed aside the values of fairness, justice, and equity. The spread of economics beyond its disciplinary borders shows no signs of abating.

83. Ellul, 1964, p. 411.

84. Ibid.

85. James Beniger, *The Control Revolution: Technological and Economic Origins of the Information Society*. Cambridge: Harvard University Press, 1986.

86. Dennis Wrong, "Introduction." In D. Wrong [ed], *Max Weber*. Englewood Cliffs, NJ: Prentice-Hall, 1970.

87. Rogers Brubaker, *The Limits of Rationality: An Essay on the Social and Moral Thought of Max Weber*. London: Allen and Unwin, 1984, p. 2.

88. Brubaker, 1984, pp. 3–4.

89. Christopher Dandeker, *Surveillance, Power and Modernity: Bureaucracy and Discipline from 1700 to the Present Day*. New York: St. Martin's Press, 1990.

90. Robert J. Holton and Bryan S. Turner, *Max Weber on Economy and Society*. New York: Routledge, 1989, p. 23.

91. David Beetham, *Max Weber and the Theory of Modern Politics*. London: Allen and Unwin, 1974, p. 65.

92. Holton and Turner, 1989, p. 44.

93. John Elster and John Roemer [eds], *Interpersonal Comparisons of Well-Being*. New York: Cambridge University Press, 1991.

94. Holton and Turner, p. 53.

95. See the discussion of the "emergence of legal rationality" in Weber's political sociology in Reinhard Bendix, *Max Weber: An Intellectual Portrait*. Garden City: Doubleday, 1962, pp. 391–496.

96. Bendix, 1962, p. 414.

97. Harry Braverman, *Labor and Monopoly Capital*. New York: Monthly Review Press, 1974.

98. Frank Webster and Kevin Robins, *Information Technology: A Luddite Analysis*. Norwood, NJ: Ablex, 1986.

99. This process of automation is discussed from the perspective of personal experience by Harley Shaiken in his *Work Transformed: Automation and Labor in the Computer Age*. New York: Holt, Rinehart & Winston, 1984.

100. Webster and Robins, 1986, pp. 328–347.

101. Beniger, 1986.

102. Kevin Robins and Frank Webster, "The revolution of the fixed wheel: Information, technology and Social Taylorism," pp. 36–91. In P. Drummond and R. Paterson [eds], *Television in Transition*. London: British Film Institute, 1986.

103. Beniger, 1986, p. 15.

104. Ibid., p. 16.

105. Spiros Simitis, "Reviewing privacy in an information society." *University of Pennsylvania Law Review* 135 (1987):733.

106. This is to say nothing about the debates in science about the impossibility of measuring anything that does not change that which is being measured. To this we add the insight that "identity" is a construct, rather than a fact. Mario Bunge argues that not only are repeated measures necessarily at variance with each other, but increasing the precision or quality of measurement only increases the unrepeatability of any measure. Mario Bunge, *Causality and Modern Science*. 3d rev. ed. New York: Dover Publications, 1979, p. 267.

107. Oscar H. Gandy, Jr., "A critical challenge: The approach of political economy to the study of communication and information." *Journal of Media Economics*. 107 (Summer 1992): 23–42.

108. Mario Bunge, op. cit., p. 271.

109. Anthony Giddens, "A reply to my critics," pp. 249–301. In D. Held and J. Thompson, 1989, op. cit., pp. 288–289.

110. The Heisenberg principle that denies the possibility of measuring anything without changing that which is being measured, however, is certainly an issue worthy of consideration.

111. Eugene Webb, Donald Campbell, Richard Schwartz, and Lee Sechrest, *Unobtrusive Measures: Nonreactive Research in the Social Sciences*. New York: Rand McNally, 1971.

112. Giddens in Held and Thompson, p. 289.

113. Bunge, 1979, pp. 14–19.

114. Bunge, 1979, p. 353.

115. Bunge, 1979, pp. 330–331.

116. Thomas L. Haskell, *The Emergence of Professional Social Science: The American Social Science Association and the Nineteenth-Century Crisis of Authority.* Urbana: University of Illinois Press, 1977, p. 16.

117. Haskell, 1977, p. 251.

118. Max Weber from *Wirtschaft und Gesellschaft.* In W. G. Runiciman [ed], *Weber: Selections in Translation.* 1978, p. 350.

119. Christopher Dandeker, *Surveillance, Power and Modernity: Bureaucracy and Discipline from 1700 to the Present Day.* New York: St. Martin's Press, 1990, p. 9.

120. The surveillance of telecommunications workers was explored in great detail in the study of workplace surveillance by the U.S. Office of Technology Assessment, *The Electronic Supervisor.* Washington, D.C.: U.S. Government Printing Office, 1987. See also: Andrew Clement, "Office automation and the technical control of information workers," pp. 217–244. In V. Mosco and J. Wasko [eds], *The Political Economy of Information.* Madison: University of Wisconsin Press, 1988.

121. Peter T. Kilborn, "Workers using computers find a supervisor inside." *New York Times.* December 23, 1990, sec. A.

122. Richard Barnet and Ronald Müller. *Global Reach. The Power of Multinational Corporations.* New York: Simon and Schuster, 1974.

123. Dandeker, 1990, p. 154. See also: Mark Hepworth, *Geography of the Information Economy.* New York: Guilford Press, 1990.

124. Dandeker, 1990, p. 210.

125. Reinhard Bendix, *Max Weber: An Intellectual Portrait.* Garden City: Doubleday, 1962, p. 482.

126. Julien Freund, *The Sociology of Max Weber.* New York: Vintage Books, 1969, p. 229.

127. Bendix, 1962, pp. 424–425.

128. Haskell, 1977, p. 89.

129. Andrew Gamble, *The Free Economy and the Strong State: The Politics of Thatcherism.* Durham, N.C.: Duke University Press, 1988.

130. Gamble, 1988, p. 184.

131. The Reagan administration's corporatist evolution began with the involvement of a privately managed and funded commission: "The President's Private Sector Survey on Cost Control," referred to as the Grace Commission, that made extensive recommendations on the transformation of the government. See: U.S. Congress. Senate Committee on Governmental Affairs. *Oversight of the Grace Commission Report.* Hearing, May 9, 1985. Washington, D.C.: U.S. Government Printing Office, 1985. The involvement of the conservative Heritage Foundation and its *Mandate for Leadership* represents another means through which an attack on the bureaucracy was designed and implemented.

132. Gamble, 1988, p. 50.

133. Weber's discussion of these problems focused on a kind of double government that might characterize an authoritarian regime, but the operation of executive power through the Office of Management and Budget was not unlike that of an army or secret police force charged with whipping the government bureaucracy into alignment with the new party line. See the discussion of this point in Bendix, 1962, p. 467.

134. Wilson Dizard, *The Coming Information Age.* 3d ed. New York: Longman, 1989, originally published in 1982.

135. Peter Hall and Paschal Preston, *The Carrier Wave: New Information Technology and the Geography of Innovation, 1846–2003.* London: Unwin Hyman, 1988. Hall and Preston

suggest that the next global economic expansion might be seen as the fifth in a series of such cyclical waves as described by Vasily Kondratieff and as widely discussed in terms of the long waves of the business cycles explored by Joseph Schumpeter.

136. Jorge Schement and Leah Lievrouw, "Capitalism and the industrial origins of the information society," pp. 33–45. In Schement and Lievrouw [eds], *Competing Visions, Complex Realities: Social Aspects of the Information Society*. Norwood, NJ: Ablex, 1987.

137. Marc Uri Porat, *The Information Economy* Vols. 1–2. Washington, D.C.: U.S. Department of Commerce, 1976.

138. See for example, Meheroo Jussawalla, Donald Lamberton, and Neil Karunaratne [eds], *The Cost of Thinking: Information Economies of Ten Pacific Countries*. Norwood, NJ: Ablex, 1988; Raul Katz, "Measurement and cross-national comparisons of the information work force." *The Information Society* 4 (4) (1986): 231–277.

139. It should be noted that a portion of Porat's work did in fact utilize an input-output table of the United States to estimate what the employment consequences might be if there were a reduction in defense expenditures.

140. Meheroo Jussawalla, "Information economies and the development of Pacific countries," pp. 15–43. In M. Jussawalla, D. Lamberton, and N. Karunaratne, 1988, op. cit.

141. Dan Schiller discusses what he sees as a counterproductive debate about a relatively useless distinction that remains as a vestige of Marx's emphasis on surplus value rather than the wage relation. See: Dan Schiller, "How to think about information," pp. 27–44. In V. Mosco and J. Wasko, 1988, op. cit. A classical Marxian analysis of the information economy that explores the implications of a growing pool of nonproductive workers is to be found in Patricia Arriaga, "Toward a critique of the information economy." *Media, Culture and Society* 7 (1985): 271–296.

142. Gales of creative destruction and swarms of innovations are constructs popularized by Joseph Schumpeter through his emphasis on the importance of the entrepreneur to the periodic crises of capitalism that we know as the business cycle. Joseph Schumpeter, *Capitalism, Socialism and Democracy*. London: Unwin University Books, 1966.

143. Peter Hall and Paschal Preston, *The Carrier Wave: New Information Technology and the Geography of Innovation, 1846–2003*. London: Unwin Hyman, 1988.

144. Stinchcombe, 1990, p. 362.

145. G. J. Mulgan, *Communication and Control*. New York: Guilford Press, 1991.

146. Murray Laver, *Information Technology: Agent of Change*. Cambridge: Cambridge University Press, 1989.

147. Theodore Roszak, *The Cult of Information*. New York: Pantheon, 1986. Roszak is especially critical of the dangers that flow from treating models, especially simulations, as though they were reality, rather than as a set of hypothetical assumptions about the nature of reality. The problem with simulations is that they tend to make reality much more neat and tidy than it actually is; pp. 68–70.

148. Arno Penzias, *Ideas and Information: Managing in a High-Tech World*. New York: W. W. Norton, 1989.

149. Steven Yearley, *Science, Technology and Social Change*. London: Unwin Hyman, 1988.

150. Charles Jonscher, "Information resources and economic productivity." *Information Economics and Policy* 1 (1983): 13–35.

151. Webster and Robins, 1986, op. cit.

152. Marcel J. Schoppers, "A perspective on artificial intelligence in society." *Communication* 9 (1986):195–227.

153. Katz, 1986, op. cit.

154. Arriaga, 1985, op. cit.

155. Klaus Lenk, "Information technology and society," pp. 273–310. In G. Friedrichs and A. Schaff [eds], *Microelectronics and Society: For Better or Worse*. Oxford: Pergamon Press, 1982.

CHAPTER 3

1. Klaus Krippendorff, *Content Analysis*. Beverly Hills, CA: Sage, 1980.

2. Krippendorff, 1980, p. 21.

3. Krippendorff, 1980, p. 27.

4. U.S. Congress. Office of Technology Assessment, *Informing the Nation: Federal Information Dissemination in an Electronic Age*. OTA-CIT-396. Washington, D.C.: U.S. Government Printing Office, October 1988, pp. 64–67.

5. Michael J. Weiss, *The Clustering of America*. New York: Harper & Row, 1988.

6. Gary D. Bass, Executive Director, OMB Watch, Washington, D.C.: "Testimony Before the Legislation and National Security Subcommittee of the House Government Operations Committee Regarding Reauthorization of the Paperwork Reduction Act." July 25, 1989.

7. Priscilla M. Regan, "Privacy, government information, and technology." *Public Administration Review* 46 (6) (November/December 1986):629–634.

8. Robert Mitgang, *Dangerous Dossiers*. New York: Donald Fine, Inc., 1988.

9. Ibid., p. 250.

10. Frank J. Donner, *The Age of Surveillance: The Aims and Methods of America's Political Intelligence System*. New York: Alfred A. Knopf, 1980.

11. Herbert N. Foerstel, *Surveillance in the Stacks: The FBI's Library Awareness Program*. New York: Greenwood Press, 1991.

12. Gary T. Marx, *Undercover: Police Surveillance in America*. Berkeley: University of California Press, 1988; see also, Gerald Dworkin, "The serpent beguiled me and I did eat: Entrapment and the creation of crime." *Law and Philosophy* 4 (1985):17–39.

13. Donner, 1980, op. cit., p. 73.

14. U.S. Congress. Office of Technology Assessment, "Update on computerized criminal history record systems." Appendix A, pp. 129–134. In *Federal Government Information Technology: Electronic Record Systems and Individual Privacy*. OTA-CIT-296. Washington, D.C.: U.S. Government Printing Office, June 1986.

15. U.S. Congress. Office of Technology Assessment, *Automated Record Checks of Firearm Purchasers: Issues and Options*. OTA-TCT-497. Washington, D. C.: U.S. Government Printing Office, July 1991.

16. Donner, 1980, op. cit., p. 321.

17. Don H. Zimmerman, "Record-keeping and the intake process in a public welfare agency," pp. 319–344. In S. Wheeler [ed], *On Record: Files and Dossiers in American Life*. New York: Russell Sage, 1969.

18. U.S. Congress. Office of Technology Assessment, June 1986, op. cit.

19. The development of mandatory screening and subsequent registry of persons with such genetic characteristics is described by Troy Duster in *Back Door to Eugenics*. New York: Routledge, 1990, p. 53.

20. David H. Flaherty, *Privacy and Government Data Banks*. London: Mansell, 1979, p. 249.

21. Paul Starr, "The sociology of official statistics." pp. 7–57. In W. and P. Starr [eds], *The Politics of Numbers*. New York: Russell Sage Foundation, 1987.

22. Ibid., p. 11.

23. David H. Flaherty, *Protecting Privacy in Surveillance Societies*. Chapel Hill: University of North Carolina Press, 1989, p. 81.

24. Ibid., p. 83.

25. A body of sophisticated research has been developed that focuses on the strategies that might be used to reduce the risk of disclosure of information about a person's identity and his or her personal attributes. See, for example, George T. Duncan and Diane Lambert, "Disclosure-limited data dissemination." *Journal of the American Statistical Asssociation* 81 (393) (March 1986):10–18; and Duncan and Lambert, "The risk of disclosure for microdata." Paper presented at the Third Annual Research Conference of the Bureau of the Census, March 29–April 1, 1987.

26. Dawn Nelson, "Record linkage: Confidentiality from the perspective of the U.S. Bureau of the Census, pp. 325–333. In European Communities Commission, *Eurostat News: Protection of Privacy, Automatic Data Processing and Progress in Statistical Documentation*. Luxembourg: Office for Official Publications of the European Communities, 1986.

27. Joseph W. Duncan and William C. Shelton, *Revolution in United States Government Statistics 1926–1976*. Washington, D.C.: U.S. Department of Commerce. Office of Federal Statistical Policy and Standards, October 1978.

28. Testimony of John A. McLain, Joint Hearing on "1990 Census Planning—Questionnaire Subjects." Subcommittee on Federal Services, Post Office and Civil Service of the Committee on Governmental Affairs, Senate; and the Subcommittee on Census and Population of the Committee on Post Office and Civil Service. House. May 14, 1987. Washington, D.C.: U.S. Government Printing Office, 1987.

29. Duncan and Shelton, 1978. Unless otherwise noted, the broad history of other government statistics has been derived from this source.

30. Max Eveleth, Jr., "How the private sector uses data and technology," pp. 24–45. In *Data Uses in the Private Sector*. Washington, D.C.: U.S. Department of Commerce, March 1974.

31. Jerome M. Clubb, "Computer technology and the source of materials of social science history." *Social Science History* 10 (2) (Summer 1986):97–114.

32. U.S. Congress. Office of Technology Assessment, *Informing the Nation: Federal Information Dissemination in an Electronic Age*. OTA-CIT-396. Washington, D.C.: U.S. Government Printing Office, October 1988.

33. Herbert I. Schiller and Anita R. Schiller, "Libraries, public access to information, and commerce," pp. 146–166. In V. Mosco and J. Wasko [eds], *The Political Economy of Information*. Madison: University of Wisconsin Press, 1988; see also Paul Starr and Ross Corson, "Who will have the numbers? The rise of the statistical services industry and the politics of public data," pp. 415–447. In Alonso and Starr, 1987, op. cit.

34. Kenneth MacCrimmon, Donald A. Wehrung, with W. T. Stanbury, *Taking Risks: The Management of Uncertainty*. New York: Free Press, 1986.

35. Arthur L. Stinchcombe, *Information and Organizations*. Berkeley: University of California Press, 1990.

36. Stinchcombe, 1990, p. 245.

37. Robert H. Coombs and Louis J. West [eds], *Drug Testing: Issues and Options*. New York: Oxford University Press, 1991.

38. Steven J. Wisotsky, "The ideology of drug testing." *NOVA Law Review* 11 (2) (Winter 1987):763–778.

39. J. Michael Walsh and Jeanne G. Trumble, "The politics of drug testing," pp. 22–49. In Coombs and West, 1991, op. cit.

40. Neil Karunaratne, "An input-output approach to the measurement of the information economy," pp. 61–70. In M. Jussawalla, D. Lamberton, and N. Karunaratne [eds], *The Cost of Thinking: Information Economies of Ten Pacific Countries*. Norwood, NJ: Ablex, 1988.

41. H. Laurence Ross, "Personal information in insurance files," pp. 203–222. In S. Wheeler [ed], *On Record: Files and Dossiers in American Life*. New York: Russell Sage, 1969.

42. Ibid., p. 219.

43. Stephen Schleifer, "Trends in attitudes toward and participation in survey research." *Public Opinion Quarterly* 50 (1986): 17–26.

44. Randall Rothenberg, "Surveys proliferete but answers dwindle." *New York Times*. October 5, 1990, p. A1.

45. Hugh M. Beville, Jr., *Audience Ratings: Radio, Television, Cable*. Hillsdale, NJ: Lawrence Erlbaum, 1988, pp. 226–227.

46. Schleifer, 1986, op. cit., p. 22.

47. Beville, 1988, op. cit.

48. Meg Cox, "Nielsen announces new technology for People Meters." *Wall Street Journal*. June 1, 1989. p. B6.

49. Frederick Bleakley, "Citicorp's Folly? How a terrific idea for grocery marketing missed the targets." *Wall Street Journal*. April 3, 1991, p. A1.

50. "American Express plans to publish 20 magazines." *Friday Report*. April 20, 1990, p. 1.

51. Timothy Noah, "Welfare recipients collect benefits with ATM cards." *Wall Street Journal*. April 10, 1991, p. B1.

52. This issue has been raised in the early days of the experimental program. Jeffrey Kutler, "U.S. Report raises privacy concerns in electronic benefit payments." *American Banker*. May 18, 1988, p. 32.

53. Thomas E. McManus, *Telephone Transaction-Generated Information: Rights and Restrictions*. Cambridge, MA: Harvard University, Program on Information Resources Policy, May 1990.

54. Patrick Barwise and Andrew Ehrenberg, *Television and its Audience*. London: Sage Publications, 1988.

55. Arbitron's "ScanAmerica" system was designed to increase the reach of a market test. Because the program would utilize a "people meter," with regular prompts to increase the reliability of estimates of viewing by persons in conjunction with a scanning unit in the home with which products with the universal products code purchases from any vendor could be scanned into the database at home, the service was not dependent upon nor limited to participating stores. ScanAmerican plans were described in Beville, 1988, op. cit., pp. 292–293.

56. Summary Scan! Marketing report. Chicago, IL, March 3, 1989.

57. Joyce Kole and Roseann Neilsen, "The coupon revolution." *Direct*. April 20, 1991, p. 33.

58. Cauzin Systems, Inc., of Waterbury, Connecticut, described the character and use of its "Softstrip" technology in 1989.

59. David Paulin, "Supermarket uses data strip to build customer profile." *Direct.* February 20, 1989, p. 87.

60. Cauzin Systems, Inc., "Frequently asked questions about Cauzin's direct response system." Promotional sheet, December 1989.

61. Roger A. Clarke, "Information technology and dataveillance." *Communications of the ACM* 31 (5) (May 1988):498–512.

62. Ibid., p. 499.

63. Ibid., p. 502.

64. Ibid.

65. John Markoff, "American Express to buy 2 top supercomputers." *New York Times.* October 30, 1991.

66. Stewart Brand, *Inventing the Future at MIT.* New York: Viking Penguin, 1988, pp. 181–200.

67. Peg Kay and Patricia Powers [eds], *Future Information Processing Technology—1983.* NBS–500–103. Institute for Computer Sciences and Technology. National Bureau of Standards. Washington, D.C.: U.S. Department of Commerce, August 1983. NBS is now the National Institute for Standards and Technology (NIST).

68. Ibid., p. 75.

69. Ibid., p. 77.

70. Barbara Elazari, "Amex designs an OLTP system." *Datamation.* November 15, 1986:96–108.

71. Ibid., p. 96.

72. Dimitris N. Chofras and Henrich Steinmann, *Expert Systems in Banking: A Guide for Senior Managers.* New York: New York University Press, 1990.

73. Ibid., pp. 39–40.

74. Ibid., pp. 227–230.

75. Ibid., p. 234.

76. Ibid., p. 270.

77. U.S. Senate. Committee on Governmental Affairs, "Report: The computer matching and privacy protection act of 1987." Washington, D.C.: U. S. Government Printing Office. 1988.

78. Anne M. Barry, "Defamation in the workplace: The impact of increasing employer liability." *Marquette Law Review* 72 (1989): 264–303.

79. Gilbert Fuchsberg, "Employers' use of accident records raises specter of blacklisted workers." *Wall Street Journal.* July 16, 1990, p. B1.

80. Troy Duster, *Backdoor to Eugenics.* New York: Routledge, 1990, p. 3. Philip Bereano, a professor of engineering and public policy at the University of Washington, convinced me of the importance of genetic testing and the technology of genetic engineering as components of the panoptic sort during a visit to the campus in Seattle in November 1991. Bereano had testified several times before congressional committees and had explored the civil liberties issues in several conference papers. See his "Testimony on DNA Identification Systems: Social Policy and Civil Liberties Concerns" before the Subcommittee on Civil and Constitutional Rights. Committee on the Judiciary. U.S. House of Representatives. March 22, 1989.

81. Ronald Frank, William Massey, and Yoram Wind, *Market Segmentation.* Englewood Cliffs, NJ: Prentice-Hall, 1972.

82. Ronald Frank and Marshall Greenberg, "Zooming in on TV Audiences." *Psychology Today.* October 1979, pp. 92–103; see also Ronald Frank and Marshall Greenberg, *Audiences for Public Broadcasting.* Beverly Hills, CA: Sage, 1982.

83. Patrick Barwise and Andrew Ehrenberg, *Television and its Audience.* London: Sage Publications, 1988. Simmons was influenced primarily by their early studies for the Independent Broadcasting Authority that focused on the choice of television programs as a reflection of a decision to invest mental effort in the processing of information.

84. Ronald I. Simmons, "The relationship between cognitive style and television preferences among African-American college students." (unpublished dissertation) Howard University, Washington, D.C., June 1987.

85. Most of these multivariate statistical techniques are described in Peter Monge and Joseph Cappella [eds], *Multivariate Techniques in Human Communication Research.* New York: Academic Press, 1980.

86. Jonathan Gutman, "Techniques for audience segmentation," pp. 123–137. In J. Dominick and J. Fletcher [eds], *Broadcasting Research Methods.* Newton, MA: Allyn and Bacon, 1985.

87. Jae-On Kim and Charles W. Mueller, *Introduction to Factor Analysis.* Beverly Hills, CA: Sage, 1978.

88. Mark Aldenderfer and Roger Blashfield, *Cluster Analysis.* Beverly Hills, CA: Sage, 1984.

89. Marija Norusis, "Stacking Beers: Cluster Analysis," pp. 165–191. In *SPSSx Advanced Statistics Guide.* Chicago: SPSS Inc., 1985.

90. William R. Klecka, *Discriminant Analysis.* Beverly Hills, CA: Sage, 1980.

91. Paul E. Green and Vithala Rao, *Applied Multidimensional Scaling.* New York: Holt, Rinehart & Winston, 1972. See also Joseph Kruskal and Myron Wish, *Multidimensional Scaling.* Beverly Hills, CA: Sage, 1978.

92. Frank, Massey, and Wind, 1972, op. cit., pp. 165–175.

93. Joseph Cappella, "Structural equation modeling: An introduction," pp. 57–110. In P. Monge and J. Cappella, 1980, op. cit.

94. James B. Rule, Douglas McAdam, Linda Stearns, and David Uglow, "Documentary identification and mass surveillance in the United States." *Social Problems* 31 (2) (1983):222–234.

95. Ibid., p. 214.

96. Jerome Svigals, "Smart Cards—A critical decision point." *Journal of Retail Banking* 19 (1) (Spring 1987):43–55.

97. Ibid., p. 47.

98. Joseph Eaton, *Card Carrying Americans.* Totowa, NJ: Rowman & Littlefield, 1986, p. 140.

99. Michel Foucault, *The Order of Things: An Archaeology of the Human Sciences.* New York: Vintage Books, 1973.

100. Edward Eugene Gallahue, "Some factors in the development of market standards, with special reference to foods, drugs, and certain other household wares." (dissertation) Washington, D.C.: Catholic University Press, 1942.

101. J. Beniger, 1986, op. cit., pp. 344–346.

102. Gerald R. Winslow, *Triage and Justice*. Berkeley: University of California Press, 1982.

103. Starr, 1987, op. cit., pp. 43–44.

104. Mary Tew Douglas, *How Institutions Think*. New York: Syracuse University Press, 1986, p. 58.

105. Ibid., p. 101.

106. Foucault, 1973, p. 131.

107. John E. Hunter, "Factor Analysis," pp. 229–257. In P. Monge and J. Cappella [eds], *Multivariate Techniques in Human Communication Research*. New York: Academic Press, 1980. Hunter suggests that one approach to factor analysis, trait theory, asks "What are the fundamental traits which underlie a given set of observed variables?" p. 228.

108. James A. Anderson, "Some preliminary thoughts on the elaboration of audiences." Conference paper. Association for Education in Journalism and Mass Communication, Washington, D.C.: August, 1989.

109. David Margolick, "Finding jury is first test in celebrated rape trial." *New York Times*. October 31, 1991, p. B8.

110. Newton N. Minow and Fred H. Cate, "Who is an impartial juror in an age of mass media?" *American University Law Review* 40 (2) (Winter 1991):660.

111. Nancy Reichman, "Managing crime risks: Toward an insurance based model of social control." *Research in Law, Deviance and Social Control* 8 (1986):151–172.

112. Ibid., p. 166.

113. Peter W. Huber, *Liability: The Legal Revolution and Its Consequences*. New York: Basic Books, 1988.

114. James K. Stewart, "From the director." *National Institute of Justice Research in Brief*. March 1987, p. 1.

115. Norval Morris and Marc Miller, "Predictions of dangerousness in the criminal law." *National Institute of Justice Research In Brief*. March 1987, p. 3.

116. Ibid., p. 4.

117. This is a point made elegantly by Troy Duster, 1990, op. cit., pp. 97–101.

118. Reichman, 1986, p. 157.

119. James Rule, *Private Lives and Public Surveillance (Social Control in the Computer Age)*. New York: Schocken Books, 1974.

120. Ibid., p. 178.

121. Ibid., p. 179.

122. Peter McAllister, "Early warning on delinquencies." *Retail Control*. March 1986, pp. 16–27.

123. Svigals, 1987, op. cit., p. 47.

124. Michael J. Weiss, *The Clustering of America*. New York: Harper & Row, 1988.

125. Eveleth, 1973, op. cit., p. 34.

126. Starr and Corson, 1987, op. cit., p. 426.

127. Philip Porado, "Tiger pause." *Campaigns and Elections*. April–May 1990, pp. 49–51.

128. *TIGER: The Coast-to-Coast Digital Map Data Base*. Washington, D.C.: U.S. Department of Commerce. Bureau of the Census, November 1990.

129. Ibid., p. 4.

130. Weiss, 1988, op. cit., p. 11.

131. Ibid., p. 13.

132. Oscar H. Gandy, Jr., and Charles E. Simmons, "Technology, privacy and the democratic process." *Critical Studies in Mass Communication* 3 (2) (June 1986):155–168. See also the "inside view" by political consultant Matt Reese. "From telephone to telelobby," p. 104. In R. Meadow, *New Communication Technologies in Politics.* Washington, D.C.: Washington Program. Annenberg School of Communications, 1985.

133. David Beiler, "Precision politics." *Campaigns and Elections.* February/March 1990, p. 33.

134. Kevin Kramer and Edward Schneider, "Innovations in campaign research: Finding the voters in the 1980s," pp. 19–52. In Meadow, 1985, op. cit.

135. Ibid., p. 23.

136. Beiler, 1990, op. cit., p. 35.

137. *Campaigns and Elections.* February/March 1990, p. 35.

138. Joel E. Book (Book and Company Marketing Services), "Target market publishing: The revolutionary marketing communications potential of database-driven magazine publishing systems." Executive briefing, Orlando, Florida, December 1989.

139. Ibid.

140. Chorafas and Steinmann, 1990, p. 232.

141. Conquest/Direct promotion, October 1989.

142. Personalized copy of 1989 Epsilon Data Management letter to shareholders, February 20, 1990, p. 2.

143. *Charting Your Course: For Fundraising and Membership Development.* Burlington, MA: Epsilon, n.d., p. 4.

144. Ibid., p. 10.

145. Gannett Co. news release, December 7, 1989.

146. Information included in a package from Gannett Telemarketing in response to a query about the business, March 12, 1990.

147. Eleanor Novek, Nikhil Sinha, and Oscar Gandy, "The value of your name." *Media, Culture and Society* 12 (1990):525–543.

148. Personal correspondence, March 9, 1990.

149. "Equifax reverses 'target marketing' policy." *Privacy Journal.* August 1991, p. 1.

150. "Privacy-risk assessment program mounted by TRW; some criticism." *DM News.* November 11, 1991, p. 238.

151. Raymond Wacks, *Personal Information: Privacy and the Law.* New York: Oxford University Press, 1989.

152. "The DBA consumer file vs. the competition—A competitive analysis." Photocopy of a broadsheet. Englewood, NJ: Database America Companies, 1990.

153. Product announcement in the direct marketing newsletter, *Friday Report.* April 13, 1990, p. 1.

154. Tom Koch, *Journalism for the 21st Century: Online Information, Electronic Databases, and the News.* New York: Praeger, 1991. That newspapers themselves have also entered the business of selling access to their files and the data they generate about their customers has been noted by Jean Ward and Kathleen Hansen, "Journalist and librarian roles, information technologies and newsmaking." *Journalism Quarterly* 68 (3) (Fall 1991):491498.

155. Starr and Corson, 1987, op. cit.

156. "Meredith Online with 'largest' database." *DM News.* October 28, 1991, p. 1.

157. Starr and Corson, op. cit., 1988, p. 420.

158. U.S. Department of Commerce. National Telecommunications and Information Administration, *NTIA Information Services Report*. 88-235. Washington, D.C.: U.S. Department of Commerce, August 1988, p. 29.

159. The RBOCs, created after the consent decree that broke up AT&T, involved restrictions on the lines of business that the still large and powerful common carriers could enter. Pressure from other information service providers who feared competition from the RBOCs was exercised through the oversight of District Judge Harold Greene. After staying his own order to allow the RBOCs into the information business, the U.S. Court of Appeals vacated the stay on October 7, 1991. The American Newspaper Publishers Association immediately began a campaign to put the giant companies back into their cages. See *Telecommunications Reports*. October 14, 1991, pp. 1–7.

CHAPTER 4

1. Meredith Mendes, "Privacy and computer-based information systems," pp. 193–264. In B. Compaine [ed], *Issues in New Information Technology*. Norwood, NJ: Ablex, 1988.

2. American Express Company, *1984 Annual Report*. New York: American Express, 1985, p. 3.

3. American Express Company, *1985 Annual Report*. New York: American Express, 1986, p. 4.

4. American Express Company, *1986 Annual Report*. New York: American Express, 1987, pp. 4–5.

5. Ibid., p. 31.

6. American Express Company, *1987 Annual Report*. New York: American Express, 1988, pp. 8–15.

7. American Express Company, *1988 Annual Report*. New York: American Express, 1989, pp. 14–15.

8. "Privacy task force being formed." *Friday Report*. January 6, 1989, p. 1.

9. There is no intention of leaving the impression that the image of American Express is one without any warts. In a case in the U.S. Court of Appeals, D.C. circuit, Amex was chided for its pursuit of its interests through its "extraordinary use of interrogatories … the various sets of interrogatories and their answers are in the hundreds of pages. They run as far afield as inquiring the name of every law firm the plaintiff had been affiliated with since 1951." In the court's view "the length, scope and detail of the interrogatories propounded by American Express suggest a strategy of attrition rather than a legitimate discovery of the facts needed to resolve a dispute over the account." *Oscar S. Gray, v. American Express Company*. No. 83–1475. U.S. Court of Appeals. 743F. 2d 10 (1984) at 20.

10. David Enscoe, "Privacy debate goes public." *Target Marketing*. January 1989, p. 35.

11. Ibid., p. 39.

12. American Express Company, *Form 10-K. Annual Report to the Securities and Exchange Commission*. New York: American Express, March 1989.

13. For a useful discussion of the changes in the United States and in advanced industrial economies, which have been labeled by some as information economies, the following represent good sources: Vincent Mosco and Janet Wasko [eds], *The Political Economy of Information*. Norwood, NJ: Ablex, 1988; Jennifer Slack and Fred Fejes [eds], *The Ideology of the Information Age*. Norwood, NJ: Ablex, 1987.

14. TRW, Inc., *1984 Annual Report.* Cleveland, OH: TRW, Inc., 1985.

15. Ibid., pp. 16–17.

16. "TRW credit data flexes its muscles." *Privacy Journal.* April 1989, pp. 1, 4, 6.

17. TRW, Inc., *1985 Annual Report.* Cleveland, OH: TRW, Inc., 1986, p. 4.

18. Ibid., p. 7.

19. Ibid.

20. Ibid., p. 11.

21. Michael Van Buskirk, cited as a source in William Ecenbarger, "They know who you are." *Philadelphia Inquirer Magazine.* February 4, 1990, p. 15.

22. "TRW credit data flexes its muscles," *Privacy Journal.* April 1989, p. 6.

23. Michael Miller, "Six states sue TRW over credit-reporting practices." *Wall Street Journal.* July 10, 1991, p. B1.

24. Equifax, Inc., *1984 Annual Report.* Atlanta, GA: Equifax, Inc., 1985, p. 2.

25. Ibid., p. 9.

26. Ibid., p. 15.

27. Ibid.

28. Equifax, Inc., *1985 Annual Report.* Atlanta, GA: Equifax, Inc., 1986, p. 2.

29. Equifax, Inc., *1986 Annual Report.* Atlanta, GA: Equifax, Inc., 1987, p. 3.

30. Ibid., p. 12.

31. Ibid.

32. Ibid., pp. 18–19.

33. Equifax, Inc., *1987 Annual Report.* Atlanta, GA: Equifax, Inc., 1988.

34. *Hovator v. Equifax, Inc.* U.S. Court of Appeals for the Eleventh Circuit, July 30, 1987, 823 F. 2d 413.

35. Equifax, Inc., *1988 Annual Report.* Atlanta, GA: Equifax, Inc., 1989, p. 14.

36. Ibid., p. 22.

37. David Linowes, *Privacy in America.* Urbana, IL.: University of Illinois Press, 1989; David Flaherty, *Protecting Privacy in Surveillance Societies.* Chapel Hill, NC: University of North Carolina Press, 1989.

38. Mark Nadel, "Rings of privacy: Unsolicited telephone calls and the right of privacy." *Yale Journal on Regulation* (1986):99–128.

39. Congress passed the Telephone Consumer Protection Act in 1991 and charged the FCC with its implementation. In its efforts to balance what it sees as legitimate privacy interests with the "continued viability of beneficial and useful business services," which generated hundreds of millions of dollars from unsolicited calls, the commission clearly favored the industry position. See: "FCC stands up for telemarketing; hits do-not-call database option." *DM News.* April 27, 1992, p. 1.

40. James Katz, "U.S. Telecommunications privacy policy." *Telecommunications Policy* (December 1988):353–368.

41. Brian Lane, quoted in: Robert M. Entman, *State Telecommunications Regulation: Toward Policy for an Intelligent Telecommunications Infrastructure.* Report of an Aspen Institute Conference, Aspen, Colorado. July 9–13, 1989. Truro, MA: Aspen Institute, p. 21.

42. James B. Ginty, vice president AT&T, Philadelphia, quoted in A. Gnoffo: "They've got your number." *Philadelphia Inquirer.* February 4, 1990, sec. C1, p. 8.

43. R. Fannin, "The last great hope?" *Marketing and Media Decisions.* February 1988, pp. 24–30.

44. The question of the sale of the company's member lists has been addressed by Ari Solomon, but there is no firm distinction between general membership lists and the identification of persons who repond to client ads. See: Ari Solomon, "The Consequences of Prodigy." *Privacy Journal.* April 1990, pp. 4–5.

45. "PRODIGY Service Member Agreement." White Plains, NY: Prodigy Services Company, 1989, p. 8.

46. Seymour Lusterman, *Managing Federal Government Relations.* Research Report No. 905. New York: Conference Board, 1988.

47. *Direct Marketing Association Guidelines for Ethical Business Practices.* Direct Marketing Association, mailed to the author, January 1990.

48. "Automated number identification systems growing." *Friday Report.* March 3, 1989, pp. 1–2.

49. Ed Burnett, "How to cope with list problems and abuses." *Directions.* March/April 1988, pp. 1–6.

50. R. Baker, R. Dickinson, and S. Hollander, "Big brother 1994: Marketing data and the IRS." *Journal of Public Policy and Marketing* 5 (1988):227–241.

51. Alexander Hoffman, "A Statement to the House Committee on the Judiciary." U.S. Congress. House. Subcommittee on Courts, Civil Liberties, and the Administration of Justice. Hearings: "1984 Civil Liberties and the National Security State." Washington, D.C.: Government Printing Office, 1984, pp. 320–321.

52. Ray Schultz, "Big compilers say no to the FBI." *DM News.* May 4, 1992, p. 1.

53. "Can direct marketers police themselves?" *Target Marketing.* April 1989, p. 16.

54. Ibid.

55. "TRW credit data flexes its muscles." *Privacy Journal.* April 1989.

56. Quoted by David Enscoe in "Privacy debate goes public." *Target Marketing.* January 1989, p. 34.

57. Robert J. Posch, "How the law(s) of 'privacy' impact your business." *Direct Marketing.* October 1987, p. 78.

58. Ibid., p. 80.

59. Ibid., p. 102.

60. Robert Posch, "Nuisance/privacy infractions—part two." *Direct Marketing.* January 1988, p. 103.

61. Roy Schwedelson, February 23, 1989. Audio tape 39–0088 LI, Hoke Communications, Inc., Garden City, NY; abstracted in: "Privacy vs. Free Speech." (May 1989). *Direct Marketing.* May 1989, pp. 41–46.

62. Ibid., p. 42.

63. Ibid., pp. 45–46.

64. David Linowes, 1989, op. cit.

65. My research throughout this entire project was aided by the fine work of a number of graduate research assistants. However, one student, Elizabeth Van Horn, was especially helpful in the design and implementation of this survey of business leaders.

66. Rose Harper, *Mailing List Strategies: A Guide to Direct Mail Success.* New York: McGraw-Hill, 1986.

67. Analysts have suggested that cross-marketing was pretty much in its infancy because the majority of firms, including those in financial services, did not have their customer data

in formats that would facilitate matching to support cross-marketing. See Dan Bencivenga, "Pinpointing Investors." *Target Marketing*. September 1988, p. 32.

68. Alan Westin and Lance Hoffman, "Privacy and security issues in the use of personal information about clients and customers on micro and personal computers used in office automation." Contractor Report prepared for the U.S. Office of Technology Assessment. February 1985.

69. Equifax, Inc., *The Equifax Report on Consumers in the Information Age*. Atlanta, GA: Equifax, Inc., 1990, p. 77.

70. David Linowes, 1989, op. cit., p. 40.

71. Arthur L. Stinchcombe, *Information in Organizations*. Berkeley: University of California Press, 1990.

CHAPTER 5

1. T. R. Young makes a distinction between public opinion, mass opinion, and social opinion. For Young, public opinion represents the primary source of democratic social change, which is the authentic product of communicative interaction within the public sphere. Young, along with Habermas and others, suggests that the public sphere has been subverted and transformed through its penetration by state and corporate interests and that manufactured mass opinion is the result. Social opinion represents the middle distance in which the emancipatory potential of public opinion is limited by the influence of history, tradition, and established cultural beliefs and serves primarily to reproduce things as they are: "Social opinion reproduces existing social forms while public opinion is pointed toward new and different forms of social life." He continues, "News is the stuff of public opinion; propaganda is the heart of social opinion. It is a mystification to conflate them and does much mischief to the public opinion policy process." See T. R. Young, "Public opinion, mass opinion, and social opinion: The constitution of political culture in the capitalist state," pp. 264–266. In V. Mosco and J. Wasko [eds], *The Critical Communications Review*. Vol. 3. Norwood, NJ: Ablex, 1985.

2. Anthony Giddens, *The Constitution of Society*. Cambridge: Polity Press, 1984, pp. 49–104.

3. Amos Tversky and Daniel Kahneman, "Rational choice and the framing of decisions," pp. 60–89. In K. Cook and M. Levi [eds], *The Limits of Rationality*. Chicago: University of Chicago Press, 1990.

4. A classic in the field of social research is the work by Eugene Webb, Donald Campbell, Richard Schwartz, and Lee Sechrest, *Unobtrusive Measures: Nonreactive Research in the Social Sciences*. Chicago: Rand McNally, 1971. For an updated assessment of approaches to the problems of measurement see Delbert C. Miller, *Handbook of Research Design and Social Measurement*. 5th ed. Newbury Park, CA: Sage, 1991.

5. Joseph Lepkowski, "Telephone sampling methods in the United States," pp. 73–98. In R. Groves et al. [eds], *Telephone Survey Methodology*. New York: John Wiley and Sons, 1988.

6. Owen Thornberry and James Massey, "Trends in United States telephone coverage across time and subgroups," pp. 25–69. In Groves, et al., 1988, op. cit.

7. My research assistants, Jerry Baber and Catherine Preston, administered each of the groups, with Baber leading the discussions through a "nominal group technique" that utilized a well-structured set of questions and exercises.

8. The term panoptic sort was never used. The letters of invitation and the question-naire each participant completed prior to beginning the group interview spoke only about privacy and practices related to information privacy.

9. Kristen Eddy, "Lit majors are not lepers." *Washington Post*. November 22, 1987, p. C5.

10. Kurt Dubowski, "Drug use testing: Scientific perspectives." *Nova Law Review* 11 (2) (1987): 416–552.

11. Raymond Wacks, *Personal Information: Privacy and the Law.* Oxford: Oxford University Press, 1989.

CHAPTER 6

1. The 1978 survey was administered by Louis Harris and Associates (Harris) for Sentry Insurance, the 1983 survey was administered by Harris for Southern New England Telephone, and the 1990 survey was administered by Harris for Equifax, Inc. All secondary analyses of the Harris data were performed without weighting. Although the Harris organization has developed a high level of precision in the construction of its samples, even their procedures generate samples that require weighting if they are to be projectable to the U.S. population. The published reports of these Harris surveys use data weighted to more closely approximate proportions in key demographic groups. My secondary analyses are focused primarily on uncovering relationships between variables, rather than emphasizing distributions in the population. This approach will, on occasion, produce estimates of distributions that are at variance with those published by Harris, Westin, or the sponsors of the surveys.

2. Oscar H. Gandy, Jr., "Telecommunication and Privacy," a study funded by a grant from AT&T through the Center for Communication and Information Science and Policy at the University of Pennsylvania, 1988–1990.

3. The limitation of the number of call-backs to three, in addition to dominance of the quota over the representativeness of the sample produced a sample that grossly overincluded female respondents. The bulk of the analyses of this dataset were performed with a weighting factor for gender that reduced the effective presence of females to 52 percent and the effective sample size to 1,008. Concerns about concentrating an oversample through weighting are quite different from those that expand categories that are underrepresented. Such is clearly not the case in this analysis.

4. One broad search was conducted through the Roper Center for Public Opinion Research in November of 1987 that collected summaries of responses to questions about privacy from 1975 to 1987 in order to compare levels of concern with attention to privacy issues in the press.

5. Alan Westin, *Privacy and Freedom*. New York: Atheneum, 1967.

6. Raymond Wacks, *Personal Information, Privacy and the Law*. Oxford: Oxford University Press, 1989.

7. "Pentagon considers data access controls." *Transnational Data and Communications Report*. August 1986, p. 5; Philip Doty, "Federal research and development (R&D) as intellectual property," pp. 139–171. In C. McClure and P. Hernon [eds], *U.S. Scientific and Technical Information (STI) Policies: Views and Perspectives*. Norwood, NJ: Ablex, 1989.

8. James Katz and Annette Tassone, "Public opinion trends: Privacy and information technology." *Public Opinion Quarterly* 54 (1990): 125–143.

9. Ibid., p. 138.

10. For the scale with eleven variables (direct marketers excluded) Chronbach's alpha = .87.

11. Comments made during conferences, seminars, and conversations about her work by Mary J. Culnan, an associate professor at the School of Business Administration, Georgetown University.

12. Hearings were held in April 1980 before the Senate Committee on Banking, Housing, and Urban Affairs. The Subcommittee on Consumer Affairs included testimony from Eugene T. Merrigan, senior vice president of marketing, Equifax Services, Inc.

13. Twenty-six variables were measured through Likert-type scales, ranging from 1 (disagree very strongly) to 5 (agree very strongly). SPSSx, principle components analysis, generated ten factors explaining 79.2 percent of the total variance.

14. John S. Detweiler, "Monitoring 'entitlement' attitudes in the '80s." *Public Relations Review* 12 (3) (Fall 1986):28–40.

15. Herbert McClosky and Alida Brill's exploration of public opinion regarding civil liberties, including those they identified with regard to personal privacy, indentified a widespread willingness of people to limit the rights of criminals and even those who might depart from a community's standards. See their *Dimensions of Tolerance: What Americans Believe About Civil Liberties.* New York: Russell Sage Foundation, 1983, especially Chapter 5, "The rights of privacy and lifestyle," pp. 171–231.

16. The factor analysis method was principal components with varimax rotation as generated by SPSSx. The four factors explained 74.8 percent of the measured variance. For the identification of the factors, those variables with factor loadings of .5 or higher were used. Additionally, those variables that were highly correlated with more than one factor were eliminated after the factors had been rotated.

17. Katz and Tassone, op. cit., p. 139.

18. Respondents' rankings were determined empirically, after-the-fact, rather than by a direct question.

19. *Whose Business is it Anyway?* Washington, D.C.: National Business League, January 1990.

20. Reported in the *Equifax Report*, p. 14.

21. Katz and Tassone, 1990, op. cit., p. 142.

22. The factor analysis method was principal axis factoring with varimax rotation. It should be noted that the original instrument generally only allowed for an affirmative, a negative, and a don't know/not sure response. Two modifications were made that have implications for the interpretation of the factors and correlation-based analyses. For the bulk of the items used in the factor analysis, the items were transformed into dichotomous dummy variables, taking the values of zero and one, whereby the value of one was assigned to those that were the privacy affirming, or most fearful, responses. All other responses, including the nonresponses, were coded as zero. This allowed the full data set to be used in all correlations. At the same time, such a coding undoubtedly served to underestimate the extent of privacy concern in that it treated all qualified (unsure) responses as not concerned. The second option, taken less frequently, was to assign the not sure response to the middle category. Because the number was always small, the resultant distribution was grossly bimodal. It was for this reason that rather conservative estimates of significance were used to guide my interpretation. The likely result is a type II error, missing relationships that might have appeared if the distributions were more appropriate to the tests applied.

23. Chronbach's alpha was utilized as a measure of reliability.

24. This might be seen as a fairly extreme view in the context of the current popularity of a cognitive science approach. Political ideology might be seen as an intervening variable that provides an indication of an information processing screen that influences how individuals understand their changing environment. In this way ideology, like personality and values, can be seen as causal or determinative of other more dynamic opinions and behaviors. That is not the position that is taken at this stage in the analysis.

25. The correlations were r = . 15 for African-Americans and r = . 09 for Hispanics.

26. Ronald Inglehart, *The Silent Revolution: Changing Values and Political Styles Among Western Publics*. Princeton: Princeton University Press, 1977; Ronald Inglehart, *Culture Shift in Advanced Industrial Society*. Princeton: Princeton University Press, 1990.

27. Inglehart, 1977, p. 7.

28. Ibid., p. 293.

29. Milton Rokeach, *The Nature of Human Values*. New York: Free Press, 1973.

30. Oscar H. Gandy, Jr., "Is that all there is to love? Values and program preference," pp. 207–219. In S. Thomas [ed], *Studies in Mass Communication and Technology*. Norwood, NJ: Ablex, 1981. This study utilized a modified version of the Rokeach value sort in combination with discriminant analysis to predict the program preferences of college students. Attributes of the programs were seen to be related to the values that were dominant in student rankings.

31. Rokeach, 1973, p. 62.

32. Ibid., p. 73.

33. For an examination of changes in ideological self-identification see John P. Robinson and John A. Fleishman, "Ideological identification trends and interpretations of the Liberal-Conservative balance." *Public Opinion Quarterly* 52 (1988): 134–145.

34. Analysis was performed with unweighted data, n = 1,250, using gender as a control variable, primarily to assess the extent of its interaction with age.

35. Westin's "concern over privacy index" was described in his testimony before the Subcommittee on Government Information, Justice, and Agriculture. House Committee on Government Operations, Washington, D.C., April 10, 1991. The additivity of the measures is questionable (alpha = .29), although its use as a basis for an ordinal classification of respondents has been shown to have considerable predictive ability with regard to other measures of privacy concern.

36. Nancy Signorielli and Michael Morgan [eds], *Cultivation Analysis: New Directions in Media Effects Research*. Newbury Park, CA: Sage, 1990.

37. The standard deviation = 2.34 hours.

38. "When you read the papers, how much attention do you pay to stories about politics, government or public affairs?"

39. Theoretical positions that suggest that television and the media system in general contain contradictory tendencies may be reintegrated from a theoretical stance that argues that different media forms play different symbolic functions. The more "selective" media serve the interests of the more elite members of the population because they deal with ideological questions that are as yet unsettled.

40. This was measured by response to the question "How concerned would you guess the average American is about threats to their privacy?" On a scale from 1–10, 1 = of no concern and 10 = of very great concern.

41. Allen Barton and R. Wayne Parsons, "Measuring belief system structure." *Public Opinion Quarterly* 41 (1977):159–180; George Bishop, "The effect of education on ideological consistency." *Public Opinion Quarterly* 40 (1976): 337–348; Pamela Conover and Stanley Feldman, "The origins and meaning of Liberal/Conservative self-identifications." *American Journal of Political Science* 25 (4) (1981):617–645; John Fleishman, "Types of political attitude structure: Results of a cluster analysis." *Public Opinion Quarterly* 50 (1986):371–386.

42. Louis Harris and Associates, "Despite gains conservatives still minority." *The Harris Survey.* February 27, 1986, p. 1.

43. John Fleishman, "Trends in self-identified ideology from 1972 to 1982: No support for the salience hypothesis." *American Journal of Political Science* 30 (3) (1986):517–541.

44. Milton Rokeach, *The Nature of Human Values.* New York: Free Press, 1973.

45. George Gerbner, Larry Gross, Michael Morgan, and Nancy Signorielli, "Living with television: The dynamics of the cultivation process," pp. 17–40. In J. Bryant and D. Zillman [eds], *Perspectives on Media Effects;* and George Gerbner, "Epilogue: Advancing on the path of righteousness (Maybe)," pp. 249–262. In N. Signorielli and M. Morgan [eds], *Cultivation Analysis: New Directions in Media Effects Research.* Newbury Park, CA: Sage, 1990.

CHAPTER 7

1. See Roger Noll, "The political and institutional context of communications policy," pp. 42–65. In M. Snow [ed], *Marketplace for Telecommunications.* New York: Longman, 1986; Vincent Mosco, "Perspectives on the state and telecommunications system," pp. 85–108. In *The Pay-Per Society.* Norwood, NJ: Ablex, 1989; Alan P. Hamlin, "Public choice, markets and utilitarianism," pp. 116–138. In D. Whynes [ed], *What is Political Economy?* Oxford: Basil Blackwell, 1984.

2. Richard F. Hixon, *Privacy in a Public Society: Human Rights in Conflict.* New York: Oxford University Press, 1987, p. 46.

3. Alan F. Westin, *Privacy and Freedom.* New York: Atheneum, 1967.

4. David Flaherty, *Protecting Privacy in Surveillance Societies.* Chapel Hill: University of North Carolina Press, 1989.

5. Richard F. Hixon, *Privacy in a Public Society: Human Rights in Conflict.* New York: Oxford University Press, 1987.

6. Barrington Moore, Jr., *Privacy: Studies in Social and Cultural History.* Armonk, NY: M. E. Sharpe, 1984, pp. 268, 285. The historical basis in levels of social development for different meanings of privacy is discussed in several other key sources, including Richard A. Posner, "Privacy, secrecy and reputation." *Buffalo Law Review* 28 (1979).

7. Leon Festinger, *A Theory of Cognitive Dissonance.* Evanston, IL: Row, Peterson and Company, 1957.

8. Elisabeth Noelle-Neumann, "Spiral of silence: A theory of public opinion." *Journal of Communication* 24 (1974): 43–51.

9. David L. Bazelon, "Probing privacy." *Gonzaga Law Review* 12 (4) (Summer 1977):587–619.

10. Gary L. Bostwick, "A taxonomy of privacy: Repose, sanctuary, and intimate decision." *California Law Review* 64 (1976):1, 451.

11. *Roe v. Wade,* 410 U.S. 113 (1973).

12. Bostwick reflects this unfortunate confusion by specifying "the privacy of intimate decision" in his suggestion that "this privacy is less 'freedom from' and more 'freedom to,'"

and cites *Griswold v. Connecticut,* 381 U.S. 479 (1965) as the case that recognized the zone of intimate decision and generated this migration from the core interests in controlling access.

13. Samuel D. Warren and Louis D. Brandeis, "The right to privacy." *Harvard Law Review* 14 (5) (December 15, 1890): 213, note 1.

14. Ibid., p. 196.

15. Ibid., p. 198.

16. Ibid., p. 204.

17. Ibid., p. 209, note 1.

18. Ibid., p. 215.

19. James H. Barron, "Warren and Brandeis. *The Right to Privacy, Harvard Law Review* (1890): Demystifying a landmark citation." *Suffolk University Law Review* 13 (4)4 (Summer 1979):874–922.

20. This is Barron's claim, ibid., pp. 910–911.

21. Edward J. Bloustein, "Privacy as an aspect of human dignity: An answer to Dean Prosser." *New York University Law Review* 39 (December 1964):962–1,007.

22. Ibid., p. 969.

23. William Patton and Randall Bartlett, "Corporate 'persons' and freedom of speech: The political impact of legal mythology." *Wisconsin Law Review* (1981):494–512; Herbert Hovenkamp, *Enterprise and American Law, 1836–1937.* Cambridge, MA: Harvard University Press, 1991; Morton J. Horwitz, "'Santa Clara' revisited: The development of corporate theory," pp. 13–63. In W. Samuels and A. Miller [eds], *Corporations and Society: Power and Responsibility.* New York: Greenwood Press, 1987; Kent Middleton, "Commercial Speech and the First Amendment." (unpublished dissertation) University of Minnesota, 1977.

24. Bloustein, op. cit., p. 971.

25. Ibid.

26. Ibid., p. 974.

27. Ibid., p. 979.

28. Ibid., p. 987.

29. *Shilbey v. Time, Inc.,* 45 Ohio App. 2d 69, 341 N.E. 2d 337 (1975) in Jonathan P. Graham, "Privacy, computers and the commercial dissemination of personal information." *Texas Law Review* 65 (7) (June 1987), pp, 1,413–1,415.

30. *Lamont v. Commissioner of Motor Vehicles,* 269 F. Supp. 880 (S.D.N.Y.), *aff'd,* 386 F. 2d 449 (2d Cir. 1967) cited in Graham, p. 1, 415.

31. Bloustein, op. cit., p. 989.

32. A great many things are bought and sold in the marketplace, and much of that involves a loss of dignity. Prostitution is only the most obvious example, and the efforts to deny the trade the protections of the law may be taken as evidence of the salience of the threat to dignity as well as the concern that its consequence is not limited to the primary parties in the transaction but is threatening to the moral fabric of the society.

33. National Public Radio story, "Weekend Edition," December 29, 1991, included a comment by a satisfied customer who uses his device faithfully, and "if he's over the limit, he doesn't drive." Counterarguments were heard from representatives of Mothers Against Drunk Driving who argued that the device encourages driving while under the influence of alcohol and that targeting those who had already demonstrated a tendency toward such dangerous behavior was irresponsible.

34. Bloustein, op. cit., p. 999.

35. Bloustein, op. cit., p. 1, 003.

36. Spiros Simitis, "Reviewing privacy in an information society." *University of Pennsylvania Law Review* 135 (1987):707–746.

37. Ibid., p. 731.

38. Anne W. Branscomb, "Property rights in information," pp. 603–642. In M. Gurevitch and M. Levy [eds], *Mass Communication Review Yearbook,* Vol. 6. Newbury Park, CA: Sage, 1987; previously published in B. Guile [ed], *Information Technologies and Social Transformation.* Washington, D.C.: National Academy Press, 1985.

39. Ibid., p. 603.

40. This refers to an advantage such as that derived from the monopoly claims on the electronic frequency spectrum provided with an exclusive broadcast license. Tax subsidies, import restrictions, patents, and copyrights all represent state guaranteed advantages that carry with them some expectation of public benefit.

41. Herbert Schiller, *Culture, Inc.: The Corporate Takeover of Public Expression.* New York: Oxford University Press, 1989.

42. The conflicting positions taken by activists and others within the homosexual community over the practice of "outing" has been discussed in Alida Brill, *Nobody's Business: The Paradoxes of Privacy.* Reading, MA: Addison-Wesley, 1990, pp. 128–142. Gay activists justify outing as a means of normalizing homosexuality by increasing public recognition of its prevalence, especially as it regards persons of importance who have avoided labeling or even as it refers to suspicion of their difference in the past.

43. As part of Title III of the federal Superfund Amendments Reauthorization Act (SARA), the Emergency Planning and Community Right-to-Know Act as passed in 1986 required manufacturers to provide public estimates of the amounts of their "routine" emissions of toxic chemicals into the environment. Six years later, the environmental movement was actively discussing the "right to know more." See for example, "The next steps for right to know." *Environmental Action* 23 (3) (November/December 1991): 19–24.

44. *U.S. v. Miller,* 425 U.S. 435 (1976).

45. Quoted in Bazelon, 1977, op. cit., from *California Bankers Association v. Shultz,* 416 U.S. 21, 78 (1974), p. 609.

46. Branscomb, op. cit., p. 615.

47. The Supreme Court in 1991 struck down a New York law, referred to as the "Son of Sam" law, which sought to limit the realization of profit by criminals who commercialized their exploits in the mass media. Part of the rationale in the New York courts, and the countless state courts that used the rule as a model, was that victims rather than criminals ought to be compensated from books about criminal activity. Although recognizing a legitimate state interest in compensating victims, the restriction on particular forms of speech was not considered to be justifiable under the First Amendment. See Paul M. Barrett, "High Court rejects 'Son of Sam' law, citing criminals' rights of free speech." *Wall Street Journal.* December 11, 1991, p. A4. The prior restraint on publication by government employees who might be working with "sensitive" information still remains as a restriction on the realization of profit.

48. Edward Ploman and L. Clark Hamilton, *Copyright: Intellectual Property in the Information Age.* London: Routledge and Kegan Paul, 1980; Sandra Braman, "Trade and information policy." *Media, Culture and Society* 12 (1990): 361–385.

49. Robert J. Posch, "How the law(s) of 'privacy' impact your business." *Direct Market-ing* (October 1987):78. That free speech rights find constitutional expression in the First Amendment and that privacy rights are found only in a penumbra of emanations is the product of a narrow and self-interested interpretation. Fourth Amendment limitations of state access seem equally explicit, even if the word privacy is not used.

50. *DM News,* a trade paper for the direct marketing industry, reported the availability of a list of recent callers to 900 numbers, including callers to adult, dating, and psychic lines. The same issue offered listings of the 50,000 "active members" of the Penthouse Book and Video Society, which "offers 'hard-to-find' adult reading and viewing material." December 2, 1991. Offering of the lists by the publication would not be seen as publication in the same way that posting of the lists might.

51. C. Edwin Baker, *Human Liberty and Freedom of Speech.* New York: Oxford University Press, 1989, especially Chapter 9.

52. Ibid., pp. 201–202.

53. Ibid., pp. 205–206.

54. Ibid., p. 211.

55. Kenneth C. Laudon, *Dossier Society: Value Choices in the Design of National Informa-tion Systems.* New York: Columbia University Press, 1986, p. 367.

56. Priscilla M. Regan, "Public use of private information: A comparison of personal in-formation policies in the United States and Britain." (unpublished dissertation) Cornell University, 1981, pp. 361–368.

57. John C. Bennett, "Regulating the computer: A comparative study of personal data protection policy." (unpublished dissertation) University of Illinois at Urbana-Champaign, 1986, p. 298.

58. Flaherty, 1989, p. 309.

59. David F. Linowes, *Privacy in America.* Urbana, IL: University of Illinois Press, 1989, p. 82.

60. "Select Committee to Study Governmental Operations with Respect to Intelligence Activities." U.S. Senate. 94th Congress. First Session, 1975.

61. Flaherty, op. cit., p. 309.

62. George B. Trubow, "Watching the watchers: The coordination of federal privacy pol-icy." *Software Law Journal* 3 (3) (Summer 1989):391–411.

63. David H. Flaherty, "The need for an American Privacy Protection Commission." *Government Information Quarterly* 1 (3) (1984):246.

64. Kenneth James Langan, "Computer matching programs: A threat to privacy?" *Co-lumbia Journal of Law and Social Problems* 15 (1979):142–180.

65. Testimony of Janlori Goldman, ACLU, on S. 496, the Computer Matching and Pri-vacy Protection Act of 1987, before the Subcommittee on Government Information, Justice and Agriculture. House Government Operations Committee, June 23, 1987, p. 8.

66. Flaherty, 1989, p. 357.

67. Herbert Hovenkamp, *Enterprise and American Law, 1836–1937.* Cambridge, MA: Harvard University Press, 1991.

68. Morton J. Horwitz, "The doctrine of objective causation," pp. 201–213, in David Kairys [ed], *The Politics of Law: A Progressive Critique.* New York: Pantheon, 1982.

69. Peter W. Huber, *Liability: The Legal Revolution and its Consequences.* New York: Ba-sic Books, 1988.

70. *Tureen v. Equifax*, 571 F 2d 411 8th Cir. 1978, cited in Jonathan P. Graham, "Privacy, computers and the commercial dissemination of personal information." *Texas Law Review* 65 (7) (June 1987):1,416.

71. Susan Gardner, "Wiretapping the mind: A call to regulate truth verification in employment." *San Diego Law Review* 21 (1984): 295–323.

72. A distinction is made between reliability and validity. Presumably, a core attribute such as honesty should not be highly variable within individuals. An unreliable instrument might produce a low honesty score one day and a high score another day, which could indicate a change in honesty that had not taken place. The reliability of the measure might be affected by the humidity in the room, the amount of coffee consumed by the person being tested, the time of the day when the test is taken, or any one of a hundred other factors that might cause the scores to vary. Although an unreliable measure can be valid only by chance, in the case of predictive validity, the concern with validity turns on the relationship between the test score and some unmeasured, but genuine, attribute of the individual's personality, which, if known, could predict a variety of behaviors. Predictive validity, then, is concerned with the accuracy of the test in the identification of persons who would, if given the opportunity, act dishonestly.

73. Ann M. Barry, "Defamation in the workplace: The impact of increasing employer liability." *Marquette Law Review* 72 (1989): 264–303. Barry discusses the emergence of a "negligent reference theory" by which employers seek actions against those who write references for not providing relevant information that they held and by which the failure to disclose information is defined as negligent, p. 301. This liability is in conflict with suits charging negligent hiring, defined as a "breach of the employer's duty to make an adequate investigation of an employee's fitness before hiring him," p. 302. A comprehensive examination of employer liability that emphasizes privacy dimensions is found in Richard M. Howe, "Minding your business: Employer liability for invasion of privacy." Paper presented to the Association of Life Insurance Counsel, White Sulphur Springs, WV, May 21, 1990.

74. Raymond Wacks, *Personal Information, Privacy and the Law.* Oxford: Oxford University Press, 1989.

75. Ibid., p. 181.

76. Ibid., p. 238.

77. Ibid., p. 230.

78. Richard A. Posner, "Privacy, secrecy and reputation." *Buffalo Law Review* 28 (1979), p. 5.

79. Amitai Etzioni takes detailed exception to this claim and provides numerous examples that indicate the influence of moral, nonselfish motivations. Amitai Etzioni, *The Moral Dimension: Toward a New Economics.* New York: Free Press, 1988.

80. Posner, op. cit., p. 9.

81. The fact that these estimates are themselves subject to race, class, and gender bias is ignored in Posner's and other neoclassical responses to critiques of discrimination.

82. This has been rather inadequately measured in terms of the proportion of African-American and Hispanic residents of the state.

83. Robert Posch, "Why are we returning to redlining?" *Direct Marketing* (March 1990):77.

84. Posner, 1979, op. cit., pp. 44–45.

85. Ibid., p. 50.

..

86. Andrew Cassel, "Loan-rejection study puts banks on defense." *Philadelphia Inquirer.* October 28, 1991, p. D1; Anthony R. Wood, "Brokers having qualms over loan criteria." *Philadelphia Inquirer.* October 28, 1991, p. D1.

87. Simitis, 1987, op. cit., p. 735.

88. Laurence A. Benner, "Diminishing expectations of privacy in the Rehnquist Court." *John Marshall Law Review* 22 (4) (Summer 1989):525–876.

89. Benner notes that the force of the warrant clause was weakened by the Court in a decision regarding the right of housing inspectors to gain access to private property without the necessity of a warrant demonstrating probable cause. Thus a distinction for *administrative*, rather than criminal searches was established. See *Camara v. Municipal Court,* 387 U.S. 523, 538–539, 1967, cited p. 831.

90. Ibid., p. 835.

91. The case of *California v. Greenwood,* 108 S. Ct. at 1,627 cited in Benner, p. 856.

92. See *Skinner v. Railway Executives' Association,* 109 S. Ct. 1,402 (1989) cited in Benner, p. 843.

93. Ibid., p. 845.

94. See *Katz v. United States,* 389 U.S. 347 (1967) cited in Benner, p. 852.

95. See *California v. Ciraolo,* 476 U.S. 207 (1986) cited in Benner, p. 859.

96. Ibid.

97. James J. Tomkovicz, "Beyond secrecy for secrecy's sake: Toward an expanded vision of the Fourth Amendment privacy province." *Hastings Law Journal* 36 (5) (March 1985):736.

98. Loretta E. Murdock, "The use and abuse of computerized information: Striking a balance between personal privacy interests and organizational information needs." *Albany Law Review* 44 (3) (April 1980):610.

99. See for example, Robert Ellis Smith, *Compilation of State and Federal Privacy Laws, 1988.* Washington, D.C.: Privacy Journal, 1988.

100. Colin J. Bennett, "Computers, personal data, and theories of technology: Comparative approaches to privacy protection in the 1990s." *Science, Technology and Human Values* 16 (1) (Winter 1991):51–69; Colin J. Bennett, "Regulating the computer: Comparing policy instruments in Europe and the United States." *European Journal of Political Research* 16 (1988):437–466.

101. David Chaum, "Security without identification: Transaction systems to make big brother obsolete." *Communications of the ACM* 28 (10) (October 1985):1,030–1,044.

102. Bennett, 1991, p. 58.

103. Flaherty, 1989, op. cit., p. 382.

104. Ibid., p. 365.

105. "How the American public views consumer privacy issues in the early '90s and why." Testimony of Alan F. Westin before the Subcommittee on Government Information, Justice and Agriculture. House Committee on Government Operations, Washington, D.C., April 10, 1991.

106. Baker, 1989, op. cit., p. 213.

107. Ibid., p. 212.

108. Robert Babe angered economists with his return to the fundamentals in the warning he delivered to them and other policymakers at a telecommunications policy conference. See his "Information industries and economic analysis: Policymakers beware," pp.

123–135. In O. Gandy, P. Espinosa, and J. Ordover [eds], *Proceedings from the Tenth Annual Telecommunications Policy Research Conference.* Norwood, NJ: Ablex, 1983.

109. Meheroo Jussawalla and Chee-Wah Cheah, Chapter 4, "Economic analysis of the legal and policy aspects of information privacy," pp. 75–102 in their book *The Calculus of International Communications.* Littleton, CO: Libraries Unlimited, 1987.

110. Rohan Samarajiva and Roopali Mukherjee, "Regulation of 976 services and dial-a-porn: Privacy and policy implications for the intelligence network." Conference paper. Seventeenth Congress of the International Association for Mass Communication Research, Bled, Yugoslavia, August 1990.

111. Jussawalla and Cheah, op. cit., p. 89.

112. Ruth Faden and Tom Beauchamp with Nancy King, *A History and Theory of Informed Consent.* New York: Oxford Unversity Press, 1986, p. 8.

113. Ibid., p. 28.

114. I am quoting Cardoza in the 1914 case of *Schloendorff v. Society of New York Hospitals,* p. 123.

115. Martin R. Gardner, "Consent as a bar to fourth amendment scope—A critique of a common theory." *Journal of Criminal Law and Criminology* 71 (4) (1980):443–465.

116. Gary T. Marx, *Undercover: Police Surveillance in America.* Berkeley: University of California Press, 1988.

117. Ibid., p. 107.

118. Edward Laumann and David Knoke, *The Organizational State: Social Choice in National Policy Domains.* Madison: University of Wisconsin Press, 1987.

119. Janlori Goldman responded to my question while she was serving as a panelist at a conference organized by *Telecommunications Reports,* "Caller-ID, ANI, and Privacy," Washington, D.C., October 15–16, 1990. We continued our discussion briefly following a panel on privacy at the Nineteenth Annual Telecommunications Policy Research Conference, Solomons, MD, September 28–30, 1991.

120. Robert Kastenmeir, opening statement (August 3, 1988), Joint Hearing on Video and Library Privacy Protection Act of 1988. Subcommittee on Courts, Civil Liberties, and the Administration of Justice of the House Committee on the Judiciary and the Subcomittee on Technology and the Law of the Senate Committee of the Judiciary. Washington, D.C.: U.S. Government Printing Office, 1989.

121. Testimony of Vans Stevenson in hearings cited above, pp. 75–78.

122. Testimony of Richard Barton in hearings cited above, p. 88.

123. "DMA comes out against video privacy legislation as written." *Friday Report.* August 5, 1988, p. 1.

124. This commission, headed by David Linowes, investigated issues of personal privacy between 1975 and 1977 and made recommendations for private as well as public sector policy regarding personal information.

125. Video Privacy Protection Act of 1988. PL 100–618, 102 Stat. 3,196; 2d, November 5, 1988.

126. Steve Bates, "A blockbuster debate about privacy." *Washington Post.* January 1, 1991, p. E1.

127. As has been noted, transaction processing is a multibillion dollar industry with high growth potential because telecommunications networks provide interconnections to countless point-of-purchase terminals that have become central to the operation of bank-

ing, retail, and transportation activities. The corporations that provide the telecommunications and computer services that define this market have made controversial claims regarding their rights to utilize the information that is generated through their delivery of these services.

128. Paul Shultz, *Caller ID, ANI and Privacy: A Review of the Major Issues Affecting Number Identification Technologies.* Washington, D.C.: Telecommunication Reports, 1990, p. 4.

129. State of New York Public Service Commission, "Proceeding on motion of the commission to review issues concerning privacy in telecommunications." 90–C–0075. January 31, 1990. The primary resource in this communication was the "Memorandum and Questions" provided by Commissioner Noam.

130. Part of the argument in *Smith v. Maryland,* 442 U.S. 735 (1979) was that persons should know that the telephone company could and would use available technology to identify the numbers from which illegal or harassing calls would be made. Thus all that would be necessary would be widespread publicity about the availability of Caller-ID or other technology to eliminate any claims based on reasonable expectations.

131. The attorney general of North Carolina called for an investigation of Southern Bell because corporate executives had written a memorandum encouraging the generation of letters to utility commissioners. The memo included copies of ten sample letters that were to be used as "guidelines" in generating this flood of public response. In addition, executives were warned to use personal rather than company stationery in writing versions of these letters. Details of this charge were presented in "N.C. attorney general seeks probe of Southern Bell Caller-ID campaign." *Privacy Times.* March 1, 1990, p. 3.

132. Police in several jurisdictions have indicated that Caller-ID has threatened several undercover operations and the lives of police and persons cooperating with police. See for example, "Florida law enforcers oppose Caller-ID, Southern Bell plan." *Privacy Times.* August 14, 1990, p. 2.

133. Thomas E. McManus, *Telephone Transaction-Generated Information: Rights and Restrictions.* Report P–90–5. Cambridge, MA: Harvard University, Program on Information Resources and Policy, May 1990.

134. U.S. Congress. Office of Technology Assessment. *Critical Connections: Communication for the Future.* OTA-CIT-407. Washington, D.C.: U.S. Government Printing Office, January 1990.

135. Signalling System No. 7 is the current standard for control signaling on digital telecommunication networks.

136. Testimony of Rohan Samarajiva, Call Management Services Trial, The Public Utilities Board of Manitoba, 1991.

137. Although Congress passed the Telephone Consumer Protection Act in 1991 to control these systems and the associated abuses, it appears that the Federal Communications Commission refused to honor the intention of the legislation. See "FCC stands up for telemarketing; Hits do-not-call database option." *DM News.* April 27, 1992, p. 1.

138. Susan Burnett Luten, "Give me a home where no salesmen phone: Telephone solicitation and the First Amendment." *Hastings Constitutional Law Quarterly* 7 (Fall 1979):129–164; Mark S. Nadel, "Rings of privacy: Unsolicited telephone calls and the right of privacy." *Yale Journal of Regulation* 4 (December 1986):99–128.

139. A regulatory rather than a voluntary option along these lines has been considered with regard to the placement of an asterisk, or other identifying mark, next to a name in a

directory that would inform callers that unsolicited calls were unwelcome. This option facilitates the mounting of a "no trespassing" sign on the telephone. Yet blanket bars against a category of calls defined as "unsolicited" appear to represent an unmanageable and inefficient response for all but a very small number of persons.

140. The problem of vagueness in the definition of those classes of callers that would be seen as intolerably harassing by a reasonable person is raised by M. Sean Royall, "Constitutionally regulating telephone harassment: An exercise in statutory precision." *University of Chicago Law Review* 56 (4) (1989):1,403–1,432.

141. We note that having an unlisted or unpublished telephone number provides no guarantee that individuals can even pay to limit access to their homes or their persons by phone. Any call made to another party, especially a commercial party that has some form of CNI, will introduce those numbers into the pool.

142. A citation is frequently made to the case of *Smith v. Maryland,* 422 U.S. 735 (1979) in which a pen register, a device that records the numbers called from a particular telephone, was used to gather evidence of obscene and harassing telephone calls. The court argued that since the device did not record the content of the communications, only the fact that they were made, it was sufficiently unlike a wiretap to make the requirement of a prior warrant unnecessary. The court argued further that because it is necessary to indicate the number one wishes to call, even if mechanically, to the telephone company, there could be no reasonable expectations of privacy in those numbers. Glenn Chatmas Smith, "We've got your number! (Is it Constitutional to Give it Out?): Caller identification technology and the right to informational privacy." *UCLA Law Review* 37 (1989):145–223. This provides a detailed critique of the Smith court's view and its limited applicability to the technology of Caller-ID.

143. "Caller-ID declared legal by South Carolina County Judge." *Privacy Times.* December 4, 1990, pp. 2–3.

144. David B. Hack, "Caller I.D. and Automatic Telephone Number Identification. *CRS Issue Brief,* IB90085. Washington, D.C.: Congressional Reference Service. Library of Congress, February 11, 1991.

145. Amy S. Rosenberg, "Rising call for unlisted numbers." *Philadelphia Inquirer.* May 6, 1990, p. A1.

146. Women frequently request that they be listed in telephone directories only by initials rather than by given name so as not to provide information to potential harassers about homes with single women. Professional women and feminists, however, have pressured the telephone companies to include individual listings of their names as well as listings for their husbands.

147. Remarks by Will Dwyer, CEO of Private Lines, Inc., of Beverly Hills, CA, as presented to the Telecommunications Reports conference on Caller-ID, ANI, and Privacy, Washington, D.C., October 15, 1990.

148. Gary Marx included such claims, as well as others, in his influential testimony before the Pennsylvania Public Utility Commission. Docket No. R-891200, May 1989.

149. Julie Johnson, "ANI leads the way." *Telephony.* April 10, 1989, p. 34.

150. American Express reportedly changed its instructions to its service operators after cardmembers reported surprise and some irritation with the knowledgeable greetings they received because operators knew who they were before they actually answered the call.

151. Ibid., p. 35.

152. This is from a presentation by Steve Mulcahy, Manager, corporate marketing, 800 Service for MCI Communications, to the Telecommunication Reports conference on Caller-ID, ANI & Privacy, Washington, DC, October 15–16, 1990.

153. James Rule and Paul Attewell. "What do computers do? *Social Problems* 36 (3) (1989):225–241, p. 237.

154. These are the comments of Brian R. Lane, Managing Director for Marketing and Regulatory Planning, NYNEX Service Company, at a conference on "State Telecommunications Regulation," Aspen, Institute, Aspen, Colorado, July 9–13, 1989.

155. Hack, 1991, op. cit., p. 7.

156. Marx, testimony, op. cit., pp. 10–11.

157. These comments are in regard to the Proceeding on the Motion of the Commission to Review Issues Concerning Privacy in Telecommunications, Case 90-C-0075, March 15, 1990.

158. These comments by Cathleen Black were delivered at an address to the National Press Club on October 7, 1991, as quoted in *Telecommunications Reports,* October, 14, 1991, p. 5.

159. We are reminded of the example of question framing, which opposes the Roper form of the question of economic justification: "Don't you agree that watching commercials is a reasonable price to pay for receiving quality television entertainment?"—which finds nearly the same proportion of the population agreeing that "television commercials represent an annoying interruption."

160. Evan Hendricks, Trudy Hayden, and Jack Novik, *Your Right to Privacy.* 2d Edition. Carbondale, IL: Southern Illinois University Press, 1990.

161. Meredith W. Mendes, "Privacy and Computer-based Information Systems," pp. 193–264. In B. Compaine [ed], *Issues in New Information Technology.* Norwood, NJ: Ablex, 1988.

162. Laumann and Knoke, op. cit., 1987.

163. The assumption of an absence of an individual's legitimate interest in records held by others, added to the already weakened standards of reasonableness following *Katz,* started a decline in privacy fortunes that has not yet begun to slow.

164. By distributing readily available information about the demographic makeup and consumer orientation of the more than 120 million households on CD-ROM discs, Lotus and Equifax expected their product to revolutionize marketing among the small businesses that had been less active users of consumer list services. After the *Wall Sreet Journal* published an article describing this proposed product, computer activists distributed copies and comments through their electronic bulletin boards and electronic mail networks. The resultant swarm of letters and threats led Lotus to withdraw the product, at a reported loss exceeding $8 million.

165. Michael W. Miller, "Coming to your local video store: Big Brother." *Wall Street Journal.* December 26, 1990, p. 9.

166. Jerry Berman and Janlori Goldman, *A Federal Right of Informational Privacy: The Need for Reform.* Washington, D.C.: Benton Foundation, 1989.

167. David F. Linowes, "The U.S. Privacy Protection Commission. A restrospective view from the chair." *American Behavioral Scientist* 26 (5) (May/June 1983):577–590.

168. Council of Europe, *Convention for the Protection of Individuals With Regard to Automatic Processing of Personal Data;* OECD. *Guidelines Governing the Protection of Privacy and Transborder Data Flows of Personal Data.*

169. Flaherty, 1989, p. 380.

170. Simitis, 1987, pp. 740–741.

171. Moore, 1984, op. cit., p. 288.

CHAPTER 8

1. Majid Tehranian, *Technologies of Power*. Norwood, NJ: Ablex, 1990.

2. Samuel Bowles and Herbert Gintis, *Democracy and Capitalism*. New York: Basic Books, 1987.

3. James Beniger, *The Control Revolution*. Cambridge, MA: Harvard University Press, 1986.

4. Robert M. Entman, *Democracy Without Citizens: Media and the Decay of American Politics*. New York: Oxford University Press, 1989, p. 128.

5. Ibid., p. 136.

6. Herbert I. Schiller, *Culture, Inc*. New York: Oxford University Press, 1989.

7. Jürgen Habermas, *Moral Consciousness and Communicative Action* (trans. C. Lenhardt and S. Nicholsen). Cambridge, MA: MIT Press, 1990, p. 133.

8. Ibid., p. 136.

9. Ibid., p. 175.

10. David Flaherty, *Protecting Privacy in Surveillance Societies*. Chapel Hill: University of North Carolina Press, 1989, pp. 393–394.

11. Jacques Ellul, *The Technological Society*. Alfred A. Knopf, 1964, p. 427.

12. Stewart Brand, *The Media Lab. Inventing the Future at M.I.T.* New York: Penguin Books, 1987.

ABOUT THE BOOK AND AUTHOR

The consensus is clear. Personal privacy will become the dominant issue of the 1990s. Yet a focus on privacy, as we have come to understand it so far, all but guarantees that we ignore the implications of the privacy debate at the more fundamental levels of individual autonomy, collective agency, and bureaucratic control. *The Panoptic Sort* helps us to understand just what is at stake when the bureaucracies of government and commerce gather, share, and make use of an almost unlimited amount of personal information to manage the social and economic systems within their spheres.

Unlike Foucault's panoptic prison, which involved continual, all-encompassing surveillance, the current panoptic system depends upon the ability of operators to classify and then separate disciplinary subjects into groups in a way that increases the efficiency with which the techniques of correct training or rehabilitation may be applied to each individual. This book describes in full detail the design and use of the panoptic operation, with examples from marketing, employment, insurance, credit management, and the provision of governmental social services.

Oscar H. Gandy, Jr., is professor of communication at the Annenberg School for Communication at the University of Pennsylvania.

INDEX